Innovation, Transparency, and Participation in Smart Government

Jorge A. Ruiz-Vanoye
https://orcid.org/0000-0003-4928-5716
Universidad Politécnica de Pachuca, Mexico

Ocotlan Díaz-Parra
Universidad Politécnica de Pachuca, Mexico

Eric Simancas-Acevedo
https://orcid.org/0000-0001-7823-709X
Universidad Politécnica de Pachuca, Mexico

IGI Global Scientific Publishing
Publishing Tomorrow's Research Today

Vice President of Editorial	Melissa Wagner
Director of Acquisitions	Mikaela Felty
Director of Book Development	Jocelynn Hessler
Production Manager	Mike Brehm
Cover Design	Jose Rosado

Published in the United States of America by
IGI Global Scientific Publishing
701 East Chocolate Avenue
Hershey, PA, 17033, USA
Tel: 717-533-8845 | Fax: 717-533-7115
Website: https://www.igi-global.com E-mail: cust@igi-global.com

Library of Congress Cataloging-in-Publication Data

LCNN: 2025036615 (CIP Data Pending)
ISBN13: 9798337355351
Isbn13Softcover: 9798337355368
EISBN13: 9798337355375

British Cataloguing in Publication Data
A Cataloguing in Publication record for this book is available from the British Library.

Table of Contents

Detailed Table of Contents

The emergence of digital technologies — cloud computing, big data analytics, the Internet of Things (IoT), artificial intelligence (AI), and blockchain — has transformed public administration into a data-driven, citizen-centred ecosystem often referred to as smart government. This paper synthesises theoretical foundations and empirical evidence on how these technologies are reshaping governance structures, decision-making processes, service delivery models, and stakeholder engagement. We further examine the policy implications — including regulatory frameworks, capacity building, and ethical considerations — and propose a framework for scaling smart government initiatives while mitigating risks such as privacy erosion, digital exclusion, and governance fragmentation. The paper concludes with recommendations for policymakers, practitioners, and researchers to foster resilient, inclusive, and evidence-based digital public services.

Technologies are essential in public management to improve efficiency, management, and availability of services and information. A smart government combines various technologies and guidelines, makes data and information from public agencies available, and makes it publicly accessible to citizens. The objective is to analyze various technologies and tools that support transparency, citizen participation, and accountability in the field of smart government, including various initiatives by international organizations that promote digital technologies, case studies, and ethical and regulatory aspects. Conceptual terms related to governance, smart governance, open data, open platforms, and others are addressed. The relationship

transparency, digital equity, and cyber resilience. The analysis demonstrates that safe cities must move beyond reactive models towards anticipatory, inclusive frameworks that embed technological innovation within democratic, human-centred urban governance. The chapter concludes by identifying future challenges—including neuro-rights, post-quantum security, and digital exclusion—and advocates for a holistic, ethically grounded vision of urban resilience.

Mario Oscar Ordaz Oliver, Tecnológico Nacional de México, Pachuca, Mexico
Evelin Gutiérrez, Universidad Politécnica de Pachuca, Mexico
Jesús Patricio Ordaz, Universidad Autónoma del Estado de Hidalgo, Mexico
Javier Hernández Pérez, Universidad Politécnica de Pachuca, Mexico
Amadeo Manuel Hernández Hernández, Tecnológico Nacional de México, Pachuca, Mexico
Justo Fabián Montiel Hernández, Universidad Autónoma del Estado de Hidalgo, Mexico

This chapter addresses smart cities not simply as a technological deployment, but as a space where different branches of engineering complement each other. It analyzes some of the contributions of mechanical, mechatronic, electrical, electronic, computational, and chemical engineering, highlighting how each of them, from its perspective, integrates innovative and preferred factors to make a city more efficient, safe, and, above all, tailored to its inhabitants. It also presents some specific examples of the implementation and management of smart cities and governments, such as Barcelona, Singapore, New York, and Amsterdam. The text details some of the actions these places have taken to become smart. It analyzes how the knowledge contributed by different branches of engineering articulates with the Internet of Things, electrical grids, and the mechatronic design of smart sensor networks to give rise to innovative systems.

Preface

The digital transformation of the public sector is redefining the foundations of governance, reshaping how decisions are made, and how citizens interact with institutions. The convergence of technologies such as artificial intelligence (AI), the Internet of Things (IoT), blockchain, and advanced data analytics is enabling governments to enhance transparency, participation, and efficiency in public management. These advances open new opportunities for optimising the provision of essential services and improving the quality of urban life. However, this transformation also entails significant challenges, including issues of data security, ethical governance, regulatory adaptation, and persistent disparities in digital access.

Innovation, Transparency, and Participation in Smart Government brings together a multidisciplinary body of research and applied knowledge that examines the responsible and effective use of technology within public administration. The chapters compiled in this volume offer a comprehensive perspective on how digital tools and data-driven strategies are being implemented in areas such as urban management, energy systems, water governance, and cybersecurity. Collectively, they provide both theoretical and empirical insights into the design of intelligent, participatory, and transparent governance systems capable of responding to contemporary social and environmental complexities.

At its core, this book argues that the success of smart governance depends not only on technological adoption but also on institutional values—particularly openness, accountability, and collaboration. Digital innovation should serve as a means to reinforce democratic legitimacy and public trust, rather than as an end in itself. By integrating conceptual analysis with case-based evidence, the volume bridges the gap between academic discourse and practical policymaking, offering a structured approach to the sustainable transformation of government systems.

Ultimately, this work aspires to serve as a reference for academics, policymakers, and technology professionals interested in the evolution of digital governance. It invites reflection on how innovation can be harnessed to create more equitable, transparent, and resilient public institutions. Through its multidisciplinary scope and emphasis on applied research, the book contributes to advancing a shared understanding of how technology can act as a catalyst for democratic renewal and sustainable urban development.

CHAPTER OVERVIEW

Chapter 1, *Fundamentals of Smart Government* (Jorge A. Ruiz-Vanoye et al.), defines Smart Government as the next stage of electronic governance, integrating open data, budget optimisation, and intelligent management of public resources. It highlights how domains such as smart economics, smart infrastructure, disaster management, and digital tourism contribute to sustainability, resilience, and citizen-centred governance.

Chapter 2, *Tools for Transparency, Accountability, and Citizen Participation in Smart Government* (Ricardo A. Barrera-Cámara et al.), examines technologies that underpin openness and accountability in public management, linking smart governance initiatives to the Sustainable Development Goals.

Chapter 3, *Smart Grids for Governments: Strategy, Technology and Energy Transition* (Juan Manuel Xicoténcatl-Pérez et al.), discusses the governmental strategies for transitioning towards resilient and sustainable electricity systems, analysing enabling tools such as AMI, SCADA, and VPPs.

Chapter 4, *Smart Cities: Integration of Technological Solutions in Urban Management* (Francisco R. Trejo-Macotela et al.), analyses the multidimensional framework of smart cities, highlighting the intersection between technology, community, and nature to promote inclusive and sustainable urban development.

Chapter 5, *Smart Water Systems for Sustainable and Participatory Urban Governance* (Francisco R. Trejo-Macotela et al.), evaluates smart water solutions and their contribution to integrated water resources management through IoT, AI, and wireless sensor networks.

Chapter 6, *Safe Cities and Smart Government for Transparency, Equity and Resilience* (Francisco R. Trejo-Macotela), examines how emerging technologies and ethical frameworks redefine urban safety, calling for human-centred and transparent digital governance.

Chapter 7, *Smart Cities as Open Governance Laboratories: A Multidisciplinary Approach from Engineering* (Mario Oscar Ordaz Oliver et al.), presents smart cities as collaborative spaces where various branches of engineering converge to create efficient, adaptive, and citizen-oriented environments.

Chapter 8, *Future Perspectives and Innovative Governance Models: Digital Innovation for Future Governance* (Miguel Ángel Ruiz Jaimes et al.), analyses emerging trends such as AI, blockchain, and predictive analytics to propose a roadmap for transparent and inclusive public institutions.

Chapter 9, *Cybersecurity, Data Protection and Ethics in Digital Government: Emotional Stability and Institutional Trust in the Age of Artificial Intelligence* (Miguel Ángel Ruiz Jaimes et al.), investigates the interplay between security, ethics, and citizen trust, proposing policy frameworks for emotionally resilient and ethically sound digital ecosystems.

Collectively, the chapters in this volume demonstrate that the future of governance lies in the strategic integration of innovation, transparency, and citizen participation. The research presented here not only advances theoretical understanding but also provides actionable insights for policymakers, practitioners, and researchers seeking to design inclusive, data-driven, and sustainable models of governance.

This book thus serves as a reference and a call to action—advocating for an informed, collaborative, and ethical approach to digital transformation in the public sector. Its contributions reflect a growing consensus: that technology, when aligned with democratic values and institutional trust, can serve as a catalyst for a more transparent, participatory, and resilient future.

Jorge A. Ruiz-Vanoye
Universidad Politécnica de Pachuca, México

Ocotlán Diaz-Parra
Universidad Politécnica de Pachuca, México

Eric Simancas-Acevedo
Universidad Politécnica de Pachuca, México

Chapter 1
Fundamentals of Smart Government

Jorge A. Ruiz-Vanoye
https://orcid.org/0000-0003-4928-5716
Universidad Politécnica de Pachuca, Mexico

Ocotlán Díaz-Parra
Universidad Politécnica de Pachuca, Mexico

Eric Simancas-Acevedo
https://orcid.org/0000-0001-7823-709X
Universidad Politécnica de Pachuca, Mexico

ABSTRACT

The emergence of digital technologies — cloud computing, big data analytics, the Internet of Things (IoT), artificial intelligence (AI), and blockchain — has transformed public administration into a data-driven, citizen-centred ecosystem often referred to as smart government. This paper synthesises theoretical foundations and empirical evidence on how these technologies are reshaping governance structures, decision-making processes, service delivery models, and stakeholder engagement. We further examine the policy implications — including regulatory frameworks, capacity building, and ethical considerations — and propose a framework for scaling smart government initiatives while mitigating risks such as privacy erosion, digital exclusion, and governance fragmentation. The paper concludes with recommendations for policymakers, practitioners, and researchers to foster resilient, inclusive, and evidence-based digital public services.

DOI: 10.4018/979-8-3373-5535-1.ch001

1. INTRODUCTION

Smart Government refers to an evolution of electronic government that incorporates open data and budget optimisation to ensure efficient public resource management. According to Ruiz-Vanoye et al. (2023), it involves the intelligent management of the city's economy-referred to as smart economics—and the enhancement of government–enterprise relationships to support civil works (smart infrastructure) and priority public services aimed at citizens' well-being. Furthermore, Smart Government integrates domains such as disaster risk management (smart disasters) and technology-driven tourism development (smart tourism), aligning itself with principles of sustainability, resilience, and citizen-centric governance.

Functionally, Smart Government represents the optimal coordination of human, economic, and technological resources within public institutions. Its development relies on the integration of emerging technologies, including combinatorial optimisation, machine learning, big data analytics, data visualisation, and the Internet of Government Things (IoGT), all of which serve to improve the quality, efficiency, and responsiveness of public service delivery.

Ruiz-Vanoye et al. (2023) outline several core technological components of Smart Government. The Internet of Government Things (IoGT) enables digital interconnection between computational and non-computational government assets using sensors and RFID technologies. Smart economics includes mechanisms for price regulation, consumer protection, quality assurance, industrial standardisation, and allocation of government budgets. Meanwhile, smart open government fosters transparent, participatory governance by maintaining continuous communication with citizens, encouraging co-creation of services, and enhancing public trust through openness.

Additionally, smart infrastructure involves the intelligent coordination of critical urban systems—such as energy grids, transport networks, water and waste systems, and telecommunications. Smart disasters utilise data-driven methods and technological tools for risk assessment, emergency logistics, shelter planning, and coordinated response and recovery efforts. Smart tourism leverages ICT to develop cultural assets, improve accessibility, and support the infrastructure of professional and recreational tourism.

Other key pillars include e-government, which digitises state–citizen interactions across domains like virtual justice, online tax administration, and electronic voting, and data science, which supports evidence-based decision-making in areas such as healthcare, crime prevention, environmental monitoring, and transport. Finally, Smart Government Policy refers to adaptive and sustainable public policies that comply with the constitutional and institutional frameworks of governance.

The foundational principle of smart government embraces the utilization of digital technologies to improve administrative tasks and service delivery. Liu and Yuan discuss how the proliferation of ICT in public administration reflects a shift towards New Public Management, where technology is pivotal in managing daily operations and enhancing interaction with citizens (Liu & Yuan, 2015). This dependency on ICT is crucial for creating responsive public services that meet contemporary societal demands (Dzvinchuk et al., 2022). Furthermore, the concept of Public Administration 5.0 posits the integration of artificial intelligence, Internet of Things (IoT), and blockchain technologies as transformative forces that could significantly increase the quality and scope of public services (Ejjami, R., 2024).

Citizen participation stands at the core of smart governance, as it emphasizes the need for public managers to engage citizens in the co-creation of services (Webster & Leleux, 2018). With the increasing implementation of online platforms, administrators are urged to improve functionalities and ensure that these platforms are user-friendly and trustworthy (Purwanti et al., 2022). Reliable service frameworks enhance citizen trust and can stimulate higher participation levels, ultimately leading to improved governance outcomes (Hartanti et al., 2021). The importance of transparency in e-government further underscores this aspect, as increased access to information bolsters accountability and promotes ethical practices (Ardielli, 2015; Galushi & Malatji, 2022).

Moreover, the notion of smart governance encompasses adaptive frameworks that allow governments to respond creatively and efficiently to the needs of their constituents. For instance, in smart cities, governance models that prioritize open data and community engagement are fundamental for developing trust and satisfaction among citizens (Guazzo & Çekani, 2023; Pereira et al., 2018). The application of technologies, such as big data analytics and AI, facilitates informed decision-making, fostering a governance climate that is not only inclusive but also proactive in addressing urban challenges (Pereira et al., 2018; Meijer & Bolívar, 2015). By employing these tools, public administrations can better align their services with the demands of the modern populace, creating an agile and resilient governance infrastructure.

In addition, the challenges posed by digital transformations in public administration necessitate effective managerial capacities. Scholars have highlighted that public institutions must navigate potential pitfalls related to the adoption of technologies, ensuring that digitalization aligns with transparency and accountability initiatives (Kropf et al., 2020; Androniceanu et al., 2022; Cordella & Paletti, 2018). The effective implementation of digital governance tools allows for significant improvements in public sector efficiency, enabling more streamlined and responsive administrative practices (Molobela & Uwizeyimana, 2023; Gualdi & Cordella, 2022). The collaborative efforts between governments and citizens, facilitated through smart technologies, promote not only enhanced service delivery but also a greater sense of community ownership in governance processes (Choo et al., 2023; Johnson et al., 2020).

2. THEORETICAL FOUNDATIONS AND CONCEPTUAL FRAMEWORKS

Smart governance has become a crucial approach in contemporary public management, characterised by key elements such as transparency, participation, efficiency, and innovation. These components are fundamental to addressing the complexity and uncertainty inherent in socio-ecological systems, as discussed in the literature on adaptive governance and other relevant theoretical frameworks. The Key Elements of Smart Governance:

2.1. Transparency:

Transparency is essential in smart governance, as it enables citizens to access information about governmental decisions and processes, thereby fostering trust in institutions. According to Fernández (2021), the use of emerging technologies allows for greater visibility in municipal decision-making, which is crucial for smart cities. This aligns with the notion that open governance contributes to empowering citizens and enhancing accountability (Franco, 2021).

Transparency mechanisms within smart governance include the use of information and communication technologies (ICT), which facilitate access to public data and promote citizen participation. *E-government*, through the use of digital platforms for public administration, plays a fundamental role in this regard (Xia, 2017; Ruijer et al., 2019). The implementation of open government data enables citizens to obtain information that was previously inaccessible, thereby fostering more effective scrutiny of governmental actions (Ruijer et al., 2019; Petrović et al., 2022). This, in turn, enhances accountability and responsiveness to social demands, cultivating an environment in which citizens become active participants in governance.

However, the mere availability of information does not guarantee transparency's effectiveness. The study by Hope et al. (2021) demonstrates that the quality of the information provided is crucial. Transparency must be accompanied by contextualisation that enables citizens to comprehend and apply the information effectively, thereby influencing the efficiency of both public and private sector operations. This represents a challenge for governments and citizens alike, requiring a collective effort to ensure that information is not only accessible but also meaningful, comprehensible, and usable.

Despite the benefits of transparency, there are inherent challenges in its implementation. A lack of trust in the government's capacity to act transparently, together with resistance from certain political actors to share information, can hinder progress towards more open and accountable governance (Mabillard & Pasquier, 2015; Ngatikoh et al., 2020; Chatfield & Brajawidagda, 2013). Some critics contend that, although transparency represents a positive step, it can at times result in superficial practices, whereby governments prioritise the public display of actions rather than addressing deeper structural issues (Mabillard & Pasquier, 2015). Furthermore, research by Voitenko et al. (2022) highlights that genuine transparency is closely linked to improved resource allocation and socio-economic development, which necessitates a sustained commitment to quality and accountability.

The future of smart governance should focus on integrating transparency more fully into decision-making processes. Approaches are needed that not only promote openness but also empower citizens to use information effectively to participate actively in governance (Fernández-Añez et al., 2018). Promoting a culture of transparency, including training for public officials and raising public awareness, is vital to moving towards a model of governance that responds to contemporary needs.

2.2. Participation

Citizen participation constitutes another fundamental pillar of smart governance. Research indicates that involving local actors in decision-making not only improves the quality of public policies but also promotes innovation and shared learning (McCool et al., 2019; Meza-Jiménez et al., 2021). The work of Trimble and Plummer underscores the importance of participatory evaluation in strengthening adaptive governance processes, thereby demonstrating how active participation can enhance the effectiveness of ecological system conservation (Trimble & Plummer, 2019).

Active citizen participation is essential for reinforcing democracy. According to Igbokwe-Ibeto and Osakede (2017), citizen involvement in the execution of development projects reflects community commitment and is associated with greater effectiveness in their implementation. This suggests that engaging citizens in decision-making processes enhances their sense of ownership and responsibility for the outcomes of implemented policies.

A key dimension of citizen participation lies in its capacity to improve the quality of public policies. Yang and Pandey (2011) argue that active collaboration between citizens and public officials can produce more effective administrative outcomes, underlining the importance of establishing spaces for civic engagement. This supports the notion that citizen participation should be understood as a dynamic process that enriches democratic deliberation and decision-making.

The incorporation of information and communication technologies (ICT) has transformed the ways in which citizens participate in governance. Hutahaean et al. (2023) note that citizens' trust in government is closely linked to their willingness to participate, underscoring the need to develop accessible and efficient digital platforms for civic interaction. Such platforms facilitate communication and collaboration among diverse social actors (Maciél et al., 2010).

Despite its numerous benefits, citizen participation continues to face significant challenges. One of the most pressing is the persistent lack of trust that many citizens hold towards their governments. Letki and Steen (2021) observe that in contexts where civic participation is low, negative perceptions of state actors prevail, limiting opportunities for meaningful collaboration. This deficit of trust represents a substantial obstacle to the advancement of participatory governance.

In addition, technological and accessibility barriers remain areas of concern in contemporary governance frameworks. Aman and Jan (2022) emphasise that in certain regions, the implementation of digital tools has not been sufficiently inclusive, potentially excluding the most vulnerable sectors of society from genuine participation. Hence, it is crucial to design approaches that ensure the inclusion of diverse voices and perspectives within governance processes.

Promoting more inclusive governance requires a deeper understanding of how citizen participation is structured and facilitated. Krawczyk and Sweet-Cushman (2016) argue that the adoption of digital technologies in governance can unlock transformative potential by enabling participation across a wider range of demographic groups. This not only enhances equity in participation opportunities but also encourages greater diversity in decision-making processes.

Furthermore, Maciél et al. (2010) suggest that well-structured participation mechanisms within e-democracy environments can be highly effective in fostering greater civic engagement, as they establish clear and accessible methods through which citizens can contribute to issues of public interest. Such processes are vital for cultivating an informed and engaged citizenry capable of interacting meaningfully with their governments.

2.3. Efficiency

Efficiency in resource use and policy implementation is a key component of smart governance. Maestre-Góngora and Nieto (2015) argue that technology plays a vital role in enabling more dynamic and effective interactions between governments and citizens, thus optimising the delivery of public services. This is particularly evident in times of crisis, when adaptability and efficiency in governmental responses become essential (Cardozo, 2024).

Mechanisms to Ensure Efficiency in Smart Governance:

- Information and Communication Technologies (ICT): The adoption of ICT enables real-time data collection and analysis, thereby facilitating more informed and evidence-based decision-making. Through the use of integrated information systems, governments can manage resources more effectively, enhance communication with citizens, and monitor the implementation of public policies. For instance, the use of digital platforms is transforming the delivery of public services, making processes more agile, transparent, and accessible.
- Policy Evaluation and Monitoring: The establishment of systematic evaluation and monitoring mechanisms allows governments to assess the effectiveness and efficiency of their policies in resource utilisation. Recent studies emphasise that continuous policy evaluation helps identify areas for improvement and enables timely adjustments to strategies, resulting in enhanced performance. The literature suggests that analytical frameworks for policy assessment should incorporate clear performance indicators and measurable, achievable objectives.
- Citizen Participation: Involving citizens in policy design and implementation processes contributes significantly to improving efficiency. Direct feedback from end beneficiaries provides valuable insights into how resources are allocated and how effective the implemented policies are. According to Krawczyk and Sweet-Cushman (2016), citizen participation can help optimise resource allocation towards initiatives that genuinely address community needs.

Despite the recognised importance of efficiency, several challenges remain. One of the most pressing is resistance to change among governmental actors. Organisational inertia and insufficient training in the use of emerging technologies can hinder the adoption of more efficient governance practices. Furthermore, unequal access to technology constrains efficiency in disadvantaged areas, where infrastructure and digital resources are limited.

Another major challenge lies in the risk of over-optimisation, whereby short-term results are excessively prioritised at the expense of long-term sustainability. Such an approach can lead to decisions that, although efficient in the immediate term, fail to consider their social and environmental implications. It is therefore essential to adopt a balanced perspective that integrates both immediate efficiency and future sustainability, ensuring that progress today does not compromise resilience tomorrow.

2.4. Innovation

Continuous innovation is necessary to sustain the relevance of smart governance, particularly in an ever-changing environment. Research by Libert-Amico et al. (2018)

reveals that integrating new approaches and technologies can foster responsiveness to emerging challenges, including climate change and natural resource conservation (Billi et al., 2020). This reinforces the idea that innovation should be regarded not merely as a tool, but as a central strategy for the resilience and sustainability of socio-ecological systems.

In a rapidly evolving world, responsiveness is paramount. As noted in the United Nations report on governance and sustainable development, adaptability is essential for addressing emerging crises and complex social challenges that demand creative and timely solutions. Innovation—understood as the implementation of new ideas, processes, or technologies—enables governments to bridge the gap between citizens' expectations and the realities of public service delivery.

Globalisation has intensified competition among cities and nations, making it vital for public administrations to pursue continual improvement in services and infrastructure. Research by Azevedo et al. demonstrates that cities adopting innovative governance approaches are better positioned to attract investment and talent. Consequently, innovation is not merely an enhancement but a strategic necessity for survival in an interconnected world.

The deployment of new technologies, such as mobile applications for service management and digital platforms for citizen participation, can profoundly transform the citizen experience. According to Jansen et al., innovation in service delivery enhances public satisfaction and fosters greater civic engagement. This results in a more collaborative relationship between citizens and government, encouraging the co-creation of solutions and shared responsibility in governance.

Cultivating an environment that nurtures innovation is central to smart governance. This involves not only embracing new technologies but also fostering a culture that values creativity, experimentation, and learning within public institutions. Burke and Tschakert argue that governments promoting continuous learning and interdepartmental collaboration are more capable of effective innovation. Training civil servants, encouraging cross-sectoral partnerships, and welcoming external ideas are essential elements of such an environment.

Collaboration among government, the private sector, and civil society serves as a powerful catalyst for innovation. Innovation labs—where governments, citizens, and technology companies jointly experiment with new solutions—are increasingly recognised as effective mechanisms for advancing collaborative innovation.

Data analytics and emerging technologies, including the Internet of Things (IoT) and Big Data, play a pivotal role in driving innovation. These tools allow governments to collect and analyse vast amounts of information, enabling them to identify needs and trends in real time. Giffinger and Fertner underscore how these technologies can optimise processes and enhance evidence-based decision-making across administrative domains.

Despite its significance, innovation in governance faces several barriers. One major obstacle is resistance to change, both within institutions and among communities. Clayton Christensen notes that organisations often cling to established practices, limiting their capacity for effective innovation. Furthermore, financial and human resource constraints can impede the adoption of new technologies and innovative approaches.

Another critical challenge concerns equity. While innovation has the potential to improve citizens' lives, not all social groups have equal access to its benefits. Governments must therefore ensure that innovation is inclusive and responsive to the needs of vulnerable populations. Achieving equitable innovation requires deliberate strategies that promote accessibility, fairness, and social cohesion within the digital transformation process.

2.5. Relevant Theoretical Models

The conceptual foundation of smart governance draws upon a range of theoretical frameworks that explain how complex systems can adapt, learn, and evolve through the interaction of human, institutional, and technological components. These models provide the intellectual scaffolding for understanding how digital transformation reshapes administrative decision-making, stakeholder engagement, and systemic resilience. From the cybernetic vision of feedback and control, through adaptive governance models that emphasise flexibility and collective learning, to socio-technical network theories that explore the co-evolution of humans and technologies, each framework contributes a distinct perspective. Together, they offer an integrated understanding of how intelligent, data-driven, and participatory governance systems emerge and sustain themselves in dynamic socio-political environments.

2.5.1. Cybernetic Systems Theory

Cybernetic theory, as introduced by Norbert Wiener (1948) and later developed in the context of organisational management by Stafford Beer (1972), posits that any complex system can be understood as a network of feedback loops that regulate its behaviour. Within the framework of *smart governance*, this theory offers valuable insights into how digital and institutional systems achieve stability through continuous data circulation and control mechanisms.

- Control loops: Performance indicators (KPIs) feed automated decision systems that monitor and adjust administrative functions.

- Positive and negative feedback: Algorithms dynamically allocate or withhold resources according to real-time demand, as observed in smart energy grids or adaptive traffic systems.
- Autonomy: Processes self-regulate to maintain institutional objectives within acceptable thresholds of efficiency and equity.

Cybernetics thus provides a formal language for describing information flows among sensors, computational systems, and human decision-makers, illustrating how these interactions establish a *dynamic equilibrium* essential for resilient governance structures.

2.5.2. Adaptive Governance

The concept of *adaptive governance*, rooted in the institutional analysis of Elinor Ostrom (1990, 2010) and later expanded by scholars such as Peter Mair (2013), emphasises the ability of political and social systems to adjust to internal and external changes while preserving institutional coherence. This model is particularly relevant for understanding flexibility in smart government operations.

Key principles include:

- Continuous interaction among actors: Persistent dialogue with stakeholders to foster collaboration and legitimacy.
- Flexible policy responses: Mechanisms for rapid adjustment based on predictive analytics and emerging evidence.
- Shared resources: Co-ownership and co-management of data infrastructures and digital assets.
- Learning institutions: Formal evaluation and feedback cycles that enable iterative improvement of public policies.

In smart governance, adaptive models translate into evidence-based policy cycles, where predictive insights guide both regulatory design and service reconfiguration, ensuring governments remain responsive, resilient, and citizen-centred.

2.5.3. Socio-Technical Network Theory

The socio-technical network perspective synthesises structural systems theory from Ludwig von Bertalanffy (1968) with the *Actor–Network Theory (ANT)* developed by Bruno Latour, Michel Callon, and John Law (1986–1999), and the *Mode 2 knowledge production* framework proposed by Gibbons et al. (1994). This integrative approach examines how social relations and technical infrastructures co-evolve within governance systems.

It is grounded in three analytical dimensions:

- Actor–Network Theory (ANT): Human and non-human entities—such as sensors, algorithms, databases, and citizens—function as interconnected nodes shaping governance outcomes.
- Heterogeneity of devices: Digital artefacts and institutional actors form an integrated ecosystem that mediates decision-making processes.
- Translation: The alignment of diverse interests through negotiation, standardisation, and shared objectives within socio-technical systems.

From this perspective, smart governance can be viewed as a dynamic network of interactions where emerging technologies (IoT, AI, data analytics) are embedded within institutional routines, redistributing agency and redefining power among actors in the digital public sphere.

3. FUTURE TRENDS AND DIRECTIONS IN SMART GOVERNMENT

The current landscape of digital governance is undergoing a critical phase of transition, in which technological progress is reshaping not only the tools available to the State but also the very logic through which it operates. Emerging technologies such as Artificial Intelligence (AI), the Internet of Things (IoT), blockchain, and data analytics are redefining the structure and dynamics of public decision-making (OECD, 2020; Janssen & van der Voort, 2020). This section explores four interrelated trends that are expected to influence the future trajectory of public governance: autonomous governance and algorithmic decision-making, digital twins in public policy, and AI-augmented digital democracy. Each subsection integrates theoretical underpinnings, applied cases, and methodological challenges to illustrate the pathways through which smart government is likely to evolve in the coming decade.

3.1. Autonomous Governance and Algorithmic Decision-Making

3.1.1. Concept and Theoretical Foundations

Autonomous governance refers to the use of algorithmic systems—based on machine learning, inference rules, and automated decision processes—to perform governance functions in real time with minimal or no direct human intervention (Meijer, 2021; Yeung, 2018). In public administration, this involves automation in key domains such as:

- Resource allocation: dynamic budgeting and fiscal adjustments driven by predictive demand models.
- Regulation: algorithmic regulation of traffic, energy consumption, or public health parameters (Danaher et al., 2017).
- Crisis management: real-time emergency responses to natural disasters or pandemics through data-driven predictive systems.

The theoretical foundations of autonomous governance can be traced to cybernetic systems theory (Wiener, 1948; Beer, 1972), which emphasises continuous feedback loops that enable systems to self-regulate and pursue institutional objectives dynamically.

3.1.2. Illustrative Cases

Practical examples include:

- Smart traffic management systems in cities such as *Barcelona* and *Singapore*, where neural networks adjust traffic lights and reroute vehicles based on real-time congestion patterns (Kitchin, 2021).
- Automated public microfinance schemes, in which AI-based credit scoring allocates financial support to small enterprises, reducing administrative delays and human bias (Zheng et al., 2020).

3.1.3. Ethical and Regulatory Challenges

The implementation of algorithmic governance raises fundamental questions regarding:

- Accountability: determining responsibility when automated systems produce unintended or harmful outcomes, requiring frameworks of *algorithmic accountability* (Wirtz et al., 2023).
- Transparency: ensuring that model interpretability allows public justification and judicial oversight (Floridi et al., 2018).
- Bias and fairness: mitigating the risk of algorithms perpetuating historical inequalities embedded in training data (Mehrabi et al., 2021).

Continuous auditing, explainable AI (XAI) approaches, and citizen oversight mechanisms are therefore critical for maintaining trust and ethical integrity.

3.2. Digital Twins in Public Policy

3.2.1. Definition

A *digital twin* is a virtual replica of a physical asset, process, or system that is synchronised with its real-world counterpart through sensors and IoT data (Tao et al., 2019). Within public governance, digital twins enable governments to simulate, monitor, and optimise complex socio-technical systems before policy implementation, supporting a more predictive and evidence-based approach.

3.2.2. Governmental Applications

Applications in public administration include:

- Urban planning: modelling congestion patterns to assess the effects of new infrastructure projects (Batty, 2018).
- Water management: simulating distribution networks to optimise pressure control and detect leaks before they occur (Min et al., 2021).
- Fiscal policy: testing taxation scenarios and their sectoral economic impacts using real-time macroeconomic data (Kitchin, 2021).

3.2.3. Benefits

Digital twin integration offers multiple advantages:

- Reduces *trial-and-error costs* by enabling pre-implementation testing.
- Increases *precision* in socio-economic impact assessments.
- Enhances *citizen participation* by visualising the projected outcomes of policy interventions (Pérez-Lara et al., 2023).

3.2.4. Technical and Organisational Challenges

Key challenges include:

- Data integration: ensuring the quality, interoperability, and temporal consistency of data sources (Tao et al., 2019).

- Scalability: managing the high computational demands of large-scale simulations, often requiring cloud or edge computing infrastructure.
- Security: protecting the integrity and confidentiality of digital twin environments from cyber threats (Min et al., 2021).

Effective governance frameworks will require multidisciplinary collaboration between policymakers, engineers, and data scientists to ensure these systems remain transparent, resilient, and ethically aligned.

3.3. Augmented Digital Democracy with Generative AI

3.3.1. Definition and Conceptual Basis

Augmented Digital Democracy (ADD) refers to a model of governance in which digital tools not only facilitate access to information and participatory processes but also enhance the collective capacity to generate, evaluate, and refine policy proposals. Unlike traditional e-consultation or electronic voting systems, ADD integrates generative Artificial Intelligence (AI) to support collaborative ideation and evidence-based decision-making (Helbing et al., 2021; OECD, 2023). Citizens interact with intelligent systems that:

- Provide simulated scenarios illustrating the potential impact of proposed decisions.
- Generate alternative policy options based on collective data and expressed preferences.
- Facilitate dialogue between diverse groups through automated translation and context-aware summarisation.

Generative AI—encompassing large language models (LLMs), generative adversarial networks (GANs), and multimodal synthesis tools—acts as a *co-author of the public agenda* (Bryson et al., 2017). It transforms raw data and fragmented opinions into coherent narratives, draft policy documents, or interactive visualisations that are accessible to non-technical audiences.

3.3.2. Participation Process

The participatory cycle in ADD typically involves six iterative phases:

1. Data acquisition: Collection of inputs through civic consultation platforms, social media, and urban sensor networks.

2. Pre-processing: AI filters noise, clusters topics, and extracts key themes for discussion.
3. Collaborative generation: Citizens propose ideas which the AI synthesises into structured drafts or scenario outlines.
4. Simulation and feedback: Predictive models estimate policy consequences, which are presented interactively for public review.
5. Guided deliberation: Human moderators—or ethically designed conversational agents—facilitate debate, ensuring AI remains a tool, not a decision-maker.
6. Voting and consensus: Weighted voting or deliberative online mechanisms (e.g., *Loomio*, *Pol.is*) finalise collective decisions (Macintosh & Whyte, 2008).

This hybrid model seeks to combine computational intelligence with human deliberation, promoting a more inclusive and transparent governance cycle.

3.3.3. Case Studies

- Barcelona – "Participa" prototype: A civic participation platform integrating GPT-4 to generate automated responses to citizen inquiries and to draft local policy proposals, enhancing both transparency and responsiveness (Ajuntament de Barcelona, 2024).
- Virtual School, Finland: A pilot project where generative AI creates personalised curricula based on collective feedback, improving measurable educational outcomes and demonstrating AI's participatory potential in the public sector (European Commission, 2023).

Augmented Digital Democracy envisions a *"democracy of ideas"* where the quality, diversity, and creativity of public proposals are shaped jointly by human intelligence and computational capability. As generative AI systems evolve towards greater transparency and contextual awareness, their integration into civic processes may enable more agile, inclusive, and evidence-informed policymaking (Helbing et al., 2021). However, realising this vision requires the convergence of explainable AI, robust cybersecurity, and adaptive digital regulation—ensuring that technological empowerment strengthens, rather than supplants, the human essence of democracy.

4. CHALLENGES IN THE ADOPTION OF SMART PUBLIC POLICIES

The adoption of intelligent public-policy frameworks faces structural, cultural and technological barriers. This section outlines the main challenges and proposes strategies to overcome them.

- Digital divides and social exclusion. Unequal access to digital technologies remains a critical obstacle. Disparities in broadband connectivity and mobile-device availability persist between urban and rural areas, as well as across socio-economic groups (López-Aguado et al., 2022). Furthermore, a lack of digital literacy prevents many citizens from effectively using online public services (Boudou, 2023). Proposed strategy: implement device-subsidy programmes, expand 5G networks in remote areas, and conduct nationwide digital-skills training campaigns, targeting both basic and advanced competencies.
- Public institutions often display rigid bureaucratic structures and risk aversion that hinder innovation. Organisational inertia and the absence of an "agile" culture reduce the ability to respond to technological change (Mergel et al., 2019). Strategy: introduce structured change-management programmes, set measurable indicators of success, and establish cross-disciplinary teams that combine technical expertise with administrative experience.
- Interoperability and infrastructure issues. Legacy systems with poor documentation often prevent the integration of new digital platforms. Fragmented data standards across agencies result in information silos and inefficiencies (Wilson-Menzfeld, 2025). Action plan: adopt open standards (e.g., RESTful APIs, JSON-LD), migrate to microservice-based architectures, and establish a *Data Stewardship Office* responsible for maintaining data quality, compatibility and ethical compliance.
- Data governance and algorithmic ethics. Algorithms trained on biased historical datasets can perpetuate social inequalities. The need for transparency, fairness and accountability in AI decision-making has been widely recognised in public governance research (Grimmelikhuijsen et al., 2022). Ensuring explainability is equally essential—citizens must understand how automated systems make decisions that affect them (Frontiers Authors, 2024). Recommendation: define ethical principles for algorithmic governance, implement independent audit mechanisms, and establish review panels to assess high-impact algorithms before deployment.
- Cybersecurity risks. Public infrastructures are vulnerable to both internal and external cyber threats, including ransomware, phishing and denial-of-

service attacks (European Union Agency for Cybersecurity [ENISA], 2023). Response: establish Business Continuity and Disaster Recovery (BCP/DR) plans, perform regular incident-response simulations, and train dedicated security teams to ensure service resilience.

- Sustainable funding. Financial sustainability remains a challenge in long-term digital transformation. Public–private partnerships, venture funding, and co-financing with international donors such as the UN or IDB have proven effective in supporting large-scale digital initiatives (Organisation for Economic Co-operation and Development [OECD], 2020). Approach: reinvest operational savings achieved through automation into new innovation projects and promote cross-sector collaboration to maintain financial continuity.
- Impact measurement and institutional learning. Continuous evaluation ensures accountability and improvement. Quantitative indicators (response time, cost reduction, citizen reach) must be complemented by qualitative metrics, such as citizen satisfaction and trust in government (Boudou, 2023). Cycle of improvement: conduct biannual reviews with stakeholders, publish transparent performance reports, and adjust strategies based on empirical findings and feedback.

5. CONCLUSIONS

The transition towards smart governance represents not merely a technological shift but a structural transformation in how states conceive, deliver, and evaluate public services. Across the diverse case studies examined, several common lessons emerge. Interoperability stands out as the central pillar of successful digital transformation, enabling seamless data exchange between government agencies and the private sector through open and standardised architectures. Evidence-based governance, supported by real-time metrics and analytics, allows governments to adapt policies dynamically, improving efficiency and citizen satisfaction while reducing operational costs. Furthermore, the cultivation of a strong digital culture among public servants has proven as crucial as technological investment. Digital literacy, continuous training, and a mindset of innovation constitute essential elements of human capital in the digital era. Equally important, robust frameworks for cybersecurity, identity verification, and auditing mechanisms underpin public trust, a prerequisite for widespread technological adoption. Finally, adaptability emerges as a defining quality of smart governance—governments must act with a "fast-learning" ethos, acknowledging that regulatory and institutional frameworks often evolve more slowly than the technologies they seek to govern.

From these findings arise several guiding principles for implementation. An open-data-first policy should be prioritised, whereby governments release public data through well-documented APIs and permissive licences to stimulate innovation and prevent duplication of effort. Modular and scalable system design—rooted in microservice architectures—enables governments to expand or upgrade services without overhauling entire infrastructures. Active citizen participation from the design stage ensures that digital solutions meet real needs, strengthening legitimacy and avoiding the disconnect that can arise between policymakers and communities. Proactive regulation is equally essential: legal frameworks must anticipate potential risks such as algorithmic bias and privacy breaches rather than react to crises after they occur. Collectively, these principles promote a resilient digital ecosystem capable of sustaining technological evolution while preserving democratic accountability and social inclusion.

Translating these principles into action requires differentiated yet coordinated efforts. Local governments should establish open data hubs with interactive dashboards for municipal services, pilot small-scale projects in areas such as waste management or urban mobility, and build partnerships with local technology firms to foster knowledge transfer and local innovation capacity. National governments should focus on enacting unified regulatory frameworks for open data and cybersecurity, creating digital innovation funds dedicated to applied research in AI, IoT, and blockchain, and introducing mandatory continuous training programmes for civil servants linked to performance incentives. Multilateral organisations, for their part, can play a catalytic role by developing international standards (e.g., ISO/IEC) for cross-border digital interoperability, funding pilot projects in developing countries to replicate successful models such as Estonia's e-Residency or X-Road, and facilitating global ethical dialogues on artificial intelligence and data governance. Ultimately, the future of smart government depends not only on technological capability but on political vision, institutional coherence, and a shared commitment to transparency, equity, and sustainability.

REFERENCES

Ajuntament de Barcelona. (2024). Participa Barcelona: Inteligencia artificial para la participación ciudadana. Barcelona City Council, Digital Innovation Report.

Aman, S., & Jan, M. (2022). Are we moving towards a managerial model of e-governance? building a case for citizen centric e-participation in khyber pakhtunkhwa, pakistan. *Biological and Clinical Sciences Research Journal, 3*(1), 500–523. DOI: 10.47264/idea.jhsms/3.1.35

ANDRONICEANU, A., Georgescu, I., & Kinnunen, J. (2022). "public administration digitalization and corruption in the eu member states. a comparative and correlative research analysis". Transylvanian Review of Administrative Sciences, (65E), 5-22. DOI: 10.24193/tras.65E.1

Ardielli, E. (2015). Public administration transparency in e-government at local level of czech government. *The International Journal of Management Science and Business Administration, 2*(8), 24–33. DOI: 10.18775/ijmsba.1849-5664-5419.2014.28.1003

Authors, F. (2024). Transparency and accountability in AI systems. *Frontiers in Human Dynamics, 6*, 1421273. DOI: 10.3389/fhumd.2024.1421273

Batty, M. (2018). Digital twins. *Environment and Planning. B, Urban Analytics and City Science, 45*(5), 817–820. DOI: 10.1177/2399808318796416

Beer, S. (1972). *Brain of the firm.* Allen Lane.

Billi, M., Delgado, V., Jiménez, G., Morales, B., Neira, C., Silva, M., & Urquiza, A. (2020). Gobernanza policéntrica para la resiliencia al cambio climático: Análisis legislativo comparado y ley marco de cambio en chile. *Estudios Públicos*, (160), 7–53. DOI: 10.38178/07183089/1028191015

Boudou, M. (2023). Digital divide, e-government and trust in public service: The key role of educational inequalities. *Frontiers in Sociology, 8*, 1140416. DOI: 10.3389/fsoc.2023.1140416 PMID: 36895333

Bryson, J. J., Diamantis, M. E., & Grant, T. D. (2017). Of, for, and by the people: The legal lacuna of synthetic persons. *Artificial Intelligence and Law, 25*(3), 273–291. DOI: 10.1007/s10506-017-9214-9

Callon, M. (1986). Some elements of a sociology of translation: Domestication of the scallops and the fishermen of St Brieuc Bay. In Law, J. (Ed.), *Power, action and belief: A new sociology of knowledge?* (pp. 196–233). Routledge.

Cardozo, N. (2024). Las crisis en la literatura de políticas públicas. *Análisis Plural*, (8). Advance online publication. DOI: 10.31391/4291h136

Cardozo, N. (2024). Las crisis en la literatura de políticas públicas. Análisis Plural, (8). Chatfield, A. and Brajawidagda, U. (2013). Political will and strategic use of youtube to advancing government transparency: an analysis of jakarta government-generated youtube videos., 26-37. https://doi.org/DOI: 10.31391/4291h136

Chatfield, A. and Brajawidagda, U. (2013). Political will and strategic use of youtube to advancing government transparency: an analysis of jakarta government-generated youtube videos., 26-37. DOI: 10.1007/978-3-642-40358-3_3

Choo, M., Choi, Y., Yoon, H., Bae, S., & Yoon, D. (2023). Citizen engagement in smart city planning: The case of living labs in south korea. *Urban Planning*, *8*(2). Advance online publication. DOI: 10.17645/up.v8i2.6416

Cordella, A., & Paletti, A. (2018). Icts and value creation in public sector: Manufacturing logic vs service logic. *Information Polity*, *23*(2), 125–141. DOI: 10.3233/IP-170061

Danaher, J., Hogan, M. J., Noone, C., Kennedy, R., Behan, A., De Paor, A., Felzmann, H., Haklay, M., Khoo, S.-M., Morison, J., Murphy, M. H., O'Brolchain, N., Schafer, B., & Shankar, K. (2017). Algorithmic governance: Developing a research agenda through the power of collective intelligence. *Big Data & Society*, *4*(2), 1–21. DOI: 10.1177/2053951717726554

Dzvinchuk, D., Borshch, H., Tsygylyk, N., Dobosh, Z., & Dziubynska, O. (2022). Public management for sustainable development: Current challenges and future trends. *Cuestiones Políticas*, *40*(73), 741–753. DOI: 10.46398/cuestpol.4073.42

Ejjami, R. (2024). Public administration 5.0: Enhancing governance and public services with smart technologies. *International Journal for Multidisciplinary Research*, *6*(4), 26086. Advance online publication. DOI: 10.36948/ijfmr.2024.v06i04.26086

European Commission. (2023). *Artificial intelligence in education: Generative models and participatory learning*. Publications Office of the European Union.

European Union Agency for Cybersecurity. (2023). *ENISA Threat Landscape 2023*. https://www.enisa.europa.eu

Fernández, J. (2021). La gobernanza inteligente de las metrópolis y la participación ciudadana. *Información Comercial Española*, (920). Advance online publication. DOI: 10.32796/ice.2021.920.7178

Fernández-Añez, V., Güell, J., & Giffinger, R. (2018). Smart city implementation and discourses: An integrated conceptual model. the case of vienna. *Cities (London, England), 78*, 4–16. DOI: 10.1016/j.cities.2017.12.004

Floridi, L., Cowls, J., Beltrametti, M., Chatila, R., Chazerand, P., Dignum, V., Luetge, C., Madelin, R., Pagallo, U., Rossi, F., Schafer, B., Valcke, P., & Vayena, E. (2018). AI4People—An ethical framework for a good AI society. *Minds and Machines, 28*(4), 689–707. DOI: 10.1007/s11023-018-9482-5 PMID: 30930541

Franco, I. (2021). Las smart cities en la agenda del plancamiento y la gobernanza urbana en américa latina. *Cuadernos de Geografia, 30*(2), 280–296. DOI: 10.15446/rcdg.v30n2.89479

Galushi, L., & Malatji, T. (2022). Digital public administration and inclusive governance at the south african local government, in depth analysis of e-government and service delivery in musina local municipality. *Academic Journal of Interdisciplinary Studies, 11*(6), 116. DOI: 10.36941/ajis-2022-0154

Gibbons, M., Limoges, C., Nowotny, H., Schwartzman, S., Scott, P., & Trow, M. (1994). *The new production of knowledge: The dynamics of science and research in contemporary societies*. SAGE Publications.

Grimmelikhuijsen, S., Wirtz, B. W., & Welch, E. W. (2022). Algorithmic transparency and trust in government: Legitimacy challenges in automated decision-making. *Public Policy and Management, 5*(3), 232–246. DOI: 10.1093/ppmg/pwac021

Gualdi, F. and Cordella, A. (2022). Techno-legal entanglements as new actors in the policy-making process.. DOI: 10.24251/HICSS.2022.298

Guazzo, G., & Çekani, V. (2023). How nudge can support smart governance in smart cities ecosystems: an a4a framework. Itm Web of Conferences, 51, 02002. DOI: 10.1051/itmconf/20235102002

Hartanti, F., Abawajy, J., Chowdhury, M., & Shalannanda, W. (2021). Citizens' trust measurement in smart government services. *IEEE Access : Practical Innovations, Open Solutions, 9*, 150663–150676. DOI: 10.1109/ACCESS.2021.3124206

Helbing, D., Frey, B. S., Gigerenzer, G., Hafen, E., Hagner, M., Hofstetter, Y., & Zwitter, A. (2021). Will democracy survive big data and artificial intelligence? *Scientific American, 317*(2), 25–33.

Hope, O., Jiang, S., & Vyas, D. (2021). Government transparency and firm-level operational efficiency. *Journal of Business Finance & Accounting, 49*(5-6), 752–777. DOI: 10.1111/jbfa.12563

Hutahaean, M., Eunike, I., & Silalahi, A. (2023). Do social media, good governance, and public trust increase citizens' e-government participation? dual approach of pls-sem and fsqca. *Human Behavior and Emerging Technologies, 2023*, 1–19. DOI: 10.1155/2023/9988602

Igbokwe-Ibeto, C., & Osakede, K. (2017). Public policy and citizens participation in ngor okpala local government area of imo state, nigeria 2011 - 2015. *Management Studies and Economic Systems, 3*(3), 149–158. DOI: 10.12816/0040228

Janssen, M., & van der Voort, H. (2020). Agile and adaptive governance in crisis response: Lessons from the COVID-19 pandemic. *International Journal of Information Management, 55*, 102180. DOI: 10.1016/j.ijinfomgt.2020.102180 PMID: 32836637

Johnson, P., Acedo, A., & Robinson, P. (2020). Canadian smart cities: Are we wiring new citizen-local government interactions? *The Canadian Geographer. Geographe Canadien, 64*(3), 402–415. DOI: 10.1111/cag.12623

Kitchin, R. (2021). *Data lives: How data are made and shape our world.* Bristol University Press.

Krawczyk, K., & Sweet-Cushman, J. (2016). Understanding political participation in west africa: The relationship between good governance and local citizen engagement. *International Review of Administrative Sciences, 83*(1, suppl), 136–155. DOI: 10.1177/0020852315619024

Kropf, M., Pope, J., Shepherd, M., & Mohr, Z. (2020). Making every vote count: The important role of managerial capacity in achieving better election administration outcomes. *Public Administration Review, 80*(5), 733–742. DOI: 10.1111/puar.13216

Latour, B. (1987). *Science in action: How to follow scientists and engineers through society*. Harvard University Press.

Law, J. (1992). Notes on the theory of the actor-network: Ordering, strategy and heterogeneity. *Systems Practice, 5*(4), 379–393. DOI: 10.1007/BF01059830

Letki, N., & Steen, T. (2021). Social-psychological context moderates incentives to co-produce: Evidence from a large-scale survey experiment on park upkeep in an urban setting. *Public Administration Review, 81*(5), 935–950. DOI: 10.1111/puar.13340 PMID: 34690373

Libert-Amico, A., Trench, T., Rodríguez, A., & Martínez-Morales, M. (2018). Experiencias de gobernanza multinivel en méxico: Innovación para la reducción de emisiones de carbono de los ecosistemas terrestres. *Madera y Bosques, 24*. Advance online publication. DOI: 10.21829/myb.2018.2401909

Liu, S., & Yuan, Q. (2015). The evolution of information and communication technology in public administration. *Public Administration and Development, 35*(2), 140–151. DOI: 10.1002/pad.1717

López-Aguado, M., Gutiérrez-Provecho, L., Quintanal-Díaz, J., & García-Llamas, J. L. (2022). *Social exclusion and the digital divide.* Journal of e-Learning and Knowledge Society, 18(3), 74–82. https://doi.org/DOI: 10.20368/1971-8829/1135660

Mabillard, V., & Pasquier, M. (2015). Transparency and trust in government: A two-way relationship. *Yearbook of Swiss Administrative Sciences, 6*(1), 23. DOI: 10.5334/ssas.78

Maciél, C., Roque, L., & García, A. (2010). Interaction and communication resources in collaborative e-democratic environments: The democratic citizenship community. *Information Polity, 15*(1,2), 73–88. DOI: 10.3233/IP-2010-0197

Macintosh, A., & Whyte, A. (2008). Towards an evaluation framework for eParticipation. *Transforming Government: People. Transforming Government, 2*(1), 16–30. DOI: 10.1108/17506160810862928

Maestre-Góngora, G., & Nieto, W. (2015). Factores clave en la gestión de tecnología de información para sistemas de gobierno inteligente. *Journal of Technology Management & Innovation, 10*(4), 109–117. DOI: 10.4067/S0718-27242015000400012

Mair, P. (2013). *Ruling the void: The hollowing of Western democracy.* Verso Books.

McCool, S., Freimund, W., & Breen, C. (2019). Beneficios del pensamiento complejo.. https://doi.org/DOI: 10.22459/GGAP.2019.10

Mehrabi, N., Morstatter, F., Saxena, N., Lerman, K., & Galstyan, A. (2021). A survey on bias and fairness in machine learning. *ACM Computing Surveys, 54*(6), 1–35. DOI: 10.1145/3457607

Meijer, A. (2021). *The algorithmic state: Towards a new digital democracy.* Oxford University Press.

Meijer, A., & Bolívar, M. (2015). Governing the smart city: A review of the literature on smart urban governance. *International Review of Administrative Sciences, 82*(2), 392–408. DOI: 10.1177/0020852314564308

Meza-Jiménez, A., Vázquez, M., Verschoor, G., Lugo, E., & García-Barrios, L. (2021). Hacia una gobernanza adaptativa centrada en los grupos domésticos rurales que habitan las áreas naturales protegidas. el caso de la sepultura, chiapas, méxico. Sociedad Y Ambiente, (24), 1-30. https://doi.org/DOI: 10.31840/sya.vi24.2340

Min, Q., Lu, Y., Liu, Z., Su, C., & Wang, B. (2021). Machine learning-based digital twin framework for smart water management. *Water Research, 197*, 117060. DOI: 10.1016/j.watres.2021.117060

Molobela, T. and Uwizeyimana, D. (2023). E-governance as a new public administration paradigm: a rhetoric or reality?. International Journal of Research in Business and Social Science (2147-4478), 12(8), 348-356. DOI: 10.20525/ijrbs.v12i8.2931

Ngatikoh, S., Kumorotomo, W., & Retnandari, N. (2020). Transparency in government: a review on the failures of corruption prevention in indonesia.. https://doi.org/ DOI: 10.2991/aebmr.k.200301.010

OECD. (2020). *Digital government index: 2019 results*. OECD Publishing., DOI: 10.1787/4de9f5bb-

OECD. (2023). *OECD digital government policy framework: Towards a digitally enabled state*. OECD Publishing.

Organisation for Economic Co-operation and Development. (2020). *Digital government in Latin America: Transforming public services and institutions*. OECD Publishing., DOI: 10.1787/6e1b64a3-

Ostrom, E. (1990). *Governing the commons: The evolution of institutions for collective action*. Cambridge University Press. DOI: 10.1017/CBO9780511807763

Ostrom, E. (2010). Beyond markets and states: Polycentric governance of complex economic systems. *The American Economic Review, 100*(3), 641–672. DOI: 10.1257/aer.100.3.641

Pereira, G., Eibl, G., Stylianou, C., Martínez, G., Neophytou, H., & Parycek, P. (2018). The role of smart technologies to support citizen engagement and decision making. *International Journal of Electronic Government Research, 14*(4), 1–17. DOI: 10.4018/IJEGR.2018100101

Pereira, G., Parycek, P., Falco, E., & Kleinhans, R. (2018). Smart governance in the context of smart cities: A literature review. *Information Polity, 23*(2), 143–162. DOI: 10.3233/IP-170067

Pérez-Lara, M. D., Trejo-Macotela, F. R., & Ruiz-Vanoye, J. A. (2023). Digital twins for participatory governance in smart cities. *Journal of Urban Technology, 30*(3), 115–133.

Petrović, N., Milić, P., & Prlinčević, B. (2022). Using open government data for economic development. *The European Journal of Applied Economics, 19*(2), 129–141. DOI: 10.5937/EJAE19-39004

Purwanti, Y., Purwanto, B., & Jamaludin, M. (2022). Citizen participation in electronic public administration: The considerations of functionality and the technology acceptance model. *International Journal of Public Policy and Administration Research*, *9*(4), 90–101. DOI: 10.18488/74.v9i4.3206

Ruijer, E., Détienne, F., Baker, M., Groff, J., & Meijer, A. (2019). The politics of open government data: Understanding organizational responses to pressure for more transparency. *American Review of Public Administration*, *50*(3), 260–274. DOI: 10.1177/0275074019888065

Ruiz-Vanoye, J. A., Díaz-Parra, O., Marroquín-Gutiérrez, F., Rodríguez-Lara, B. M., Fuentes-Penna, A., Barrera-Cámara, R. A., Ramos-Fernández, J. C., Xicoténcatl-Pérez, J. M., & Aguilar-Ortiz, J. (2023). Smart Government and Future Trends. In Ruiz-Vanoye, J. (Ed.), *Management, Technology, and Economic Growth in Smart and Sustainable Cities* (pp. 37–59). IGI Global Scientific Publishing., DOI: 10.4018/979-8-3693-0373-3.ch003

Tao, F., Zhang, H., Liu, A., & Nee, A. Y. C. (2019). *Digital twin driven smart manufacturing*. Academic Press.

Trimble, M. and Plummer, R. (2019). Evaluación participativa para la gobernanza adaptativa de sistemas socio-ecológicos. Tekoporá Revista Latinoamericana De Humanidades Ambientales Y Estudios Territoriales, 1(1). https://doi.org/DOI: 10.36225/TEK.1.1.5

Trimble, M. and Plummer, R. (2019). Evaluación participativa para la gobernanza adaptativa de sistemas socio-ecológicos: participatory evaluation for adaptative governance of social-ecologic systems. Tekoporá Revista Latinoamericana De Humanidades Ambientales Y Estudios Territoriales, 1(1). https://doi.org/DOI: 10.36225/tekopora.v1i1.8

Voitenko, O., Shults, S., Bilyk, I., & Kaplenko, H. (2022). Government transparency as ukrainian territorial communities' economic development factor. *Financial and Credit Activity Problems of Theory and Practice*, *5*(46), 387–397. DOI: 10.55643/fcaptp.5.46.2022.3879

von Bertalanffy, L. (1968). *General system theory: Foundations, development, applications*. George Braziller.

Webster, C., & Leleux, C. (2018). Smart governance: Opportunities for technologically-mediated citizen co-production. *Information Polity*, *23*(1), 95–110. DOI: 10.3233/IP-170065

Wiener, N. (1948). *Cybernetics: Or control and communication in the animal and the machine*. MIT Press.

Wilson-Menzfeld, G. (2025). Digital inclusion and governance frameworks for community resilience. *Behaviour & Information Technology*, *44*(1), 1–18. DOI: 10.1080/0144929X.2024.2368087

Wirtz, B. W., Weyerer, J. C., & Sturm, B. J. (2023). Algorithmic transparency in the public sector: Toward responsible artificial intelligence. *Government Information Quarterly*, *40*(2), 101824. DOI: 10.1016/j.giq.2022.101824

Xia, S. (2017). E-governance and political modernization: An empirical study based on asia from 2003 to 2014. *Administrative Sciences*, *7*(3), 25. DOI: 10.3390/admsci7030025

Yang, K., & Pandey, S. (2011). Further dissecting the black box of citizen participation: When does citizen involvement lead to good outcomes? *Public Administration Review*, *71*(6), 880–892. DOI: 10.1111/j.1540-6210.2011.02417.x

Yeung, K. (2018). Algorithmic regulation: A critical interrogation. *Regulation & Governance*, *12*(4), 505–523. DOI: 10.1111/rego.12158

Zheng, Y., Capra, L., Wolfson, O., & Yang, H. (2020). Urban computing: Concepts, methodologies, and applications. *ACM Transactions on Intelligent Systems and Technology*, *11*(4), 1–33. DOI: 10.1145/3383261

ADDITIONAL READING

Bryson, J. J. (2022). The standard model of governance for AI: A call for ecosystem alignment. *AI & Society*, *37*(1), 405–417. DOI: 10.1007/s00146-021-01283-2

Chapter 2
Tools for Transparency, Accountability, and Citizen Participation in Smart Government

Ricardo A. Barrera-Cámara
https://orcid.org/0000-0002-3170-4671
Universidad Autónoma del Carmen, Mexico

David H. Fuque-Ehuan
https://orcid.org/0009-0005-5032-8076
Universidad Autónoma del Carmen, Mexico

Alejandro Fuentes-Penna
https://orcid.org/0000-0002-4303-3852
El Colegio de Morelos, Mexico

ABSTRACT

Technologies are essential in public management to improve efficiency, management, and availability of services and information. A smart government combines various technologies and guidelines, makes data and information from public agencies available, and makes it publicly accessible to citizens. The objective is to analyze various technologies and tools that support transparency, citizen participation, and accountability in the field of smart government, including various initiatives by international organizations that promote digital technologies, case studies, and ethical and regulatory aspects. Conceptual terms related to governance, smart governance, open data, open platforms, and others are addressed. The relationship between sustainable development goals and smart government tools and initiatives

DOI: 10.4018/979-8-3373-5535-1.ch002

is established. As a result, information technologies, public policies, sustainable development goals, and citizen participation are of great importance in transparency and accountability; however, there are still challenges in their application.

INTRODUCTION

Technological development has reached all organizations, changing the way they communicate with citizens, manage resources, and handle transparency. The smart digital government demonstrates how the development of an open data access model is shifting to a governance model based on emerging technologies that enable analysis, availability, and data-driven decision-making, while considering the needs and concerns of citizens

To understand what smart government supported by recent technologies implies, it is important to understand various conceptual elements such as governance, e-government, open government, civic technologies, and open government data platforms. This allows us to understand the differences and conceptual links for a transparent and inclusive government, where citizen participation is essential.

A large number of proposals, technologies, tools, frameworks, and regulations have been developed and implemented by governments and organizations external to government, with the aim of making communication with governments and citizens more participatory, open, sustainable, and accessible. This allows citizens and organizations to access data and information on the public administration of their governments, keeping them informed in a responsible manner and in line with national and international technological and regulatory changes. Evidence on transparency and accountability platforms, citizen participation platforms, digital governments, open data platforms, mobile applications, intelligent systems, and others.

In addition, various cases are analyzed to understand how different countries applied technologies as part of their strategies to promote and strengthen transparency, accountability, and participation. Successful experiences and specific or common obstacles are identified to support the improvement of strategies and policies under smart or e-government.

Governments must transform their processes, structures, and technological innovation to respond to social needs, sustainability, social participation, and accountability. This is part of the commitments that public institutions and countries have under the 2030 Agenda to contribute to the achievement of sustainable development goals.

BACKGROUND

Related Works

There are several international programs, frameworks, and efforts aimed at promoting transparency, accountability, and citizen participation in governments, especially through digital technologies.

The Open Government Partnership (OGP) is a multilateral initiative that brings together more than 76 countries with the aim of promoting transparency in public management, strengthening citizen participation, combating corruption, and harnessing the potential of new technologies to build more open, effective, and accountable governments (Onufreiciuc, 2022).

The 2030 Agenda for Sustainable Development (SDGs): The UN promotes more open and accountable governance through SDG 16, which promotes effective and accessible institutions through the use of digital technologies to facilitate citizen participation and access to information (Stringhini, 2020). Artificial intelligence and digital services are used to strengthen accountability and improve services (Sherif & Labib, 2025). In addition, the UN promotes multisectoral partnerships that combine resources and knowledge to expand the scope of these digital transformations, strengthening the fulfillment of the SDGs through collaboration and shared transparency (Leal Filho et al., 2024).

OECD. The OECD has developed a comprehensive framework for strengthening democratic governance through digital tools, highlighting initiatives that promote citizen oversight, participation in public policy, and financial transparency. Through the Digital Government Index, it promotes digital transformation in its member countries, while its inventory of social initiatives shows how governments and civil society organizations use ICT to bring public power closer to citizens (Peixoto, 2007; Sysoyeva & Martínez-Usarralde, 2025). It also promotes the fight against disinformation with principles of open government (Matasick et al., 2020) and reinforces accountability through standards of budget transparency and consumer protection in digital environments (Mishra & Varshney, 2024).

CONCEPTUAL ASPECTS

Governance

Governance is the process of decision-making and the process by which decisions are implemented or not implemented (UN & ESCAP, 2009). Good governance means being participatory, consensus-oriented, accountable, transparent, effective and efficient, equitable and inclusive, responsive, and based on the rule of law. Good governance relates to the political and institutional processes and outcomes necessary to achieve development goals and the extent to which the promise of human rights, civil, cultural, economic, political, and social is fulfilled (OHCHR, 2025). With transparency, accountability, participation, and responsiveness (to people's needs) as key elements OECD (OECD, 2020b), defines public governance as the government's ability to organize, coordinate, implement, and oversee public policies in an effective, ethical, and transparent manner, involving all relevant actors and ensuring results oriented toward the common good and sustainable development.

E-Government

E-government, digital government, or e-governance involves the use of information technologies to enable citizens, government, and businesses to exchange and provide information and services, which they can access through any device such as computers or phones (Akhter Shareef et al., 2009; Setiya et al., 2021) It involves a set of activities carried out through information technologies to make public administration and public services more efficient and to make the activities of the state more transparent (SABG, 2013).

An e-government model describes the stages of evolution in which a government uses ICT to move from a simple online presence to full integration of digital services that enable interaction, transactions, and collaboration with citizens, businesses, and other entities (Seyyed Reza Khademi1Seyyed Mousa Khademi, 2021). The factors that make up a digital government model:

– Online presence, i.e., has basic government information available on the internet.
– Interaction between the government and citizens, enabling two-way communication.
– Digital transactions, where procedures can be completed online automatically without the need to visit in person.
– Integration, collaboration between different government agencies, and the adoption of mechanisms that encourage citizen participation in digital democratic life.

The model proposed by the United Nations (UN, 2024) aims to be a comprehensive guide that supports countries in designing digital policies and strategies. Its goal is to build more efficient, inclusive, and sustainable governments, always with a focus on the real needs of the population, businesses, and public servants. This model promotes the use of digital technologies to improve public services, strengthen governance, encourage citizen participation, and advance the Sustainable Development Goals, particularly Goal 16, which promotes more effective, open, and accountable institutions. This model for sustainable development is based on the following governance principles (CEPA, 2024):

1. Competence. To fulfill their responsibilities, institutions need to have the necessary expertise, resources, and tools to adequately address the mandates entrusted to them.
2. Formulation of sound policies. In order to achieve the desired results, public policies must be consistent with each other and based on truthful or well-established arguments, in full accordance with facts, reason, and common sense.
3. Collaboration. On issues that affect everyone, institutions, regardless of their level of government or sector, we must work in a coordinated manner and together with non-governmental actors to advance toward the same goal and achieve real impact.
4. Integrity. Officials must behave with honesty, impartiality, and in a manner consistent with their moral principles.
5. Transparency. If accountability is to be ensured and people are to be able to monitor what institutions do, it is essential that institutions act with honesty and transparency. Facilitate access to information, subject to cases where the law clearly limits it.
6. Independent oversight. The agencies that oversee governments must be professional and act independently, without being influenced by them, in order to maintain confidence in the government.
7. Inclusion (Leaving no one behind). Public policies must consider what society needs and expects, especially those who live in difficult conditions, face inequalities, or have been discriminated against.
8. Non-discrimination. All citizens have equal access to public offices without distinction.
9. Participation. All individuals, as members of society, should be involved in policy design and decision-making processes.
10. Subsidiarity. The national government should focus solely on those responsibilities or needs that local or regional governments cannot effectively fulfill.
11. Intergenerational equity. Administrative decisions must consider both present and future well-being, seeking a balance between current needs and those of future generations.

The European Maturity Model eGovernment Benchmark (European Union, 2025) assesses the progress of European digital public services towards an efficient, user-centric, interoperable, and secure digital administration. The dimensions it assesses are:

- Provision of online services. Availability of services, use from any mobile device, and transparency of services.
- Interoperability indicators. Presence of national and international authentication mechanisms, transparency in the processing of personal data, and digitization services.
- User-friendly portals: online help and feedback, accessibility, security, and ease of finding information.

Open Government

Open government is an approach that uses technology and leadership to achieve a more ethical, collaborative, and people-centered government, as it seeks to strengthen transparency, accountability, and citizen participation (Robertson et al., 2013) It can be effectively applied in smart cities, helping to establish a governance model where citizen participation is key (Agustí i Hernàndez, 2022).

Smart Government

On the other hand, smart governance refers to the use of modern technologies and digital tools to create an environment where citizens and governments work together in a transparent, open, participatory, and sustainable manner, all supported by effective communication (İkizer, 2022). Smart government combines technological, social, economic, and political aspects that integrate citizen participation, transparency, interoperability, and the use of open data and emerging technologies to improve governance, public services, and quality of life for the benefit of society in a sustainable manner. (Natalya & Ella, 2020) Technologies such as artificial intelligence, IoT, and big data are used to improve service efficiency, encourage citizen participation, protect data, and strengthen collaboration between different sectors focused on sustainable well-being (Kaiser, 2024).

Civic Technology

Civic technology, or citizen technologies, is the set of information and communication technologies, such as various platforms and applications, available to citizens to participate and communicate with authorities on issues related to public administration (Zhang et al., 2022). Some civic technologies (Cardullo & Kitchin, 2025) highlight digital participatory voting platforms, platforms for citizen reporting and monitoring of local issues, platforms for consultation and participatory policy or constitution drafting, and global digital petition platforms.

Open Government Data

Open data is public digital data that is accessible online for use, reuse, and sharing by anyone (INAFED, 2024), which has the following characteristics (Congreso de la Unión, 2025c):

– Accessible: They are available to anyone and for any purpose.
– Integrals: contain the topic they describe in detail and with the corresponding metadata.
– Free: there is no cost to purchase them.
– Non-discriminatory: No registration is required for access.
– Timely: updated periodically as they are generated.
– Permanent: historical versions are preserved and remain available for public use.
– Primary: come from the producers of the information with the highest level of disaggregation
– Computer-readable: they are processed and interpreted automatically by electronic equipment.
– In open formats: digital assets in public formats for reading and use.
– Free to use: citing the source is the only requirement for use.

In Shaharudin (2020), principles are proposed instead of characteristics, which are similar to those proposed (Congreso de la Unión, 2025c):

– Completeness: Data available, except for restrictions (privacy, security).
– Primacy: Original data, with the highest level of detail.
– Opportunity: Rapid publication to ensure the usefulness of the data.
– Accessibility: Access for everyone via the internet.
– Machine-processable: formats that allow automatic processing.
– Non-discrimination: Access without registration or discrimination.
– Open formats: open formats and standards to maintain interoperability.
– Free licensing: No restrictions on use, respecting privacy, and security
– Permanence: Versions and files must be available and accessible online.
– Zero costs No cost for accessing and using the data.

SUSTAINABLE DEVELOPMENT GOALS

The Sustainable Development Goals aim to eradicate poverty, protect the planet, and ensure well-being for all by 2030. In this regard, smart government can support the implementation of multiple SDGs through technology, transparency, innovation, and citizen participation. The goals that can be linked to smart government are described below.

– SDG 16. Peace, justice, and strong institutions: Build effective, transparent, and accountable institutions. Digital technologies promote transparency, access to information, the fight against corruption, and greater citizen participation in public decision-making.
– SDG 11. Sustainable cities and communities: Sustainable cities through the use of technologies to improve waste management, transportation, urban development, energy use, and citizen participation.
– SDG 9. Industry, innovation, and infrastructure: Modernize infrastructure, promote innovation, use new technologies to improve services, reduce costs, and increase administrative efficiency.
– SDG 17. Partnerships for the goals: Work collaboratively with various sectors, sharing technology, data, and information.
– SDG 4. Quality education: The use of platforms in education supports open access to knowledge and the strengthening of digital literacy.
– SDG 10. Reduced inequalities: Supports reducing geographical, economic, or social barriers to accessing public services.
– SDG 13. Climate action: Applying platforms and technologies for environmental management and monitoring helps to tackle climate change and protect the environment by making data-driven decisions.

DIGITAL TOOLS FOR TRANSPARENCY AND ACCOUNTABILITY

Open or Public Data Portals

Represented by online portals with open data, where citizens can access information from public bodies, this strengthens transparency and accountability among officials and trust in institutions (Públicas, 2019). Users can download data and reuse data in various formats, as well as access APIs for the development of applications or services based on government data and information.

Examples of European portals or platforms:

– The city of Paris developed an open data web platform based on the Lutèce platform, which it called Paris Data, with data corresponding to the city of Paris (Ville de Paris, 2025). It contains a search engine for words and sections corresponding to topics such as administration and public finance, citizenship, trade and tourism, culture, environment, facilities, services, social affairs, mobility and public space, urban planning and housing, data news, and the use of technology by the police.

– Data.gouv.fr is a portal based on the Udata platform where citizens can access French public data through sections such as Data Catalog, APIs for accessing various data sources, reuses, organizations, and news (DINUM, 2025). The platform's data search engine contains filters that combine searches for organizations, types, tags, formats, licenses, data schema locations, coverage, and spatial granularity.

– Dati Piemonte is a platform of the Piedmont Region (Piemonte, 2025), with a set of 1,426 data sets to consult and download, covering topics such as agriculture, fishing, forestry, and food products; the environment; economics and finance; energy; justice, the legal system, and public safety; government and the public sector; education, culture, and sports; population and society; regions and cities; health; science and technology; international issues; transportation; and others. Searches can be general, using filters by topic, tags, or title. It offers tools for graphical data visualization, stories, and queries from the institutions participating in the initiative. Institutions must use the YUCCA platform to publish their resources on the dati piemonte portal.

– The Italian public administration's open data platform (AGID, 2025a) It has 22,907 datasets on topics such as administration, culture and leisure, economy, finance, housing, international affairs, agriculture, migration and integration, nature and the environment, education and science, public order and security, law, space and infrastructure, social security, traffic, labor, health and healthcare, and data exploration by metadata.

– Yucca (AGID, 2025b) is an open cloud-based intelligent data platform with tools to aggregate, manage, analyze, and experiment with data from various sources such as the Internet of Things, the Internet of People, and public/private data, enabling selective information sharing, real-time data processing, and advanced data analysis. Developed and managed by the Piedmont Region, it is used as an open data platform.

– data.government.nl (Dutch government, 2025), It is a platform of the Dutch government with a total of 22,900 open data sets available for consultation, with information on topics such as administration, culture and leisure, economy, finance, housing, environment, education, health, and many more, with a total of 22,900 data sets available for consultation.

– Data.gob.es (Gobierno de España & Pública, 2025), Spain's open data platform, where citizens can access and use data from a total of 93,898 datasets organized into sectors such as science and technology, commerce, culture and leisure, demography, sports, economy, education, employment, energy, finance, industry, legislation and justice, environment, rural areas, health, public sector, security, society and welfare, transportation, tourism, urban planning and infrastructure, and housing. Various applications built from the data on the portal are also available. Searches can be performed by category, publisher, format, level of administration, update frequency, and tags and exported or accessed in various formats.

Examples of US portals or platforms:

– Open data portal of the United States government that offers various tools and applications to support research tasks and report on the decisions and results of public administration (GSA, 2025). Queries are performed by dataset or by organization. The data search tool offers filtering options by location, topics, topic categories, dataset type, tags, formats, organization types, organizations, publishers, and offices.

Examples of Latin American portals and platforms:

– Mexico has several open data platforms: historico.datos.gob.mx is one of the Mexican government's open access portals where historical data on culture/tourism, development, economy, education, energy and the environment, finance and procurement, geospatial data, local governments, infrastructure, health, security, and justice can be consulted (Gobierno de México, 2025a). The search engine has filters: categories, level of government, organizations, groups, tags, and formats. INEGI (2025) provides a range of geographical and statistical data for consultation and use for various purposes through a variety of publicly accessible formats. Examples include censuses and counts, surveys, administrative-statistical records, and sociodemographic characteristics in small areas.
– Argentina's open data portal (Gobierno de Argentina, 2025), It has a set of 1,231 datasets and 40 organizations with data related to agriculture and livestock, fishing and forestry, science and technology, economy and finance, education, culture, and sports; energy; government and the public sector; justice, security, and legal matters; the environment; population and society; and regions and cities. Time series tools, access to organizations, and availability of APIs for data sources.

– On the other hand (Gobierno de Chile, 2025), the Chilean government has a portal providing access to 2,700 datasets from 602 institutions, allowing citizens to access and use public data. The portal includes Datasets, Featured Datasets, Reuses, Help Center, Statistics, and a forum. The data search engine includes filters by institution, category, and file format.

Examples of Asian portals and platforms:

– Dat.gov.in (Government of India, 2025) is India's open data platform with centralized government data, visualization tools, statistics, metrics, data analysis, and APIs for accessing data sources. Data can be searched by sectors, groups, central government entities, and states/union territories. Users can propose new data sets, new visualizations, generate ideas, participate in blogs, or generate infographics.

– e-Gov Data Portal is the Japanese government's open data portal for improving transparency and access to public data (Government of Japan, 2025). Its data is organized by categories that include population and households, transportation and tourism, social security, sanitation, education, culture, sports and life, domestic trade and services, business, home, economy, public administration and finance, information and communication, science and technology, agriculture, forestry and fisheries, energy and water, land and climate, international, and justice, security, and environment. The search offers filtering options by organizations, category, tags, formats, license, type of delivery, status, and date of last metadata update, offering a total of eighteen thousand eight hundred and sixty-three data sets.

– Singapore has a free open data portal with more than 5,000 data sets on topics such as art and culture, education, economics, the environment, housing, health, and social issues, sourced from various government agencies (Singapore Government, 2025). It also offers graphical and interactive tools, access to APIs, notifications of data updates, and specific searches: by topic, month, frequency, format, agencies, and relevance.

Examples of African portals and platforms:

– Nigeria has an open portal with public data that is accessible to the public free of charge, with reports and graphical data visualization tools that are part of the Open Data for Africa initiative (African Development Bank, 2025b). The available data includes health, agriculture, education, trade and investment, women's and children's issues, and demographics.

– The Kenyan government's data portal provides access to public government data through a catalog organized by various categories, sources, and regions (African Development Bank, 2025a), with interactive and analytical tools, user management, information, and help

Citizen Reporting Platforms and Digital Oversight Channels

Platforms through which it is possible to file complaints promote transparency and accountability, in which citizens participate in the monitoring of public issues. Public bodies, civil society, or international organizations can administer these tools.

The Comprehensive Citizen Complaint System (SIDEC) (Gobierno de México, 2025b) ensures that anyone can file complaints, reports, and citizen petitions related to acts of corruption, administrative misconduct, abuse of power, or irregularities on the part of federal public servants. Its goals include promoting citizen participation, providing a mechanism for registration and response, offering various means of reporting, ensuring confidentiality and anonymity, classifying the types of complaints, providing follow-up, and establishing a legal basis. Furthermore, the national transparency platform (INAI, 2025). It is a data portal where citizens can access public information, submit requests for information, and file complaints if they do not receive a response or are dissatisfied with it. Some of its sections include public information, requests, complaints, notices, open data and statistics, guaranteeing authorities, and thematic search engines. The thematic search engine allows users to search for information by gender, directories, salaries, services, procedures, contracts, beneficiary lists, sanctioned public servants, annual budgets, budgetary exercises, and transparency and data resolutions.

The organization Transparency International Rwanda (Rwanda, 2025) focuses on the fight against corruption and good governance in Rwanda, with the "IFATE Next Generation" tool making it possible to report corruption.

Transparency Portals

Transparency portals aim to demonstrate transparency in the use of public resources and enable citizens to access them.

Chile has a transparency portal through which citizens can request and access information, track requests, and file complaints regarding public information from various agencies and institutions (CPLT, 2025).

On the other hand (Ministerio para la Transformación Digital, 2025), presents a platform that works for transparency in government, open government, and citizen participation. It has main sections on active disclosure, right of access, integrity, open government, participation, and more information. The sections related to transparency are active disclosure, right of access, and open government; channels of oversight, integrity, and right of access; and, regarding citizen complaints, the integrity section.

Brazil's transparency portal offers transparency and open data platform functionality (União, 2025) allows users to consult and download information in various formats for further analysis related to public expenditure, civil servants and pensioners, sanctions, citizen benefits, public tenders and contracts, public revenue, individuals and legal entities, payment cards, parliamentary amendments, transferred resources, tax receipts, public budget, states and municipalities, agreements, business travel, and functional real estate. Citizens can submit requests and complaints on the platform, which also offers educational resources on public administration.

Citizens can access information on Argentina's public administration by visiting the transparency portal sections (AAIP, 2025): government transparency, access to information, and opportunities for participation. This portal offers citizens the opportunity to participate in public policy.

Paraguayan citizens use a transparency and access to information tool through which they can request and access public information called the Unified Portal for Access to Public Information (Gobierno del Paraguay, 2025), where they can search for applications, submit new applications, find instructions or guides, contact details, statistics, and access educational materials.

USAspending.gov is a US government portal that displays information on annual government spending, making it available in a transparent and public manner (United States government, 2025). Expenses may include federal grants, data exploration, and access to technological tools and resources for data analysis or teaching.

The national portal of Bangladesh (Government of Bangladesh, 2025) aims to ensure transparency in government information and services by centralizing resources and information. Users must submit a request for information in order to make inquiries. Information inquiries cover institutional information, budgetary and financial data, public procurement and contracting, asset declarations, regulatory information, audit and evaluation results, information on government personnel, government plans and programs, and statistics on access to information.

Social Media and Chatbots

Complaint platforms or oversight channels where citizens interact through social media and chatbots allow citizens to report irregularities, request information, reduce administrative times, and monitor government activities. Chatbot is a tool that functions as a complementary means of receiving and redirecting complaints in contexts related to public administration (Larsen & Følstad, 2024). On the other hand, the information must be verified, as it may lead to misinformation or defamation. For their incorporation in this context, they must be designed and regulated to maintain proper functioning, protect security, and respect fundamental rights (Maldonado-Meléndez, 2023). The ideal citizen complaint chatbot, or DCI Chatbot (OLACEFS & EFS, 2024), is included in the websites of countries such as Argentina, Guatemala, Panama, and Uruguay, with the intention of guiding citizens of these entities to file complaints appropriately with the Supreme Audit Institutions.

Social media is used as a means to identify irregularities, report them, and follow up on complaints. It is also used to identify possible tax evasion by analyzing public data, and specialized software supports the detection of informal commercial activities on social media (Márquez et al., 2024). Justina del Mar is a WhatsApp chatbot for artisanal fishermen to answer questions related to fishing regulations and sanctions and as a channel for reporting irregularities in the fishing sector (WWF Peru, 2024). Chatbot Teo (TOJIL, 2024) It runs on WhatsApp, Facebook Messenger, and Telegram. Designed to report corruption, malpractice, and intent, and to receive legal advice. OneService Kaki Chatbot supports users in filing complaints or reports related to Singapore municipal issues or services. The tool is available for WhatsApp, Telegram, Instagram, and Facebook Messenger (Government of Singapore, 2025). The municipalities of Guadalajara and Zapopan developed GuaZap, a chatbot that runs on WhatsApp, where citizens can file reports and follow up on their requests. It serves as a means of reporting public servants and receiving personalized attention from a public servant via chat (Cruz-Meléndez et al., 2024).

Social media is used to communicate citizen co-production initiatives through content analysis via the official Twitter account of the Bandung (Indonesia) government using G2C, enabling citizens to report urban problems and monitor (Cho & Melisa, 2021).

Emerging Technologies

Blockchain. Blockchain improves internal and external control in the public sector by recording all transactions and operations, reducing potential fraud, and enabling continuous auditing (Wanden-Berghe Lozano & Fernández Daza, 2020). Blockchain supports transparency, accountability, public management, and collaboration through (Benitez Eyzaguirre, 2021): inherent transparency and auditability, elimination of intermediaries and reduction of administrative discretion, technical impossibility of falsifying or deleting records, improved governance and participatory management, and prevention of irregularities through simplified audits. Its effectiveness depends on the legal, political, technical, and social factors of the context in which it is applied; it cannot eliminate the risks of corruption that exist outside the electronic system (World Economic Forum, 2020). Initiatives such as GovBlockchain propose improving transparency, accountability, and efficiency in open data, complete auditability, and traceability of all recorded transactions; and minimizing risks, especially in public procurement processes, facilitating data extraction (Alotaibi et al., 2025). Smart contracts, decentralized autonomous organizations, self-sovereign identity, and token economies are blockchain-based technologies that aim to improve transparency and reduce corruption (Ibrahimy et al., 2024).

Big Data. The use of big data enables fast and efficient public management, promotes transparency and cost reduction, and helps identify hidden patterns; however, its implementation presents technical challenges, a lack of knowledge on the part of employees regarding its use, and legal or regulatory issues (Dci, 2024). Through e-government, transparency and accountability in processes are possible, but it also presents ethical challenges in data selection, privacy, and centralization, where it is necessary to create regulatory frameworks that protect citizens' rights in relation to their data (Hochstetter-Diez et al., 2023). Combining the use of platforms, big data, and artificial intelligence promotes the fight against corruption and demands accountability. Its use strengthens the transparency of institutions and encourages greater citizen participation (Bonilla Gutiérrez, 2025).

Artificial intelligence. Artificial intelligence with the Internet of Things improves transparency, accountability, and efficiency in government services, enables data-driven decision-making, and ensures data privacy and security (Al-Besher & Kumar, 2022). AI optimizes bureaucratic processes, facilitates agile access to public information, and reaches citizens. This is possible through the automation of responses and processes, optimizing navigation and search; through database connectivity; and with initiative-taking citizen participation, but with ethical challenges to consider (Ibarra Vazquez et al., 2025). Artificial intelligence (AI) is a tool that governments can use to promote transparency and accountability through various means (Novelli et al., 2024): reporting and accountability, oversight and monitoring, regulatory compliance, limitation and control of power, and fostering public trust.

DIGITAL TOOLS FOR CITIZEN PARTICIPATION

Citizen participation involves activities through which citizens express their ideas, report situations, collaborate in policy design, and supervise their governments. This is possible through various technological tools or platforms (RICI, 2024): online consultation platforms, mobile applications, social media discussion forums, collaborative mapping or geospatial information systems, and e-government.

– Citizen participation platforms. Citizens can propose, vote, and express their opinions on issues of interest to the city through the "Mexico City Electoral Institute's Digital Platform for Citizen Participation," where they can participate in participatory budgeting, citizen assemblies, community participation commissions, and citizen consultations. Authorities submit issues that impact the city for consideration through citizen consultations (IECM, 2025). Paraguay has a digital platform where citizens can make proposals, support existing proposals, and propose changes to initiatives (agesic, 2025). Osoigo (FEDER, 2025), a Spanish platform supported by the European Regional Development Fund, where citizens ask questions to associations, institutions, politicians, and parties, who then consider and evaluate the questions raised by citizens; it also has survey and debate systems.

– Civic platforms. Hackity App (Hackity, 2025), a civic platform that allows citizens of a city and its neighborhoods to propose ideas, collaborate, and carry out joint actions to improve their community in areas such as urban facilities, cleanliness, mobility, green spaces, and others. The proposals are brought to the attention of city councils to improve public services and support transparency.

– Citizen participation platforms are supported by artificial intelligence. Make.org and MAPLE use artificial intelligence to analyze and prioritize citizens' responses through artificial intelligence (Combaz et al., 2025). Make.org (Make.org, 2025) is a European citizen platform where citizens collaborate with organizations, companies, and authorities to support decision-making. It uses AI based on citizen ideas and proposals based on votes to summarize and synthesize citizen testimonies in public discussion. MAPLE or Massachusetts Platform for Legislative Engagement for Legislative Engagement (MAPLE, 2025), helps users write their testimonials, publishes them for the community, and sends them directly to the relevant legislators; it uses artificial intelligence to support the compression of legislative information and access policies of interest to citizens.

– Platforms for exposing information of public interest. WikiLeaks (WikiLeaks, 2015) is an organization that stores, analyzes, and publishes large sets of data and official documents that have been censored or restricted in order to promote them later. It has agreements with organizations around the world to improve the protection of sources and the impact these documents generate. Document authentication and resistance to censorship are key features. MexicoLeaks (LATINNO, 2017a) It was a platform based on the WikiLeaks format where citizens share sensitive documents and data as a means of making anonymous reports and publishing leaked information with the aim of fighting corruption, exposing abuses of power, and human rights violations. The data and information are verified, analyzed, and published by various organizations and media outlets. Chileleaks (Ciudadanía Inteligente, 2025), a platform developed by the non-profit organization Ciudadanía Inteligente, with the aim of anonymously reporting cases of bribery and corruption in Chile involving public officials who engage in malpractice. The cases to be reported must involve the participation of at least one public official and one private individual. The payment, compensation, or benefit received by the official must be considerable in relation to their income, and evidence must be presented to support the crime committed. Distributed Denial of Secrets (SCIDSG, 2025) a non-profit platform with the aim of storing and publishing documents and leaks of public interest, which can be downloaded by users. The documents originate from cyberattacks or leaks from various public or private organizations, including databases, emails, financial records, media, among others.

– Electronic voting. Mexican citizens residing abroad can vote electronically in elections through electronic voting (INE, 2024). Bogotá has an Electronic Voting System (VOTEC), where citizens of any age can vote electronically online (IDPAC, 2025). Estonia has an online voting system called e-voting (VVK, 2025), which requires an ID card with a reader or mobile ID, also provides information on Estonian elections (Riigikogu, local, European Parliament, presidential), statistics, rules for candidates, and voting procedures. In Switzerland (Swiss Post, 2024) an electronic voting system developed by Swiss Post was developed in Neuchâtel, where cities can vote both in Switzerland and abroad using a computer or electronic device.

– Citizen consultations and surveys. Through the DemocraciaOS platform, citizens and organizations can conduct digital consultations, comments, votes, surveys, polls, and debates and collect opinions related to public issues (Democrcia en Red, 2025). Your Priorities (Citizens Foundation, 2025) It allows you to generate ideas, deliberate, and make decisions using tools that include voting, forums, surveys, and opinion gathering for collaborative decision-making. On behalf of (Change.org, 2025), Change.org is a mass citizen consultation platform based on petitions on specific issues, where citizens who sign voluntarily give their support to the petition.

– Mobile applications focused on citizen services. Linea Verde is a mobile application in Spain that allows citizens to report various incidents, including potholes, damaged street lighting, and litter. It provides updates and alerts on the status of the report. (Ambientum.com, 2025). FixMyStreet (MYSOCIETY, 2024) allows users to report issues related to streets, roads, the environment, potholes, and damaged lights to UK authorities. It requires the use of GPS to locate the location of the report and a description of the incident. BOS:31 (City of Boston Digital Service, 2025) It is an app from the city of Boston for reporting basic problems, which are automatically directed for attention and follow-up and can be viewed on a map.

– Mobile applications aimed at citizen participation and transparency. Congress 2.0 (Hierro, 2013) was a Spanish app that allowed citizens to check the activity of members of the Spanish Congress. The app allowed users to identify the status of a legislative initiative and the person responsible for its presentation, check which laws had been approved or rejected (user data remained anonymous), and cast symbolic votes with no legal validity, just like a member of Congress. Pleno Ciudadano (EXPANSIÓN, 2015) It was an app designed to enable citizens to communicate with and monitor the work, initiatives, and expenses of federal deputies and senators. The app's features allow users to identify legislators, verify whether they have submitted their 3 of 3 declarations, rate their responsiveness, consult their professional backgrounds, and send messages to legislators. Yoveoveo (LATINNO, 2017b) is an Ecuadorian app designed to serve as a means of communication between citizens and the public administration, allowing users to report on public services and community problems and propose solutions for community improvement without involving decision-making. Agreements were established between the private company that administered it and the governments of Quito, Guayaquil, and Cuenca. Its final design incorporates the support of government programs as a tool to promote citizen participation, inclusion, and accountability. Colap app (Colab, 2025), a Brazilian app where citizens participate in city administration by reporting garbage problems, evaluating services, responding to surveys, making suggestions, proposing new transportation routes, and participating in civic activities. The app is available in cities and regions throughout Brazil, such as Aracaju, Maceió, Rio de Janeiro, and the state of Rio Grande do Sul. It also has a complementary website (Colab, 2025), where citizens' reports and complaints can be viewed, including data such as the user's name, address, type of problem, a brief description, and a timestamp indicating when it was posted.

ANALYSIS OF INTERNATIONAL EXPERIENCES

When discussing digital transformation in government processes, and especially transparency, it is important to analyze the adoption of infrastructure and software by different governments around the world and, above all, to understand the factors that led to the success or failure of the projects implemented and the lessons that these experiences can provide for future implementations. Below are some examples of government portals:

– Decide on Madrid. Spain's attempt to create an open, digital democracy was the Decide Madrid portal. It was created in response to the demands of 15M, a political and social movement in which protesters, also known as the indignados movement, demanded transparency and civil society participation in public administration decision-making (Royo et al., 2020). As a result, in 2015, Madrid City Council developed a solution called Decide Madrid, which was created using Consul software. Decide Madrid served as a channel of communication between citizens and the public administration. The main strength of this portal was the fact that citizens could make proposals and, above all, vote on participatory budgets (Royo et al., 2023). However, despite the promising outlook, the change in government meant that the project lost continuity, which affected the sustainability of Decide Madrid (Tseng, 2022).

– Particpa.br. Meanwhile, in America, the Secretary General of the Presidency of Brazil created Brasil.br in 2015. Using Hangouts technology, this digital initiative integrated forums, surveys, thematic communities, and public consultations, encouraging citizen participation with these tools (Steibel, 2018). Its main source of success was based on its ability to structure spaces for interaction between civil society and the state (da Costa Peixoto, 2015). Despite this, the platform also had its weaknesses, the main one being institutional fragility in the face of political polarization. Due to a lack of regulatory protection and the change of government, participa.br was deactivated in 2016 (Fagundes, 2017).

– National Platform. In 2016, as part of a constitutional obligation arising from the 2014 reform, Mexico committed to the National Transparency Platform (PNT), whose main objective was to centralize access to public information from more than 7,400 obligated entities in the country (INEGI, 2023). Its interoperability, under a national standard, brought together subsystems such as Declaranet, CompraNet, and the information access request system (SEP, 2023). With legal backing that allowed it to continue under different administrations and consolidate itself as the main source of the right to know, PNT was extraordinarily successful in Mexico. Despite the usefulness of this platform, the 2024 initiative to eliminate the INAI promoted uncertainty about its future and, above all, alerted citizens to the possible loss of autonomy and quality of open data (Castillo Jiménez, 2024).

– VTaiwan. The Taiwanese government's civic experiment emerges in response to the crisis of legitimacy caused by the Sunflower Movement (Chung, 2015). Its main promotion came from civic activists such as the G0v collective and Audrey Tang (O'Flaherty, 2018). The architecture of this platform includes systems such as Pol.is for consensus and forums that allow proposals to be iterated between citizens, officials, and experts (Tseng, 2022). This digital tool, implemented by the Taiwanese government, draws its strength from the social and political legitimacy it has achieved as a hybrid model of innovation in civic engagement. However, its reach within the formal state apparatus was limited due to its dependence on volunteers and the difficulties in institutionalizing its processes, since vTaiwan did not arise from a formal law, but rather from a collaborative civic institutional process that was recognized by the Ministry of Digital Affairs. In reality, the purpose of this platform was to institutionalize an open and deliberate response to controversial bills.

– e-People. For its part, the South Korean government opted for the e-People platform as part of a digital administrative reform, which was consolidated in 2005 (Government of the Republic of Korea, 2018). This tool enabled the channeling of complaints, reports, and citizen requests into a single national system. The success of this public CRM was due to its proven effectiveness in resolving more than 90% of the cases received in a timely manner (Pan et al., 2024). However, the software was more geared toward management than deliberation. The primary purpose of this tool was to centralize, standardize, and receive complaints, reports, and suggestions electronically, thereby increasing transparency and administrative efficiency.

– State digital infrastructure. In the case of Estonia's digital transformation, the country opted for a remarkably interesting initiative. The state launched three strategic solutions, such as the Tiigrihüpe program, the creation of the e-ID, and the X-Road interoperability platform (EU Commission, 2024). This set of tools enabled the digitization of nearly 99% of public services and approximately 51.1% of the electorate to vote online in 2023. X-Road's modular architecture makes it secure and widely used by citizens, which is its greatest strength. Despite this robustness, although it may not seem so, this system faces challenges such as a shortage of ICT personnel in governments and the rural digital divide (Rajamäe-Soosaar & Nikiforova, 2024). One point in favor of this digital proposal is that Estonia consolidated its legal framework with the Digital Signature Act, the Electronic Document Act, and the Personal Data Protection Act. The government's goal was to create an interoperable, secure, and efficient digital state that offers citizens 100% online public services, as well as civic participation through digital solutions.

ETHICAL, LEGAL, AND INSTITUTIONAL CONSIDERATIONS

The laws, frameworks, regulations, and ethical aspects of digital and smart government are legal provisions that establish principles, rules, rights, and obligations for the use and regulation of digital technologies in public management. This aims to ensure transparency, accountability, and the protection of personal data.

Ethical

– The Ibero-American Charter of Open Government (CLAD, 2016) proposes a series of principles and criteria for good governance to be applied by Ibero-American countries to promote collaboration, transparency, and citizen participation in order to form open, efficient, and inclusive governments. The Ibero-American Charter of Principles and Rights in Digital Environments (Secretaría General Iberoamericana, 2023) proposes a series of principles related to the protection of individual rights, which should be considered in the design of policies for the implementation of digital environments by any person or organization.
– Open Government Partnership (OGP, 2025) is based on transparency, citizen participation, and public accountability, where open governments collaborate with everyone to strengthen democracy and achieve better results. This is achieved through dialogue, action, accountability, and learning.
– The Universal Declaration of Human Rights, in Article 19 (UN, 1948), specifies that "Everyone has the right to freedom of opinion and expression; to not be harassed because of their opinions; to seek, receive, and impart information and ideas without regard to frontiers, through any media."
– Within the OECD Digital Government Policy Framework (OECD, 2020a), six principles are established: Digital by default, data as strategic assets, Government as a platform, open government by default, user orientation, and proactivity. These principles aim to make governments more inclusive, efficient, and transparent, where public trust is increased through digital technologies and data.

Legals

– The General Data Protection Regulation (GDPR) (Parliament, 2016) protects individuals' data in relation to its processing and distribution within the European Union and European Economic Area and applies to any organization, company, or individual.
– European Union Digital Services Regulation (Parliament, 2022) requires all commercial and service organizations that use digital platforms to prevent crime, avoid spreading misinformation, protect user data and rights, and build transparent and open platforms.

Institutional

– The OECD Recommendations on Digital Government Strategies consider (OECD, 2025): transparency, openness, and inclusion; participation and engagement; data-driven culture; leadership and coordination; effective governance; clear business cases; and international cooperation. These are aimed at designing strategies, processes, and services using technologies for participation, transparency, and reliability.

National

– Spanish Law on Transparency, Access to Public Information, and Good Governance (BOE, 2013) aims to increase transparency and the right to information and compel the government to make its activities and obligations transparent.
– General Law on Transparency and Access to Public Information (Congreso de la Unión, 2025b) defines principles and procedures for accessing public information and regulates how authorities should handle and disclose information, ensuring transparency and accountability.
– The General Law on the Protection of Personal Data Held by Obligated Subjects establishes that any public or non-public body that holds personal data must guarantee the protection of data and the rights of individuals (Congreso de la Unión, 2025a).
– Law on Access to Public Information in Argentina (Ministerio de Modernización, 2024) It establishes that individuals have the right to request and receive information from public bodies, makes data transparent, limits access to information considered classified or personal, and establishes the use of technological platforms to track access and online requests.

Adversity and Vulnerability

The evidence in the literature shows that there are a large number of initiatives, regulations, and intentions to promote and maintain transparency, accountability, and data protection. In contrast, approaches or initiatives have emerged that tend to weaken the control and surveillance tools of agencies, including the very institutions responsible for guaranteeing them.

The reform of Mexico's Telecommunications Law authorizes authorities to access users' personal data without their authorization and without justification, including device geolocation. It also opens up the possibility of blocking or suspending broadcasts at the discretion of the authorities, including radio and television (Canal del Congreso, 2025), and even blocking digital platforms (Castillo Jiménez, 2025).

On the other hand, with (Riquelme, 2025) found that citizen researchers identified various AI-based applications in the Mexican government, for which they requested information from agencies about how the AI applications work, the data they use, the objectives of their implementation, responses to transparency requests, and whether the applications meet AI criteria. Most of the institutions responded with a lack of clarity and resistance to providing the requested information (Riquelme, 2025).

The Madrid Transparency and Data Protection Council has accumulated a large number of unresolved complaints since 2022 (Mateo, 2025), affected by a lack of resources and control by the local government.

The DC Council amended the proposed Open Meetings Act so that council meetings and deliberations would be public. The amendment and approval exclude public access to many of its meetings; the only meetings allowed are those involving voting. This amendment uses as its justification the facilitation of deliberation and the avoidance of frustration among legislators when discussing issues that require greater privacy (Flynn & Gathright, 2025). This is seen as a way of undermining transparency.

CONCLUSIONS

In the strategies adopted by various countries, projects that had legal and regulatory support were able to continue providing their services. On the other hand, those lacking a policy related to their implementation and use tended to fail and even disappear due to the lack of a regulatory framework for their operation. It is also important to note that another relevant factor for success is the type of service provided through government digital portals. In some cases, these portals were limited to being mere administrators of procedures, but others focused more on including citizen participation and, above all, on increasing trust between the public administration and citizens.

Smart government requires an updated legal framework based on international standards that include transparency, data protection, accountability, and citizen participation. However, its implementation requires technical and legal adaptations, changes in organizational culture, and economic resources. In contrast, in recent years, initiatives have emerged and changed that put transparency, accountability, public access, and even possible censorship at risk.

The focus on digital government and transparent government is closely related to the sustainable development goals, specifically SDG 16, which is linked to transparency (Ríos et al., 2024), accountability (Ishengoma & Shao, 2025), and inclusive governance.

FUTURE RESEARCH DIRECTIONS

As lines of work, to deepen in the algorithms and artificial intelligence models incorporated in the management platforms and information attention. Evaluation of the platforms from the perspective of citizens in matters of transparency and citizen participation. Develop a study of the behavior of intelligent agents or chatbots for service assistance, responses, and referrals to public agencies or servers. Also analyze cybersecurity and data protection on government platforms.

CONFLICT OF INTEREST

The authors declare that they have no conflict of interest in the publication of this chapter.

REFERENCES

AAIP. (2025). Agencia de Acceso a la Información Pública Retrieved May 14, 2025 from https://portal.transparencia.gob.ar/

African Development Bank. (2025a). Kenya Data Portal. Retrieved June 26, 2025 from https://kenya.opendataforafrica.org

African Development Bank. (2025b). Nigeria Data Portal. Retrieved June 29, 2025 from https://nigeria.opendataforafrica.org/

agesic. (2025). Plataforma de Participación Ciudadana Digital. Retrieved July 3, 2025 from https://plataformaparticipacionciudadana.gub.uy/

AGID. (2025a). dati.gov.it i dati aperti della pubblica amministrazione. Retrieved June 15, 2025 from https://www.dati.gov.it/

AGID. (2025b). Yucca Smart Data Platform Smart Data Platform. Retrieved June 16. 2025 from https://developers.italia.it/en/software/d5da261d-68f6-4c81-9ba8-6f2984515c85.html

Agustí i Hernàndez, C. (2022). Promoting platforms for bottom-up participatory governance: a policy instrument approach through the facilitation of strategic smart city governance. In Vacca, J. R. (Ed.), *Smart Cities Policies and Financing* (pp. 297–304). Elsevier. https://doi.org/https://doi.org/10.1016/B978-0-12-819130-9.00043-7

Akhter Shareef, M., Kumar, V., Kumar, U., & Akhter Hasin, A. (2009). Diffusion of Innovation and Capability Theory in the Context of E-Government. In Dwivedi, Y. K., Lal, B., Williams, M. D., Schneberger, S. L., & Wade, M. (Eds.), *Handbook of Research on Contemporary Theoretical Models in Information Systems* (pp. 193–211). IGI Global Scientific Publishing. DOI: 10.4018/978-1-60566-659-4.ch011

Al-Besher, A., & Kumar, K. (2022). Use of artificial intelligence to enhance e-government services. *Measurement. Sensors*, *24*, 100484. https://doi.org/https://doi.org/10.1016/j.measen.2022.100484

Alotaibi, E. M., Issa, H., & Codesso, M. (2025). Blockchain-based conceptual model for enhanced transparency in government records: A design science research approach. *International Journal of Information Management Data Insights*, *5*(1), 100304. https://doi.org/https://doi.org/10.1016/j.jjimei.2024.100304

Ambientum.com. (2025). Línea Verde. In (Version May 5, 2025) https://play.google.com/store/apps/details?id=lineaVerde.App

Benitez Eyzaguirre, L. (2021). Blockchain para la transparencia, gestión pública y colaboración. Teknokultura. *Revista de Cultura Digital y Movimientos Sociales, 18*(1), 23–32. DOI: 10.5209/tekn.71514

BOE. (2013, December 10). Ley de transparencia, acceso a la información pública y buen gobierno. Retrieved June 11, 2025 from https://www.boe.es/eli/es/l/2013/12/09/19

Bonilla Gutiérrez, J. C. (2025). Las plataformas digitales como herramientas anticorrupción: democracia, tecnología y transparencia en la era digital. Universita Ciencia, 13(36). https://doi.org/https://doi.org/10.5281/zenodo.15121040

Canal del Congreso. (2025, June 30). Senado aprueba Ley de Telecomunicaciones. Retrieved July 4, 2025 from https://www.canaldelcongreso.gob.mx/noticia/senado-aprueba-ley-de-telecomunicaciones#:~:text=Al%20respecto%2C%20la%20nueva%20normativa,Registro%20de%20Poblaci%C3%B3n%20(CURP)

Cardullo, P., & Kitchin, R. (2025). Provincialising platform citizenship: Citizen participation in and through civic platforms. *Digital Geography and Society*, *8*, 100123. DOI: 10.1016/j.diggeo.2025.100123

Castillo Jiménez, E. (2024, November 8). La desaparición del INAI amenaza con dejar 15 000 millones de datos en el limbo. El País. https://elpais.com/mexico/2024-11-09/la-desaparicion-dcl-inai-amenaza-con-dejar-15000-millones-de-datos-en-el-limbo.html

Castillo Jiménez, E. (2025, July 1). Claudia Sheinbaum, sobre la Ley de Telecomunicaciones: "No hay censura, ni espionaje". El Paiss, Mexico. https://elpais.com/mexico/2025-07-01/claudia-sheinbaum-sobre-la-ley-de-telecomunicaciones-no-hay-censura-ni-espionaje.html?utm_source=chatgpt.com

CEPA. (2024). Principles of Effective Governance for Sustainable Development Retrieved June 22, 2025 from https://www.un.org/ssr/sites/www.un.org.ssr/files/news_articles/_principles_of_effective_governance_for_sustainable_development.pdf

Change.org. (2025). Change.org. Retrieved July 3, 2025 from http://change.org

Cho, W., & Melisa, W. D. (2021). Citizen Coproduction and Social Media Communication: Delivering a Municipal Government's Urban Services through Digital Participation. *Administrative Sciences, 11*(2), 59.

Chung, C.-S. (2015). The Introduction of e-Government in Korea: Development Journey, Outcomes and Future. Gestion et management public, 3(4), 107-122. DOI: 10.3917/gmp.034.0107

Citizens Foundation. (2025). Your Priorities. Retrieved June 2, 2025 from yrpri .org/domain/3

City of Boston Digital Service. (2025). BOS:311. In (Version 6.4.24) https://play .google.com/store/apps/details?id=gov.cityofboston.citizensconnect

Ciudadanía Inteligente. (2025). Chileleaks de la ciudadania inteligente. Retrieved July 5, 2025 from https://chileleaks.org

CLAD. (2016). Carta Iberoamericana de Gobierno Abierto. Bogotá, Colombia Retrieved from https://segib.org/es/publicacion/declaracion-de-la-xvii-conferencia -de-ministros-de-administracion-publica-y-reforma-del-estado/

Colab. (2025a). Colab. In (Version 7.6.11) https://play.google.com/store/apps/details ?id=thirtyideas.colab_android&hl=pt_BR

Colab. (2025b, July 4). Colab a rede social paa cidadania. Retrieved July 4, 2025 from https://app.colab.re/

Combaz, A., Mas, D., Sanders, N., & Victor, M. (2025). Applications of Artificial Intelligence Tools to Enhance Legislative Engagement: Case Studies from Make. Org and MAPLE.

Congreso de la Unión. (2025a, March 20). Ley General de Protección de Datos Personales en Posesión de Sujetos Obligados. Diario Oficial de la Federación. https:// www.diputados.gob.mx/LeyesBiblio/pdf/LGTAIP.pdf

Congreso de la Unión. (2025b). Ley General de Transparencia y Acceso a la Información Pública. Diario Oficial de la Federación. https://www.diputados.gob.mx/ LeyesBiblio/ref/lgtaip/LGTAIP_orig_20mar25.pdf

Congreso de la Unión. (2025c). Ley General de Transparencia y Acceso a la Información Pública: Artículo 3, Fracción VIII. Diario Oficial de la Federación. https:// www.diputados.gob.mx/LeyesBiblio/ref/lgtaip/LGTAIP_orig_20mar25.pdf

Controladoria-Geral da União. (2025, June 10). Portal da Transparência. Retrieved June 29, 2025 from https://portaldatransparencia.gov.br/

CPLT. (2025). Portal de Transparencia. Retrieved June 30, 2025 from https://www .portaltransparencia.cl/PortalPdT/

Cruz-Meléndez, C., Jiménez Canseco, J. M., & Martínez Gutiérrez, R. (2024). La implementación de chatbots en gobiernos municipales mexicanos. Exploración y diagnóstico de uso. *Revista Mexicana de Análisis Político y Administración Pública, 13*(26), 119–153. DOI: 10.15174/remap.v13i26.441

da Costa Peixoto, A. (2015). Instrumentos da Democracia Participativa: Um estudo sobre o Participa.br e o Dialoga Brasil Universidade de Brasília]. Brasília, DF. https://bdm.unb.br/bitstream/10483/12701/1/2015_AbnerdaCostaPeixoto.pdf

Dei, H. (2024). The role of big data in ensuring transparency and accountability of public authorities. *Health Leadership and Quality of Life*, *3*, 421. DOI: 10.56294/hl2024.421

Democrcia en Red. (2025). democraciaOS: Public Consultation. Retrieved July 3, 2025 from https://www.democraciaos.org/consultadigital

DINUM. (2025). The French public data platform. Retrieved June 2, 2025 from https://www.data.gouv.fr

Dutch government. (2025). National Data Portal of the Dutch government. Retrieved June 16, 2025 from https://data.overheid.nl/

EU Commission. (2024). Estonia 2024 Digital Decade Country Report. Retrieved July 5,2025 from https://digital-strategy.ec.europa.eu/en/factpages/estonia-2024-digital-decade-country-report

European Union. (2025). eGovernment Benchmark Report 2025: On track for user-friendly online public services. Luxembourg: Publications Office of the European Union. DOI: 10.2759/0837457

EXPANSIÓN. (2015, September 7). Pleno ciudadano. Retrieved June 19, 2025 from https://expansion.mx/nacional/2015/09/07/pleno-ciudadano-una-app-para-vigilar-a-los-legisladores-mexicanos

Fagundes, V. S. Jonice de Oliveira. (2017). Análise da Plataforma de Participação Social: Participação do Cidadão e Organizações na Elaboração de Políticas Públicas. XXXVII Congresso da Sociedade Brasileira de Computação, São Paulo.

FEDER. (2025). Osoigo, El portal de los políticos que escuchan. Fondo Europeo de Desarrollo Regional. Retrieved July 4, 2025 from https://www.osoigo.com/

Flynn, M., & Gathright, J. (2025, April 1). Transparency law slashed by D.C. Council as lawmakers want more privacy. Retrieved July 7, 2025 from https://www.washingtonpost.com/dc-md-va/2025/04/01/dc-vote-closed-meetings-council/

Gobierno de Argentina. (2025). Datos Argentina. Retrieved June 30, 2025 from https://datos.gob.ar/

Gobierno de Chile. (2025). Datos.Gob, el portal de datos abiertos del Estado. Retrieved June 20, 2025 from https://datos.gob.cl/

Gobierno de España, & Pública. (2025). Open data initiative of the Government of Spain. Retrieved June 15, 2025 from https://datos.gob.es/es

Gobierno de México. (2025a). Datos abiertos de Mexico. Retrieved June 28, 2025 from https://historico.datos.gob.mx

Gobierno de México. (2025b). Sistema Integral de Denuncias Ciudadanas (SIDEC). Retrieved May 25, 2025 from https://sidec.buengobierno.gob.mx/

Gobierno del Paraguay. (2025). Portal Unificado de Acceso a la Información Pública. Retrieved May 24, 2025 from https://informacionpublica.paraguay.gov.py/#!/

Government of Bangladesh. (2025, June 29). Bangladesh National Portal. Retrieved June 29, 2025 from https://bangladesh.gov.bd/index.php

Government of India. (2025). Open Government Data (OGD) Platform India. Retrieved June 30, 2025 from https://www.data.gov.in/

Government of Japan. (2025). e-Gov Data Portal. Retrieved June 30, 2025 from https://data.e-gov.go.jp/info/en

Government of Singapore. (2025, April 3). Kaki Chatbot Retrieved July 1, 2025 from https://www.oneservice.gov.sg/kaki

Government of the Republic of Korea. (2018). End-of-Term Self-Assessment Report 2016–2018 [Government Report](Open Government Partnership, Issue. https://www.opengovpartnership.org/documents/south-korea-end-of-term-self-assessment-report-2016-2018/

GSA. (2025). The Home of the U.S. Government's Open Data. Retrieved June 22, 2025 from https://data.gov/

Hackity. (2025). Hackity App. Eusebio Reyero. Retrieved July 1, 2025 from https://hackityapp.com/

Hierro, L. (2013, July 4). Congreso 2.0. EL Pais. Retrieved July 4, 2025 from https://elpais.com/politica/2013/07/04/actualidad/1372930254_072779.html

Hochstetter-Diez, J., Negrier-Seguel, M., Diéguez-Rebolledo, M., Vásquez-Morales, F., & Sancho-Chavarría, L. (2023). Governance Democratic and Big Data: A Systematic Mapping Review. *Sustainability*, *15*(16), 12630.

Ibarra Vazquez, A., Lara Ramos, B. G., & Soto Karass, J. G. (2025). Transparencia en México mediante inteligencia artificial: La ruta digital emergente hacia una nueva rendición de cuentas. *Encrucijada Revista Electrónica del Centro de Estudios en Administración Pública*, (50), 98–122. DOI: 10.22201/fcpys.20071949e.2025.50.90895

Ibrahimy, M. M., Norta, A., & Normak, P. (2024). Blockchain-based governance models supporting corruption-transparency: A systematic literature review. Blockchain: Research and Applications, 5(2), 100186. https://doi.org/https://doi.org/10.1016/j.bcra.2023.100186

IDPAC. (2025). El Sistema de Votación Electrónica Ciudadana. Retrieved July2, 2025 from https://votec.participacionbogota.gov.co/votec-ciudadano

IECM. (2025). Plataforma Digital de Participación Ciudadana del Instituto Electoral de la Ciudad de México. Retrieved June 1, 2025 from https://plataformaciudadana.iecm.mx/#/inicio

İkizer, İ. (2022). Do Smart City Solutions Contribute to the Achievement of the Sustainable Development Goals?: Case of Istanbul. In Pego, A. C. (Ed.), *Smart Cities, Citizen Welfare, and the Implementation of Sustainable Development Goals* (pp. 22–44). IGI Global Scientific Publishing., DOI: 10.4018/978-1-7998-7785-1.ch002

INAFED. (2024, April 12). Datos abiertos. Retrieved May 30, 2025 from https://www.gob.mx/inafed/documentos/datos-abiertos-347532#:~:text=Los%20Datos%20Abiertos%20son%20los,redistribuidos%20por%20cualquier%20persona%20interesada

INAI. (2025). Plataforma Nacional de Transpaencia. Retrieved June 29, 2025 from https://www.plataformadetransparencia.org.mx

INE. (2024). Voto de mexicanos residentes en el extranjero. Retrieved June 2, 2025 from https://votoextranjero.mx/web/vmre/modalidades-de-voto

INEGI. (2023). Censo Nacional de Transparencia, Acceso a la Información Pública y Protección de Datos Personales. Retrieved July 4, 2025 from https://www.inegi.org.mx/programas/cntaippdpf/2023/

INEGI. (2025). Datos abiertos. Retrieved June 25, 2025 from https://www.inegi.org.mx/datosabiertos/

Ishengoma, F., & Shao, D. (2025). A framework for aligning e-government initiatives with the sustainable development goals. Journal of Innovative Digital Transformation. DOI: 10.1108/jidt-09-2024-0025

Kaiser, Z. R. M. A. (2024). Smart governance for smart cities and nations. *Journal of Economy and Technology*, *2*, 216–234. DOI: 10.1016/j.ject.2024.07.003

Larsen, A. G., & Følstad, A. (2024). The impact of chatbots on public service provision: A qualitative interview study with citizens and public service providers. *Government Information Quarterly*, *41*(2), 101927. https://doi.org/https://doi.org/10.1016/j.giq.2024.101927

LATINNO. (2017a). MexicoLeaks. Berlin: WZB. Retrieved July 5,2025 from https://latinno.wzb.eu/en/case/13145/

LATINNO. (2017b). Yoveoveo. Berlin: WZB. Retrieved July 5,2025 from https://latinno.net/es/case/8091/

Leal Filho, W., Dibbern, T., Pimenta Dinis, M. A., Coggo Cristofoletti, E., Mbah, M. F., Mishra, A., & Aina, Y. A. (2024). The added value of partnerships in implementing the UN sustainable development goals. *Journal of Cleaner Production*, *438*, 140794. DOI: 10.1016/j.jclepro.2024.140794

Make.org. (2025). Make.org. Retrieved June 4, 2025 from https://make.org/US

Maldonado-Meléndez, M. A. (2023). La regulación (necesaria) de la actuación administrativa automatizada: el uso de la robótica mediante chatbots y asistentes virtuales en la administración pública peruana. Revista Iberoamericana de Gobierno, 23(Junio· 2023).

MAPLE. (2025). Massachusetts Platform for Legislative Engagement (MAPLE). Retrieved June 4, 2025 from https://www.mapletestimony.org/

Márquez, M., Velasco, M., Ochoa, R., & Delfin, F. (2024). Inteligencia artificial en el sector público en México: Actos de fiscalización. *Newman Business Review*, *10*, 124–147. DOI: 10.22451/3002.nbr2024.vol10.2.10103

Matasick, C., Alfonsi, C., & Bellantoni, A. (2020). Governance responses to disinformation: How open government principles can inform policy options. OECD Working Papers on Public Governance(39), 46. https://doi.org/https://doi.org/10.1787/d6237c85-en

Mateo, J. J. (2025, January 1). La transparencia se atasca en el Madrid de Ayuso: reclamaciones sin resolver desde 2022 y 335 casos en un limbo. elpais.com. Retrieved July 4, 2025 from https://elpais.com/espana/madrid/2025-01-02/la-transparencia-se-atasca-en-el-madrid-de-ayuso-reclamaciones-sin-resolver-desde-2022-y-335-casos-en-un-limbo.html?utm_source=chatgpt.com

Ministerio de Modernización. (2024). Derecho de Acceso a la Información Pública. Boletín Nacional. Retrieved Sep 5, 2025 from https://www.argentina.gob.ar/normativa/nacional/decreto-780-2024-403572

Ministerio para la Transformación Digital. (2025). Portal de la Transparencia de la Administración del Estado. Retrieved June 28, 2025 from https://transparencia.gob.es/

Mishra, R., & Varshney, D. (2024). Consumer Protection Frameworks by Enhancing Market Fairness, Accountability and Transparency (FAT) for Ethical Consumer Decision-Making: Integrating Circular Economy Principles and Digital Transformation in Global Consumer Markets. *Asian Journal of Education and Social Studies*, *50*(7), 640–652. DOI: 10.9734/ajess/2024/v50i71494

MYSOCIETY. (2024). FixMyStreet. In (Version 3.0.2) https://play.google.com/store/apps/details?id=org.mysociety.FixMyStreet

Natalya, V. B., & Ella, M. L. (2020). Conceptualization of Smart Government: A scientometric approach. *Upravlenets*, *11*(3), 33–45. DOI: 10.29141/2218-5003-2020-11-3-3

Novelli, C., Taddeo, M., & Floridi, L. (2024). Accountability in artificial intelligence: What it is and how it works. *AI & Society*, *39*(4), 1871–1882. DOI: 10.1007/s00146-023-01635-y

O'Flaherty, K. (2018). Taiwan's revolutionary hackers are forking the government. Wired, (July 2, 2025).

OECD. (2020a). *The OECD Digital Government Policy Framework: Six dimensions of a Digital Government*. OECD Publishing. DOI: 10.1787/f64fed2a-

OECD. (2020b). Policy Framework on Sound Public Governance: Baseline Features of Governments that Work Well. OECD Publishing. https://www.oecd.org/en/publications/policy-framework-on-sound-public-governance_c03e01b3-en.html

OECD. (2025). *Recommendation of the Council on Digital Government Strategies*. OECD.

OGP. (2025). *Foundations for Open Government* OGP National Handbook.

OHCHR. (2025). OHCHR and good governance. Retrieved May 20, 2025 from https://www.ohchr.org/en/good-governance

OLACEFS & EFS. (2024, July). Chatbot DCI: Chatbot de denuncia ciudadana idónea. Retrieved July 1, 2025 from https://olacefs.com/giz/iniciativa/chatbot-de-denuncia-ciudadana-idonea/

Onufreiciuc, R. (2022). Principle of Transparency as reflected in OGP National Action Plans in Romania. Logos Universality Mentality Education Novelty. *Law*, *10*, 60–71. DOI: 10.18662/lumenlaw/10.1/71

Pan, T. H., Aung, M. N., & Nam, E. W., & al., e. (2024). Digital inclusion among community older adults in the Republic of Korea: Measuring digital skills and health consequences. *European Journal of Investigation in Health, Psychology and Education, 14*(8), 2314–2336. DOI: 10.3390/ejihpe14080154

Parliament, E. (2016, April 27). Reglamento General de Protección de Datos (RGPD – UE 2016/679). Retrieved April 4, 2025 from https://eur-lex.europa.eu/eli/reg/2016/679/oj

Parliament, E. (2022, October 19). Reglamento de Servicios Digitales. European Parliament. Retrieved April 12, 2025 from https://eur-lex.europa.eu/eli/reg/2022/2065/oj

Peixoto, T. (2007). Peixoto, Tiago, Stocktaking of Social Accountability Initiatives in OECD Countries. *SSRN.*

Piemonte, R. (2025). Open Data della Regione Piemonte. Retrieved June 15, 2025 from https://www.dati.piemonte.it/#/home

Públicas, A. D. P. (2019). *Herramientas para la transparencia y la rendición de cuentas. Claves para un Gobierno abierto. LABgobar.* Subsecretaría de Innovación Pública y Gobierno Abierto, Secretaría de Modernización.

Rajamäe-Soosaar, K., & Nikiforova, A. (2024). Exploring Estonia's Open Government Data Development as a Journey towards Excellence. https://doi.org/https://doi.org/10.48550/

Reza, S. (2021). Investigating electronic government maturity models. Sociología y tecnociencia, 11(Extra_1), 160-176. https://doi.org/https://doi.org/10.24197/st.Extra_1.2021.160-176

RICI. (2024, August). Participación Ciudadana Digital. https://redciudad.org/posts/post-4/

Ríos, A. M., Guillamón, M. D., & Benito, B. (2024). The influence of local government transparency on the implementation of the sustainable development goals in municipalities. Journal of Public Budgeting, Accounting &amp. *Financial Management.* Advance online publication. DOI: 10.1108/jpbafm-12-2023-0229

Riquelme, R. (2025, March 3). Gobiernos en México usan al menos 119 aplicaciones de Inteligencia Artificial. Retrieved July 3, 2025 from https://www.eleconomista.com.mx/tecnologia/gobiernos-mexico-119-aplicaciones-inteligencia-artificial-20250311-750004.html

Robertson, S. P., Bertot, J. C., & Nahon, K. (2013). Introduction to Open Government and Participation Minitrack. 2013 46th Hawaii International Conference on System Sciences

Royo, S., Bellò, B., Torres, L., & Downe, J. (2024). The success of e-participation: Learning lessons from Decide Madrid and We asked, You said, We did in Scotland. *Policy and Internet*, (16), 65–82. https://doi.org/https://doi.org/10.1002/poi3.363

Royo, S., Pina, V., & Garcia-Rayado, J. (2020). Decide Madrid: A Critical Analysis of an Award-Winning e-Participation Initiative. *Sustainability*, *12*(4), 1674. DOI: 10.3390/su12041674

Rwanda, T. I. (2025). Transparency International Rwanda web site. Retrieved May 30, 2025 from https://www.tirwanda.org/#

SABG. (2025). Gobierno diogital o electrónico. Retrieved June 1, 2025 from https://www.gob.mx/buengobierno/documentos/gobierno-digital-o-electronico

SCIDSG. (2025). Distributed Denial of Secrets. Retrieved July 7, 2025 from https://ddosecrets.com

Secretaría General Iberoamericana. (2023). Carta Iberoamericana de Principios y Derechos en los Entornos Digitales. https://www.segib.org/wp-content/uploads/Carta_iberoamericana_derechos_digitales_ESP_web.pdf

Setiya, R., Pandey, S., Singh, A. K., & Sharma, D. K. (2021). Citizen e-governance using blockchain. In Krishnan, S., Balas, V. E., Julie, E. G., Robinson, Y. H., & Kumar, R. (Eds.), *Blockchain for Smart Cities* (pp. 119–152). Elsevier. https://doi.org/https://doi.org/10.1016/B978-0-12-824446-3.00010-7

SFP. (2023). Política Nacional de Datos Abiertos. https://canalonce.mx/REST/data/transparencia/datosabiertos/politica-nacional-de-datos-abiertos-dof-09102023-dof-10112023.pdf

Shaharudin, A. A. A. (2020). Open Government Data: Principles, Benefits and Evaluations. Khazanah Research Institute, 12(20).

Sherif, S., & Labib, G. (2025). Digital Transformation and the SDGs: A Case Study on Egypt's E-government and SDG-16. *Governance and Politics*, *3*, 8–20. DOI: 10.24833/2782-7062-2024-3-4-8-20

Singapore Government. (2025). Singapore's open data portal. Retrieved Jun 23, 2025 from https://data.gov.sg

Steibel, F. (2018). Brazil Midterm Progress Report 2016–2018. https://www.opengovpartnership.org/wp-content/uploads/2018/10/Brazil_Mid-Term_Report_2016-2018_EN.pdf

Stringhini, A. (2020). Open government, emerging technologies and public information. Revue internationale des Gouvernements Ouverts, 9, 121-132.

Swiss Post. (2024). E-voting: Online voting and elections. Retrieved July 3, 2025 from https://digital-solutions.post.ch/en/e-government/digitization-solutions/e-voting

Sysoyeva, L., & Martínez-Usarralde, M.-J. (2025). From security to digital governance in OECD: Evolution and some current considerations since the digital transformation. *Salud, Ciencia y Tecnología*, *4*(1401). Advance online publication. DOI: 10.56294/sctconf20251401

TOJIL. (2024). Teo Chatbot. Retrieved July 1, 2025 from https://tojil.org/teo/

Tseng, Y. (2022). Algorithmic Empowerment: A Comparative Ethnography of Two Open-Source Algorithmic Platforms – Decide Madrid and vTaiwan. *Big Data & Society*, *9*(2). Advance online publication. DOI: 10.1177/20539517221123505

UN. (1948). Universal Declaration of Human Rights, Article 19. Retrieved July 4, 2025 from https://www.un.org/en/about-us/universal-declaration-of-human-rights

UN. (2024). A Digital Government Model Framework for Sustainable Development. In Affairs, U. N. D. E. S. (Ed.), *United Nations E-Government Survey 2024 Accelerating Digital Transformation for Sustainable Development - With the addendum on Artificial Intelligence* (pp. 1–33). United Nations Department of Economic and Social Affairs. DOI: 10.18356/9789211067286

UN & ESCAP. (2009). What is good governance? Retrieved May 11, 2025 from https://hdl.handle.net/20.500.12870/3794

United States government. (2025). The official source of government spending data. Retrieved June 27, 2025 from https://www.usaspending.gov/

Ville de Paris. (2025). Paris Open Data. Retrieved June 2, 2025 from https://opendata.paris.fr/pages/home/

VVK. (2025). Internet voting in Estonia: i-Voting. Retrieved July 1, 2025 from

Wanden-Berghe Lozano, J. L., & Fernández Daza, E. (2020). Blockchain: instrumento de transparencia y control del sector público.

WikiLeaks. (2015, November 3). What is WikiLeaks. Retrieved July 5, 2025 from https://wikileaks.org/What-is-WikiLeaks.html

World Economic Forum. (2020). Exploring Blockchain Technology for Government Transparency: Blockchain-Based Public Procurement to Reduce Corruption. https://www3.weforum.org/docs/WEF_Blockchain_Government_Transparency_Report.pdf

WWF Peru. (2024, June 11). Justina del Mar. Retrieved July 1, 2025 from https://www.wwf.org.pe/?389250/

Zhang, W., Lim, G., Perrault, S., & Wang, C. (2022). A Review of Research on Civic Technology: Definitions, Theories, History and Insights. arXiv.Org.

KEY TERMS AND DEFINITIONS

Smart Government: Combines emerging technologies and regulations to speed up transparency and accountability, enabling citizen participation.

Chapter 3
Smart Grids for Governments:
Strategy, Technology, and Energy Transition

Juan Manuel Xicoténcatl-Pérez
https://orcid.org/0009-0008-8554-4192
Universidad Politécnica de Pachuca, Mexico

Jorge A. Ruiz-Vanoye
https://orcid.org/0000-0003-4928-5716
Universidad Politécnica de Pachuca, Mexico

Ocotlán Díaz-Parra
Universidad Politécnica de Pachuca, Mexico

José M. Liceaga-Ortiz-De-La-Peña
Universidad Politécnica de Pachuca, Mexico

Julio César Ramos-Fernández
https://orcid.org/0000-0002-9997-6550
Universidad Politécnica de Pachuca, Mexico

Rubén Oswaldo Hernández-Terrazas
Universidad Politécnica de Pachuca, Mexico

ABSTRACT

This chapter presents a comprehensive overview of Smart Grid implementation from a governmental perspective, structured into five thematic modules. These modules range from the technical diagnosis of legacy electricity grids to the assessment of technological maturity levels, and they include enabling tools such as AMI, SCADA, and VPPs. The chapter also examines the integration of renewable energy sources, the emergence of new actors such as prosumers and electric vehicles, and the importance of appropriate regulatory frameworks and incentives. Overall, it articulates strategy, technology, and governance to support governments in the transition toward smarter, more resilient, and more sustainable electricity systems.

DOI: 10.4018/979-8-3373-5535-1.ch003

1. INTRODUCTION

The transition to sustainable and resilient energy systems has become a challenge for governments in the 21st century. In this context, Smart Grids or smart grids emerge to achieve the objectives of decarbonisation, energy efficiency, security of supply and citizen participation. Far from being a mere technological modernization, Smart Grids represent a change in the way electricity is generated, distributed and consumed, allowing a more flexible, dynamic energy ecosystem adapted to future needs.

For governments, adopting a strategic vision on Smart Grids not only implies investing in sensors, smart meters or advanced control software, but also in public policies, updated regulatory frameworks, collaborative governance models and green financing instruments. The implementation of smart grids requires the articulation of multiple dimensions: from territorial and energy planning to the development of institutional and citizen capacities, including technological interoperability, cyber-security and social equity. Smart Grids offer the possibility of integrating variable renewable energies, enabling prosumers and energy communities, reducing technical and non-technical losses, improving resilience to extreme events and facilitating the automation of electricity management at all levels. In addition, they allow the energy transition to be addressed with an inclusive and territorially differentiated perspective: rural microgrids, digital urban platforms, distributed energy industrial hubs, among others.

This chapter provides a comprehensive view of how governments can plan, implement, and scale smart grids as part of their national energy strategy. Through thematic modules, they explore everything from technical bases to governance frameworks, from maturity models to public policy instruments, based on scientific evidence, international cases and emerging regulatory frameworks. The aim is to provide decision-makers with a robust, adaptable and informed roadmap to move towards smarter, cleaner and more democratic electricity systems.

2. DIAGNOSING THE POWER GRID AND PUBLIC CHALLENGES

Many countries, especially in Latin America and other emerging regions, face ageing, fragmented, and poorly automated electricity infrastructures, designed for a centralized and passive energy reality. In this first section, it is proposed to carry out a technical, institutional and regulatory analysis of the current network, as a starting point for planning its modernization. Diagnosis is an exercise that reveals bottlenecks, identifies opportunities for improvement, and informs investment and regulatory decisions. This section discusses issues such as the lack of sensors, the low digitization of substations, weak interoperability between technologies, the limited availability of real-time data, and cybersecurity challenges. Tools for conducting audits, assessing reliability (SAIDI, SAIFI), reviewing the current regulatory framework, and mapping key stakeholders are also presented.

2.1 Current State of the Electrical Infrastructure

In the global context, electricity losses during transmission and distribution range from 2% to 22%, depending on the country and network configuration (CEER, 2025). These losses are associated with additional costs and effects on continuity of supply, reflected in the service quality indicators. In this framework, the use of automated real-time monitoring systems is proposed to prevent operational degradations and support the restoration of operations. Historically, electrical infrastructure was designed under a centralized model, in which generating plants (thermal, hydroelectric, or nuclear) delivered power to consumers without feedback or bidirectionality. This design has restrictions to incorporate variable renewable sources, measure flows in real time, enable the participation of prosumers or establish distributed responses to failures (Khalid, 2024).

Technological solutions are currently being implemented to overcome these restrictions. Technologies such as advanced metering (AMI), sensors, and SCADA networks make it possible to record variations in consumption, non-technical losses, or other events with defined temporal resolution, enabling operation and maintenance actions. Recent literature also addresses the integration of renewable energies, the use of AI and IoT, and cybersecurity requirements (Campana et al., 2025). The figure of the prosumer – who generates, stores and injects energy – requires regulatory frameworks and bidirectional mechanisms for its interaction with the system (Kabeyi, 2023). Some strategies combine blockchain and artificial intelligence to enable distributed energy transactions and improve system operation (Hua et al., 2022). Additionally, the deployment of advanced features allows for the implementation of distributed responses to failures, with automatic reconfiguration and contingency management capabilities. In summary, various sources indicate that the evolution towards electricity grids with higher levels of digitalization, automation, integration of renewable resources and user participation is technically feasible and consistent with the modernization of the electricity system.

2.2 Technical Challenges in Legacy Infrastructure

In the global environment, much of the legacy electrical infrastructure maintains limited analog equipment and control schemes for measurement, monitoring, and protection, restricting operational visibility and responsiveness under varying conditions (Mansour et al., 2023; Mchirgui et al., 2024). To address connectivity and the gradual integration of existing assets, modernization strategies have been documented that combine sensor networks, gateways, and interoperable software layers, along with incremental incorporation schemes of IoT modules and digital twins (Alavikia & Shabro, 2022; Kirmani et al., 2022). In parallel, recent technical literature describes the convergence of monitoring, analysis, and control with high-resolution temporal data to support operation and maintenance decisions (Sievers et al., 2023). In practice, solutions that incorporate cellular and NB-IoT modules are employed for telemetry and control in remote locations, with hubs and gateways that prioritize the use of the communications link according to the available quality (Burczyk et al., 2022). In addition, investments and pilots are registered in different regions aimed at very high voltage lines, digitalization of substations and management of distributed resources, with an emphasis on observability and resilience (Wang et al., 2024).

Interoperability is addressed through standardized information models and protocols that allow the integration of equipment and applications from multiple vendors (Ayello & Lopes, 2023). Heterogeneous devices and protocols often coexist, so gateways and semantic mappings are used to facilitate data exchanges between transmission and distribution systems, as well as between operations, markets, and customers (JRC, 2022). To facilitate convergence, IEC 61850 has evolved in profiles and services (e.g., GOOSE, Sampled Values IEC 61850-9-2), complemented by canonical models such as CIM (IEC 61970/61968) to standardize information exchange between applications (Ayello & Lopes, 2023; Song et al., 2023). Hardware-in-the-loop testing is used to validate controls and protections prior to deployment, reducing integration risks and verifying performance under representative operational scenarios (von Jouanne et al., 2023; Chintapalli et al., 2024). In Europe, technical assessment frameworks and interoperability laboratories are promoted to verify compliance and performance of digital network solutions (JRC, 2022).

Cybersecurity is incorporated as a cross-cutting requirement, with a focus on segmentation, continuous authentication, and least-trust access control, as well as protecting data exchange between operational and IT domains (He et al., 2022; Wu et al., 2023). In parallel, the extension of observability in medium and low voltage networks has been documented using PMUs and micro-PMUs for time synchronization, state estimation, and event detection, taking into account cost and coverage constraints (Fiorucci et al., 2025; Tangi et al., 2024).

2.3 Impact of Renewable Intermittency Without Smart Grids

The growing incorporation of renewable energies such as solar photovoltaic and wind energy has transformed the operational dynamics of electricity systems. These sources have variable and intermittent production, depending on weather conditions and schedules, which presents significant stability, control, and predictability challenges. In traditional electricity grids, which operate with unidirectional flows and without real-time monitoring, the variability of these sources can lead to frequency and voltage imbalances, affecting the quality of supply and increasing the risk of partial or regional blackouts (Reif et al., 2023). Without the support of Smart Grids, which enable distributed control, advanced automation, and two-way communication, the electricity system lacks mechanisms to dynamically respond to fluctuations in renewable generation. This translates into a greater reliance on fossil sources as a backup, which contradicts energy decarbonization goals (Liu et al., 2023). In addition, in the absence of energy management systems (EMS), prediction algorithms, and resources such as battery storage, the massive integration of renewables can lead to congestion on lines, discharge of surplus energy, and difficulties in maintaining the balance between generation and consumption in real time (Liu et al., 2023). This phenomenon shows how the lack of smart grids and adequate storage can limit renewable potential (Federal Electricity Commission (CFE), 2022). The above discussed can be seen in the following table.

Table 1. Impact of non-smart grids

Indicator	Ideal for smart grids	Latin American average (2023)	Derived problems
Technical and non-technical losses	< 7%	15–22%	Costs, overhead, fraud
SAIDI (duration of interruptions)	< 1 h/year	14–45 h/year	Frequent power outages, economic damages
AMI Penetration	> 80%	< 20%	Lack of real-time data
Quality of service measurement	Automated	Manual or Reagent	There are no early warnings or predictive analytics
Operating Voltage	Controlled ±5%	Variations > ±10%	Equipment damage and loss

2.4 Technical Modernization and Mitigation Strategies

To overcome the technical challenges associated with legacy electrical infrastructure, a modular diagnostic strategy is proposed. This strategy begins with the progressive installation of sensors, Fasorial Measurement Units (PMUs) and smart meters (AMIs) in critical areas such as cities, industrial parks and isolated communities, where the impact of a smart grid can be more immediate and measurable (International Renewable Energy Agency (IRENA), 2023). The adoption of international technical standards, such as IEC 61850, for substation automation and IEEE 1547, for the interconnection of distributed energy resources, facilitates interoperability between devices from different manufacturers, ensuring safe and efficient integration of new components (International Energy Agency (IEA), 2023). In cybersecurity, it is recommended to implement Zero Trust architecture, segment networks according to operational priority levels, and apply end-to-end encryption in communications between critical nodes in the network. These practices help mitigate attacks such as command injections, denial of service (DoS), and unauthorized access to controllers or SCADA systems (Inter-American Development Bank (IDB), 2023). The use of PMUs offers the ability to detect jitter events such as frequency swings or voltage imbalances, with time accuracy on the order of milliseconds. This improves the dynamic response of the electrical system and allows for more efficient control of the synchronization of distributed grids and variable generation (California ISO, 2023). Finally, computational simulations using open-source tools such as GridLAB-D or OpenDSS allow complex network scenarios to be modeled before physical investments are made. This reduces the technical and financial risks associated with modernization, especially in systems that include the integration of renewables, batteries, and distributed charging (Song & Lee, 2024).

2.5 Initial Recommendations for Government Diagnosis

To move forward with the transition to smart grids, governments must start with a technical and regulatory diagnosis of their current infrastructure. A first recommendation is to carry out an audit of the electrical infrastructure, which allows evaluating the state of the substations, distribution lines, measurement equipment, installed sensors and existing communication and control protocols. This technical diagnosis will make it possible to identify technological bottlenecks, such as the lack of interoperability or the absence of automation in medium and low voltage networks (California ISO, 2023).

At the same time, an analysis of the reliability data of the electrical system must be carried out. Indicators such as the SAIDI (Average Duration of Service Interruption Index) and the SAIFI (Average Frequency of Service Interruption Index) make it possible to measure the quality of the energy supply and establish comparisons by region. It is also essential to assess losses and map the areas with the highest number of complaints or recurring failures (Song & Lee, 2024). This data-driven approach helps prioritize interventions according to social and economic impact.

A third line of action is to carry out a regulatory inventory that evaluates current legislation on key issues such as advanced metering (AMI), the interconnection of distributed renewable energies, the rights of prosumers, electricity service quality standards and energy data privacy policies. Many jurisdictions still lack modern regulatory frameworks that allow for the digital transformation of the electricity system or have contradictory regulations that curb private investment (European Union Agency for Cybersecurity (ENISA), 2023).

Finally, it is recommended to draw up a map of key actors in the energy ecosystem, identifying distribution companies, network operators, regulatory bodies and technical agencies that can lead modernization processes. In addition, opportunities for international cooperation and climate financing should be considered with entities such as CAF, the IDB, GIZ, or the UN, which have supported multiple smart grid pilot projects in emerging countries (U.S. Department of Energy (DOE), 2022).

3. IMPLEMENTATION LEVELS AND MATURITY MODELS

The transition to smart grids is not a change that happens instantaneously or uniformly. It requires a gradual, staggered adoption adapted to the local context, both technologically and institutionally. This is based on the SGMM (Smart Grid Maturity Model), which allows evaluating the stage of an electricity system in terms of its digitalization, automation and integration of renewable sources. This section also explores differentiated models according to the context: urban, rural, industrial and energy communities. Each faces particular challenges and opportunities, requiring specific solutions in infrastructure, regulation and financing. Likewise, the technical, regulatory and financial criteria to scale successful pilots are analyzed, guaranteeing sustainability and replicability.

3.1 Smart Grid Maturity Model (SGMM)

The Smart Grid Maturity Model (SGMM), developed by Carnegie Mellon's Software Engineering Institute (SEI), is a comprehensive tool to guide the adoption of smart technologies in an orderly and strategic manner (ORNL (Oak Ridge National Laboratory), 2013). This model proposes six levels of maturity, from pilot projects to fully intelligent operations, and covers eight key domains, including technology, operations, customers, and security.

In the initial phase, Level 1 – Initiation, organizations often promote isolated projects to explore emerging technologies. There is no defined strategy or clear organizational integration. As Level 2 – Enablement progresses, smart meters (AMIs) or sensors are installed in pilot areas, beginning to generate useful data, albeit without operational cohesion. During Level 3 – Integration, the priority is interoperability: systems such as SCADA and EMS are connected, demand response applications are integrated, and sufficient information exchange is established to make coordinated decisions. In the next step, Level 4 – Optimization, the network achieves self-healing capabilities and advanced automation, reducing outage times and improving operational efficiency. The advancement to Level 5 – Pioneer brings with it the incorporation of disruptive technologies such as distributed storage, artificial intelligence and the implementation of virtual plants (VPPs). At this stage, prosumers have an active role, and regulated structures are in place for energy communities. Finally, Level 6 – Innovate represents the highest maturity: resilient grids, with 24/7 real-time operation, dynamic energy markets and total integration of energy services (ORNL (Oak Ridge National Laboratory), 2013). In addition, recent studies show that in developing countries, moving to levels 4 and 5 is critical to ensure resilient electricity systems, adapt to solar generation peaks, and reduce dependence on fossil fuels (Song & Lee, 2024).

An example of the above can be found in Chattanooga (Tennessee, USA)., where the EPB exemplifies the advanced step between SGMM levels 4 and 5. After initially using an infrastructure of smart meters and sensors, they moved towards an automatically switched self-healing network supported by real-time data analytics. Since 2010, the installation of 1,200 smart switches and a fiber optic network has reduced outages by 40%, generating annual savings of close to $100 million and obtaining PEER certifications for energy efficiency (Utility Dive (March 12), 2024). In Italy, Enel deployed its "Telegestore" project in 2005, considered one of the first on a global scale. By manufacturing smart meters domestically and integrating them into a centralized system, he was able to save close to €500 million per year. This case represents an early application from level 3, with interoperability between AMI, distribution systems and information management (Song & Lee, 2024).

Finally, China has carried out a large-scale modernization of the existing substations, associated with phases 3 and 4. With UHV and AMI projects covering mass between 2016 and 2020, more than 60% of substations were upgraded to interoperate using IEC 61850. This strengthens coordination between transmission and distribution networks, aiming towards levels 4-5 in the SGMM (Nguyen et al., 2024).

3.2 Incremental Initiatives: From AMI to Fully Intelligent Grids

From the government's perspective, the transition to smart grids should focus on gradual implementations, combining technological innovation with strategic and regulatory management. Firstly, smart meters (AMIs) are implemented that provide real-time data and facilitate user/government participation in schemes as a response to demand. A recent study by the ICEEE2023 shows that AMIs integrate hardware and software (meters, communication networks, and data management systems), allowing instant decisions to be made about the consumption and support of renewables (Utility Dive (March 12), 2024).

Once the AMI infrastructure has been consolidated, the next step consists of distribution monitoring with IoT sensors and PMUs, an infrastructure that allows interconnection with SCADA/EMS systems. In the U.S., pilots with HIL have validated smart sensors prior to deployment, reducing failures by up to 30% (Song & Lee, 2024). This enhancement allows for early detection of failures and activates "self-recovery" mechanisms, avoiding prolonged outages.

The third step introduces advanced automation, where SCADA and EMS are integrated with AMIs and sensors to execute autonomous actions in emergencies. A study in European urban networks indicated a 20% reduction in operational disruptions, thanks to this automation layer (Australian Energy Market Operator (AEMO), 2023). Finally, the last phase promotes the creation of virtual plants (VPPs), distributed storage and the use of artificial intelligence to stabilize the network. According to Utility Dive, in the US, several states launched VPP policies and programs in 2024-2025, highlighting their speed in deploying operational flexibility in the face of consumption growth, especially driven by data centers and electric vehicles (Australian Energy Market Operator (AEMO), 2023). VPPs allow DERs (batteries, controllable loads, EVs) to be grouped together and offer peak or frequency regulation services with a speed and efficiency superior to conventional plants. Below is a table with information about it:

Table 2. Technologies associated with the different phases

Phase	Technologies involved	Observed Benefits	APA Examples / References
1. AMI (Smart Metering)	Smart meters, GPRS/ PLC, MDM	Real-time remote reading, load control, dynamic speeds, active user participation	(Utility Diving (March 12, 2024) ICEEE (2023)
2. Sensors in distribution	IoT, Voltage/Current Sensors, PMU, SCADA	Visibility in medium and low voltage, early detection of faults, proactive diagnostic capability	(Luong et al., 2023) Song & Lee (2024)
3. Advanced automation	SCADA, EMS, Distributed Control, Auto Response	Reduced power outages, operational efficiency, resilience after failures	(Australian Energy Market Operator (AEMO), 2023) Utility Diving (2024)

In the United States, the staggered adoption of Smart Grid technologies has advanced significantly, particularly in the states of California and Texas, which have opted for Virtual Power Plant (VPP)-based models. This type of VPP has demonstrated the ability to respond quickly to imbalance events and has reduced dependence on natural gas by nearly 5% in some high-demand areas such as the Bay Area (Kraft & Luh, 2024).

Australia has been a pioneer in the use of phased implementation strategies, starting with large-scale MIL since 2010. However, in the last three years a second stage has been strengthened, where state governments, such as that of Victoria and New South Wales, have invested in dynamic residential network management technologies. This strategy allows renewable integration to be scaled without saturating existing infrastructure and avoids millionaire investments in additional transformers (Li et al., 2023).

3.3 Implementation Models: Urban, Rural, Industrial, Microgrids

The transition to smart grids is not a uniform process; its implementation varies depending on the type of environment you are targeting. For this reason, it is crucial to distinguish between different implementation models that respond to the needs and conditions of the urban, rural, industrial and community sectors (microgrids). Each model presents specific technical, economic, and societal challenges, but also offers unique opportunities to optimize energy efficiency, improve the resilience of the electricity system, and facilitate the integration of renewable energy.

3.3.1 Urban Model

In urban environments, Smart Grids have a great potential for impact due to the density of users and access to existing electricity and telecommunications infrastructure. The City of Sacramento, USA, implemented the "SmartSacramento" project through the Sacramento Municipal Utility District (SMUD), where PMUs, demand response systems and state-of-the-art SCADA control were incorporated. This made it possible to reduce failure times, improve the quality of supply, and apply dynamic tariff schemes to promote efficient consumption (Khan & Ahmed, 2024). In Europe, the case of HafenCity, a smart district in Hamburg, Germany, demonstrated that the use of virtual buffers and dynamic control over integrated renewable sources (solar panels on buildings, charging stations for electric vehicles, and distributed storage) managed to reduce operating costs by up to 32%, as well as avoid dangerous load peaks for the grid (Alex Bazigu & Johnson Mwebaze, 2025).

3.3.2 Rural Model

Rural and isolated areas present challenges for electrification, so Smart Grids are adapted through the use of hybrid microgrids, where distributed generation (such as solar + batteries + biomass) is key. In Tanzania, a smart microgrid was developed that, through autonomous control and local communication, managed to provide reliable energy 24 hours a day, improving the quality of life of rural communities without access to the national grid (Khan & Ahmed, 2024). Likewise, in Indonesia, a system based on operational risk models was tested using stochastic programming, allowing planning the operation of a rural microgrid with high renewable penetration in variable climatic conditions. This strategy improved operational efficiency and reduced reliance on diesel (Ezeigweneme et al., 2024).

3.3.3 Industrial Model

Modern industries demand reliable and efficient power with strict quality standards. In this context, the industrial model of Smart Grid implementation is key to transforming plants, factories and industrial areas into smart and resilient energy environments. The process begins with a comprehensive energy audit. This methodology was used in a Power-to-X study in European factories, where IoT sensors and SCADA platforms were installed to monitor the behavior of pumps, motors, and HVAC systems in real time, reducing consumption by 18% and improving failure forecasting (Skjølsvold, 2021).

A critical evolution in the industrial model is the adoption of advanced industrial SCADA, powered by artificial intelligence and IoT networks. For example, factories in Asia applied SCADA 5.0 with predictive AI to automatically adjust pressure, temperature, and energy consumption parameters, achieving efficiencies of over 15% and reducing downtime (Losa, 2024).

In Europe, ports and manufacturing facilities integrated batteries and solar energy systems connected to a smart grid. This made it possible to change the consumption of energy peaks, avoiding costly surcharges and reducing the need for investments in additional infrastructure (Alex Bazigu and Johnson Mwebaze, 2025). A study revealed the use of embedded learning to protect against energy fraud and vulnerabilities in industrial IoT systems, thereby strengthening system integrity and avoiding costly outages (EDF North America, 2022).

3.3.4 Autonomous Microgrid Model

In Calistoga, California, an autonomous microgrid with high-capacity battery backup and hydrogen cells was developed, which guarantees supply for up to 48 hours even in the event of disconnection from the main grid, offering a key solution for regions prone to natural disasters (Song & Lee, 2024). In Africa, Husk Power Systems has installed more than 150 hybrid microgrids (solar + biomass + batteries), benefiting more than 5,000 customers with continuous access to clean energy, local storage, and smart meters. These networks have digital payment systems and automatic control, promoting economic development and sustainability (Losa, 2024).

While cities benefit from dense smart grids and advanced management technologies, rural areas require more autonomous and resilient solutions that ensure reliable access to energy. In parallel, industrial environments demand highly robust grids, with predictive monitoring capabilities and operational efficiency, while microgrids offer flexibility and energy security on a local scale.

3.4 Evaluation and Escalation of Pilot Cases

A pilot case, in the context of Smart Grids, is a controlled implementation that allows testing technologies, business models, regulatory frameworks and citizen participation mechanisms. It is not just a matter of observing whether a technology "works", but of studying its behavior in real conditions, its degree of interoperability with existing systems, its economic impact and its social acceptance. To structure a sound assessment, four main types of analysis are generally employed. The first is the technical-operational evaluation, which measures the performance of the devices and systems involved: sensors, smart meters, PMUs, storage, and controllers. This assessment includes interoperability testing (often with hardware-in-the-loop simulations) that determine whether devices from different manufacturers can communicate and operate together, a prerequisite for scaling without excessive technological dependency (Smart Grid Interoperability Panel (SGIP), 2023).

The second type is the economic-financial evaluation, which analyzes the viability of the pilot in terms of investment costs, operation, projected savings, and expected return. In Europe, for example, projects supported by the BRIDGE program have established assessment frameworks that integrate net present value (NPV), internal rates of return (IRR) and risk-adjusted social benefit analysis (Song & Lee, 2024).

The third dimension of evaluation addresses scalability and replicability. A successful pilot should not be seen as a unique and unrepeatable solution, but as a model adaptable to other territories and contexts. European projects such as EUniversal and Platone have generated standardized scalability indicators that can be adopted in Latin America (Song & Lee, 2024).

Finally, the social impact and citizen acceptance are evaluated. This often-underestimated aspect has proven to be key to the success of initiatives. Evaluations should incorporate metrics of user satisfaction, energy equity, and community participation in project design and monitoring (Losa, 2024).

In addition to these evaluation categories, there are international regulations and standards that guide the structuring of pilots. In the United States, the "Assessment Framework for Smart Grid Implementation Plans" guide from the Electric Power Research Institute (EPRI) and EDF North America proposes a set of metrics for operational performance, distributed resource share, and real-time demand response (Skjølsvold, 2023). Internationally, IEEE standards (such as P2030 on interoperability) and Smart Grid Interoperability Panel (SGIP) guidelines have been widely used to ensure pilots meet minimum quality and compatibility requirements (EDF North America, 2022).

A key aspect of convincing decision-makers is the establishment of objective criteria. These criteria include technical interoperability, superior operational performance, proven financial performance, evidence of scalability, measured social acceptance, and compliance with the current regulatory framework. The case of the European CROSSBOW project illustrates this process. The results showed improvements of 12% in efficiency, reduction of losses and high acceptance by users. This evidence influenced their inclusion in national European digital network policies (Song & Lee, 2024).

3.5 Strategy for Progressing in Phases

For a Smart Grid pilot not to remain just a technical experiment, a strategy structured in phases is required: first phase, design and technical execution of the pilot, the specific objectives of the pilot project are established: to reduce losses, improve reliability, enable demand response or evaluate new tariff frameworks (Smart Grid Interoperability Panel (SGIP), 2023). A slight preliminary cost-benefit (CBA) analysis is also performed in this phase to determine whether the initial investment is modest and potentially profitable. Finally, the community gets involved, especially in urban or rural areas, through informative workshops and participatory pilots (Siano et al., 2022).

Second phase, multidimensional evaluation and SRA, once the pilot is concluded, its results are analyzed in four dimensions: technical, regulatory, financial and social. In technical analysis, operational indicators, interoperability, and stability are validated. From the regulatory side, it is verified that the current legal framework allows replication and sustainable businesses; gaps are identified such as the lack of regulations on shared storage or the rights of prosumers (EDF North America, 2022). At the financial level, the CBA analysis is completed to include indirect benefits, such as reducing emissions or improving resilience to extreme events. Socially, adoption, equity, and citizen perception are evaluated after the pilot (Siano et al., 2022).

Third phase: validation and adjustments. Based on this assessment, technical adjustments are made (e.g., renewing protocols or adding cybersecurity), regulatory (establishing regulation, data, or AMI participation), and operational (including training plans or predictive maintenance). A technical-articulated report is prepared that recommends whether the pilot is ready to climb. At this stage, resources, timelines, and key sponsors are already defined.

Fourth phase: progressive scaling. With the strengthened pilot, progress is being made towards sectoral or territorial replication, adjusting investment by user density, type of networks and local characteristics. The strategy may include several waves of deployment, each aligned with robust regulatory frameworks, this ensures that each stage is supported by proven evidence and an aligned institutional framework (He et al., 2023) (Song & Lee, 2024). This phased approach allows any government to move forward safely and efficiently.

3.6 Factors that Speed Up or Slow Down Progress

First, the quality of the technical design and interoperability define the pace of implementation. When projects include proven technologies and ensure compatibility through testing such as Hardware-in-the-Loop, the risk of errors in the field is significantly reduced and deployment is accelerated (Song & Lee, 2024). On the other hand, the lack of common standards causes delays by requiring rigorous complementary validations. When regulations are ambiguous or require change, projects tend to get stuck in jurisdictional validations, losing momentum and funding (Siano et al., 2022).

Sustainable finance is another key factor. Well-designed pilots with business models based on cost-benefit analysis (CBA), which include intangible benefits such as emissions reductions or energy resilience, tend to attract investment from public and private entities. Otherwise, a lack of financial support can paralyze the project after the early stages (He et al., 2023).

User acceptance and engagement are vital. When citizens are actively involved in the design, they feel part of the solution and facilitate implementation. Instead, a lack of communication or concern about additional costs breeds resistance, which can lead to the abandonment of technology-intensive initiatives (Song & Lee, 2024). Studies show that settings with political support and specialized human resources manage to meet milestones in weeks, while in weak contexts the process takes several years and raises the cost of change (Zhao et al., 2022).

3.7 Examples of Successful Pilots

The InterFlex – France pilot (2016-2023) was implemented in several French regions, such as Nice and Nantes, and focused on the integration of storage, distributed generation and demand response. The initiative used adaptive regulatory frameworks and European technical standards, such as IEC 61850, to ensure replicability. In addition, it incorporated a clear scaling strategy and evaluation metrics, following methodologies aligned with EDF North America's practices (Deloitte, 2023). The Bogotá pilot, Enel Colombia's AMI Project, consisted of installing thousands of smart meters in key sectors of Bogotá. Despite international funding and a clear technological vision, the project faced delays due to regulatory barriers and societal concerns about data privacy. This was documented in Enel's reports and directly relates to the findings of (Skjølsvold et al., 2023) (Zhao et al., 2022) on the importance of citizen participation in smart grids. The pilot carried out by SmartNet Project in Italy was carried out between 2017 and 2022, although it began in 2017, the subsequent analysis in 2023 reveals key aspects. SmartNet explored coordination between transmission system operators (TSOs) and distribution system operators (DSOs). The project advanced with technical success thanks to the use of advanced simulators and interoperability tests using HIL (Song & Lee, 2024). However, it faced delays in scale due to a lack of alignment between institutional actors and rigid regulatory frameworks that prevented the exchange of operational data between companies. This case illustrates the need for regulatory synchronization and clear governance as central elements of pilot success, as emphasized (Losa and Cossent, 2024) (He et al., 2023).

4. ENABLING TECHNOLOGY AND TOOLS

The section focuses on the enabling technology layers that underpin a distributed smart grid: sensors, advanced meters, SCADA systems, communication networks, substation automation, demand management, simulation platforms, and cybersecurity. Mature technologies such as Advanced Metering Infrastructures (AMIs) and more advanced solutions such as Virtual Power Plants (VPPs), which allow multiple distributed energy resources to be orchestrated in a coordinated and optimized way, are analyzed. It also addresses international technical standards such as IEC 61850 and IEEE 1547, which ensure interoperability between equipment and platforms from different manufacturers. The convergence of automation, sensing, and digitization not only enables more accurate network management, but lays the groundwork for incorporating artificial intelligence, predictive algorithms, and real-time control. Cybersecurity is also recognized as an essential component. Finally, the importance of energy simulation and analysis platforms, such as GridLAB-D, HOMER or OpenDSS, which allow the behavior of the grid, validate investment scenarios and predict responses to contingencies, is highlighted.

4.1 Distributed Smart Infrastructure

Modern Smart Grids are based on an intelligent, distributed and digitized infrastructure, capable of collecting real-time data, automating decisions and orchestrating dispersed energy resources. This infrastructure is not a surface layer, but the technical basis that allows the implementation of efficiency policies, demand response, renewable integration, electrification of transport and resilience to extreme weather events. In this context, the deployment of IoT sensors, advanced metering networks (AMIs), distributed control systems and centralized management platforms represents not only an operational improvement, but a prerequisite for achieving energy transition and sustainability goals at the national level.

The design of this distributed architecture is based on the principle of edge intelligence, where each component of the network acts as an active node. These nodes not only consume energy, but also produce, store, and decide how to interact with the grid. This level of local autonomy requires new forms of communication, synchronization, and decision-making, supported by open standards, interoperability, advanced cybersecurity, and distributed computing capacity (Deloitte, 2023) (Yoldaş et al., 2023).

At the foundation of a distributed electrical infrastructure, sensors and smart meters (AMIs) function as active nodes that measure, communicate, and execute automated functions. Their role is not limited to the replacement of analog meters; They enable an operation scheme where the network is observed and managed with greater granularity and in close time to the real one. In bidirectional metering and edge control, the meters record consumption at frequent intervals (e.g., every 5 or 15 minutes) and maintain two-way communication: they send data and receive operating instructions (Deloitte, 2023). This exchange supports tools such as demand response, dynamic load management and home control. In addition, IoT sensors located in transformers, distribution lines, and substation busbars monitor voltage, current, and losses, offering a detailed view of power quality variables (Yoldaş et al., 2023). To support interoperability and integration, the adoption of standards (e.g., IEC 61850) and Hardware-in-the-Loop (HIL) testing are employed as a pre-verification practice. Evidence reports reductions in integration errors during the incorporation of new devices when these testing and certification methods are applied (IEA, 2023).

In terms of management and efficiency, the extended functionality of smart meters reduces displacements for manual readings, facilitates the detection of non-technical losses, and provides useful information for operating decisions and users (Deloitte, 2023; Siemens, 2023). Likewise, decreases in residential consumption have been observed, typically in the order of 3% to 5%, associated with direct feedback and efficiency programs (Taqi et al., 2022). Regarding connectivity and resiliency, the evolution towards "AMI 2.0" platforms incorporates edge computing, connectivity options (Wi-Fi or cellular) and upgradable applications that extend the life cycle of equipment and enable future functional improvements (Deloitte, 2023). This type of connectivity also helps events to be detected and addressed in a more timely and remote manner.

Bidirectional measurement, for example, not only improves the quality of information for utilities, but also enables dynamic demand response mechanisms, distributed generation, and flexible pricing. This is essential in a context where the participation of the user as a "prosumer" (producer and consumer) grows exponentially (Deloitte, 2023).

Distributed sensors, on the other hand, allow granular monitoring of the network, detecting incipient faults or technical losses in real time. This ability for early diagnosis is essential to reduce interruption times, improve reliability indices (SAIDI/SAIFI) and increase resilience to extreme events (Yoldaş et al., 2023). In terms of interoperability, the adoption of open technical standards and validation through hardware-in-the-loop testing have proven to be effective strategies to avoid bottlenecks in the integration of new equipment. This characteristic, which is often underestimated, represents one of the key factors for the success or failure of large-scale pilot projects (IEA, 2023). From an economic and operational point of view, AMI systems allow for more efficient management, by reducing operation and maintenance costs, detecting non-technical losses (fraud), and enabling energy efficiency programs for residential and industrial consumers (World Bank, 2022).

4.2 Substation Automation and Demand Management

After the deployment of sensors, the integration of this distributed layer with SCADA and ADMS systems connects field supervision with central operation, enabling two lines of action: automating the location, isolation and restoration of service in the event of failures, and coordinating demand with operational or tariff signals in close to real time. Recent literature documents that, in networks with remote switching and automation schemes, continuity indicators (e.g., SAIDI/CAIDI) can be significantly improved in controlled case studies (Shafik et al., 2023; Sánchez-Ixta et al., 2024).

Substation automation comprises IEDs, remote switching, and operating schemes that identify and isolate affected sections without continuous manual intervention. In recent evaluations, the incorporation of distributed automation and remote maneuvering is associated with relevant reductions in restoration times and minutes of interruption for users (Shafik et al., 2023; Sánchez-Ixta et al., 2024). In parallel, interoperability frameworks based on IEC 61850 support integration and coordinated operation tests between equipment from different manufacturers (Ayello & Lopes, 2023).

Demand management uses signals flowing through meters and platforms to adjust shiftable consumption during periods of increased system stress. Recent evidence indicates observable reductions in peak usage under hourly rates (TOU) and automatic responses in residential and commercial loads, with effects concentrated on peak demand days (Fu et al., 2024). These capabilities are extended through automated control and standardized communication protocols at the network edge (Wu et al., 2024; Bienert, 2023).

Smart substations integrate IEDs, digital relays and distributed control that operate in near-real-time on SCADA/ADMS platforms. With this architecture, it is possible to detect events, isolate sections and reconfigure the service with less dependence on manual maneuvers. Studies from 2023–2024 report substantial improvements in outage rates and restoration times when automation and remote switching are implemented on selected circuits (Shafik et al., 2023; Sánchez-Ixta et al., 2024).

A complementary evolution is the virtualization of Protection, Automation and Control (vPAC) functions, which transfers protection and control logics to standardized computing platforms while maintaining time and observability requirements. Recent literature describes use cases and cost-benefit models for vPAC and for software-defined approaches based on IEC 61850 (Leiva Vilaplana et al., 2024; Kabbara et al., 2022).

Demand response adjusts consumption based on price or operation signals. In homes with automation and smart thermostats, the adoption of TOU shows clear decreases in peak usage times, especially on days of high demand, which contributes to smoothing load profiles and deferring infrastructure reinforcements in certain contexts (Fu et al., 2024). To orchestrate these interactions, communication frameworks such as OpenADR are used, which establish standardized messaging between operators, aggregators, and end-user devices, facilitating coordinated responses (Bienert, 2023; Wu et al., 2024). Together, these practices allow automated programs—for example, temporary HVAC adjustments or non-critical loads—to be articulated when grid conditions require it.

5. PARTICIPATION OF SOCIAL ACTORS AND INTERNATIONAL CASES

The participation of social actors, users, companies, aggregators, grid operators and energy communities are articulated through regulatory instruments, tariff designs and market rules. Recent evidence indicates that this institutional architecture conditions who participates, with what rights, under what obligations and with what incentives (European Commission, Joint Research Centre [JRC], 2022; Radtke & Renn, 2024; Silva et al., 2023). In recent years, the comparison between jurisdictions has documented the relationship among: i) regulatory enablement of distributed energy resource aggregators; ii) retail price signals with temporal variation; and iii) frameworks for collective action through energy communities (Barone et al., 2023; Losada-Puente et al., 2023; Muttaqee et al., 2024). The analysis of these components offers elements to contrast public policies and draw lessons that can be transferred to other contexts (Häseler & Wulf, 2024; Zeng et al., 2024).

5.1 Stakeholder Participation in Smart Grids

The literature indicates that the economic signal facilitates consumption adjustments if there is granular measurement, settlement rules, and, in certain cases, automation at the edge (Silva et al., 2023). Studies for households under time-of-use prices describe strategies for displacing activities and time windows where the response is concentrated, with implications for estimating the potential for flexibility and for designing programs by type of load (Muttaqee et al., 2024). Recent methodological proposals examine alternatives for configuring time-of-use tariffs based on demand profiles and load equivalence criteria, which can support regulatory design processes (Zeng et al., 2024).

In the aggregation of distributed energy resources, an entity groups multiple loads, distributed generation or storage and represents them in markets or on flexibility platforms. In the European Union, the state of openness to independent aggregators, the measurement and settlement requirements, and the remaining barriers for small users have been systematized (European Commission, JRC, 2022). Financial and product analysis suggests representing flexibility as volumetric options, which facilitates the packaging of heterogeneous resources under a uniform contract and the valuation of their contribution (Geman et al., 2023). The comparison of policy styles indicates that the way in which competencies are distributed among regulators, operators, and marketers conditions the aggregator's space of action and the relationship with users (Radtke & Renn, 2024). On the other hand, collective action through energy communities can manage distributed generation, storage and, in some cases, local services. Comparative evaluations show that internal sharing rules, compatibility with network rules, and available incentives influence operational viability and its contribution to the network (Barone et al., 2023; Losada-Puente et al., 2023). Energy communities are inserted into smart grids through metering, data exchange platforms, and settlement arrangements, which allow local flows to be related to system signals (Silva et al., 2023). Recent literature classifies these forms of participation as components of energy policy design, rather than as objectives in themselves, and explores how they are integrated with public decision-making processes (Radtke & Renn, 2024).

5.2 International Cases and Comparison of Public Policies

At the European level, the 2022 analyses describe the state of explicit demand response in small users, access by independent aggregators, and the measurement and settlement procedures required for their participation (European Commission, JRC, 2022). This framework regulates responsibilities between the aggregator and the marketer, as well as mechanisms to avoid double counting. In parallel, reviews on energy communities in Spain, Italy and Greece describe the regulatory transposition process, the legal figures enabled, the administrative procedures and the energy-sharing practices (Losada-Puente et al., 2023). The case analysis suggests that clarity in roles and procedures is associated with a higher probability of completing projects and with a more fluid interaction with network operators (Barone et al., 2023; Losada-Puente et al., 2023). These conclusions are complemented by cross-sectional diagnoses that compare the implementation of demand response programs in Europe and the United States, highlighting convergences in objectives and divergences in the implementation sequence (Silva et al., 2023).

In Germany, a 2024 analysis proposes policy options for real-time tariffs in households, including adjustments to legal definitions, network charges and taxes, and consumer protection mechanisms (Häseler & Wulf, 2024). The study contrasts four configurations and describes their expected effect on incentives for adjusting consumption and on the adoption of automation tools. This case illustrates a policy design process that aligns retail signals with technical and market conditions, with the aim of expanding participation without mandatory membership.

In California, United States, a 2024 study analyzes the probability of shifting activities and the timing of consumption changes under time-of-use rates. The results identify schedules where adjustment is most likely and strategies that combine manual action and technological support, informing program sizing and automation design (Muttaqee et al., 2024). This case relates to the discussion on aggregation, insofar as individual behavior can be aggregated at scale to participate in markets or platforms, subject to measurement and settlement rules (European Commission, JRC, 2022; Geman et al., 2023).

The 2023 reviews compare the implementation of demand response and advanced metering integration. In the United States, the adoption of measurement and programs with behavioral and technological components shows a broad deployment trajectory; in Europe, openness to aggregators and articulation with flexibility platforms are advancing at different speeds depending on the country (Silva et al., 2023). In both cases, stakeholder participation is related to the existence of stable rules, to the compatibility between measurement and settlement, and to the availability of tools to reduce transaction costs in participation (Radtke & Renn, 2024). In assessments on grid balancing, it is described that communities with clear rules for distribution and access to incentives can coordinate distributed generation and storage to cover part of their demand and, under certain frameworks, provide services to the system (Barone et al., 2023). These results depend on proper measurement, internal governance and compatibility with policy instruments. Comparative analyses underscore that measurement standardization and settlement mechanisms are conditions for scaling up this type of initiative (Losada-Puente et al., 2023; Silva et al., 2023).

The conclusions are that the cases reviewed show that the participation of social actors in smart grids depends on regulatory and market arrangements that determine access, measurement, and settlement of services. Three elements are repeated in the jurisdictions studied. First, enabling aggregators with defined rules for responsibilities and data facilitates the onboarding of small resources into markets and platforms (European Commission, JRC, 2022; Geman et al., 2023). Second, tariff designs with temporal variation expand opportunities for freight movement, with empirical evidence on schedules and strategies, and with methodological proposals to configure price signals (Häseler & Wulf, 2024; Muttaqee et al., 2024; Zeng et al., 2024). Third, energy communities with stable frameworks, sharing rules, and access to incentives can coordinate local resources and, under specific conditions, provide services to the system (Barone et al., 2023; Losada-Puente et al., 2023). The EU–US comparison suggests that the sequence of implementation, institutional competencies, and standardization of measurement explain part of the differences in scale and modalities of participation (Radtke & Renn, 2024; Silva et al., 2023).

REFERENCES

Alavikia, Z., & Shabro, M. (2022). A comprehensive layered approach to implementing IoT technologies in smart grid. *Digital Communications and Networks*, *8*(4), 506–520. DOI: 10.1016/j.dcan.2022.01.002

Alex Bazigu and Johnson Mwebaze. (2025). A framework for IoT-enabled smart manufacturing for energy and resource optimization. arXiv. /arXiv.2502.03040. DOI: 10.48550

Australian Energy Market Operator (AEMO). (2023). DER Integration Projects – Flexible Export Test. https://aemo.com.au/en/initiatives/major-programs/der-program/flexible-exports

Ayello, M. F., & Lopes, Y. (2023). Interoperability based on IEC 61850 standard: Systematic literature review, certification method proposal, and case study. *Electric Power Systems Research*, *220*, 109355. DOI: 10.1016/j.epsr.2023.109355

Barone, G., Buonomano, A., Forzano, C., Palombo, A., & Russo, G. (2023). The role of energy communities in electricity grid balancing: A flexible tool for smart grid power distribution optimization. *Renewable & Sustainable Energy Reviews*, *187*, 113742. DOI: 10.1016/j.rser.2023.113742

Bienert, R. (2023). Standardizing Demand-Side Management: The OpenADR Standard. In Demand-Side Management (Ch. 5). Wiley. DOI: 10.1002/9781119899457.ch5

Burczyk, S., Kozłowski, M., & Kułaszka, A. (2022). LTE and NB-IoT performance estimation based on indicators measured by the radio module. *Electronics (Basel)*, *11*(18), 2892. DOI: 10.3390/electronics11182892

California, I. S. O. (2023). Duck Curve Management: Smart Grid Tools and Challenges. https://www.caiso.com

Campana, P., Censi, R., Ruggieri, R., & Amendola, C. (2025). Smart Grids and Sustainability: The Impact of Digital..... *Energies*, *18*(9), 2149. Advance online publication. DOI: 10.3390/en18092149

CEER. (2025). 3rd CEER Report on Power Losses. https://www.ceer.eu/publication/3rd-ceer-report-on-power-losses

Chintapalli, S., Arzamasov, V., & Monti, A. (2024). From prototype to interoperable DERs: A Hardware-in-the-Loop interoperability approach. *2024 IEEE International Conference on Industrial Cyber-Physical Systems (ICPS)*, 1–6. DOI: 10.1109/ICPS61098.2024.10662284

Deloitte. (2023). The benefits of demand response in network modernization: economic and operational perspectives. https://www2.deloitte.com

European Commission, Joint Research Centre. (2022). Explicit demand response for small end-users and independent aggregators: Status, context, enablers and barriers (EUR 31190 EN). Publications Office of the European Union. DOI: 10.2760/625919

European Union Agency for Cybersecurity (ENISA). (2023). Cybersecurity for Smart Grids: Threat Landscape 2023. https://www.enisa.europa.eu (2023).

Ezeigweneme, C. A., Nwasike, C. N., Adefemi, A. O., Adegbite, B. O., & Gidiagba, J. O. (2024). Smart Grids in Industrial Paradigms: A Review of the Progress, Benefits, and Implications of Maintenance. *Journal of Engineering Science and Technology*, *5*(1), 1–20. DOI: 10.51594/estj/v5i1.719

Federal Electricity Commission (CFE). (2022). Operational continuity report after instability events 23/06/2022. https://www.cfe.mx

Fiorucci, E., Musolino, A., Ferri, M., Pacioni, A., & Luiso, M. (2025). Driving sustainable development with PMU systems in distribution grids. *Sustainability*, *17*(12), 5280. DOI: 10.3390/su17125280

Fu, Z., Novan, K., & Smith, A. (2024). Do time-of-use prices deliver energy savings at the right time? *Journal of Environmental Economics and Management*, *128*, 103054. DOI: 10.1016/j.jeem.2024.103054

Geman, H., Hamida, S. B., & Roncoroni, A. (2023). Distributed energy resources flexibility as volumetric options. *Frontiers of Mathematical Finance*, *2*(3–4), 247–330. DOI: 10.3934/fmf.2023018

Häseler, S., & Wulf, A. J. (2024). Promoting real-time electricity tariffs for more demand response from German households: A review of four policy options. *Energy, Sustainability and Society*, *14*, 59. DOI: 10.1186/s13705-024-00490-z

He, Y., Liu, C., Liu, C.-C., & Wang, Y. (2023). Smart Monitoring and Fault Diagnosis in Smart Grids: A Review. *Energy Reports*, *9*, 584–596. DOI: 10.1016/j.egyr.2022.11.071

He, Y., Yang, F., & Hua, Q. (2022). A survey on Zero Trust architecture: Challenges and future research directions. *Wireless Communications and Mobile Computing*, *6476274*(1), 6476274. Advance online publication. DOI: 10.1155/2022/6476274

Hua, W., Chen, Y., Qadrdan, M., Jiang, J., Sun, H., & Wu, J. (2022). Applications of blockchain and artificial intelligence technologies for enabling prosumers in smart grids: A review. arXiv preprint. /arXiv.2202.10098.DOI: 10.48550

Inter-American Development Bank. (2023). *The economics of electricity losses in Latin America and the Caribbean*. IDB Publications.

Inter-American Development Bank (IDB). (2023). Smart Infrastructure for Latin America: Policy Priorities and Lessons Learned. https://www.iadb.org

International Energy Agency (IEA). (2023). Grid integration of variable renewable energies: a key priority for system stability. https://www.iea.org

International Energy Agency (IEA). (2023). Latin America Energy Outlook 2023. https://www.iea.org/reports/latin-america-energy-outlook-2023

International Energy Agency (IEA). (2023). Monitoring the reliability of the energy system. https://www.iea.org/reports/tracking-power-system-reliability

International Renewable Energy Agency (IRENA). (2023). Smart grid policy frameworks for the energy transition. https://www.irena.org

JRC (Joint Research Centre). (2022). *Smart Grid Interoperability Laboratory—Annual Report 2022*. Publications Office of the European Union., DOI: 10.2760/066580

Kabbara, N., Zografopoulos, I., & Antoniou, A. (2022). Towards software-defined protection, automation, and control in power systems: A survey. *Energies*, *15*(24), 9362. DOI: 10.3390/en15249362

Kabeyi, M. J. B. (2023). Smart grid technologies and application in the sustainable power sector. *Energy and Environment Research*, *10*(2), 123–139. DOI: 10.1080/14786451.2023.2222298

Khalid, M. (2024). Smart grids and renewable energy systems: Perspectives. *Energy Reports*. Advance online publication. DOI: 10.1016/j.egyr.2024.05.105

Khan, F. & Ahmed, Z. (2024). Smart grid integration with Industry 5.0: Applications, challenges. Sustainable energy systems. .DOI: 10.1016/j.sesj.2024.02.031

Kirmani, S., Khurshid, F., & Karim, S. (2022). A survey on IoT-enabled smart grids: Technologies, architectures, applications, and challenges. *Sustainability (Basel)*, *15*(1), 717. DOI: 10.3390/su15010717

Kraft, J., & Luh, P. Y.-S. (2024). Improving energy access in rural areas: Smart microgrid in Tanzania. *Energy for Sustainable Development*. Advance online publication. DOI: 10.1016/j.esd.2024.100452

Leiva Vilaplana, J. A., Kabbara, N., & Coste, T. (2024). Virtualized Protection, Automation, and Control in Electrical Substations: An Open-Source Dynamic Cost-Benefit Assessment Model. *IEEE Access : Practical Innovations, Open Solutions*, *12*, 1–1. DOI: 10.1109/ACCESS.2024.3435972

Li, Y., & Cao, J.. (2023). Operational risk awareness planning for rural multi-energy microgrids. *Frontiers in Energy Research*, *11*, 112164. DOI: 10.3389/fenrg.2023.112164

Liu, C.-C., McArthur, S. J., & Lee, S.-J. (2023). *Smart Grid Handbook* (Vol. 1–3). Wiley.

Losa, I., & Cossent, R. (2024). Scalability and replicability analysis in smart grid demonstration projects: Lessons learned and future needs. *Energies*, *17*(21), 5312. DOI: 10.3390/en17215312

Losada-Puente, L., Blanco, J. A., Dumitru, A., Sebos, I., Tsakanikas, A., Liosi, I., & Rodríguez, E. (2023). Cross-case analysis of the energy communities in Spain, Italy, and Greece: Progress, barriers, and the road ahead. *Sustainability*, *15*(18), 14016. DOI: 10.3390/su151814016

Luong, H. T., ... (2023). Innovating the Smart Grid: A SmartSacramento Utility Case Study from SMUD. EBA-Net Reports https://www.smud.org/en/Corporate/About-Us/News-and-Media

Mansour, R. F., Mafarja, M., Bruzzone, A., & Al-Azab, M. (2023). Digital twins and IoT-assisted smart electric power systems: A review. *IET Generation, Transmission & Distribution*, *17*(23), 5581–5597. DOI: 10.1049/gtd2.12940

Mchirgui, M., Frikha, M., Dhaou, I., & Jemaa, M. B. (2024). Digital twin for smart grid: A comprehensive review. *Applied Sciences (Basel, Switzerland)*, *14*(23), 10933. DOI: 10.3390/app142310933

Muttaqee, M., Stelmach, G., Zanocco, C., Flora, J., Rajagopal, R., & Boudet, H. S. (2024). Time-of-use pricing and likelihood of shifting energy activities, strategies, and timing. *Energy Policy*, *187*, 114019. DOI: 10.1016/j.enpol.2024.114019

Nguyen, L.-H., Nguyen, V.-L., Hwang, R.-H., Kuo, J.-J., Chen, Y.-W., Huang, C.-C., & Pan, P.-I. (2024). Towards a Secure Smart Grid 2.0: Exploring Security Threats, Protection Models, and Challenges. arXiv. /arXiv.2404.12371.DOI: 10.48550

North America, E. D. F. (2022). *Evaluation framework for smart grid deployment plans*. EDF.

ORNL (Oak Ridge National Laboratory). (2013). Chattanooga Electric Power Board Smart Grid Analysis. Technical report. .DOI: 10.2172/1376469

Radtke, J., & Renn, O. (2024). Participation in energy transitions: A comparison of policy styles. *Energy Research & Social Science, 114*, 103743. DOI: 10.1016/j.erss.2024.103743

Reif, V., Strasser, T. I., Jimeno, J., ... (2023). Towards an interoperability roadmap for the energy transition. arXiv. /arXiv.2304.10394.DOI: 10.48550

Sánchez-Ixta, C., Vázquez-Abarca, J. R., López-Sosa, L. B., & Golpour, I. (2024). Analysis of the Restoration of Distribution Substations: A Case Study of the Central–Western Division of Mexico. *Energies, 17*(16), 4154. DOI: 10.3390/en17164154

SGMM Team. The. (2011, September 1). Smart Grid Maturity Model, Version 1.2: Model Definition (Technical Report CMU/SEI-2011-TR-025). Institute of Software Engineering. DOI: 10.1184/R1/6583835.v1

Shafik, M. B., Elbarbary, Z. M. S., Bu, S., Azmy, A. M., & Hussien, M. G. (2023). Distribution network's reliability assessment considering distributed automation system with penetration of DG units and SOP devices. *Energy Reports, 9*, 6199–6210. DOI: 10.1016/j.egyr.2023.05.224

Siano, P., De Marco, C., Rola, P., Loia, V., & Vasirani, M. (2022). Advanced smart metering infrastructures for distribution networks: A review. *Electric Power Systems Research, 211*, 108000. DOI: 10.1016/j.epsr.2022.108000

Sievers, T., Mata-Vázquez, M., & Schuller, A. (2023). A systematic review of data-driven energy management in distribution grids. *Energies, 16*(4), 1688. DOI: 10.3390/en16041688

Silva, C., Faria, P., & Vale, Z. (2023). Demand response implementation: Overview of Europe and United States status. *Energies, 16*(10), 4043. DOI: 10.3390/en16104043

Skjølsvold, T. M., Ryghaug, M., & Heidenreich, S. (2023). Citizen participation in smart grid pilots: A review of frameworks and impacts. *Energy Research & Social Science, 98*, 103123. DOI: 10.1016/j.erss.2023.103123

Smart energy. (2024, February). IEC 61850 – The standard for digitizing and automating power grids. Smart energy.

Smart energy. (2025, June). IEC 61850 Ed. 2.1: A new milestone in smart grid interoperability. Smart energy.

Song, E. & Lee, K. B. (2024). Interoperability testing based on hardware-in-the-loop simulation of smart sensors. IEEE ICPS 2024 Proceedings.

Song, J.-U., Oh, Y.-S., Ahn, J.-G., & Lee, S.-I. (2023). A topology-based local identifier mapping scheme for power system resources in a CIM framework for interoperability. *Applied Sciences (Basel, Switzerland)*, *13*(18), 10341. DOI: 10.3390/app131810341

Tangi, S., Majumdar, A., & Das, D. (2024). Smart distribution network voltage estimation using PMU measurements. *PLoS One*, *19*(2), e0293616. DOI: 10.1371/journal.pone.0293616

Taqi, H. M., Naeem, M., & Javaid, N. (2022). Implementation of IoT in smart grids. *Future Energy Proceedings*, *1*(2), 66–78. DOI: 10.1016/j.fep.2022.04.006

U.S. Department of Energy (DOE). (2022). Cybersecurity Capability Maturity Model (C2M2). https://www.energy.gov/ceser/c2m2 (2022).

Von Jouanne, A., Agamloh, E. B., & Yokochi, A. (2023). Power hardware-in-the-loop (PHIL): A review to advance smart inverter-based grid-edge solutions. *Energies*, *16*(2), 916. DOI: 10.3390/en16020916

Wang, Z., Yang, Q., & Qiu, S. (2024). The construction effect of ultra-high-voltage power grid based on multilevel index analysis method. *Sustainability*, *16*(18), 8083. DOI: 10.3390/su16188083

World Bank. (2022). Energy Data Landscape – Latin America and the Caribbean. https://databank.worldbank.org/source/sustainable-energy-for-all)

World Bank. (2022). Energy Infrastructure Cost Benchmarking Toolkit. https://www.worldbank.org)

Wu, J., Li, Y., & Xu, H. (2023). Design and implementation of the Zero Trust model in power IoT networks. *International Transactions on Electrical Energy Systems*, *6545323*, 1–13. Advance online publication. DOI: 10.1155/2023/6545323

Wu, Y.-C., Chang, C.-S., & Li, W.-H. (2024). Development of a Low-Cost Automated Demand Response Controller for Home Energy Management. *Applied Sciences (Basel, Switzerland)*, *14*(23), 11434. DOI: 10.3390/app142311434

Yoldaş, Y., Önen, A., Muyeen, S. M., Vasilakos, A. V., & Alan, İ. (2023). Improving Smart Grid Flexibility with Virtual Power Plants: Recent Developments and Future Directions. *Renewable & Sustainable Energy Reviews*, *180*, 113298. DOI: 10.1016/j.rser.2022.113298

Zeng, X., Chen, L., Wang, D., Zhang, Z., He, S., Liu, S., & Wang, L. (2024). An effective method of equivalent load-based time-of-use electricity pricing strategy. *Mathematics*, *12*(9), 1408. DOI: 10.3390/math12091408

Zhao, L., Wang, X., Li, Z., & Li, Z. (2022). Self-healing control strategy in intelligent distribution networks based on data-driven decision-making. *Applied Energy, 313*, 118807. DOI: 10.1016/j.apenergy.2022.118807

Chapter 4
Smart Cities:
Integration of Technological Solutions in Urban Management

Francisco R. Trejo-Macotela
https://orcid.org/0000-0003-2133-3456
Universidad Politécnica de Pachuca, Mexico

Jaime Aguilar-Ortiz
https://orcid.org/0009-0003-5302-1454
Universidad Politécnica de Pachuca, Mexico

Esther Citlali Garcia-Contreras
Universidad Politécnica de Pachuca, Mexico

ABSTRACT

This chapter explores the conceptual evolution and multidimensional implementation of smart cities as socio-technical systems. It investigates how the integration of digital technologies—including the Internet of Things (IoT), Artificial Intelligence (AI), Building Information Modelling (BIM), and Geographic Information Systems (GIS)—reshapes urban governance, service delivery, and participatory planning. Emphasis is placed on the triadic framework of technology, community, and nature, offering a holistic analytical lens for sustainability and inclusivity. Through global case studies (e.g., Singapore, Barcelona, New York), the chapter critically evaluates governance models, data ethics, infrastructural innovation, and policy design. Emerging challenges—cybersecurity, digital inequality, and environmental impacts—are addressed alongside future trajectories in generative AI, biophilic urbanism, and autonomous mobility. Ultimately, the chapter argues that smart cities must transcend technocentric paradigms, fostering equitable, resilient, and democratically governed urban futures.

DOI: 10.4018/979-8-3373-5535-1.ch004

1. INTRODUCTION

Urbanisation has emerged as one of the most significant and transformative phenomena of the twenty-first century, exerting profound influence over demographic distribution, resource allocation, and socio-economic development on a global scale. According to the United Nations (2019), over 56% of the world's population now resides in cities—a figure projected to rise to approximately 68% by 2050. This unprecedented urban expansion presents both formidable challenges and transformative opportunities for sustainable development. Amid this complex scenario, the concept of the "smart city" has assumed a pivotal role in addressing the multifaceted demands of modern urban life, serving as an integrated platform that amalgamates technology, governance, and social innovation.

Originally conceived from a technocentric paradigm that prioritised the optimisation of infrastructure through Information and Communication Technologies (ICT), the smart city model has undergone a substantial conceptual metamorphosis (Albino et al., 2015). Initial efforts concentrated primarily on the deployment of digital technologies such as automated lighting systems, traffic control mechanisms, and intelligent grid infrastructure to improve operational efficiency and reduce administrative costs. However, these narrow interpretations have progressively yielded to a more nuanced, interdisciplinary perspective that incorporates the values of environmental sustainability, social inclusion, participatory governance, and long-term resilience (Mora et al., 2019; Meijer & Bolívar, 2016).

Today, the smart city is no longer defined solely by its technological sophistication, but rather by the capacity of that technology to enhance the quality of urban life, mitigate ecological impact, and foster democratic engagement. The shift from purely digital to socio-technical paradigms underscores the growing recognition that technological infrastructure alone is insufficient to resolve the deep-seated structural issues afflicting contemporary cities. Instead, meaningful integration of community participation, environmental consciousness, and cultural awareness is required to ensure that technological interventions are equitable, context-sensitive, and sustainable (Angelidou, 2017; Yu, 2024).

Central to this evolving discourse is the triadic framework of technology, community, and nature, which constitutes an essential analytical lens for understanding the dynamics of smart urbanism. This triad accentuates the interdependence of digital infrastructure, civic agency, and ecological stewardship, offering a comprehensive basis for evaluating the effectiveness of smart city initiatives. Within this context, urban development must not only accommodate technological advancement but must do so in ways that are ecologically responsible, socially inclusive, and culturally grounded (Dilip, 2024).

Moreover, smart city initiatives are increasingly aligned with global development agendas, most notably the United Nations' Sustainable Development Goals (SDGs). In particular, SDG 11—"Sustainable Cities and Communities"—emphasises the necessity for urban spaces to be inclusive, resilient, safe, and sustainable (United Nations, 2021). By leveraging advanced technologies to manage natural resources more judiciously, optimise transport systems, and reduce pollution, smart cities offer viable pathways for achieving these objectives. Initiatives such as Singapore's Smart Nation, the European Urban Agenda, and various Latin American smart city strategies exemplify the global commitment to harnessing technology in service of urban sustainability (ITU, 2021; OECD, 2022).

The implementation of smart city technologies must be supported by robust data governance structures and an ethical framework that prioritises privacy, transparency, and inclusiveness. The massive proliferation of data generated by Internet of Things (IoT) devices, urban sensors, and digital platforms necessitates a careful balance between innovation and the protection of citizens' rights. As Batty (2024) articulates, the mere existence of data is not sufficient—its utility arises from contextualisation and interpretation within the social and political realities of urban life. Consequently, data must be managed not only for operational efficiency but also for public accountability and democratic legitimacy.

Technological infrastructure—comprising IoT systems, edge computing, urban data platforms, and advanced connectivity networks—constitutes the backbone of smart urban systems. These components function synergistically to collect, process, and analyse data in real time, facilitating informed decision-making and anticipatory governance. For example, the deployment of smart parking sensors, adaptive traffic lights, and environmental monitoring devices allows cities to enhance mobility, reduce emissions, and improve public safety (Abdulsaheb et al., 2024; Mehta et al., 2024). Nonetheless, the efficacy of these technologies depends upon their interoperability, scalability, and alignment with citizen needs.

Emerging technologies such as Artificial Intelligence (AI), blockchain, and robotics are extending the operational capacity of smart cities beyond data collection and into the realms of predictive analytics, decentralised governance, and automated service delivery. In New York City, AI-driven platforms have led to measurable reductions in emergency response times, while blockchain applications in Dubai have enhanced the transparency of government transactions (Makanadar & Shahane, 2023; Bishr, 2019). These examples highlight the transformative potential of intelligent systems to improve urban functionality and public trust.

Despite these promising developments, critical challenges persist. Concerns regarding cybersecurity, digital inequality, environmental impact, and regulatory fragmentation threaten the sustainability and legitimacy of smart city projects. Addressing these challenges necessitates the adoption of comprehensive public policies that integrate technological innovation with ethical oversight and civic participation. Successful smart cities are those that transcend sectoral boundaries, build cross-institutional partnerships, and empower citizens as co-creators of urban solutions (Cardullo et al., 2019; Cowley et al., 2018).

In sum, the smart city represents both a technological and a socio-political endeavour. Its success hinges not merely on the sophistication of its digital tools, but on the intentional and inclusive design of its governance models, participatory frameworks, and ecological practices. As this chapter demonstrates, the smart city is not a static entity or a singular template, but a continuously evolving construct shaped by the interplay of innovation, inclusion, and integrity. By embracing a holistic approach that integrates technology, community, and nature, cities can move beyond superficial digitisation towards meaningful and enduring transformation.

1.1. Definition and Historical Evolution of the Concept of "Smart City"

The concept of the "smart city" has undergone a remarkable transformation and expansion over the past two decades. What initially emerged as a predominantly technocentric vision, focused on optimising the efficiency of infrastructures through the application of Information and Communication Technologies (ICT), has today evolved into a much richer and more holistic perspective. In its early stages, the discourse revolved around the implementation of sensors to manage traffic, automated systems for public lighting, or smart grids for energy distribution. The primary objective was operational optimisation and cost reduction, approached from a purely engineering and technological standpoint (Albino et al., 2015).

However, as global urbanisation progressed and socio-environmental challenges became increasingly evident, the definition expanded significantly. At present, a smart city encompasses a vision that fundamentally integrates environmental sustainability, social inclusion, and participatory governance (Mora et al., 2019). It is no longer solely about equipping a city with technology, but rather about how that technology is employed to substantially enhance the quality of life of its inhabitants, optimise urban services, and, crucially, ensure resilient urban planning in the face of complex contemporary challenges such as climate change, resource scarcity, or public health crises (Meijer & Bolívar, 2016; Gil-Garcia et al., 2015).

This conceptual evolution has been marked by a critical transition: from a merely digital approach, wherein technological solutions were viewed as panaceas, towards socio-technical models. These new paradigms acknowledge that technology is merely a tool, and that its true impact depends on how it is integrated with human, cultural, and ecological factors in the design, operation, and evolution of the city (Angelidou, 2017; Yu, 2024). Within this broader and more nuanced context, the triad of “technology–community–nature” emerges as a fundamental analytical axis. This triad not only aids in understanding contemporary urban complexities but also provides a framework for assessing the long-term effectiveness and sustainability of smart city initiatives, ensuring that solutions are not only efficient, but also equitable and environmentally respectful.

1.2. Global Importance of the Urban Phenomenon and the Role of Smart Cities

The urban phenomenon is undoubtedly one of the principal drivers of change in the twenty-first century. Urbanisation is advancing inexorably: over 56% of the global population currently resides in cities, and United Nations projections indicate that this figure will rise to an astonishing 68% by 2050 (United Nations, 2019; UN-Habitat, 2022). This unprecedented growth, while generating economic and cultural opportunities, also brings with it a host of significant challenges that test the resilience and management capacity of urban administrations. Among the most pressing are pressures on natural resources (water, energy, land), air and water pollution, the exponential increase in municipal solid waste, urban insecurity, traffic congestion, and, critically, social inequality and spatial segregation.

In the face of this scenario, smart cities are proposed as an integral and multifaceted solution. Their inherent design enables more efficient resource use through intelligent monitoring and management of water and energy consumption, optimisation of public transport routes, or smart waste collection. Furthermore, they significantly enhance the management of urban services—from healthcare and education to public safety—by integrating data and technologies to deliver faster and more personalised responses. The ability to collect and analyse real-time data facilitates evidence-based decision-making, enabling authorities to anticipate problems and design more effective policies tailored to the specific needs of the population (Sharifi et al, 2024).

In this context, the role of smart cities has been essential in advancing the implementation of the 2030 Agenda and the Sustainable Development Goals (SDGs). In particular, their comprehensive approach aligns directly with SDG 11: “Sustainable Cities and Communities” (United Nations, 2021), which aims to make cities and human settlements inclusive, safe, resilient, and sustainable. From promoting sustainable transport to reducing cities’ environmental impact and improving habitability, smart city initiatives actively contribute to these global goals.

The growing global interest in this paradigm is also reflected in national and municipal strategies across various regions. Large-scale initiatives such as Singapore’s Smart Nation—a bold project to integrate technology into all aspects of civic life; the European Urban Agenda, which promotes sustainable urban development across the European Union; and the various smart city policies in Latin America, which aim to adapt these solutions to their socio-economic realities—are consolidating technological ecosystems. These efforts not only foster technological innovation but also explicitly prioritise social well-being and environmental efficiency as foundational pillars of urban development (ITU, 2021; OECD, 2022). This global commitment underscores the conviction that smart cities are not merely a trend, but an urgent necessity for building a more liveable and sustainable urban future.

1.3. Analytical Framework: Technology, Community, and Nature as Fundamental Axes

In order to conduct a robust and meaningful study of smart cities, it is imperative to establish a sound analytical framework that transcends mere technological implementation. This framework is founded upon the intrinsic interconnection between technology, community, and nature. Such an approach recognises that no technological solution, however advanced, can be truly effective, sustainable, or equitable without being complemented by participatory governance that actively involves citizens, and without a respectful and attentive approach to the natural environment and the ecosystems that sustain urban life (Dilip, 2024). This implies that technology must be designed and applied with a deep understanding of social needs and dynamics, as well as the constraints and opportunities presented by the environment.

Accordingly, an interdisciplinary convergence that transcends traditional knowledge silos is required. This approach must actively engage specialists in urban planning and spatial design, who understand the morphology and function of the city; computer science and artificial intelligence, to develop the necessary platforms and algorithms; user-centred design, to ensure that technological solutions are intuitive, accessible, and responsive to real citizen needs; and, crucially, urban ecology, which offers the perspective of natural systems, biodiversity, and environmental sustainability within the urban context.

Within this framework, urban data become fundamental inputs for decision-making. These data—collected from a diverse array of sources, ranging from strategically located IoT (Internet of Things) sensors monitoring traffic, air quality, or water consumption, to big data platforms aggregating information from various origins, or citizen monitoring systems enabling residents to report incidents or contribute to data collection—constitute the raw material. However, their value lies not solely in their volume or technical precision, but in their social and political contextualisation (Batty, 2024). A datum is merely a number; it becomes useful knowledge only when interpreted within a specific social, cultural, and political context, and when utilised to inform decisions that benefit the community.

Therefore, the architecture of smart cities must go beyond technological infrastructure alone. It must consider open data models that facilitate transparency and participation, while simultaneously implementing robust privacy mechanisms to protect citizens' personal information. Equally important is the creation of citizen deliberation spaces—both physical and virtual—where inhabitants can express their needs, participate in the design of solutions, and monitor urban policies. In this way, a model of the city is consolidated that is not solely centred on technical efficiency or the accumulation of technologies per se, but rather on the creation of public value. This is achieved through democratic innovation, which empowers citizens, and ecological sustainability, which ensures a liveable future for coming generations (Cardullo et al., 2019; Cowley et al., 2018). It is a path towards cities that are not only more "intelligent" in technological terms, but also more humane and greener.

Figure 1 illustrates the triadic analytical framework underlying smart city paradigms, demonstrating the interdependence of digital infrastructure, civic participation, and ecological resilience. This model supports a holistic understanding of urban transformation, emphasising the importance of socially and environmentally contextualised technological solutions (Dilip, 2024).

Figure 1. Triadic Framework of Smart Urbanism: Integration of Technology, Community, and Nature.

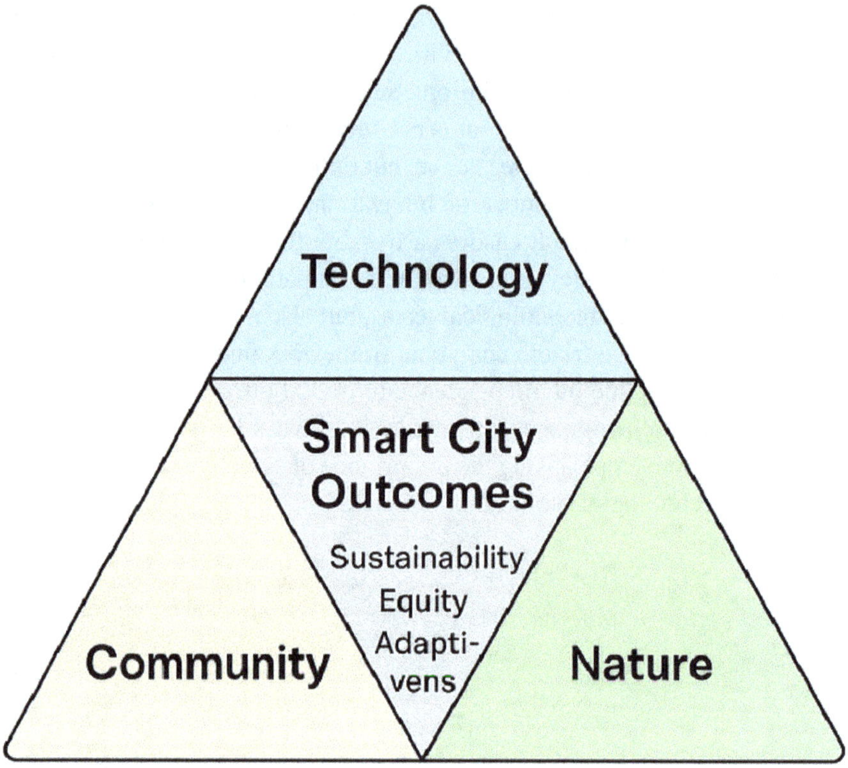

2. TECHNOLOGICAL INFRASTRUCTURE: THE FOUNDATION OF SMART CITIES

The conceptual and operational success of smart cities is inextricably linked to the robustness, scalability, and intelligence of their technological infrastructure. Far from being an ancillary element, this infrastructure constitutes the digital nervous system of the urban environment, enabling the continuous capture, transmission, and processing of vast volumes of real-time data generated across diverse domains. It is this infrastructure that underpins the capacity of a city to evolve from reactive administration to anticipatory governance—transforming the urban fabric into a dynamic ecosystem capable of self-regulation, adaptation, and optimisation in response to both routine and exceptional conditions. As cities contend with unprecedented pressures—including population growth, environmental degradation, and infrastructure ageing—technological infrastructure emerges not merely as a tool for enhancement but as an existential requirement for resilience and sustainability (Feng et al., 2019).

The foundational components of this infrastructure encompass a synergistic assembly of IoT (Internet of Things) sensors, edge computing devices, urban data platforms, and advanced connectivity systems such as 5G and LPWAN. Each of these elements performs a vital and interdependent role in the urban digital ecosystem. IoT sensors function as the perceptive organs of the city, detecting variations in environmental conditions, mobility flows, and resource consumption patterns with unparalleled granularity. Edge computing allows for the immediate processing of data at or near its source, significantly reducing latency and enabling real-time responses essential for critical functions such as traffic control and public safety (Sydle, n.d.; Iberdrola, n.d.). Urban data platforms, including digital twins and data lakes, serve as central processing units, aggregating, modelling, and visualising multisectoral data to support evidence-based decision-making. This approach aligns with visualisation tools integrating open urban datasets and unsupervised learning to support spatial decision-making (Estrada et al., 2018).

Moreover, the importance of connectivity infrastructure cannot be overstated. The convergence of high-bandwidth, low-latency communication systems with decentralised sensor networks permits a seamless integration of digital services. This technological mesh ensures not only operational efficiency but also equity, by enabling scalable digital inclusion strategies. As demonstrated by successful case studies in cities such as Singapore and New York, it is precisely the strategic deployment of these infrastructural components—interoperable, secure, and responsive—that enables cities to harness the full potential of smart technologies to improve quality of life, optimise urban systems, and ensure sustainable urban development (Du et al., 2024; Makanadar & Shahane, 2023).

2.1. Key Components of the Infrastructure

The successful implementation of smart city models necessitates the coordinated deployment of a multifaceted technological infrastructure composed of interconnected systems. To elucidate the structural underpinnings of such infrastructure, Table 1 offers a comparative overview of the core technological components, outlining their respective operational functions and the benefits observed in applied urban contexts. This analytical synthesis facilitates a more comprehensive understanding of how these elements contribute individually and synergistically to the optimisation of urban governance, service provision, and sustainable development. By identifying the strategic roles of each component—from IoT sensors to advanced communication networks—this table provides a functional taxonomy that supports the design, evaluation, and continuous improvement of smart city initiatives.

Table 1. Core Components of Smart City Technological Infrastructure: Functions and Observed Benefits.

Component	Primary Function	Observed Benefits
IoT Sensors	Real-time monitoring of urban variables such as air quality, traffic, energy use, and public space occupancy.	Enhanced situational awareness; data granularity for dynamic decision-making; reduced emissions (Abdulsaheb et al., 2024).
Edge Computing Devices	Local processing of data at the point of collection, reducing the need for cloud-based latency-sensitive operations.	Real-time responsiveness; reduced bandwidth usage; optimised traffic and safety systems (Iberdrola, n.d.; Sydle, n.d.).
Urban Data Platforms	Aggregation, modelling, and visualisation of multisource urban data; includes digital twins and data lakes.	Predictive planning; traffic and resource optimisation; proactive governance (Feng et al., 2019).
Advanced Connectivity Systems (5G, LPWAN)	Enable seamless, high-speed, and low-latency communication among urban devices and platforms.	Supports autonomous systems, distributed energy management, and inclusive connectivity (Ogbodo et al., 2022).

The functional core of a smart city is composed of various interconnected elements operating in synergy:

- **IoT Sensors (Internet of Things):** These are the components closest to the city's pulse, acting as its "senses". These devices, which may be tiny and discreet or part of more complex systems, are designed for the continuous monitoring of a wide range of urban variables. These include air quality (measuring pollutants such as PM2.5 or gases like CO_2 and ozone), noise levels in different areas, energy consumption in public and private buildings, the occupancy of public spaces (parks, squares), and, crucially, the real-time status of vehicular traffic. A notable example of the tangible impact of IoT sensors is observed in parking management. The installation of smart parking sensors in densely populated urban areas has proven highly effective. Studies, such as that cited by Abdulsaheb et al. (2024), indicate that this implementation can reduce the average time spent searching for a parking space by up to 25%. This reduction not only improves drivers' experience but also has a significant environmental impact by decreasing pollutant emissions from vehicles circulating in search of parking, thereby alleviating congestion and contributing to improved urban air quality. Other examples include sensors that detect leaks in underground water pipes, optimising water management and preventing losses.

- **Edge Computing Devices:** As the volume of data generated by IoT sensors increases exponentially, the need to process this information efficiently becomes critical. This is where edge computing comes into play. Unlike sending all data to a cloud data centre for processing—which may introduce latency—edge computing allows data to be processed as close as possible to its source, that is, at the "edge" of the network. This is fundamental for applications requiring real-time responses, such as smart traffic light systems that adjust timings according to vehicle flow or security systems that must instantly identify and respond to threats. By reducing latency and bandwidth requirements, edge computing enhances the efficiency and resilience of the urban network, enabling faster and more autonomous local responses (Iberdrola, n.d.; Sydle, n.d.).
- **Urban Data Platforms:** The vast stream of raw data collected by sensors and processed at the edge must be organised, stored, and, above all, interpreted. Urban data platforms serve as the brains of the smart city. These include data lakes—massive repositories capable of storing structured and unstructured information from diverse sources without a predefined schema—and digital twins. A digital twin is a real-time virtual representation of a physical object, system, or, in this case, an entire city or a section thereof. It enables the simulation of complex urban flows—such as traffic patterns, pedestrian movement, energy consumption, and even the spread of diseases or the impact of extreme weather events—to optimise urban planning and improve real-time responsiveness. The city of Chattanooga, USA, provides an excellent example of the practical application of digital twins. Its system has optimised traffic light synchronisation, achieving a 30% reduction in vehicular congestion (Feng et al., 2019). These platforms transform data into actionable information, enabling urban planners to make more informed and proactive decisions.
- **Advanced Connectivity Systems:** For all these components to communicate seamlessly and efficiently, next-generation connectivity infrastructure is essential. 5G networks are rapidly emerging as the standard for low-latency, high-volume data communications. Their speed and capacity are vital for supporting critical applications such as autonomous vehicles (which require millisecond-level response times for safety), distributed energy management (where smart systems balance supply and demand in real time), and emergency response systems (which require instantaneous and reliable communication). In parallel, LPWAN (Low-Power Wide-Area Networks), such as LoRaWAN, are ideal for low-power IoT devices that need to transmit small amounts of data over long distances with exceptional energy efficien-

cy, thereby extending sensor battery life by years (Ogbodo et al., 2022; TE Connectivity, n.d.). The combination of 5G and LPWAN provides a scalable, resilient, and diversified communication infrastructure, fundamental for the operability of a truly interconnected smart city.

Figure 2 graphically synthesises the relationship between key components of technological infrastructure—IoT, edge computing, urban data platforms, and connectivity networks—emphasising their systemic interdependence in enabling real-time urban management and anticipatory governance (Feng et al., 2019; Ogbodo et al., 2022).

Figure 2. Functional Interdependence of Core Technological Infrastructure in Smart Cities.

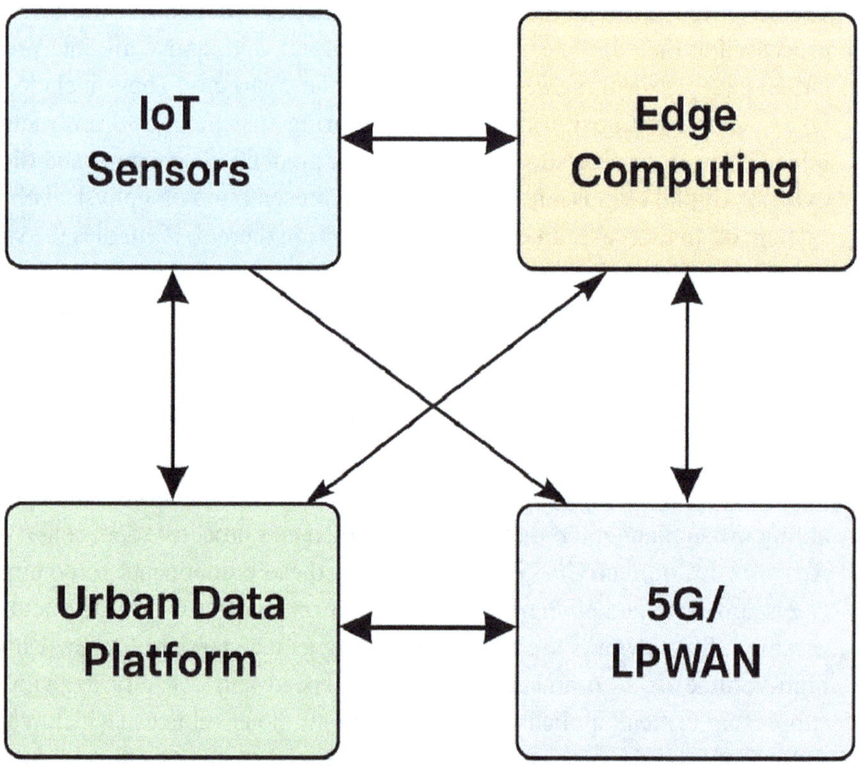

2.2. Emerging Technologies Driving Urban Transformation

Beyond the fundamental components, a range of emerging technologies is redefining and expanding the capabilities of smart cities, enabling not only the collection and processing of data but also its intelligent interpretation and innovative application.

- **Artificial Intelligence (AI):** AI represents the brain behind the predictive and optimising capabilities of smart cities. It enables the dynamic optimisation of urban resources and the forecasting of future demands by analysing vast quantities of data to identify patterns and generate predictions. For instance, AI algorithms can optimise waste collection routes, predict energy usage in buildings, or anticipate public transport demand during peak hours. A notable case is that of New York City, which implemented AI algorithms in its 311 urban incident management system. This resulted in a 12% reduction in emergency service response times (Makanadar & Shahane, 2023), demonstrating how AI can directly enhance the safety and efficiency of critical public services. AI also plays a crucial role in intelligent video surveillance for crime prevention and traffic management (Naifman, 2025).
- **Blockchain Technology:** This distributed ledger technology offers a decentralised, immutable, and transparent database. In the urban context, blockchain ensures transparency and traceability in administrative operations and information flows between public and private actors. Its applications include secure management of citizens' digital identities, property registry administration (preventing fraud and streamlining processes), optimisation of electronic voting for increased trust, and facilitation of energy transactions between prosumers in smart grids. Dubai is a global leader in this domain; in 2021, the city announced that 100% of its government procedures would be processed via blockchain, promoting a more secure, efficient, and less corruption-prone digital administration (Bishr, 2019; Use of Blockchain Technologies in Smart Cities, 2023). This not only enhances bureaucratic efficiency but also reinforces public trust in governance.
- **Urban Robotics:** Urban robotics is becoming a viable solution for automating critical tasks that are often repetitive, hazardous, or require high efficiency. These include autonomous waste collection (robots that optimise their routes and empty containers), surveillance and security (drones and ground robots monitoring large areas or events), product delivery (last-mile delivery robots), and urban maintenance (infrastructure inspection, street cleaning). These solutions can reduce operational costs, improve efficiency, and address demographic challenges such as population ageing and labour shortages in specific sectors. Tokyo, for example, is at the forefront, with projections to

deploy 250,000 autonomous robots for various municipal functions by 2035, in preparation for the challenges of an ageing population and the need to optimise services (Rivera et al., 2020; Tomorrow.city, 2024).

The convergence of these technologies is not coincidental; it is the driving force behind next-generation smart urban ecosystems. They enable cities not only to collect data but to process it using advanced intelligence and act upon it in real time, proactively and predictively. This results in more agile, inclusive, and evidence-based urban governance, where decisions are made with a deep and real-time understanding of the city's state. The ultimate outcome is cities that are more efficient, more liveable, more sustainable, and, fundamentally, better prepared for the challenges of the twenty-first century.

3. SMART MOBILITY: A FUNDAMENTAL PILLAR FOR FUTURE CITIES

Mobility represents one of the most critical dimensions of urban functionality, directly impacting economic productivity, environmental sustainability, and social equity. In the context of smart cities, mobility is no longer conceptualised merely as the movement of people and goods, but as an integrated system optimised through real-time data, intelligent infrastructure, and user-centric design. Smart mobility transcends traditional transport planning by embedding digital technologies across all modalities, including public transit, private vehicles, cycling, and pedestrian flows, thereby enabling adaptive, sustainable, and inclusive mobility ecosystems. As cities face escalating congestion, pollution, and spatial fragmentation, the reconfiguration of mobility through intelligent systems has emerged as a strategic imperative for ensuring the long-term resilience and livability of urban environments (Feng et al., 2019).

At the core of smart mobility lies the convergence of advanced technologies such as Internet of Things (IoT), Artificial Intelligence (AI), Geographic Information Systems (GIS), and real-time communication networks. These tools facilitate dynamic route optimisation, predictive maintenance of transport assets, and integrated multimodal transport planning. For example, the deployment of smart traffic signals, connected vehicle systems, and digital platforms for mobility-as-a-service (MaaS) allows urban authorities to minimise travel times, reduce carbon emissions, and improve commuter experience (Makanadar & Shahane, 2023). Furthermore, smart mobility contributes decisively to the fulfilment of Sustainable Development Goals (SDG 11) by promoting equitable access to transport, enhancing safety, and supporting low-emission mobility alternatives.

The implementation of smart mobility strategies requires not only technological investment but also institutional coordination, regulatory innovation, and robust civic engagement. Successful smart mobility systems are those that align digital capabilities with social needs and environmental priorities, ensuring that mobility infrastructures serve as enablers of urban inclusiveness, rather than as instruments of exclusion or technocratic control.

3.1. Key Technologies and Applications in Smart Mobility

To better comprehend the technological foundations underpinning smart mobility, Table 2 provides a structured overview of the principal digital tools currently employed in advanced urban transport systems. Each technology is examined in terms of its core function and the empirical benefits observed in real-world implementations. By synthesising these insights, the table highlights the synergistic relationship between digital innovation and mobility efficiency, offering a valuable reference for urban planners, policymakers, and transport engineers. The integration of these technologies not only enhances operational capabilities but also contributes to the broader objectives of sustainable development, citizen-centred mobility, and systemic resilience.

Table 2. Key Technologies in Smart Mobility and Their Observed Benefits.

Technology	Primary Function	Observed Benefits
Internet of Things (IoT)	Sensor-based data collection on traffic flow, public transport usage, and road conditions.	Enhanced traffic monitoring; real-time congestion management; optimised service provision.
Artificial Intelligence (AI)	Predictive modelling for demand forecasting, route optimisation, and incident detection.	Reduced travel times; intelligent traffic light coordination; energy efficient transport planning.
Mobility-as-a-Service (MaaS)	Integration of various transport modes into a unified digital platform for user access.	Seamless multimodal transport; improved accessibility; increased use of public transport alternatives.
Geographic Information Systems (GIS)	Spatial analysis and visualisation for mobility planning and infrastructure deployment.	Data-driven infrastructure investment; equitable transport distribution; hazard identification.
Real-time Communication Networks	Instantaneous data transmission between vehicles, infrastructure, and central control units.	Improved safety through vehicle-to-infrastructure (V2I) alerts; adaptive traffic control; reduced response time.

The integration of technology is the driving force that unlocks the potential and efficiency of smart mobility, enabling a more proactive and reactive management of urban transport:

- **Connected Transport Systems (Vehicle-to-Everything, V2X):** V2X communication represents a revolutionary advancement that is redefining road safety and efficiency. This technology allows vehicles not only to communicate with one another (V2V – Vehicle-to-Vehicle), alerting each other of sudden braking or accidents, but also to connect with road infrastructure (V2I – Vehicle-to-Infrastructure), such as smart traffic lights, road signs, or embedded sensors to optimise flow. Furthermore, it facilitates communication with pedestrians and cyclists equipped with smart devices (V2P – Vehicle-to-Pedestrian), alerting drivers to their presence in blind spots or at dangerous crossings. Finally, connection to broader networks (V2N – Vehicle-to-Network) enables vehicles to access real-time traffic information, weather updates, and advanced mapping services. This continuous, real-time connectivity provides unprecedented situational awareness. Vehicles may receive early alerts about upcoming congestion, unexpected incidents, construction zones, or even the approach of emergency vehicles. By delivering critical data to drivers—or directly to autonomous driving systems in the near future—V2X systems possess immense potential to dramatically enhance road safety and traffic flow. The U.S. Federal Highway Administration (U.S. Department of Transportation, 2024) has estimated that widespread adoption of V2X systems could prevent up to 80% of traffic accidents involving human impact, a staggering statistic that underscores the transformative power of this technology in reducing fatalities and injuries, and in minimising the economic and social costs of accidents. Major automotive manufacturers such as BMW and Ford are already heavily investing in the integration of V2X protocols in their vehicles, aiming not only at active collision prevention but also at mitigating urban congestion by facilitating real-time vehicle communication regarding optimal routes and traffic warnings.
- **Adaptive Traffic Management Based on Artificial Intelligence (AI):** Traditional traffic light systems operate with fixed, pre-programmed cycles, often misaligned with the complex and ever-changing reality of urban traffic. AI-powered adaptive traffic management revolutionises this model by introducing dynamic responsiveness. Using a continuous stream of real-time data from a dense network of sensors (traffic cameras, inductive loops, radar, GPS data from vehicles), AI algorithms can synchronise and adjust traffic light timings dynamically based on instantaneous vehicle load at each intersection and along major arteries. This means green light durations are extended or shortened to allow optimal traffic flow, minimising wait times at junctions and reducing congestion during peak hours. Moreover, these advanced systems are capable of prioritising emergency routes (providing uninterrupted green lights to ambulances, fire engines, or police vehicles) and public trans-

port (accelerating the movement of buses and trams through priority signalling). A notable success story is that of Barcelona, where the implementation of such intelligent traffic management strategies has resulted in a reduction of up to 15% in vehicle congestion, optimising the use of public space and significantly improving the efficiency and punctuality of collective transport (Mehta et al., 2024). This not only saves time for drivers and passengers, but also leads to substantial reductions in fuel consumption and, consequently, greenhouse gas emissions.

- **Mobility as a Service (MaaS):** The MaaS model represents a fundamental and strategic shift in how citizens access and utilise urban transport. Instead of the traditional reliance on private vehicle ownership, with its associated costs and concerns (maintenance, parking, fuel, insurance), MaaS seeks to offer seamless integration of multiple transport modes through a single digital platform. This platform may synergistically combine bus, metro, commuter train timetables and routes, shared bicycles, electric scooters, taxis, ride-hailing services (such as Uber or Lyft), and even car-sharing options. Users can plan, book, and pay for all their journeys through a single application, drastically simplifying the mobility experience and eliminating the need to interact with multiple providers. Cities such as Pittsburgh have pioneered the development and implementation of MaaS applications that integrate real-time timetables, routes, and payments, enabling users to identify the most efficient, cost-effective, and convenient travel options tailored to their individual needs (Phonsitthangkun & 2024). This not only significantly enhances the user experience—making it more seamless, personalised, and accessible—but also actively promotes the adoption of multimodal and sustainable transport, reducing reliance on private cars, easing parking pressures, and contributing to the development of greener, less congested, and more liveable cities. This paradigm shift encourages collaborative, sustainable, and data-driven mobility, in which efficient access to a range of options and intelligent decision-making take precedence over vehicle ownership.

3.2. Innovative Policies Complementing Technology for Sustainable Mobility

The deployment of smart mobility technologies alone cannot engender comprehensive and sustainable urban transformation. For a profound and lasting impact, these technological innovations must be supported, reinforced, and guided by intelligent and innovative urban policies. Such policies are essential to regulate the use of public space, guide citizen behaviour towards more sustainable practices, and ensure that the benefits of smart mobility are inclusive, equitable, and accessible to all population groups.

- **Congestion Pricing:** One of the most effective and widely adopted urban policies globally for managing traffic demand is congestion pricing. This measure seeks to discourage the use of private vehicles in central city areas or during peak traffic hours by imposing charges on drivers entering or circulating within designated zones. The principal objective is to alleviate pressure on the most saturated road infrastructure and, simultaneously, encourage drivers to adopt alternative modes of transport such as public transport, micromobility, or to modify their travel schedules. Visionary cities such as London and Singapore have successfully implemented this strategy, consistently demonstrating its capacity to reduce vehicular traffic in charged zones by up to 30%, resulting in significantly improved travel times, lower pollutant emissions, and reduced stress associated with traffic jams. Moreover, the revenues generated by these congestion charges are often reinvested directly into the improvement, expansion, and modernisation of public transport, creating a virtuous cycle of financial and environmental sustainability (Sheller, 2020).
- **Low Emission Zones (LEZs):** Increasing concern regarding urban air quality and its direct impacts on public health has led to the widespread implementation of Low Emission Zones (LEZs), particularly across major European cities. These strategically designated areas restrict or prohibit access to more polluting vehicles (based on age, engine type, or emission level), with the primary goal of reducing citizens' exposure to harmful airborne pollutants such as nitrogen dioxide (NO_2), particulate matter (PM2.5), and tropospheric ozone. Cities such as Madrid, Berlin, and Paris have implemented LEZs with varying degrees of rigour and coverage, actively promoting the transition of vehicle fleets towards cleaner alternatives (electric, hybrid), and, equally importantly, incentivising the adoption of alternative and sustainable transport modes. In Madrid, for instance, the implementation of its LEZ in 2021 led to a notable reduction of over 20% in nitrogen dioxide emissions, a key pollutant directly associated with respiratory and cardiovascular conditions (European Environment Agency, 2022).
- **Promotion of Micromobility:** Micromobility, which includes lightweight vehicles such as bicycles, electric bicycles, and electric scooters, has gained increasing prominence as a sustainable, efficient, and health-promoting solution for short- and medium-distance urban journeys. Innovative urban policies actively seek to facilitate and promote its use through diverse strategies. These include the installation of smart, secure parking facilities (often incorporating charging stations for electric vehicles), the creation of safe,

segregated, and well-connected cycle lanes forming a coherent city-wide network, and the implementation of subsidy schemes or fiscal incentives for the purchase or use of such modes. Amsterdam, a city globally recognised for its deep-rooted cycling culture, has continued to strengthen these measures and has observed a 15% increase in daily use of shared bicycles, consolidating its reputation as a resilient, vibrant, healthy, and low-emission urban network (Attard & Balbontin, 2024; Lee, 2023). These initiatives not only offer viable and attractive alternatives to private cars but also directly contribute to a more active lifestyle, the improvement of public health, and the significant reduction of the city's carbon footprint.

Collectively, these visionary policies and cutting-edge technologies converge and mutually reinforce one another to catalyse a profound and systemic transformation of urban mobility. The ultimate goal is to transition from a traditional transport system—often dominated by private cars and characterised by congestion and pollution—to a smart mobility system that is cleaner, safer, more efficient, more inclusive, and fundamentally centred on citizens' needs and well-being. It is an essential path towards building cities in which mobility is easier, healthier, more sustainable, and, ultimately, enhances the quality of life for all inhabitants.

4. DIGITAL URBAN PLANNING: ENABLING THE CITIES OF TOMORROW

Urban planning, historically grounded in spatial design and infrastructural regulation, is experiencing a paradigmatic transformation catalysed by the advent of digital technologies. As contemporary cities face increasingly complex, multi-scalar challenges—including demographic pressure, environmental degradation, and infrastructure obsolescence—digital urban planning emerges not as a mere enhancement of traditional methods but as a fundamentally reconfigured epistemological and operational framework. This shift is not solely technological; it is epistemic, situating data-driven simulation, participatory visualisation, and real-time responsiveness at the core of urban governance. Within this new paradigm, tools such as digital twins, Geographic Information Systems (GIS), Building Information Modelling (BIM), and Augmented Reality (AR) enable urban planners to anticipate, model, and mitigate the unintended consequences of planning decisions with unprecedented precision, transparency, and inclusivity.

Digital urban planning epitomises a move from reactive to anticipatory governance—transforming static masterplans into dynamic, adaptive systems capable of continuous recalibration in response to evolving urban conditions. The integration of real-time data from distributed IoT networks and edge computing devices allows for situational awareness at multiple granularities, from individual buildings to entire metropolitan regions. Furthermore, the capability to conduct scenario-based simulations facilitates the evaluation of environmental, economic, and social trade-offs prior to implementation, thereby reducing the risk of path dependency and inefficient capital deployment (Lim et al., 2020; Fu & Li, 2025; Feng et al., 2019).

Beyond operational efficiencies, digital urban planning also enhances democratic legitimacy through participatory mechanisms that employ immersive visualisation technologies. By integrating AR into consultative processes, stakeholders—including marginalised communities—can engage meaningfully with complex spatial data and proposed interventions, thus fostering more equitable and context-sensitive outcomes (Othengrafen et al., 2023). These technologies constitute a triadic nexus of simulation, spatial analysis, and civic interaction that reshapes the praxis of urban planning into a continuous, collaborative, and evidence-based process. Consequently, digital planning frameworks are not only essential for addressing the contingent demands of twenty-first-century urbanism but also foundational to realising the broader goals of sustainable, inclusive, and resilient cities, in alignment with SDG 11 and the normative imperatives of smart urban governance (United Nations, 2021).

4.1. Simulation and Design Tools for Proactive Planning

The imperative to anticipate and mitigate the multifaceted consequences of urban interventions has positioned digital simulation tools as indispensable instruments in contemporary planning practice. Traditional models, often linear and static, have proven insufficient in the face of complex, dynamic urban ecosystems. In contrast, the integration of high-fidelity simulation platforms—such as Urban Digital Twins, Geographic Information Systems (GIS), and Building Information Modelling (BIM)—now affords urban planners a multidimensional and evidence-based approach to decision-making (Table 3). These tools collectively enhance strategic foresight, facilitate the efficient allocation of resources, and foster participatory governance frameworks grounded in transparency and precision.

- **Urban Digital Twins** represent a convergence of real-time data analytics, spatial modelling, and system dynamics, allowing the continuous visualisation and testing of urban scenarios across multiple domains including mobility, energy distribution, climate adaptation, and land-use change. Their capacity to integrate live sensor data, simulate hypothetical futures, and iteratively refine spatial configurations has significantly reduced both planning costs and infrastructure delivery timelines, as demonstrated in Singapore's national-scale deployment (Lim et al., 2020). Moreover, their use enables the simultaneous assessment of environmental, economic, and social impacts, thus aligning with the holistic objectives set out in the Sustainable Development Goals (SDG 11) (United Nations, 2021).

- **Geographic Information Systems (GIS)** augment this capacity by enabling the layered analysis of geospatial data—revealing patterns of inequality, risk, and opportunity often obscured in tabular datasets. Through GIS-based modelling, planners can delineate zones of urban vulnerability, assess accessibility to critical services, and identify infrastructural disparities, thereby informing more equitable urban design (Fu & Li, 2025; Feng et al., 2019). The ability to integrate diverse datasets (e.g., demographic, ecological, infrastructural) enhances both micro and macro-scale planning decisions.
- **Building Information Modelling (BIM)**, though traditionally associated with architectural and construction domains, is increasingly instrumental in city-scale digital planning. BIM enables the generation of parametric, information-rich models that encompass the full lifecycle of built assets—from conception and construction to maintenance and retrofitting. Its integration with GIS and digital twins fosters a comprehensive urban information environment where vertical and horizontal infrastructure systems coalesce. When deployed in conjunction with real-time IoT data, BIM models evolve from static design tools into dynamic cyber-physical interfaces, capable of informing operational decision-making and predictive maintenance regimes. Additionally, BIM supports sustainable design by facilitating life-cycle carbon assessments and energy performance simulations prior to construction (Volk et al., 2014).
- **Augmented Reality (AR) in Participatory Planning:** Augmented reality, specifically applied in participatory urban design processes, is revolutionising the way citizens engage with and contribute to urban planning proposals. Unlike virtual reality, which immerses the user in a fully digital and isolated environment, AR overlays virtual elements (such as 3D models of buildings, trees, urban furniture) onto a real-time view of the physical world. This means that by using a tablet, smartphone, or AR glasses, citizens can visualise how proposed interventions – such as new parks, pedestrian streets, cycle lanes, or large-scale residential and commercial developments – would appear in their actual location. For instance, by pointing the camera at an existing street, an AR application could display what a new bike lane or proposed building would look like in its real context. This technology has proven to significantly enhance the quality and inclusivity of citizen participation, as it allows inhabitants to understand and interact with proposals in a far more intuitive, tangible, and accessible manner than via complex 2D plans or static models

(Othengrafen et al., 2023). By making design proposals more tangible and easier to visualise, AR empowers citizens to provide more informed, constructive, and valuable feedback, fostering genuine collaboration and a sense of ownership in the urban planning process.

Table 3. Key Digital Tools for Urban Simulation and Their Functional Integration.

Tool	Core Functionality	Strategic Contribution
Digital Twins	Real-time simulation and prediction of urban systems	Enhances dynamic scenario modelling and anticipatory governance
GIS	Spatial analysis and multi-layer geodata integration	Supports equitable service distribution and risk mapping
BIM	Parametric modelling of building systems with lifecycle data	Informs design, construction, and operational optimisation
AR (Augmented Reality)	Immersive visualisation of urban interventions in physical contexts	Empowers participatory planning and stakeholder engagement

Together, these technologies provide a robust, interoperable ecosystem for proactive urban planning. Their integration not only improves spatial logic and decision rationality but also enshrines democratic values by enabling transparent, data-informed public discourse. The synergy between BIM, GIS, AR, and digital twins forms the bedrock of smart urban design—where simulation is not a discrete stage, but an ongoing, adaptive process.

4.2. Optimised Urban Service Management with IoT: Efficiency and Sustainability in Action

The operational resilience and environmental sustainability of urban systems are increasingly dependent on the seamless integration of Internet of Things (IoT) technologies. These intelligent infrastructures enable real-time monitoring, predictive control, and responsive maintenance across critical service domains—ranging from waste management and public lighting to energy and water networks. The transition from static service provision models to adaptive, data-driven frameworks marks a paradigm shift in municipal governance, wherein urban management becomes anticipatory rather than reactive.

- **IoT-enabled lighting**, as exemplified in cities such as Montreal and San Diego, achieves considerable energy efficiency by dynamically adjusting light intensity based on environmental conditions and pedestrian movement. Beyond reducing electricity consumption by over 40%, such systems also diminish light pollution and improve public safety (Dabhade et al., 2024; Krizanovic, 2024). Embedded fault-detection mechanisms further minimise downtime and operational costs by enabling automated maintenance alerts.

- **Smart waste management** leverages fill-level sensors and route-optimisation algorithms to ensure that collection services are precisely aligned with demand. This approach, implemented in cities like Barcelona, has led to operational cost savings of up to 20% and a concomitant reduction in vehicle-related emissions by 15% (Fernandez-Monge et al., 2023). Integration with digital dashboards allows municipal authorities to adjust logistics in near real-time, responding to seasonal variations or unforeseen events with agility.
- **Water and energy services**, traditionally plagued by inefficiencies and latent system failures, now benefit from a proliferation of IoT nodes capable of detecting leaks, abnormal consumption patterns, and grid imbalances. In Augusta, Georgia, for example, the use of pressure and flow sensors across 1,200 miles of water pipeline allowed for unprecedented precision in leak detection, preserving millions of gallons of water (Vani et al., 2024). When such sensors are embedded into BIM models, facility managers gain access to predictive maintenance insights and long-term performance data, facilitating more sustainable asset management.

The convergence of IoT with BIM yields a powerful "digital-physical twin" infrastructure. While BIM supplies a richly detailed digital representation of built assets—including material properties, energy systems, and spatial configurations—IoT sensors provide the real-time data required to monitor performance and detect inefficiencies (Table 4). When synchronised, these systems enable closed-loop optimisation, wherein sensor feedback continuously informs adaptive operational adjustments. For example, a BIM-integrated building can autonomously regulate heating and ventilation based on occupancy patterns and external temperatures, enhancing comfort while reducing energy consumption.

Table 4. Urban Services Enhanced by IoT and BIM Integration

Urban Service	Enabling Technologies	Observed Benefits
Public Lighting	Smart LEDs + motion/light sensors	>40% reduction in energy use and improved public safety
Waste Management	Fill-level sensors + route algorithms	20% lower operational costs, 15% fewer emissions
Water Management	Pressure/flow sensors + BIM data	Early leak detection, reduced water losses
Energy Management	Smart meters + predictive BIM models	Dynamic load balancing, reduced peak demand, enhanced grid stability

In summation, the intelligent management of urban services via IoT and BIM integration represents a foundational strategy for achieving operational efficiency, environmental stewardship, and infrastructural resilience. It enables a shift from fragmented, siloed systems towards holistic, synergistic networks capable of learning and evolving in real time. This integrated model is not only technologically feasible but economically and environmentally imperative in the transition towards truly smart and sustainable cities.

5. URBAN PUBLIC POLICIES BASED ON TECHNOLOGY: GOVERNING THE DIGITAL TRANSFORMATION

The digital transformation of urban systems, while offering unparalleled opportunities for innovation, efficiency, and sustainability, simultaneously demands a comprehensive reconfiguration of public policy frameworks to ensure that technological advancements serve the collective public interest. The mere deployment of digital infrastructure—however advanced—does not, in itself, guarantee equitable outcomes, institutional legitimacy, or long-term viability. Rather, the governance of such technologies must be embedded within a multidimensional policy architecture that addresses ethical, legal, socio-political, and environmental dimensions in a coherent and anticipatory manner. As the smart city paradigm matures, it becomes increasingly evident that technological determinism must give way to policy-led urbanism—where innovation is guided not only by technical feasibility but by normative commitments to inclusiveness, transparency, and democratic accountability (Cardullo et al., 2019; Cowley et al., 2018).

In this context, urban public policies must evolve from fragmented, sector-specific interventions to integrated governance models capable of harmonising diverse digital initiatives under a unified strategic vision. Effective governance must strike a delicate balance between enabling technological experimentation—through instruments such as regulatory sandboxes—and safeguarding fundamental rights, particularly those concerning data privacy, algorithmic fairness, and digital equity (European Commission, 2018; OECD, 2025). This reflects how mathematical models can be deployed to forecast and optimise national smart-city initiatives, such as Mexico's PRONACES programme (Fuentes-Penna et al., 2023). Moreover, the formulation of such policies must be deeply participatory, incorporating co-creation mechanisms that empower citizens as co-authors of the urban digital agenda rather than passive recipients of top-down solutions. Cities like Singapore and Helsinki illustrate how strategic governance—rooted in institutional coherence and citizen engagement—can operationalise technological transformation as a vehicle for public value and social resilience (Du et al., 2024; Nuutinen et al., 2022).

Ultimately, governing the digital transformation of cities is not solely a technical challenge but a profound political endeavour. It necessitates the establishment of adaptive regulatory ecosystems that are not only legally robust and ethically grounded but also socially responsive and environmentally sustainable. In doing so, public policy becomes the critical interface between technological potential and urban justice.

5.1. Governance Frameworks for Technological Implementation

The manner in which cities adopt and manage technology has varied significantly, giving rise to distinct implementation models, each with its own advantages and challenges:

- **Project-Based Approach**: This model represents the most basic level and is often the initial starting point for many cities embarking on their digital transformation journey. It entails the implementation of isolated and targeted technological solutions, lacking centralised coordination. Common examples include the deployment of intelligent video surveillance in specific areas, adaptive traffic lights at key intersections to alleviate congestion, or smart parking sensors in commercial districts. While this approach enables rapid execution and short-term visibility of outcomes in very specific areas, it is frequently carried out without clear articulation with other technological initiatives or with a broader and integrated urban vision. Consequently, it tends to generate redundancies (incompatible systems, non-interoperable platforms, duplicated data inputs), information fragmentation (creating data silos that fail to intercommunicate, thereby impeding a holistic urban overview), and significant scalability issues (making it difficult to replicate or integrate the solution across other city areas or services). This can result in long-term inefficiencies, underutilisation of technological investment, and an inability to maximise the benefits of interconnectivity (Gil-Garcia et al., 2015).
- **Incremental Approach**: This model represents a more mature and strategic step forward. It typically begins with the development and deployment of pilot projects or the designation of specific "smart districts" to test, validate, and refine technological solutions at a manageable and controlled scale. Once these initiatives are thoroughly evaluated in terms of their actual impact, technical and economic viability, and public acceptance, their scope is gradually expanded across the city. Cities such as Helsinki have successfully adopted this model in innovation districts such as Kalasatama—a residential and business area that functions as a "living urban laboratory" to test solutions related to smart energy, sustainable mobility, waste management, and digital com-

munity life prior to their broader deployment. This approach enables cities to learn from experience, make necessary adjustments to solutions, and mitigate risks before large-scale investments, thereby ensuring that technologies are suitably adapted to the local context (Nuutinen et al., 2022; Flood, 2023).

- **Holistic Approach**: This is the most ambitious, complex, and ultimately desirable model for the creation of a truly integrated and sustainable smart city. It is grounded in the development and implementation of long-term national or metropolitan strategies that integrate technology not as an end in itself, but as a powerful means to achieve goals such as environmental sustainability, citizen well-being, social equity, and sound governance. A paradigmatic example of this approach is Singapore's *Smart Nation* initiative, a comprehensive strategy aimed at leveraging technology to improve every aspect of citizens' lives and city management across all domains. This strategy encompasses interconnected pillars such as healthcare (featuring personalised health monitoring and telemedicine systems), education (via adaptive learning platforms), transportation (with advanced and autonomous mobility systems), and governance (through frictionless digital public services and open data), all articulated within a single interoperable platform with a shared and forward-looking vision among stakeholders (Du et al., 2024). This model seeks to maximise synergies across sectors and achieve full coherence in the use of technology for the common good.

A transversal and absolutely fundamental element across all these approaches—especially critical in the incremental and holistic models—is data governance. Smart cities, by their very nature, generate vast volumes of information from diverse sources (environmental sensors, security cameras, public service transactions, citizen contributions). All such information must be managed in accordance with strict principles of privacy, transparency, security, and interoperability. Cutting-edge regulations such as the European Union's General Data Protection Regulation (GDPR) (European Commission, 2018) establish rigorous standards for the processing of personal data in urban environments, particularly that obtained through sensors or citizen platforms, thereby guaranteeing individual rights and fostering public trust. Furthermore, influential organisations such as the World Economic Forum (WEF) have actively promoted specific ethical frameworks for urban data governance, which include essential principles such as algorithmic fairness (ensuring that decision-making algorithms do not perpetuate or amplify bias or social discrimination) and inclusive participation in the design and use of data-based and technological solutions (World Economic Forum, & Deloitte, 2021).

Institutional architectures in cities must be sufficiently agile and adaptable to integrate existing regulatory frameworks with emerging technologies that continuously evolve at an unprecedented pace—such as blockchain, generative artificial intelligence, or digital twins. This necessitates not only the creation of new laws and regulations but also flexible regulatory frameworks that allow for controlled experimentation and rapid adaptation. A notable example of this are the *regulatory sandboxes*, which have been successfully adopted in countries such as the United Kingdom, Finland, and Colombia (Allam & Newman, 2018; OECD, 2025). These frameworks provide companies, start-ups, and governments with the opportunity to test new technologies and innovative business models in real-world but closely monitored environments under regulatory oversight. This facilitates innovation, accelerates the adoption of new solutions, and reduces time to market—without compromising safety, privacy, or the protection of citizen rights.

Figure 3 compares three governance models for implementing smart city technologies, highlighting their structural features, benefits, and limitations. It offers a strategic framework for urban stakeholders to evaluate the scalability, integration, and coherence of their digital transformation initiatives (Gil-Garcia et al., 2015; Nuutinen et al., 2022; Du et al., 2024).

Figure 3. Comparative Typology of Smart City Governance Models: Project-Based, Incremental, and Holistic Approaches.

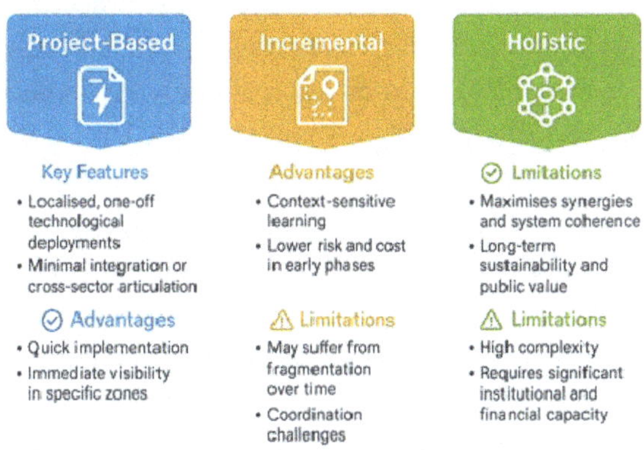

5.2. Citizen Participation and Equity: The Social Heart of the Smart City

The social dimension is, without doubt, the most critical component and the barometer for the long-term legitimacy of smart cities. It emphasises that smart city strategies must address growing inequalities and centre on social well-being—not only technological capability (Fuentes-Penna et al., 2023). The mere deployment of cutting-edge technologies and the mass collection of data do not, in themselves, guarantee substantial improvements in quality of life—unless robust participatory processes and policies explicitly oriented towards digital and social equity are actively incorporated (Cardullo et al., 2019; Cowley et al., 2018). A technologically advanced city that excludes its citizens or exacerbates existing inequalities is neither truly smart nor sustainable.

In this regard, citizen co-creation platforms have gained increasing relevance as essential tools to empower residents and convert them into active stakeholders in the governance, design, and evolution of their own cities. Intuitive mobile applications and collaborative digital platforms enable citizens to adopt a proactive role in urban governance. For example, they can report urban incidents (such as potholes, streetlight failures, refuse collection issues, or graffiti) directly to municipal authorities, thereby expediting response times and improving service efficiency. Citizens can also participate in participatory budgeting processes (deciding directly how public funds are invested in projects for their neighbourhoods or the wider city) or contribute actively to urban planning (by offering ideas, suggestions, and feedback on infrastructure projects, green space design, or local regulations). A prominent example of such transparency and collaboration is *NYC Open Data* in New York City, where residents can freely access and reuse over 3,000 public datasets, covering everything from air quality and traffic patterns to health inspection results and government expenditure. This not only promotes radical transparency in public administration but also enables the co-creation of innovative solutions driven by the community itself (NYC Office of Data Analytics, 2022).

Moreover, digital inclusion is a growing concern and an inescapable responsibility of smart governance. The persistent digital divide—whether in terms of access to high-speed connectivity or possession of the digital skills needed to engage with new platforms—significantly limits the effective participation of vulnerable population sectors in digital urban processes. To counteract this inequality and ensure that no one is left behind in the urban digital transformation, several cities have implemented ambitious, multifaceted programmes. These include the provision of free connectivity in public and community spaces (parks, libraries, plazas), the development of digital literacy training for all ages and skill levels, and the establishment of community technology centres in underserved or peripheral neighbourhoods. For instance, cities such as Bogotá and Mexico City have established free internet access points and digital education programmes in low-income and marginal areas, actively seeking to bridge the digital gap and empower more citizens to participate fully in the city's digital life (OECD, 2025; UN-Habitat, 2021).

In addition, institutional transparency is greatly enhanced—and forms a pillar of public trust—through the establishment of open data portals. These platforms, as exemplified by forward-thinking cities such as Amsterdam, Buenos Aires, and

Seoul, enable any citizen, researcher, journalist, or business to access, download, and freely reuse non-personal data generated by public administration. This not only facilitates governmental performance evaluation, fosters accountability, and curtails corruption, but also empowers the development of civic technologies (*civic tech*) and community-driven solutions, thereby reinforcing a vibrant ecosystem of civic innovation (Janssen et al., 2017).

Finally, public innovation ecosystems flourish and benefit significantly from the synergy between key stakeholders: *GovTech* (technologies developed to modernise and improve government efficiency), *CivicTech* (technologies designed to empower citizen participation and enhance the citizen-government relationship), and *UrbanTech* (technologies applied to urban management and development in areas such as energy, transport, and infrastructure). These collaborative environments bring together local governments, universities, research centres, technology companies (both disruptive start-ups and established corporations), and organised civil society to address complex urban problems. By uniting multidisciplinary knowledge, diverse resources, and varied perspectives, intelligent and inclusive governance is fostered—capable of generating innovative solutions tailored to local realities and directly benefiting the community (Angelidou, 2014; Meijer & Bolívar, 2016). In essence, a smart city is not merely a city with advanced technologies, but more importantly, a city that uses technology ethically, participatively, and equitably to build a more prosperous, sustainable future with a higher quality of life for all its inhabitants.

6. CRITICAL CHALLENGES AND SOLUTIONS

While the digital transformation of urban environments has ushered in a new era of efficiency, inclusivity, and sustainability, it simultaneously exposes cities to a constellation of critical challenges that threaten the coherence, equity, and resilience of smart city strategies. The complex interplay between technological innovation and socio-political governance has revealed deep structural tensions that must be addressed through integrative, adaptive, and ethically robust policy frameworks. Indeed, the promise of smart urbanism cannot be fully realised unless these challenges are systematically confronted through informed planning, inclusive dialogue, and context-sensitive solutions (Batty, 2024; Oliha et al., 2024).

Among the most salient of these obstacles are concerns over cybersecurity and data privacy, as the proliferation of IoT devices and data-driven systems heightens vulnerability to breaches, surveillance, and algorithmic opacity (Zuboff, 2019; Cerrillo, 2023). Moreover, financial asymmetries persist, particularly in developing regions, where limited access to capital and institutional capacity constrains the implementation of advanced technologies (UN-Habitat, 2021). Similarly, the lack of interoperability and standardisation continues to fragment smart city ecosystems, inhibiting scalability and cross-sectoral integration (Batty et al., 2012; FIWARE Foundation, 2023). Furthermore, concerns regarding environmental sustainability have emerged, given the energy demands of digital infrastructure and the lifecycle impacts of electronic waste (Ruggieri et al., 2020; United Nations Environment Programme, 2022).

These challenges, while formidable, are not insurmountable. Cities must embrace multi-scalar and multisectoral approaches that integrate regulatory innovation, public–private partnerships, inclusive digital literacy programmes, and environmental stewardship into the core of their governance agendas. As this section will demonstrate, addressing the vulnerabilities and constraints of smart city development is not merely a technical requirement, but an ethical and strategic imperative for ensuring the long-term viability, justice, and legitimacy of digital urban futures.

6.1. Privacy and Security

One of the principal challenges lies in cybersecurity, particularly in light of the exponential proliferation of IoT devices and the mass collection of data. Interconnected urban systems are increasingly vulnerable to attacks that may compromise critical infrastructure such as power grids, water supplies, transport networks, or emergency services (Oliha et al., 2024).

Citizen privacy is likewise jeopardised by algorithmic surveillance and the utilisation of personal data without informed consent. As noted by Zuboff (2019), many cities operate under a logic of "surveillance capitalism", in which data are transformed into economic assets without due respect for digital rights.

To mitigate these risks, a variety of urban cybersecurity strategies have been developed, including end-to-end encryption, the application of blockchain technologies to ensure traceability, and the implementation of periodic audits of algorithms and digital systems. Additionally, legal frameworks such as the General Data Protection Regulation (GDPR) in Europe and Spain's Digital Rights Charter provide a normative foundation for the protection of personal data (Cerrillo, 2023).

6.2. Project Financing

Urban transformation entails substantial financial investments. Deploying sensors, 5G networks, data centres, or advanced analytics platforms involves high upfront costs—particularly in cities located in developing countries (UN-Habitat, 2021).

The lack of technical and financial capacity leads to a growing divide between "advanced" cities and those left behind.

A common solution lies in the adoption of public–private partnerships (PPPs), which allow for risk-sharing and the incorporation of private-sector innovation. In Europe, initiatives such as Horizon Europe have financed dozens of smart city pilot projects, with over €1 billion allocated between 2021 and 2027 (European Commission, n.d.).

At the local level, results-based financing models are also being trialled, whereby returns on investment are measured in terms of energy efficiency, emissions reductions, or operational savings, as demonstrated in cities such as Vienna, Toronto, and Medellín (OECD, 2020; OECD, 2025).

6.3. Interoperability and Standardisation

Technological fragmentation constitutes another major barrier. In many urban contexts, systems for transport, energy, health, and waste management operate on disparate platforms that lack the capacity for intercommunication. This hampers comprehensive analysis and the development of cross-cutting solutions (Batty et al., 2012).

To address this, international bodies have promoted the adoption of open and interoperable standards. Platforms such as FIWARE, based on the NGSI-LD specification, enable the real-time integration of urban data across multiple domains, fostering collaboration between cities and solution providers (FIWARE Foundation, 2023).

Furthermore, standardisation facilitates the scaling up of technological solutions, streamlines public procurement processes, and reduces technological dependence on single suppliers (Monzon, 2015).

6.4. Environmental Sustainability

Although smart cities encourage improved resource management, they also raise ecological concerns. The expansion of sensor networks, data centres, and electronic equipment generates a significant carbon footprint, particularly if powered by fossil fuels (Ruggieri et al., 2020).

One growing alternative is edge computing, which decentralises data processing and thereby reduces the need for constant data transmission and the load on central data centres. Additionally, the deployment of data centres powered by renewable energy sources or equipped with heat recovery systems is becoming more widespread (Hoheisel et al., 2022).

Moreover, digital sustainability criteria have been proposed, including the use of environmentally friendly hardware, the recycling of electronic devices, and life-cycle assessments of the technologies deployed in urban environments (United Nations Environment Programme, 2022).

7. GLOBAL CASE STUDIES

The conceptual advancement and operational implementation of smart city frameworks have been shaped not only by theoretical models and technological paradigms but, crucially, through empirical insights derived from real-world experiences. Global case studies offer invaluable evidence of how diverse urban contexts—each with their unique socio-economic, cultural, and institutional configurations—have embraced digital transformation to enhance urban governance, public service delivery, and environmental sustainability. These examples serve not merely as success narratives but as critical reference points for assessing both the potential and the limitations of smart city initiatives across varying geographical and governance landscapes.

By systematically examining emblematic cities such as Barcelona, Singapore, and New York, this section elucidates the heterogeneous strategies employed in the pursuit of urban digitalisation. Each city exemplifies a distinct governance model, ranging from Barcelona's emphasis on technological sovereignty and citizen data rights, to Singapore's highly centralised, state-coordinated infrastructure for digital integration, and New York's pioneering use of predictive analytics and open data to drive public accountability (Fernandez-Monge et al., 2023; Lim et al., 2020; NYC Office of Data Analytics, 2022). These cities demonstrate that there is no singular or universally applicable blueprint for smart urban development; rather, successful implementation depends on the alignment of digital strategies with contextual realities, institutional capacities, and citizen priorities.

Furthermore, cross-case analysis reveals common success factors such as strong political will, coherent regulatory frameworks, participatory mechanisms, and investment in digital inclusion. Conversely, challenges related to privacy, data governance, and systemic scalability persist even in highly developed contexts. As such, global case studies function as dynamic laboratories for innovation, offering policy-makers, urban planners, and technologists a nuanced understanding of how to operationalise smart city principles in ways that are equitable, resilient, and future-oriented.

7.1. Barcelona, Spain

Barcelona has been a pioneer in the deployment of a citizen-centred smart city strategy, combining emerging technologies with public participation. Through the

Barcelona Smart City project, launched in 2011 and consolidated over the past decade, the city has rolled out IoT sensors across multiple services such as waste management, lighting, water, and transport (March & Ribera-Fumaz, 2016).

One of its most notable achievements has been the implementation of smart waste management systems: by using fill-level sensors in containers and analytical platforms, the city succeeded in reducing collection costs by 20% and cutting emissions associated with waste transport (Fernandez-Monge et al., 2023). Furthermore, the adaptive LED lighting system has enabled an energy saving of 33% (Ajuntament de Barcelona, 2022).

Barcelona has also actively promoted technological sovereignty through the adoption of open-source software (e.g., Linux and LibreOffice) and the DECODE programme, which offers citizens enhanced control over their digital data (Kitchin, 2021).

7.2. Singapore, Singapore

Singapore represents an emblematic case of a nationally coordinated, integrated, and forward-looking approach. Since the launch of the *Smart Nation* initiative in 2014, the government has integrated technology across all aspects of urban life, including transport, health, education, energy, and public safety.

Among its key innovations is the use of urban digital twins, which allow for the real-time simulation of development, mobility, and environmental management scenarios. This system has contributed to a 10% reduction in planning costs and a significant improvement in resource allocation (Lim et al., 2020).

In the transport sector, Singapore has implemented autonomous vehicles in designated areas, supported by V2X (vehicle-to-everything) systems and synchronised smart traffic lights, leading to reduced travel times and enhanced public transport efficiency (Du et al., 2024).

The Singaporean model is grounded in a unified data architecture, wherein various government agencies operate within a shared, secure digital infrastructure governed by strict privacy and ethical frameworks (Allen et al., 2025).

7.3. New York, USA

New York City has focused its digital urban transformation on two core pillars: open data and predictive analytics. In 2012, the city launched the *NYC Open Data* portal, which today provides access to over 3,000 public datasets that have catalysed hundreds of civic solutions and research initiatives (NYC Office of Data Analytics, 2022).

Among the most significant outcomes was the development of a predictive analytics platform that helped reduce police response times by 12% and enabled the prioritisation of patrols in high-risk areas by applying artificial intelligence to both historical and real-time data (Ashraf, 2020).

In the area of mobility, a system of sensors and algorithms deployed across more than 6,300 miles of streets has made it possible to optimise traffic flows, synchronise traffic lights, and alleviate congestion in critical zones such as Manhattan and Brooklyn (Makanadar & Shahane, 2023).

Additionally, the *LinkNYC* programme has installed over 7,500 free internet terminals, providing connectivity to marginalised communities and significantly narrowing the digital divide in urban areas (Wray, 2022).

7.4. Case Comparison

The comparative Table 5 synthesises the strategic orientations and measurable impacts of three globally recognised smart cities—Barcelona, Singapore, and New York—each exemplifying a distinct governance model and technological trajectory. Barcelona's emphasis on IoT integration in waste and energy management demonstrates the potential of decentralised sensor networks to deliver operational efficiencies and environmental benefits. In contrast, Singapore's adoption of digital twins and autonomous vehicles illustrates a nationally coordinated, top-down strategy aimed at predictive planning and systemic optimisation. Meanwhile, New York's deployment of artificial intelligence and open data platforms reflects a data-centric approach geared towards enhancing service responsiveness and fostering transparency. While each city operates within unique institutional and socio-political contexts, the table reveals commonalities in their pursuit of integrated, citizen-responsive, and sustainability-driven urban innovation.

Table 5. Smart City Case Studies: Strategic Orientations and Measurable Impacts.

City	Key Strategy	Impact
Barcelona	IoT in waste and energy	-20% collection costs, +33% energy savings
Singapore	Digital twins + AVs	-10% planning costs, improved urban efficiency
New York	AI + open data	-12% police response time, expanded digital access

These case studies serve as critical benchmarks, providing transferable lessons and empirical insights for other municipalities seeking to navigate the complexities of digital urban transformation, likewise these case studies illustrate that there is no singular, universally successful model; however, common patterns do emerge: data governance, digital inclusion, interoperability, and ongoing evaluation. The most successful strategies combine long-term vision, public innovation, and active citizen participation.

8. FUTURE TRENDS

The trajectory of smart cities is undergoing a profound transformation, moving beyond the initial stages of digital infrastructure deployment towards more integrated, anticipatory, and ethically grounded urban models. As the convergence of technological, environmental, and social imperatives intensifies, the future of smart urbanism will be characterised not merely by innovation, but by its capacity to reconcile technological advancement with democratic governance, ecological sustainability, and social equity. This emerging paradigm acknowledges that technological sophistication alone is insufficient; rather, it is the intentional design and governance of innovation that will determine the resilience and inclusivity of future cities (Batty et al., 2012; Gajjar & Sharma, 2022).

Against this backdrop, a series of transformative trends are poised to redefine the landscape of urban planning, management, and civic participation. The integration of Generative Artificial Intelligence with predictive modelling capabilities will enable municipalities to simulate complex scenarios, anticipate systemic failures, and formulate adaptive responses with unprecedented granularity (Xu et al., 2024; Fan et al., 2023). Simultaneously, the adoption of biophilic urbanism, supported by IoT-monitored ecological infrastructures, will reinforce climate resilience while enhancing public health outcomes (Beatley, 2016).

Moreover, the expansion of autonomous mobility, participatory governance platforms, and digitally resilient infrastructure signals a move towards decentralised, user-driven, and environmentally conscious urban ecosystems. These trends are not isolated developments but represent an interconnected evolution towards a holistic urban intelligence. As outlined in the subsequent sub-sections, understanding and anticipating these trends is essential for urban stakeholders seeking to remain not only technologically relevant but also socially responsive and environmentally accountable in an era of rapid and irreversible urban change.

8.1. Generative Artificial Intelligence and Predictive Modelling

Generative Artificial Intelligence (AI), including advanced language models and simulation systems, will enable the mass personalisation of urban services and the forecasting of complex scenarios. This technology will facilitate proactive crisis management—such as pandemics, natural disasters, or infrastructure failures—through real-time simulations (Zu et al., 2024).

Furthermore, AI-based predictive models targeting social and economic inequalities offer the prospect of a more just and efficient urbanism, allowing planners to anticipate needs and allocate resources more equitably (Fan et al., 2023). The integration of AI with digital twins will further enhance urban adaptability and responsiveness.

8.2. Biophilic Urbanism and Nature Integration

The concept of biophilic urbanism promotes the integration of smart green corridors equipped with IoT sensors that monitor biodiversity, air quality, and citizen well-being (Beatley, 2016; Gajjar & Sharma, 2022). Such infrastructure not only improves public health but also contributes to climate resilience through ecologically-based urban management.

Intelligent green spaces are expected to evolve into active nodes within the city, combining environmental data with citizen participation to support conservation and continuous improvement.

8.3. Advanced Automation and Autonomous Mobility

The deployment of autonomous vehicle fleets, urban delivery drones, and public service robots will revolutionise urban logistics and mobility (Fagnant & Kockelman, 2015; Shladover, 2020). Greater integration with V2X (vehicle-to-everything) systems and intelligent traffic management will optimise travel times, reduce emissions, and enhance road safety.

Automation will also impact waste management, urban maintenance, and emergency response, significantly reducing operational costs and response times.

8.4. Predictive and Participatory Governance

The progression toward predictive governance models supported by AI will enable cities to anticipate infrastructure failures, detect hotspots of social inequality, and design adaptive public policies (Nam & Pardo, 2011; Kitchin, 2019).

These systems will incorporate open data and citizen participation platforms to co-create solutions in real time, thereby strengthening public trust and transparency (Waza, 2024).

8.5. Sustainability and Digital Resilience

The future of smart cities will be defined by efforts to balance technological advancement with environmental sustainability. There will be an intensified adoption of renewable energy, edge computing, and clean technologies, alongside the design of infrastructures that are resilient to climate change (Batty et al., 2012; United Nations Environment Programme, 2022).

Cities will adopt digital resilience indicators and technological circularity frameworks to minimise the ecological footprint of their smart systems.

9. CONCLUSIONS

The ongoing transformation of urban systems through digital innovation marks a profound shift in the governance, design, and lived experience of contemporary cities. The emergence of the smart city paradigm represents not merely a technological evolution, but a systemic redefinition of how urban environments function, are governed, and serve their inhabitants. The multifaceted integration of advanced technologies—such as Artificial Intelligence (AI), Internet of Things (IoT), Geographic Information Systems (GIS), Digital Twins, Building Information Modelling (BIM), and blockchain—has laid the groundwork for an unprecedented capacity to optimise service delivery, anticipate urban dynamics, and enhance environmental and social resilience (Batty et al., 2012; Lim et al., 2020).

However, the success of these initiatives is contingent upon the effective articulation of technology with democratic governance, ethical oversight, and ecological stewardship. As demonstrated throughout this chapter, technological capacity alone does not ensure urban wellbeing. Rather, the smart city must be conceptualised as an iterative, participatory, and context-sensitive endeavour—anchored in inclusive public policy, transparent data governance, and citizen empowerment (Cardullo et al., 2019; Cowley et al., 2018).

9.1. Key Insights and Strategic Priorities

From the detailed analysis of technological systems, governance models, and global case studies, several critical conclusions emerge:

1. **Triadic Integration of Technology, Community, and Nature**: The sustainable evolution of smart cities depends on the harmonious interplay between digital infrastructure, civic engagement, and ecological resilience. The triadic framework—technology–community–nature—serves as a guiding principle for

designing urban ecosystems that are simultaneously efficient, inclusive, and environmentally sustainable (Dilip, 2024).

2. **Digital Equity as a Foundational Principle**: Digital inclusion is not a secondary concern but a core pillar of smart city legitimacy. Programmes that provide universal access to connectivity, promote digital literacy, and address the digital divide are essential to prevent the deepening of existing socio-economic inequalities in the wake of urban digitalisation (UN-Habitat, 2021; OECD, 2020).
3. **Data Governance and Ethical Oversight**: The widespread use of data-generating technologies necessitates robust frameworks for privacy protection, transparency, and algorithmic accountability. Legal instruments such as the European Union's General Data Protection Regulation (GDPR), coupled with participatory ethical oversight mechanisms, must be integral to any smart city agenda (European Commission, 2018; Cerrillo, 2023).
4. **Operational Resilience through Integrated Technologies**: Smart urban systems must be designed for interoperability, real-time responsiveness, and predictive capacity. The integration of IoT sensors, edge computing, and BIM platforms allows for a dynamic and decentralised infrastructure that can adapt to fluctuations in service demand and external shocks, including environmental and public health crises (Feng et al., 2019; Vani et al., 2024).
5. **Participatory and Predictive Governance**: Cities must transition from reactive administration to anticipatory, data-informed governance. This transformation hinges on the convergence of AI, digital twins, and participatory platforms that not only simulate future scenarios but incorporate citizen input into strategic urban planning processes (Nam & Pardo, 2011; Waza, 2024).

9.2. Summary Table of Strategic Dimensions for Smart Cities

To consolidate these insights, Table 6 presents a synthesis of key strategic dimensions, their enabling mechanisms, and expected outcomes.

Table 6. Strategic Pillars for Future-Oriented Smart Cities

Strategic Dimension	Enabling Mechanisms	Expected Outcome
Digital Infrastructure	IoT, 5G, edge computing, urban data platforms	Real-time responsiveness, system optimisation
Governance and Regulation	GDPR, regulatory sandboxes, public data charters	Ethical oversight, adaptive legislation
Civic Participation	Open data portals, participatory budgeting, co-creation tools	Democratic legitimacy, citizen empowerment

continued on following page

Table 6. Continued

Strategic Dimension	Enabling Mechanisms	Expected Outcome
Environmental Sustainability	Smart energy systems, water sensors, biophilic design	Reduced emissions, climate resilience
Social Inclusion	Digital literacy programmes, public internet access	Bridged digital divide, equitable access to services
Predictive Urban Planning	AI, GIS, digital twins, BIM	Anticipatory policy, improved infrastructure delivery

REFERENCES

Abdulsaheb, J. A., Nafea, R. M., Al-Jawher, W. A. M., & Hayyawi, M. L. (2024). IoT Based Smart Parking System. *Journal Port Science Research*, *7*(3), 196–203. DOI: 10.36371/port.2024.3.1

Ajuntament de Barcelona. (2022). Informe Smart City Barcelona 2022. https://ajuntament.barcelona.cat

Albino, V., Berardi, U., & Dangelico, R. M. (2015). Smart Cities: Definitions, Dimensions, Performance, and Initiatives. *Journal of Urban Technology*, *22*(1), 3–21. DOI: 10.1080/10630732.2014.942092

Allam, Z., & Newman, P. (2018). Redefining the Smart City: Culture, metabolism and governance. *Smart Cities*, *1*(1), 4–25. DOI: 10.3390/smartcities1010002

Allen, J. G., Loo, J., & Luna Campoverde, J. L. (2025). Governing intelligence: Singapore's evolving AI governance framework. 1. DOI: 10.1017/cfl.2024.12

Angelidou, M. (2014). Smart city policies: A spatial approach. *Cities (London, England)*, *41*, S3–S11. DOI: 10.1016/j.cities.2014.06.007

Angelidou, M. (2017). The Role of Smart City Characteristics in the Plans of Fifteen Cities. *Journal of Urban Technology*, *24*(4), 3–28. DOI: 10.1080/10630732.2017.1348880

Ashraf, M. J. (2020). Precision policing: a way forward to reduce crime. https://www.hsdl.org/?abstract&did=839420

Attard, M., & Balbontin, C. (2024). Workshop 6 report: Micromobility movement in urban transport. Recherche En Matière d'économie Des Transports. DOI: 10.1016/j.retrec.2023.101399

Batty, M. (2024). *The Computable City: Histories, Technologies, Stories, Predictions. MIT Press*. MIT Press., DOI: 10.7551/mitpress/14099.001.0001

Batty, M., Axhausen, K. W., Giannotti, F., Pozdnoukhov, A., Bazzani, A., Wachowicz, M., & Portugali, Y. (2012). Smart cities of the future. *The European Physical Journal. Special Topics*, *214*(1), 481–518. DOI: 10.1140/epjst/e2012-01703-3

Beatley, T. (2016). *Handbook of Biophilic City Planning and Design*. Island Press. DOI: 10.5822/978-1-61091-621-9

Bishr, A. (2019). Dubai: A City Powered by Blockchain. *Innovations: Technology, Governance, Globalization*, *12*(3-4), 4–8. DOI: 10.1162/inov_a_00271

Cardullo, A., Di Feliciantonio, C., & Kitchin, R. (2019). *The right to the smart city*. Emerald Publishing Limited., DOI: 10.1108/9781787691391

Cerrillo, I., & Martínez, A. (2023). *Ciudades inteligentes y derechos digitales. De las Smart Cities a las Ciudades integradoras. Propuestas socio-jurídicas para una administración local del s. XXI*. Dykinson., DOI: 10.14679/2245

Cowley, R., Joss, S., & Dayot, Y. (2018). The smart city and Its publics: Insights from across six UK cities. *Urban Research & Practice*, *11*(1), 53–77. DOI: 10.1080/17535069.2017.1293150

Dabhade, V., Shah, R., & Nikam, D. (2024). Smart street lighting using IoT. *International Research Journal of Modernization in Engineering Technology and Science*. Advance online publication. DOI: 10.56726/IRJMETS50033

Dilip, D. (2024). *Exploring the Symbiotic Relationship between Digital Transformation*. Infrastructure, Service Delivery, and Governance for Smart Sustainable Cities., DOI: 10.3390/smartcities7020034

Du, Y. F., Sun, T., & Huang, Y. (2024). A Comprehensive Review of Smart City Initiatives in Singapore Technological Advancements and Urban Planning from 2015 to 2023. DOI: 10.31219/osf.io/yqfsv

Estrada, E., Maciel, R., Ortíz Zezzatti, C. A. O., Bernabe-Loranca, B., Oliva, D., & Larios, V. (2018). Smart City Visualisation Tool for the Open Data Georeferenced Analysis Utilizing Machine Learning. *International Journal of Combinatorial Optimization Problems and Informatics*, *9*(2), 25–40.

European Commission. (2018). General Data Protection Regulation (GDPR). https://eur-lex.europa.eu/eli/reg/2016/679/oj

European Commission. (n.d.). Smart cities and communities. Retrieved from https://digital-strategy.ec.europa.eu/en/policies/smart-cities-and-communities

European Environment Agency. (2022). Air quality in Europe — 2022 report. https://www.eea.europa.eu/publications/air-quality-in-europe-2022

Fagnant, D. J., & Kockelman, K. (2015). Preparing a nation for autonomous vehicles: Opportunities, barriers and policy recommendations. *Transportation Research Part A, Policy and Practice*, *77*, 167–181. DOI: 10.1016/j.tra.2015.04.003

Fan, C., Xu, J., Natarajan, B. Y., & Mostafavi, A. (2023). Interpretable machine learning learns complex interactions of urban features to understand socio-economic inequality. *Computer-Aided Civil and Infrastructure Engineering*, *38*(14), 2013–2029. Advance online publication. DOI: 10.1111/mice.12972

Feng, S., Chen, L., Sun, R., Feng, Z., Li, J., Khan, M. S., & Jing, Y. (2019). The Distribution and Accessibility of Urban Parks in Beijing, China: Implications of Social Equity. *International Journal of Environmental Research and Public Health, 16*(24), 4894. DOI: 10.3390/ijerph16244894 PMID: 31817222

Fernandez-Monge, F., Barns, S., Kattel, R., & Bria, F. (2023). Reclaiming data for improved city governance: Barcelona's New Data Deal. *Urban Studies (Edinburgh, Scotland)*. Advance online publication. DOI: 10.1177/00420980231204835

Flood, D. (2023). #kalasatama: Discursive Views of the Helsinki Landscape Through the Virtual Window. *Philosophy of the City Journal, 1*(1), 112–126. DOI: 10.21827/potcj.1.1.40448

Fu, M., & Li, Y. (2025). Optimizing Sustainable Community Spatial Layouts and Public Service Facility Accessibility: A GIS and Machine Learning Approach. *Applied and Computational Engineering, 129*(1), 103–108. DOI: 10.54254/2755-2721/2025.20489

Fuentes-Penna, A., Gómez Cárdenas, R., Hernández González, O. D., González Ibarra, J., Cuesta Gómez, E., Morales Prado, W. L., & Vera Jiménez, M. A. (2023). Smart Cities facing the growth of poverty. *International Journal of Combinatorial Optimization Problems and Informatics, 14*(3), 1–2. DOI: 10.61467/2007.1558.2023.v14i3.371

Fuentes-Penna, A., Ruiz-Vanoye, J. A., Gómez-Cárdenas, R., Salgado Ramírez, J. C., Trejo-Macotela, F. R., Díaz-Parra, O., Poblano Verastegui, A., & Rentería Torres, P. L. (2023). Mexico and PRONACES towards to become a smart city. *International Journal of Combinatorial Optimization Problems and Informatics, 14*(3), 31–41. DOI: 10.61467/2007.1558.2023.v14i3.387

Gajjar, V., & Sharma, U. (2022). Relevance of Urban Ecosystem Services for Sustaining Urban Ecology in Cities-A Case Study of Ahmedabad City. In Piselli, C., Altan, H., Balaban, O., & Kremer, P. (Eds.), *Innovating Strategies and Solutions for Urban Performance and Regeneration. Advances in Science, Technology & Innovation*. Springer., DOI: 10.1007/978-3-030-98187-7_18

Gil-Garcia, J. R., Pardo, T. A., & Nam, T. (2015). What makes a city smart? Identifying core components and proposing an integrative and comprehensive conceptualization. *Information Polity, 20*(1), 61–87. DOI: 10.3233/IP-150354

Hoheisel, A., Betterman, B., Dunham, I., O'Leary, H., & Mahmoud, M. (2022).. . *Green Computing from a Holistic Perspective., 1299–1302*, 1299–1302. Advance online publication. DOI: 10.1109/CSCI58124.2022.00233

ITU. (2021). ITU smart sustainable cities brochure. International Telecommunication Union. Retrieved from https://www.itu.int/en/ITU-T/ssc/united/Documents/Reports-on-SSC/ITU_smart_sustainable_cities_brochure.pdf?csf=1&e=yIueWP

Janssen, M., Charalabidis, Y., & Zuiderwijk, A. (2017). Benefits, adoption barriers and myths of open data and open government. *Information Systems Management, 29*(4), 258–268. DOI: 10.1080/10580530.2012.716740

Kitchin, R. (2019). *The data revolution: Big data, open data, data infrastructures & their consequences*. Sage Publications Ltd., DOI: 10.4135/9781473909472

Kitchin, R. (2021). *Data Lives: How Data Are Made and Shape Our World*. Bristol University Press., DOI: 10.1080/02513625.2024.2510128

Krizanovic, V., Pejković, A., Pracny, P. (2024). Smart Street Lighting for Enhancing Energy Efficiency in Urban Environments. 1–6. DOI: 10.23919/SoftCOM62040.2024.10721821

Lee, T. L. C. (2023). Redesigning streets for micromobility: improving mobility and access to transportation for less able users. DOI: 10.32920/24085086.v1

Lim, K. Y. H., Zheng, P., Zheng, P., & Chen, C.-H. (2020). A state-of-the-art survey of Digital Twin: Techniques, engineering product lifecycle management and business innovation perspectives. *Journal of Intelligent Manufacturing, 31*(6), 1313–1337. DOI: 10.1007/s10845-019-01512-w

Makanadar, A., & Shahane, S. (2023). Urban Mobility: Leveraging AI, Machine Learning, and Data Analytics for Smart Transportation Planning- A case study on New York City. 1–6. DOI: 10.1109/ICCCNT56998.2023.10307632

March, H., & Ribera-Fumaz, R. (2016). Smart contradictions: The politics of making Barcelona a Self-sufficient city. *European Urban and Regional Studies, 23*(4), 816–830. DOI: 10.1177/0969776414554488

Mehta, K. S., Raj, K. N., & Brahmbhatt, K. N. (2024). Machine learning solutions for adaptive traffic signal control: A review of image-based approaches. *World Journal of Advanced Engineering Technology and Sciences, 13*(1), 476–481. DOI: 10.30574/wjaets.2024.13.1.0437

Meijer, A., & Bolívar, M. P. R. (2016). Governing the smart city: A review of the literature on smart urban governance. *International Review of Administrative Sciences, 82*(2), 392–408. DOI: 10.1177/0020852314564308

Monzon, A. (2015). *Smart cities concept and challenges: Bases for the assessment of smart city projects*. IEEE., DOI: 10.1007/978-3-319-27753-0_2

Mora, L., Deakin, M., Aina, Y. A., & Appio, F. P. (2019). Smart City Development: ICT Innovation for Urban Sustainability. In Leal Filho, W., Azul, A., Brandli, L., Özuyar, P., & Wall, T. (Eds.), *Sustainable Cities and Communities. Encyclopedia of the UN Sustainable Development Goals*. Springer., DOI: 10.1007/978-3-319-71061-7_27-2

Nam, T., & Pardo, T. A. (2011). Conceptualizing smart city with dimensions of technology, people, and institutions. In *Proceedings of the 12th Annual International Digital Government Research Conference* (pp. 282–291). ACM. DOI: 10.1145/2037556.2037602

Nuutinen, M., Kaasinen, E., Hyvärinen, J., Mölsä, A., & Siltanen, S. (2022). Making a Building Smart with a Co-Created and Continuously Evolving Enjoyable Service Entity—Insights from a Collaborative Study. *Smart Cities*, *5*(1), 1–21. DOI: 10.3390/smartcities5010001

NYC Office of Data Analytics. (2022). NYC Open Data Portal. https://opendata.cityofnewyork.us

OECD. (2020), Smart Cities and Inclusive Growth: Building on the outcomes of the 1st OECD Roundtable fon Smart Cities and Inclusive Growth, OECD Regional Development Papers, No. 91, OECD Publishing, Paris, DOI: 10.1787/267a6231-en

OECD. (2022). Harnessing the power of AI and emerging technologies: Background paper for the CDEP Ministerial meeting. In *OECD Digital Economy Papers, No. 340*. OECD Publishing., DOI: 10.1787/f94df8ec-

OECD. (2025). *Closing Broadband Connectivity Divides for All: From Evidence to Practice*. OECD Publishing., DOI: 10.1787/d5ea99b2-

OECD. (2025). *Regulatory sandbox toolkit: A comprehensive guide for regulators to establish and manage regulatory sandboxes effectively*. OECD Publishing., DOI: 10.1787/de36fa62-

Ogbodo, E. U., Abu-Mahfouz, A. M., & Kurien, A. M. (2022). A Survey on 5G and LPWAN-IoT for Improved Smart Cities and Remote Area Applications: From the Aspect of Architecture and Security. *Sensors (Basel)*, *22*(16), 6313. DOI: 10.3390/s22166313 PMID: 36016078

Oliha, J. S., Biu, P. W., & Chimezie, O. (2024). Securing the smart city: A review of cybersecurity challenges and strategies. Open Access Research Journal of Multidisciplinary Studies, 7(1), 094–101. DOI: 10.53022/oarjms.2024.7.1.0013

Othengrafen, F., Sievers, L., & Reinecke, E. (2023). Using augmented reality in urban planning processes: Sustainable urban transitions through innovative participation. *Gaia (Heidelberg)*, *32*(1), 54–63. DOI: 10.14512/gaia.32.S1.9

Phonsitthangkun, S., & Arreeras, T. (2024). Mobility as a Service (MaaS): A Bibliometric Analysis of Research Trends, Technology Acceptance, and Urban Logistics Integration. 1–6. DOI: 10.1109/DASA63652.2024.10836433

Rivera, R. M., Amorim, M., & Reis, J. (2020). Robotic Services in Smart Cities: *An Exploratory Literature Review. Iberian Conference on Information Systems and Technologies*. DOI: 10.23919/CISTI49556.2020.9141099

Ruggieri, R., Ruggeri, M., & Vinci, G. (2020). Efficient energy and electric transport in a Smart City: Evaluation of sustainability and competitiveness. *International Conference on Environment and Electrical Engineering*. DOI: 10.1109/EEEIC/ICPSEurope49358.2020.9160676

Sharifi, A., Allam, Z., Bibri, S. E., & Khavarian-Garmsir, A. R. (2024). Smart cities and sustainable development goals (SDGs): A systematic literature review of co-benefits and trade-offs. Cities, Volume 146, 2024, 104659, ISSN 0264-2751, DOI: 10.1016/j.cities.2023.104659

Sheller, M. (2020). Chapter 1 Mobility justice. In Handbook of Research Methods and Applications for Mobilities. Cheltenham, UK: Edward Elgar Publishing. Retrieved Jul 25, 2025, from DOI: 10.4337/9781788115469.00007

Shladover, S. E. (2020). Connected and automated vehicle systems: Introduction and overview. *Journal of Intelligent Transport Systems*, *22*(3), 190–200. DOI: 10.1080/15472450.2017.1336053

UN-Habitat. (2021). People-Centered Smart Cities. https://unhabitat.org/people-centered-smart-cities

UN-Habitat. (2021). Smart Cities for All: Bridging the Urban Digital Divide. https://unhabitat.org

UN-Habitat. (2022). *World Cities Report 2022: Envisaging the future of cities*. United Nations Human Settlements Programme.

United Nations. (2019). *World Urbanization Prospects: The 2018 Revision*. Department of Economic and Social Affairs, Population Division.

United Nations. (2021). Sustainable Development Goals: Goal 11. https://sdgs.un.org/goals/goal11

United Nations. (2021). *The Sustainable Development Goals Report 2021.* United Nations.

United Nations Environment Programme. (2022, 3 May). Build Back Better: Using green and digital technologies to reduce food waste at consumer level. UN Environment Programme. Retrieved 26 July 2025, from https://www.unep.org/explore-topics/green-economy/build-back-better

U.S. Department of Transportation. (2024, April 17). Connected Vehicle Pilot Deployment Program (2024 update). ITS Knowledge Resource Service. Last updated May 2025. Retrieved 26 July 2025, from https://www.itskrs.its.dot.gov/briefings/executive-briefing/connected-vehicle-pilot-deployment-program-2024-update

Use of Blockchain Technologies in Smart Cities. (2023). International Journal For. *Kexue Jishu Yu Gongcheng, 11*(5), 4942–4947. DOI: 10.22214/ijraset.2023.52111

Vani, S., Joshi, P., Shinde, R., Kadam, S., & Matkamwad, M. (2024). *Smart Water Management Grid.* International Journal of Innovative Science and Research Technology., DOI: 10.38124/ijisrt/IJISRT24MAY931

Volk, R., Stengel, J., & Schultmann, F. (2014). Building Information Modeling (BIM) for existing buildings — Literature review and future needs. *Automation in Construction, 38*, 109–127. DOI: 10.1016/j.autcon.2013.10.023

Waza, A. M. (2024). Examining the Role of Artificial Intelligence in Improving Decision Making Processes in Governance. DOI: 10.59890/ijatss.v2i7.2319

World Economic Forum, & Deloitte. (2021, 13 July). Governing Smart Cities: Policy benchmarks for ethical and responsible smart city development. In collaboration with Deloitte. Retrieved 26 July 2025, from https://www.weforum.org/publications/governing-smart-cities-policy-benchmarks-for-ethical-and-responsible-smart-city-development/

Wray, S. (2022, July 25). LinkNYC programme gets a reboot with 5G kiosks. ITU. Retrieved from https://www.itu.int/hub/2022/07/linknyc-5g-kiosks-cities-today/

Xu, H., Omitaomu, O. A., Sabri, S., Li, X., & Song, Y. (2024). Leveraging Generative AI for Smart City Digital Twins: A Survey on the Autonomous Generation of Data, Scenarios, 3D City Models, and Urban Designs. https://doi.org//arxiv.2405.19464DOI: 10.48550

Yu, M. Y. (2024). Key Challenges and Potential Solutions in Smart City Governance. *Scientific and Social Research Articles., 6*(8), 2024. DOI: 10.26689/ssr.v6i8.7818

Zuboff, S. (2019). The Age of Surveillance Capitalism: The Fight for a Human Future at the New Frontier of Power. Harvard Business School Faculty & Research. Retrieved 26 July 2025, from the Harvard Business School website.

Chapter 5
Smart Water Systems for Sustainable and Participatory Urban Governance

Francisco R. Trejo-Macotela
https://orcid.org/0000-0003-2133-3456
Universidad Politécnica de Pachuca, Mexico

Uriel Amado Ramírez-Hernández
Universidad Politécnica de Pachuca, Mexico

Daniel Robles-Camarillo
https://orcid.org/0000-0002-7637-5904
Universidad Politécnica de Pachuca, Mexico

Edgar López-López
Universidad Tecnológica de Mineral de la Reforma, Mexico

ABSTRACT

This chapter presents a critical analysis of smart water systems as strategic responses to water scarcity, quality decline, and distribution inefficiencies. It explores the integration of advanced technologies—including the Internet of Things (IoT), Artificial Intelligence (AI), Wireless Sensor Networks (WSNs), and remote sensing—across domains such as intelligent irrigation, leak detection, decentralised treatment, and urban water governance. Through case studies from Spain, Mexico, South Africa, and Singapore, it highlights the transformative role of data-driven, modular, and participatory models in enhancing sustainability, equity, and resilience. Emphasis

DOI: 10.4018/979-8-3373-5535-1.ch005

is placed on predictive analytics, simulation tools, and real-time monitoring to support adaptive and efficient decision-making. The chapter also identifies technical, institutional, and socio-political barriers to implementation, offering strategic insights into the future integration of smart water technologies within Integrated Water Resources Management (IWRM) paradigms.

1. INTRODUCTION

Water is a finite yet fundamental resource essential to the preservation of life, the maintenance of ecosystems, and the stability of socio-economic development. In the context of the twenty-first century, escalating pressures stemming from climate change, urbanisation, population growth, and agricultural expansion have compounded the challenges associated with water security, availability, and quality. These pressures have necessitated the advancement and implementation of intelligent systems that optimise water management through the integration of modern technologies such as the Internet of Things (IoT), Artificial Intelligence (AI), Wireless Sensor Networks (WSNs), and advanced data analytics. This document provides a comprehensive examination of smart water technologies, with a particular emphasis on the use of intelligent monitoring, predictive modelling, decentralised systems, and case-based learning to enhance water governance. The discussion is structured into several key themes, each addressing a specific aspect of the smart water ecosystem: intelligent irrigation systems, watershed monitoring through sensors and remote sensing, leak detection and predictive maintenance, modular smart treatment plants, and smart city water infrastructure.

The deployment of smart irrigation systems represents a significant technological leap in the agricultural sector, aimed at enhancing water-use efficiency and crop productivity. The integration of IoT sensors, AI-based algorithms, and automated control mechanisms enables real-time monitoring of critical environmental variables such as soil moisture, temperature, solar radiation, and evapotranspiration. Studies including those by Touil et al. (2022), Sloat (2025), and Kunt (2025) demonstrate the effectiveness of such systems in reducing water consumption by up to 92% without compromising yield, highlighting their potential to mitigate the impact of water scarcity in agriculture. Simultaneously, advancements in watershed monitoring underscore the importance of remote sensing and IoT-enabled systems in the conservation and assessment of hydrological resources. These technologies facilitate precise data acquisition across vast and often inaccessible terrains, enabling early detection of anomalies and informed decision-making. Case studies from Greece and the United States illustrate the benefits of LoRaWAN-based architectures and cloud-integrated platforms in the automation and optimisation of irrigation in olive groves and plasticulture tomato production respectively (Liopa-Tsakalidi et al., 2024; Zhang et al., 2022).

Water loss due to leakage within urban and domestic distribution networks remains a critical concern. In response, predictive maintenance and real-time leak detection systems have been developed using machine learning algorithms, flow monitoring devices, and smart metering. Research conducted in Peru and Ecuador provides insights into AI-powered potability classification systems and IoT-based domestic meters that allow for real-time user interaction and anomaly management (Zevallos Apaza et al., 2022; León Lazo & Macancela Sumba, 2024). Equally important are the innovations in decentralised water treatment technologies. Modular wastewater treatment plants with simulation-aided optimisation—such as those implemented at IIT Jammu—demonstrate how software tools like GPS-X can significantly improve treatment outcomes while reducing operational costs (Srivastava et al., 2024). Greywater reuse, analysed through systematic reviews and practical trials in India, Malaysia, and Vietnam, further reinforces the viability of decentralised and low-cost systems for sustainable urban water management (Shaikh & Ahammed, 2020; Ngo et al., 2024).

Finally, the concept of smart cities is exemplified by notable case studies including Singapore's *WaterWiSe* system and Mexico's *PUMAGUA* programme. These initiatives integrate sensor networks, cloud platforms, and predictive analytics to reduce non-revenue water, monitor quality parameters in real time, and engage communities in water-saving practices. The case of Singapore, for instance, demonstrates how algorithm-based hydraulic modelling can identify incipient leaks and ensure efficient service delivery (Allen et al., 2012). Similarly, UNAM's experience with SWM (Smart Water Management) technology affirms the role of participatory and decentralised governance in the sustainable transformation of institutional water management (González-Villareal et al., 2018). This perspective aligns with broader reflections on the development of water smart cities, as outlined by Ruiz-Vanoye et al. (2023).

This document thus seeks to explore, consolidate, and synthesise current knowledge, technological advances, and practical implementations of smart water systems, offering a multi-scalar perspective that bridges theoretical models and field-based evidence. It underscores the pressing need for adaptive, resilient, and data-driven solutions to meet the evolving challenges of global water management.

2. INTEGRATED WATER RESOURCES MANAGEMENT (IWRM)

The Integrated Water Resources Management (IWRM) paradigm embodies a holistic and coordinated approach to the governance of water resources, aiming to reconcile competing demands across agricultural, urban, industrial, and ecological domains. It promotes the equitable, efficient, and sustainable allocation of water through integrated planning that spans spatial, temporal, and institutional dimensions. In the context of accelerating climatic variability, demographic expansion, and escalating anthropogenic pressures, IWRM emerges not merely as a theoretical construct but as a necessary operational framework for adaptive and resilient hydrological governance. The imperative for IWRM is underscored by recent empirical advancements, where intelligent technologies have been embedded within watershed-scale monitoring and decision-making architectures. For instance, artificial intelligence-driven systems deployed in the Segura River Basin (Spain) illustrate the integration of hydrological models, remote sensing, and agronomic forecasting to optimise allocation through Mixed-Integer Linear Programming (MILP), thus enabling data-informed, equitable, and ecologically protective water management strategies (Otamendi et al., 2024). This confluence of AI and IWRM demonstrates a replicable model capable of enhancing institutional compliance and operational efficiency in complex river basin systems.

Concurrently, innovative applications of wireless sensor networks and remote sensing platforms have facilitated the real-time monitoring of physico-chemical parameters across vast aquatic systems. Such technologies, as exemplified in Brussels and South Africa, enable anomaly detection and predictive modelling for both potability and environmental integrity, minimising latency in response and improving governance transparency (Singh & Walingo, 2024; Lamrini et al., 2024). Therefore, IWRM—augmented by smart monitoring systems and predictive analytics—constitutes an indispensable tool in the strategic planning of urban hydrological cycles and transboundary watershed governance. It not only fosters cross-sectoral coherence and inter-institutional collaboration but also aligns with the broader objectives of environmental sustainability, technological innovation, and participatory decision-making under the tenets of sustainable development.

2.1. Implementation of Watershed Monitoring Systems through Sensors and Remote Sensing

In 2024, Yurav Singh and Tom Walingo developed an intelligent system to monitor water quality by employing wireless IoT sensor networks and artificial intelligence models. The system was implemented in four treatment plants in South Africa, where it collected data such as pH, turbidity, and electrical conductivity. However, given that not all pollutants can be directly measured, the researchers trained machine learning models—such as AdaBoost and Random Forest—to predict these parameters based on the available sensor data. AdaBoost emerged as the most effective model, delivering promising results. This system contributed to real-time monitoring, broad spatial coverage, reduced laboratory costs, and rapid response to public health risks (Singh & Walingo, 2024).

Researchers from the Vrije Universiteit Brussel (Belgium) and Abdelmalek Essaadi University (Morocco) developed an intelligent system to ensure the reliability of water quality monitoring. This system employs IoT sensors that collect real-time parameters—such as pH, temperature, electrical conductivity (EC), and dissolved oxygen (DO)—in lakes, rivers, and ponds across Brussels. The data are transmitted via LoRaWAN (Low Range Wide Area Network) to a cloud-based infrastructure, where they undergo preprocessing. The dataset is split into 80% training and 20% testing sets, values are labelled, and anomalies are detected using four classical machine learning models: Support Vector Machine (SVM), Artificial Neural Network (ANN), Decision Tree (DT), and Isolation Forest (iForest). This system enables real-time detection of anomalies in water quality data, enhances monitoring reliability, reduces technical errors, and allows for timely reactions to deviations indicative of sensor failures or environmental contamination (Lamrini et al., 2024).

2.2. Integrated Water Resources Management / Strategic Planning of the Urban Hydrological Cycle

In the Segura River Basin (Spain), a research team led by Urtzi Otamendi, in collaboration with the University of the Basque Country (UPV/EHU) and Vicomtech IK4, implemented a comprehensive water management system integrating hydrological data, agronomic models, and artificial intelligence algorithms to forecast water availability, estimate agricultural demand, and optimise resource allocation. The system receives data from sensors and remote sensing platforms, models hydrological evolution, calculates precise crop water requirements through agronomic simulations, and solves an optimisation problem via Mixed-Integer Linear Programming (MILP) to allocate water efficiently. As a result, the system achieved more sustainable, equitable, and environmentally efficient water management, as it supports both short- and long-term informed decision-making, avoids unnecessary extractions and pumping, and has been integrated into the daily operational strategy of the Segura River Basin Authority. It enhances governance compliance and presents a replicable model for other river basins. In summary, it constitutes an artificial intelligence-based platform for water management that balances supply and demand, protects ecosystems, and strengthens climate resilience (Otamendi et al., 2024).

3. REAL-TIME MONITORING AND SMART SENSORS

The evolution of real-time monitoring systems and smart sensor technologies has become instrumental in revolutionising water management practices in both urban and rural contexts. The integration of distributed Wireless Sensor Networks (WSNs), Internet of Things (IoT) frameworks, and artificial intelligence (AI)-enabled data analytics has enabled a paradigm shift from conventional, reactive approaches to predictive, responsive, and cost-effective methodologies for water governance. Real-time monitoring plays a critical role not only in early anomaly detection but also in fostering transparency, improving efficiency, and promoting data-driven decision-making across the entire water infrastructure lifecycle.

One noteworthy example of this transition is the QoW Pro platform developed by the LAMIE Laboratory at the University of Batna 2 in Algeria, in partnership with the LEREESI Laboratory of HNS-RE^{2}SD. This integrated system harnesses the capabilities of distributed IoT nodes that collect real-time parameters including flow, pressure, and water quality metrics. These data are relayed wirelessly to cloud-based platforms where AI models compare expected and actual flow dynamics, allowing the system to identify anomalies with remarkable precision (Guezouli et al., 2024). In its six-month pilot implementation, the platform achieved a 30% reduction in undetected leaks and a 94% leak detection accuracy, underscoring its technical efficacy. Additionally, operational costs were lowered by 20%, attributable to more targeted maintenance interventions and reduced water loss.

Beyond leak detection, the role of smart sensors in aquaculture and agricultural applications has drawn significant academic attention. In a comprehensive bibliometric review encompassing 217 studies from 2020 to 2024, Flores-Iwasaki et al. (2025) highlighted the growing reliance on real-time sensor data to monitor water quality parameters in aquaculture systems such as biofloc technology (BFT), recirculating aquaculture systems (RAS), and aquaponics. Sensors for pH (e.g., SEN0169, Grove pH), temperature (e.g., DS18B20), and dissolved oxygen (e.g., SEN0237, OxyGuard DO 420) were reported as the most prevalent. This systematic monitoring has enabled early detection of toxic compounds such as ammonia and significantly enhanced fish health, productivity, and survival rates. Moreover, in aquaponics systems, these sensors facilitate predictive modelling for plant growth and seed germination by capturing key physicochemical fluctuations. For water-quality assessment, data-mining techniques such as decision trees and K-NN have been shown effective in classifying contamination in lotic systems, as in Puebla, Mexico (Denicia Carral et al., 2024).

However, despite the evident advantages, certain challenges persist. Chief among these are issues related to sensor calibration, maintenance in rural environments, and the automation of parameter regulation. Sensor degradation, data drift, and environmental interferences can compromise accuracy, particularly in regions lacking technical support or stable infrastructure.

In urban water distribution systems, the development of IoT-based smart water meters using LoRaWAN technology further exemplifies the potential of real-time monitoring. Lei et al. (2025) detailed the construction of a modular system centred on an STM32 development board equipped with a water flow sensor. This system not only tracked flow data and transmitted it via LoRa to a central server, but also employed an adaptive algorithm that dynamically modulated transmission frequency to conserve energy. Notably, energy consumption was reduced by up to 88.5%, and data traffic was reduced by 76–87% compared to traditional NB-IoT devices. This intelligent modulation facilitated longer battery lifespans and improved scalability, making the system suitable for large-scale deployments in both developed and resource-constrained settings.

To assess the technical maturity and comparative performance of different smart sensing systems, Table 1 provides an overview of widely used sensor types, their functional domains, and associated challenges.

Table 1. Common Sensor Types for Real-Time Water Monitoring.

Sensor Type	Monitored Parameter	Typical Applications	Advantages	Limitations
pH Sensors	Acidity/alkalinity	Aquaculture, wastewater, agriculture	High precision, compact	Requires regular calibration
Dissolved Oxygen (DO)	Oxygen levels in water	Aquaculture, river monitoring	Real-time response	Susceptible to membrane fouling
Flow Sensors	Flow rate/volume	Domestic and industrial networks	Easy integration with IoT nodes	Can be affected by pressure fluctuations
Temperature Sensors	Thermal regulation	Aquaculture, irrigation	Low power, accurate	Limited to point-based measurement
Pressure Transducers	Systemic pressure levels	Urban water grids	Enables anomaly detection	Prone to drift in harsh environments
Conductivity Sensors	Salinity and EC	Quality monitoring, agricultural reuse	Indicates contamination trends	Sensitive to scaling and biofouling

Source: Compiled from Flores-Iwasaki et al. (2025), Lei et al. (2025), Guezouli et al. (2024).

The increasing miniaturisation and energy efficiency of these devices have enabled their deployment in remote areas, including those with intermittent connectivity and limited access to conventional energy sources. Solar-powered nodes and sleep-mode-enabled firmware have extended the operational life of monitoring systems, which is particularly crucial in large-scale environmental or agricultural applications where human intervention is limited.

Moreover, the integration of AI algorithms with smart sensor data has unlocked new frontiers in predictive analytics. For instance, models such as AdaBoost and Random Forest, as implemented in South African treatment plants, have been employed to predict water quality parameters that cannot be directly measured by sensors (Banda & Kumarasamy, 2024; Rajitha et al., 2024). The AI models infer these parameters from correlated sensor data—such as turbidity, pH, and conductivity—thereby reducing laboratory costs and response times while enabling wider spatial coverage.

These advancements are particularly valuable in the context of early warning systems, where the real-time identification of deviations can pre-empt health risks or infrastructural damage. Lamrini et al. (2024) exemplify this through the use of machine learning-based outlier detection in Brussels, wherein IoT nodes relay real-time sensor readings to the cloud for classification using SVM, ANN, and Isolation Forest models. The resulting alerts enable immediate technical interventions, enhancing system reliability and minimising downtime.

Nonetheless, the broader implementation of these systems is constrained by a number of critical factors. These include:

- **Interoperability barriers**: Variations in communication protocols (e.g., LoRaWAN, Zigbee, NB-IoT) and data formats can inhibit seamless integration between devices and platforms.
- **Data governance concerns**: Issues surrounding data ownership, privacy, and cybersecurity are of particular concern in residential and institutional applications.
- **Skill and capacity gaps**: The successful operation of these systems often requires technical expertise not readily available in all local utilities or agricultural cooperatives.

To address these limitations, scholars advocate for the development of open-source software platforms, modular hardware architectures, and community-based training programmes. Such approaches can not only enhance user engagement but also ensure that the benefits of smart water monitoring are equitably distributed across socio-economic and geographic boundaries.

In conclusion, the convergence of real-time monitoring, intelligent sensing, and adaptive analytics is reshaping the landscape of water management. These systems have demonstrated quantifiable improvements in operational efficiency, sustainability, and responsiveness. Yet, their successful deployment requires a holistic strategy encompassing technological innovation, institutional capacity-building, and inclusive policy frameworks that prioritise interoperability, data ethics, and resilience.

4. WATER LEAKAGE DETECTION SYSTEMS

Water leakage within urban and rural distribution networks represents a persistent and complex challenge for water utilities worldwide. The adverse implications of undetected leaks are manifold, encompassing resource wastage, elevated operational expenditures, public health risks, and infrastructural degradation. Given that Non-Revenue Water (NRW) can account for up to 50% of total distributed volume in some networks (González-Villareal et al., 2018), the imperative for advanced detection technologies becomes evident. The integration of smart systems, rooted in the convergence of AI, the IoT, wireless communication technologies, and precision sensing, offers an innovative and robust approach to mitigating these challenges. A recent implementation for residential water consumption optimisation demonstrated how IoT-based flow monitoring and machine learning can detect toilet-system leakages in real time (Ramírez-Hernández et al., 2025).

Traditional leakage detection methods, such as acoustic analysis and manual inspection, are increasingly being supplanted or supplemented by intelligent systems that operate in real time, allowing for autonomous anomaly identification, flow analysis, and immediate response protocols. These technologies enable the transition from reactive maintenance to predictive and condition-based interventions, thereby increasing efficiency and service reliability. A Smart Water Meter is a system composed of both hardware and software capable of recording readings and providing remote, real-time data on water consumption. These artificial intelligence systems are commonly employed in agricultural irrigation and within smart cities. Despite being a viable option for the efficient conservation of water, not all cities currently implement this technology, either due to its perceived high cost or a lack of adaptation to such advanced systems designed to prevent water loss and mitigate future challenges arising from water scarcity (Rodríguez, 2024).

4.1. Technological Framework and Detection Models

Modern leak detection systems typically comprise three fundamental layers: sensing, data transmission, and analytical modelling. The sensing layer includes vibration sensors, ultrasonic meters, flow monitors, and pressure sensors, all of which are capable of capturing physical anomalies indicative of leakage. These data are transmitted via Low-Power Wide-Area Networks (LPWANs), including LoRaWAN, Zigbee, and NB-IoT, to cloud-based or edge-processing platforms. Subsequently, AI algorithms—such as decision trees, random forests, support vector machines, and gradient boosting models—are employed to classify, predict, and localise leakage events with high accuracy.

An exemplary case of this integration is the leak detection model developed by Lee and Kim (2023), in which vibration sensors were installed at strategic nodes within cast iron and non-metallic pipelines. The sensors monitored signals across a wide frequency range (10 Hz to 5120 Hz), which were then preprocessed and transformed into statistically representative features for machine learning analysis. The XGBoost classifier demonstrated a detection accuracy of 99.79%, significantly outperforming other tested algorithms such as KNN, LightGBM, and CatBoost. Moreover, the system's modular design enabled scalability, making it suitable for deployment across both urban and peri-urban infrastructures.

In parallel, IoT-based smart meters—such as those developed by León Lazo and Macancela Sumba (2024)—combine flow sensors (e.g., YF-S201), microcontrollers (ESP32), and electromechanical valves to facilitate autonomous shutdowns in the presence of anomalies. These systems also provide user-facing interfaces, such as Telegram bots, for real-time notifications, historical data access, and consumption visualisation. This approach not only enhances technical responsiveness but also fosters consumer participation and behavioural change.

4.2. Comparative Assessment of Detection Techniques

Various technologies have been evaluated for their suitability across different application environments. Table 2 provides a structured comparison of prevalent leak detection methods, including their operating principles, advantages, limitations, and typical use cases, as adapted and extended from Mohd Yussof & Ho (2022).

Figure 1 offers a structured comparative representation of the principal water leak detection techniques employed within urban infrastructures, encompassing both conventional and intelligent methodologies. Specifically, the figure encompasses acoustic detection, fibre optic sensing, surface moisture sensors, thermal imaging technologies, tracer gas methods, vibration-based systems, and advanced statistical or AI-driven anomaly detection models. Each method is systematically assessed across three core performance dimensions: detection accuracy, scalability potential across network sizes, and cost-efficiency in terms of deployment and maintenance. A radar chart or multi-bar format is utilised to convey the comparative advantages and limitations of each technique with visual clarity. This graphical analysis consolidates findings detailed by Mohd Yussof and Ho (2022), thereby substantiating the critical discourse surrounding the technological appropriateness and economic feasibility of these detection systems across varying operational contexts and infrastructure typologies.

Figure 1. Comparative Performance of Conventional and Intelligent Water Leak Detection Techniques Based on Accuracy, Scalability, and Cost Efficiency.

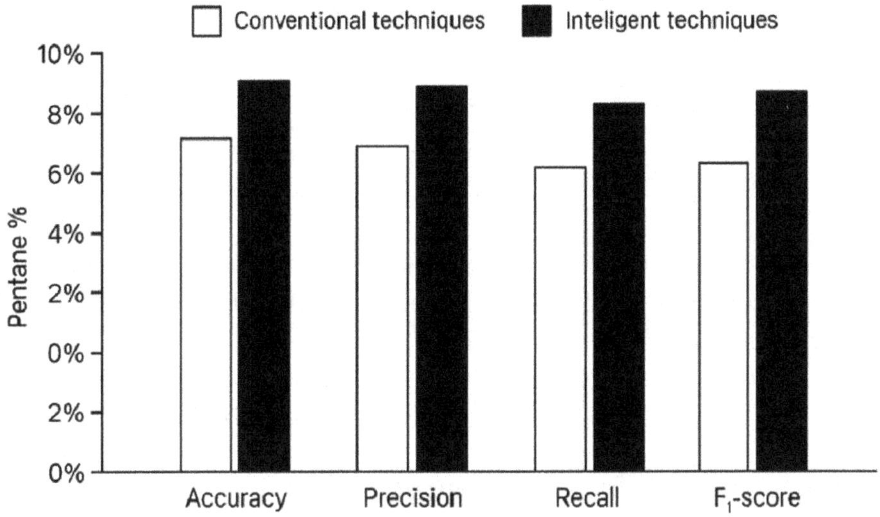

Table 2. Comparative Analysis of Water Leak Detection Methods.

Detection Method	Operating Principle	Advantages	Limitations	Common Application
Acoustic	Detects sound generated by escaping water	Non-invasive; large coverage range	Environmental noise interference	Buried metallic pipelines
Fibre Optic	Monitors light signal disruption along cables	High precision; continuous real-time monitoring	High installation cost; complexity	Critical infrastructure
Moisture Sensors	Detects water on surfaces or insulation	Economical; easy to deploy	Limited to surface detection	Building interiors, plumbing
Thermal Imaging	Captures heat anomalies caused by wet areas	Visual tool; useful in initial inspections	Susceptible to ambient temperature variation	Preventive maintenance
Tracer Gases	Introduces pressurised gas for leak detection	Effective in closed systems	Requires specialised equipment	Industrial pipelines

continued on following page

Table 2. Continued

Detection Method	Operating Principle	Advantages	Limitations	Common Application
Statistical/AI Models	Identifies anomalies in consumption patterns	Real-time alerts; scalable; adaptive	Needs historical data; calibration critical	Smart grids, household networks
Vibration Sensors	Detects frequency patterns associated with leaks	High accuracy; suitable for various pipe materials	Potential attenuation in non-metallic pipelines	Urban distribution systems

The combination of AI with vibration or flow-based sensing not only enhances detection precision but also reduces latency in reporting and intervention. Moreover, systems leveraging LPWAN communication protocols, such as LoRaWAN, allow for extended-range, low-energy deployments across dispersed geographies, making them ideal for rural or semi-urban water systems (Lei et al., 2025).

4.3. Integration with Smart Infrastructure

Leak detection systems are increasingly being embedded into broader smart water network infrastructures. The QoW Pro platform, developed by Guezouli et al. (2024), exemplifies this trend by incorporating real-time monitoring of flow, pressure, and water quality within urban distribution systems. The integration of distributed IoT nodes and cloud-based analytics led to a 30% reduction in undetected leaks and an accuracy rate of 94% in identifying flow anomalies. Additionally, operational costs were reduced by 20%, primarily through predictive maintenance and the elimination of unnecessary extractions.

Similarly, the *PUMAGUA* initiative at the National Autonomous University of Mexico illustrates the long-term institutional benefits of smart water infrastructure. The incorporation of automated metering, real-time sensor networks, and online monitoring platforms significantly reduced leak-related water losses—from 50 L/s to 25 L/s—while also improving service quality and user accountability (González-Villareal et al., 2018).

4.4. Challenges and Future Prospects

Despite the evident advantages, the deployment of smart leak detection systems is not without its challenges. Key limitations include:

- **Interoperability Issues**: Heterogeneity among sensor types, communication standards, and data platforms can hinder seamless integration.

- **Data Governance and Privacy**: Ensuring the security and ethical handling of consumption data remains an ongoing concern, particularly in residential applications.
- **Energy Constraints**: Many remote systems rely on battery-powered sensors, necessitating optimisation of energy use and communication frequency.
- **Skill Gaps**: The operation and maintenance of intelligent systems require technical proficiency, often lacking in local utilities or community operators.

Addressing these constraints calls for the development of modular, open-source platforms; the implementation of secure data protocols; and the provision of targeted capacity-building initiatives. Furthermore, the future landscape of leakage detection is likely to be shaped by advances in deep learning, edge computing, and spectrogram-based classification models, which offer enhanced accuracy and real-time processing capabilities (Lee & Kim, 2023).

The integration of these systems with smart valves, automated shutoff mechanisms, and decision-support tools will further elevate the operational responsiveness and sustainability of water networks. As AI algorithms evolve to become more context-aware and less reliant on extensive datasets, their applicability in low-resource environments will increase substantially.

Water leakage detection systems have transitioned from isolated diagnostic tools to integral components of intelligent water infrastructure. The convergence of IoT, AI, and wireless communication technologies has enabled the development of adaptive, scalable, and highly accurate solutions. From academic campuses and smart cities to rural household networks, these systems are redefining the parameters of water resource efficiency, operational transparency, and infrastructural resilience.

As water scarcity intensifies and the demand for sustainable solutions grows, investment in smart detection technologies will not only mitigate resource losses but also lay the groundwork for broader digital transformation in water governance. By ensuring real-time responsiveness and data-driven intervention, leak detection systems are no longer ancillary—they are indispensable.

5. LEAK DETECTION AND PREDICTIVE MAINTENANCE

At the Universiti Sains Malaysia (USM), researchers Nurfarah Anisah Mohd Yussof and Hann Woei Ho conducted a scientific review of existing methodologies for water leak detection in smart buildings, aiming to identify the most effective approaches and their current limitations. Both authors are affiliated with the university as academic researchers—not students—and possess expertise in systems engineering, automation, and intelligent technologies applied to water management

(Mohd Yussof & Ho, 2022). The study offers a detailed analysis of various detection techniques, including acoustic methods, fibre optics, thermal imaging, tracer gases, statistical models, and artificial intelligence-based algorithms. The review highlights that, although several technologies have shown promise in urban and industrial contexts, key challenges remain. These include achieving real-time accuracy, minimising false alarms, and developing systems capable of autonomous operation with low energy consumption and minimal human intervention. Furthermore, the authors emphasise that the future development of such systems should focus on integration with IoT platforms and intelligent building management systems. This would enable automated and efficient responses to potential leaks, safeguarding water resources and reducing maintenance costs (Mohd Yussof & Ho, 2022). The findings of this article provide a solid technical foundation for researchers, engineers, and planners seeking to implement or enhance leak detection systems in smart environments. It is evident that the field continues to hold substantial potential for growth towards more scalable, reliable, and sustainable solutions.

In order to provide an integrated view of the technologies involved in intelligent leak detection systems, Table 3 illustrates the key technological components, their functions, and application examples.

Table 3. Intelligent Technologies for Water Leak Detection: Components, Functions, and Practical Applications.

Technological Component	Primary Function	Technologies / Devices	Example of Implementation
Vibration Sensors	Detect frequency patterns associated with leakage events	MEMS, piezoelectric sensors	Urban network monitoring using XGBoost in South Korea (Lee & Kim, 2023)
Smart Water Meters	Enable remote flow monitoring and automated control	ESP32 microcontroller, YF-S201 sensor, electromechanical valve	Domestic prototype in Ecuador (León Lazo & Macancela Sumba, 2024)
Cloud-Based Platforms	Data storage, real-time analytics, and visualisation	UBIDOTS, LTE/Wi-Fi servers	Domestic integration with Telegram bot for user interaction
Communication Protocols	Transmit sensor data to processing platforms	LoRaWAN, Zigbee, NB-IoT	Distributed monitoring in urban systems (QoW Pro; Guezouli et al., 2024)
AI / Machine Learning Algorithms	Perform classification and predictive anomaly detection	XGBoost, Random Forest, Decision Trees	Multi-class signal classification system (Lee & Kim, 2023)
User Interfaces	Facilitate alert generation, system control, and data access	Mobile applications, bots, dashboards	Telegram-based interaction with smart meters

According to a study conducted by Suan Lee and Byeonghank Kim (2023), from the School of Computer Science at Semyung University (South Korea), entitled Machine Learning Model for Leak Detection Using Vibration Sensors in Water Pipelines, a leak detection system was developed using machine learning and vibration sensors installed on water pipelines to achieve high detection accuracy. This approach is based on the premise that many water distribution networks—particularly those built with ageing cast iron or non-metallic pipes—exhibit leak issues that are difficult to identify due to infrastructure degradation and ambient or electrical noise. The proposed system deploys vibration sensors at key points in the network, such as meter boxes and pipe outlets. These sensors capture signals across a wide frequency range (10 Hz to 5120 Hz), enabling the identification of both leak events and normal or interfering noise. The collected data undergo a preprocessing scheme that groups signals by frequency bands, filters out non-informative frequencies (e.g. 0 Hz), and subsequently transforms them into tabular format. Relevant statistical features—such as maximum values, averages, and band-specific correlations—are extracted, reducing dimensionality and enhancing model efficiency. A large dataset was used: 62,564 samples for training and 7,820 for testing. The samples were categorised into five classes: external leak, internal leak, electrical noise, other noise, and normal noise. This classification enabled the training and comparison of several machine learning algorithms, including K-Nearest Neighbours (KNN), Decision Trees, Random Forest, Extra Trees, LightGBM, CatBoost, and XGBoost. Among these, XGBoost delivered the highest performance, achieving a 99.79% leak detection accuracy, significantly outperforming other models. The system was tested on both metallic and non-metallic pipelines, demonstrating robustness and adaptability to various materials, although non-metallic pipes showed lower vibration transmission, potentially requiring future calibration. The XGBoost model excelled not only in accuracy but also in its ability to manage noisy data and maintain computational efficiency. A "leaf-wise" training architecture was employed, optimising decision tree performance and improving the model's generalisation in real-world scenarios. The complete system is designed for real-time operation. The process begins with data acquisition from sensors, which are transmitted to a server via wireless technologies (e.g. IoT or LTE). The data are then processed, and the trained model determines whether a leak is occurring. If an anomaly is detected, an automatic alert is triggered, which can be integrated into graphical interfaces or APIs for operator visualisation. The system offers numerous advantages: a significant improvement in leak detection accuracy, reduction in water waste, optimisation of operational costs, and the ability to integrate with broader intelligent water network management systems. Moreover, its modular architecture makes it scalable, supporting deployment in urban areas with sensors spaced every 150 to 300 metres. The model also lays the groundwork for future advancements, such as the adoption of deep neural networks or spectrogram-based models using visual learning (e.g. CNNs or Transformers), and direct integration with smart valves for automated response to detected leaks. In conclusion, this study demonstrates that the combined use of vibration sensors, advanced signal preprocessing techniques, and machine learning models such as XGBoost can provide an effective, scalable, and highly accurate solution for early leak detection in water distribution networks. Its applicability to various pipe materials, resilience to noisy environments, and low-cost, rapid implementation make it a valuable alternative to traditional detection methods (Lee & Kim, 2023).

Researchers at the Universidad Nacional de San Agustín de Arequipa in Peru proposed and implemented a predictive model for water potability based on a decision tree, employing artificial intelligence to enhance the automated assessment of water suitability for human consumption (Zevallos Apaza et al., 2022). They utilised a public dataset from Kaggle, containing 3,276 water samples, each labelled as either potable or non-potable. The dataset includes multiple physicochemical variables relevant to water quality. Using Python's Pandas and Scikit-Learn libraries, they developed a decision tree classifier, whose performance was evaluated using standard classification metrics: accuracy, precision, recall, and F1-score. This study underscores the relevance of such solutions in contexts where access to laboratories is limited, or real-time physicochemical analysis is unfeasible. The system enables automatic classification of water samples, thereby reducing costs, time, and human error, with a direct impact on public health protection. From a technical standpoint, Zevallos Apaza et al. (2022) describe the data preprocessing procedure, including handling missing values, feature selection, training and testing set division, and the construction, tuning, and validation of the decision tree. Although the final model structure is not detailed, it proved both efficient and interpretable, allowing for the identification of parameters directly influencing potability. This research demonstrates that with low-cost artificial intelligence technologies, open-source code, and accessible data, it is possible to develop effective tools for water quality assessment. The decision tree offers a transparent and robust analytical method, suitable for implementation in web or mobile platforms, with the potential to be deployed in rural or urban communities with infrastructure constraints.

Researchers León Lazo and Macancela Sumba (2024) from the Universidad Católica de Cuenca developed a prototype smart water meter aimed at reducing water losses in household distribution systems. The project is part of the university's Electricity Research Group and seeks to improve operational efficiency for both water service providers and consumers, particularly in areas where leakage or reading errors increase costs and reduce water availability. To achieve this, the authors implemented an IoT-based technological solution using the ESP32 module, a YF-S201 flow sensor, and an electromechanical shut-off valve. The meter is installed at the household's main water inlet and continuously measures flow data, processed by the ESP32 microcontroller, which also enables remote valve control to interrupt the flow in the event of anomalies such as leaks or unusual excessive use. The system architecture is supported by the UBIDOTS platform for cloud-based data storage and querying, and a communication gateway via LTE or Wi-Fi managed by the ESP32. A Telegram bot was also integrated, allowing users to interact directly with the meter via their mobile devices. Through this bot, consumers can request daily or monthly consumption readings, receive automatic 24-hour notifications, and make informed decisions regarding water use. The system was designed with clear objectives: to improve water resource management, reduce response times in the event of outages or silent losses, eliminate manual reading errors, and generate direct economic benefits for both the water provider and end users. Functionality is based on real-time flow monitoring, detection of unusual patterns (e.g., continuous night-time consumption suggesting a leak), and optional valve activation or alerting of relevant personnel. The smart meter is self-configurable and modular, enabling its deployment in households, small buildings, or even rural distribution points, at a significantly lower cost compared to traditional commercial systems. The combination of hardware (ESP32, YF-S201 sensor, valve), cloud platform, and automated communication via Telegram creates a more sustainable, reliable, and cost-effective water management system. Although the document does not detail a large-scale field study, it highlights the technical feasibility and potential economic and social impact of this solution, facilitating consumption transparency, reducing error margins, and strengthening local water infrastructure.

Ayala et al. (2011) developed a didactic prototype of a wireless data acquisition node, designed for educational and experimental purposes. It is intended to facilitate learning and application of Wireless Sensor Networks (WSNs) across various disciplines such as environmental monitoring, crop control, home automation, and agricultural monitoring, with special focus on Zigbee topologies (star, tree, and mesh) and low power consumption. The authors, professors and engineers at the Instituto Tecnológico de Los Mochis, constructed a compact device (80 × 80 mm) with a double-layer PCB integrating the Digi XBee module (compatible with IEEE 802.15.4 and Zigbee), analogue/digital input and output ports, and PWM outputs. The prototype can operate for up to 30 months on a single 9V battery due to low power modes. It includes 5V and 3.3V regulators, LED indicators, buttons, and a USB port for programming. Electronically, the node offers two digital inputs, two digital outputs, two analogue inputs, two PWM outputs, a serial USB interface, and employs LM35DZ sensors to measure temperature with 1 °C accuracy. External power supply is managed via selectors to choose between USB or a 9V adapter, and the PCB features thermal insulation and heat dissipation grids. Space was also allocated for an external XBee antenna and clearly marked terminals. During the experimental phase, the nodes were confirmed to operate under both star and point-to-point topologies (IEEE 802.15.4) as well as tree and mesh (Zigbee), allowing for extended battery life and network range through repeater nodes. Communication and analogue-to-digital conversion tests were successful, and the USB interface facilitated configuration and monitoring from a PC or tablet. A monitoring software was developed to visualise variable graphs, configure nodes, store data, and execute control actions. Although tested in a laboratory environment, the prototype demonstrated robustness, stability, and potential for diverse real-world applications. The authors emphasise the contribution to technical education and training, enabling students to apply theoretical concepts in microelectronics, communications, and WSNs through hands-on experience. They also highlight its applicability in environmental monitoring, agricultural control, crop management, early wildfire detection, aquaculture monitoring (pH, oxygen, temperature), and home automation. In conclusion, the work presents a functional, low-cost, and high-autonomy didactic module, suitable for academic and industrial environments in the study and development of Zigbee networks. This prototype combines hardware and software with real connectivity and lays the foundation for more advanced projects in wireless monitoring and control.

6. IMPLEMENTATION OF WATERSHED MONITORING SYSTEMS THROUGH SENSORS AND REMOTE SENSING

Smart irrigation refers to the automated and efficient management of water for crops through the integration of IoT sensors, AI algorithms, and remote control systems. These systems enable real-time monitoring of key variables such as soil moisture, temperature, solar radiation, and weather forecasts, thereby allowing irrigation to be adjusted locally according to the specific conditions of each crop. According to Touil et al. (2022), controllers based on soil moisture and evapotranspiration sensors can achieve water savings ranging from 20% to 92%, while maintaining both crop yield and quality. Recent studies by Sloat (2025) confirm that the combination of IoT devices with AI technologies—such as fuzzy logic, neural networks, and machine learning—enhances irrigation precision, reduces the need for human intervention, and supports more sustainable and resilient agricultural practices. For example, an AI-based system utilising IoT nodes significantly reduced water consumption while simultaneously increasing agricultural yield. More recently, Kunt (2025) developed an autonomous system using an ESP32 microcontroller and an LSTM model to predict soil moisture and regulate irrigation, highlighting the trend toward autonomous systems capable of dynamically adapting to environmental conditions.

Figure 2 provides a comprehensive depiction of the operational architecture of a smart irrigation system, highlighting the integration of Internet of Things (IoT) sensors, advanced machine learning algorithms, and cloud-based control platforms. The diagram illustrates the flow of information from soil moisture sensors, temperature sensors, and weather stations to a central microcontroller unit (e.g., ESP32). This microcontroller processes environmental data and communicates wirelessly via a LoRaWAN network. The system incorporates predictive irrigation models—such as Long Short-Term Memory (LSTM) networks and Model Predictive Control (MPC) algorithms—that analyse sensor inputs to determine optimal irrigation timing and volume. These predictions are transmitted to a visualisation and control interface which, in turn, activates irrigation actuators (e.g., solenoid valves). The architectural framework represented in the figure synthesises key technological components and their interactions, as discussed in Touil et al. (2022) and Kunt (2025), thereby offering a strategic visualisation of how precision agriculture is enhanced through cyber-physical systems and AI-enabled decision support mechanisms.

Figure 2. Functional Architecture of a Smart Irrigation System Integrating IoT Sensors, Machine Learning Algorithms, and Cloud Platforms for Precision Agriculture.

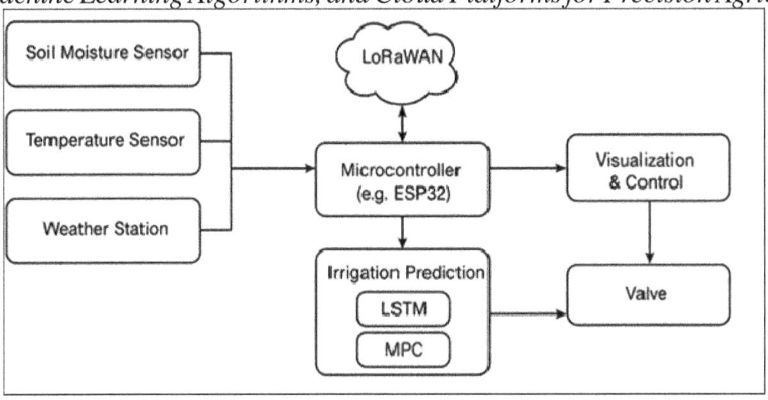

A team of researchers from the University of Patras, in collaboration with Aristotle University of Thessaloniki, developed, designed, and tested a comprehensive agricultural monitoring platform focused on the efficient use of water for olive cultivation in Greece (Liopa-Tsakalidi et al., 2024). This project responds to growing concerns over water scarcity and the need to optimise water resources in the agricultural sector. Traditionally, farmers in the region irrigate based on empirical practices, which often leads to excessive or inefficient water use. Olive cultivation, particularly in Greece, holds substantial economic and cultural importance. Due to its extensive nature, it requires modern strategies to reduce costs, conserve water resources, and enhance productivity. The technological solution developed by the researchers consists of a smart irrigation platform based on the Internet of Things (IoT) with LoRaWAN connectivity, specifically designed to operate in rural environments with low energy requirements. The system architecture relies on a network of sensor nodes deployed in the field to measure soil moisture at varying depths (30, 60, and 90 cm), as well as ambient temperature, in order to generate accurate and continuous information regarding the hydric status of the olive grove. These nodes are connected via LoRaWAN technology, allowing long-range data transmission (10–40 km) without the need for complex infrastructure or high energy demands. The captured data are sent to a central gateway with 4G connectivity, stored in cloud servers using InfluxDB databases, and displayed on real-time dashboards accessible to both farmers and technical staff responsible for monitoring and decision-making. The system was implemented and validated in a 22-hectare olive grove in Peta, Achaea region, Greece, containing 300 trees of the Kalamon variety. Previously, a conventional drip irrigation system was operated manually every 15 to 20 days for approximately 7 to 8 hours per session, based solely on the farmer's experience. The effectiveness of the system was validated both technically and economically, as it not only reduced water and energy costs, but also improved crop health by preventing water stress caused by over-irrigation.

Among the main benefits identified by Liopa-Tsakalidi et al. (2024) are:

- **Significant water savings**, contributing positively to environmental sustainability.
- **Reduction of operational costs** related to pumping, maintenance, and irrigation supervision.
- **Increased autonomy for farmers**, who now rely on accurate and up-to-date information to make informed decisions.
- **Adaptability and scalability** of the system for replication in other agricultural regions with similar needs.
- **Promotion of digital agriculture**, supporting the modernisation of rural areas through low-cost, high-impact technologies.

Researchers from Pennsylvania State University (Penn State, USA) and the University of Foggia (Italy) developed a precision irrigation system based on the Internet of Things (IoT), employing LoRaWAN technology and specifically applied to fresh tomato cultivation in greenhouses using plastic mulch systems—commonly known as plasticulture (Zhang et al., 2022). The primary aim of the study was to optimise water usage in horticultural tomato production through automated irrigation and real-time remote soil data collection, thereby minimising water waste, maximising efficiency, and increasing crop yield. To achieve this, the researchers designed a smart monitoring platform consisting of Watermark 200SS-5 tensiometric soil moisture sensors connected to IoT nodes that transmit data to a central gateway via a LoRaWAN network. LoRaWAN was chosen for its ability to cover long distances with low energy consumption, making it ideal for extensive agricultural environments and rural areas lacking conventional Wi-Fi coverage. The central gateway was connected to the internet via a 4G cellular network, allowing farmers and technicians to access real-time irrigation and soil data from any location. The system was implemented at the Russell E. Larson Agricultural Research Center at Penn State. Four different irrigation scheduling treatments were used to compare the system's efficiency: one based on reference evapotranspiration (ET), another that activated irrigation when soil moisture reached –60 kilopascals (MP60), a third at –40 kilopascals (MP40), and an additional one using the GesCoN model, a decision support tool developed for fertigation in horticultural crops. The experimental design followed a randomised complete block scheme with four replications per treatment. The data collected enabled measurement of water use efficiency and fresh tomato yield under each treatment. Results indicated a 28 % increase in water use efficiency compared to the ET-based method, while the MP60 treatment improved efficiency by 19 %, with a significant increase in yield. This demonstrates that accurate data collection and intelligent use of agronomic information can lead to better-informed irrigation decisions tailored to actual soil conditions and crop physiological needs. One of the system's standout features is its low cost. The authors estimated that the entire IoT system—including sensors, microcontrollers, gateway, power supply and connectivity—could be built for under USD 1,000, making it accessible for small- and medium-sized agricultural producers. The system was powered by rechargeable batteries and solar panels, enabling uninterrupted autonomous operation throughout the entire growing season. This development not only showcases a technological advancement but also addresses pressing challenges in agriculture: climate change, water scarcity, sustainability, and the need to improve the efficiency of agricultural production systems. Through this approach, farmers can significantly reduce water use, avoid over- or under-irrigation, improve soil and crop health, and lower operational costs by reducing energy usage for pumping and monitoring. Finally, the study's results validate that the use of IoT technologies, LoRaWAN networks, and decision support models such as GesCoN in plasticulture environments is not only viable but highly recommended. This solution can be replicated and adapted to other horticultural or open-field crops at various scales. By integrating sensors, remote connectivity, intelligent software, and advanced agronomic techniques, the study contributes to the development of efficient, resilient, and digital agriculture (Zhang et al., 2022).

In response to the challenges of climate change and the need for water-use efficiency, researchers from the CVR College of Engineering in Mangalpalli, Telangana, India, developed and implemented a sustainable smart irrigation platform based on the Internet of Things (IoT) and cloud services (Sreelatha Reddy et al., 2024). The objective was to deliver an automated, low-cost system that combines real-time soil moisture data, weather forecasts, and crop-specific parameters to optimise water use and increase agricultural productivity. The system architecture relies on soil moisture sensors distributed across the field, continuously transmitting data to a NodeMCU microcontroller based on the ESP8266. This device processes the data using statistical analysis (e.g. standard deviation) and compares the results with crop-critical parameters. Based on this evaluation, the system automatically activates the water pump and solenoid valves, initiating or halting irrigation as needed. Furthermore, it integrates online weather forecast data, enabling dynamic adjustment of irrigation plans to prevent watering during rainfall or periods of high soil moisture. The system makes irrigation decisions based on moisture levels, climatic trends, and crop requirements, achieving an optimal balance between water consumption and productivity. A key component of the design is cloud integration, where sensor data and control commands are securely stored and accessed via web or mobile applications. This allows remote monitoring of soil moisture, irrigation scheduling, and real-time data visualisation. Additionally, the platform enables higher-level analytics, such as time-series analysis, statistical summaries, inter-plot comparisons, yield forecasting, and agronomic recommendations based on historical data. Its use promotes more efficient and sustainable agriculture with minimal human intervention, thereby reducing operational costs, increasing yield, conserving water, and mitigating climate impact. The system was tested under real-world conditions over several months, demonstrating continuous functionality, stable connectivity, and adaptability to various environmental conditions and crop types. Its design, using low-cost components (NodeMCU, sensors, relays, 4G access, cloud services), makes it replicable for small- and medium-scale farms. Furthermore, its modularity and use of open communication standards allow for integration with other IoT devices and additional sensors (e.g. temperature, EC, pH), as well as more advanced agronomic systems (Sreelatha Reddy et al., 2024).

Regarding the publication "Smart irrigation monitoring and control strategies for improving water use efficiency in precision agriculture: a review", the authors highlight the importance of closed-loop systems, which adjust irrigation in real time in response to sensor measurements, as opposed to open-loop systems, which rely on fixed schedules and disregard environmental uncertainties (Bwambale et al., 2022). The review argues that integrating data from soil (e.g. moisture, temperature), the plant (e.g. phenological stage, stress indicators), and the climate (e.g. evapotranspiration, precipitation) allows for the development of predictive models. These models, when combined with advanced control techniques such as Model Predictive Control (MPC) or fuzzy logic, enable optimal irrigation scheduling and significant improvements in water-use efficiency. Among the recommended practices, proper placement of sensors at multiple depths is emphasised as essential for capturing variability in the soil moisture profile—thus avoiding both over-irrigation and water deficits that could compromise crop performance. The review also covers the use of WSNs operating via LoRa, Zigbee, or NB-IoT, along with IoT architectures that support real-time data collection, local processing, and cloud-based monitoring and control. After analysing case studies and experimental outcomes, the authors conclude that multi-variable, MPC-based irrigation systems can save between 20 % and 40 % more water than traditional methods, without sacrificing high productivity. These savings are especially impactful in fruit production and semi-arid regions, where optimised irrigation can lead to substantial improvements in sustainability and food security. The review also addresses key challenges: limited connectivity in rural areas, the cost and maintenance of specialised sensors, the training required for farmers and technicians, and the lack of interoperability among devices and platforms. Proposed solutions include modular system design, the use of solar-powered energy systems, participatory training programmes for producers, and the development of open standards. Lastly, Bwambale et al. (2022) and colleagues identify several future opportunities: the use of artificial intelligence and deep learning to improve predictive accuracy, the integration of satellite or drone imagery for more detailed modelling, and the advancement of climate-smart, resilient agriculture capable of addressing the challenges of the 21st century.

These examples illustrate how smart irrigation has evolved significantly between 2020 and 2025, through diverse yet complementary approaches. Universities and research institutions have played a pivotal role in developing the core technologies, while companies have adapted and commercialised them for various agricultural contexts. All of these systems share the common objective of optimising water use through precise soil and crop monitoring, real-time data analysis, and automated irrigation decisions. Concrete results across different crops and geographic regions confirm the potential of these technologies to address the challenges of water scarcity in modern agriculture.

A research team affiliated with the School of Civil Engineering and the Centre for Water Resources and Environment at Sun Yat-sen University in Zhuhai and Guangzhou, China, addresses the issue of centralised water management systems, which are often characterised by high costs, low efficiency, and vulnerability to failures in data storage and reliability. In response to these challenges, they propose a decentralised blockchain-based framework covering the entire water cycle: supply, use, consumption, and discharge (Xia et al., 2022). They developed an architecture integrating several functional modules:

1. **Water source management**, overseeing permits and authorisations.
2. **Water supply management**, coordinating distribution.
3. **Water consumption management**, using real-time monitoring.
4. **Drainage management**, tracking wastewater quality.

In this platform, monitoring data and operational information are encrypted and transmitted via a peer-to-peer network, rather than relying on a centralised system. Each node in the network participates in verifying, storing, and validating information. This addresses typical problems in traditional systems, such as permit forgery, data tampering, and management bottlenecks.

Two key application scenarios were designed:

- A **permit issuance and supervision system**, where water withdrawal authorisations recorded on the blockchain become immutable and transparent, allowing anyone to verify them without intermediaries.
- A **water quality traceability system**, which logs each sampling point on an immutable ledger, enabling the identification of areas with health concerns and the clear attribution of responsibility.

The benefits of the framework are manifold: high traceability, cryptographic security, improved data operation efficiency, and total transparency, which rebuilds institutional trust by eliminating the risks associated with central points of failure and manipulated records. However, the authors also acknowledge significant challenges: the technical complexity of blockchain, the need for participating institutions to modify their management models, integration with legacy centralised systems, and legal considerations related to distributed technology adoption. The project was supported by Chinese innovation programmes (National Key R&D Program, NSFC) and stands out as one of the first practical proposals to apply blockchain to water management. It demonstrates that decentralised technologies can transform traditional water governance models, which are often dependent on single central authorities (Xia et al., 2022).

7. MODULAR SMART TREATMENT PLANTS (COMPACT, AUTOMATIC, DECENTRALISED)

The authors (Srivastava et al., 2024), affiliated with the Indian Institute of Technology (IIT) Jammu and other research universities in India, identified operational issues in a modular WasteWater Treatment Plant (WWTP) with a capacity of 100 m^3/day, located on the institute's campus. The plant suffered from biological and mechanical failures that affected treatment efficiency, resulting in effluent discharges below environmental standards and incurring high operational costs due to frequent maintenance. To address this, they designed a comprehensive evaluation strategy using the GPS-X simulation model, a leading industry tool for simulating wastewater treatment processes. This tool enabled replication of the real plant's behaviour and diagnosis of the root causes of the problems. The model recreated various process units, including the anoxic tank, aerobic tank, primary and secondary settlers, and the internal recirculation system. The simulations revealed significant deficiencies, particularly in the anoxic tank, where insufficient Hydraulic Retention Time (HRT) led to poor nitrogen removal and suboptimal performance in organic matter elimination. Deficiencies were also observed in the aeration system of the aerobic reactor, resulting in inadequate dissolved oxygen levels and denitrification failures. Based on this diagnosis, the authors proposed several operational improvements: increasing the volume of the anoxic tank by adding a 15 m^3 module, optimising internal recirculation rates (nitrate return to anoxic), and improving the aeration set-up. By reconfiguring the HRT and adjusting operational parameters, simulations in GPS-X showed substantial improvements, achieving effluent standards in line with local regulations, enhancing carbon and nitrogen removal efficiency, and reducing overall retention time across the system. Following simulation, these operational improvements were implemented in the actual campus plant: the additional module was installed in the anoxic tank, and the recirculation pumps and aeration system were recalibrated. Subsequently, performance aligned with the model's predictions, as confirmed through real monitoring conducted over several months. This study clearly demonstrates the value of software modelling (GPS-X) as an effective tool for identifying operational deficiencies, evaluating alternatives, and guiding technical interventions prior to executing costly or disruptive modifications. Furthermore, it contributes to capacity building within the institution, as the model and insights gained are integrated into postgraduate academic training.

Shaikh and Ahammed (2020) offer a systematic review on the availability and quality characteristics of greywater—the effluent generated from sinks, showers, washing machines, and kitchen basins—with the aim of understanding its potential as an alternative resource, particularly in water-scarce regions. The authors, researchers from the Sardar Vallabhbhai National Institute of Technology in India, present a study examining both the volume and composition of greywater to determine which treatment processes are appropriate and safe for reuse. In terms of quantity, the review covers studies from various countries, noting that greywater constitutes approximately 65–80% of total domestic wastewater, generating between 20 and 90 litres per person per day, depending on lifestyle and climate. Sinks and showers contribute around 30–40% of the volume, while kitchen and laundry sources—ranging from 20–60%—stand out due to their high pollutant loads. Regarding quality, the review examines parameters such as organic matter (BOD, COD), nutrients (nitrogen, phosphorus), microorganisms, heavy metals, and organic micropollutants. Kitchen and laundry greywater exhibit high concentrations of organic matter and nutrients; for example, BOD/COD levels can reach 1000–2000 mg/L, whereas greywater from showers and sinks shows lower concentrations, typically 200–500 mg/L.

Microorganisms such as total coliforms appear in significant quantities in personal washing water, although heavy metal concentrations are generally below health risk thresholds due to dilution. One key conclusion of the article is the high temporal and source-based variability of greywater. Its composition can vary significantly from day to day, meaning any treatment system must be adaptable and based on real-time data. In this context, the authors emphasise that choosing an appropriate treatment technology requires understanding fluctuations in both quality and quantity. The review also analyses that, at the concentrations observed, heavy metals and emerging contaminants in greywater do not pose a health risk if appropriate treatment processes are applied—such as filtration, biological treatment, membrane processes, and disinfection. This suggests that reuse for non-potable applications—such as irrigation, cleaning, or aquifer recharge—is a viable and safe option, provided there is proper technical adaptation.

On the other hand, the authors (Ngo et al., 2024), mainly affiliated with Ton Duc Thang University (Vietnam) and Universiti Sains Malaysia (Malaysia), present a practical approach for treating and reusing domestic greywater (from sinks, bathrooms, and kitchens) in home irrigation systems, aiming to reduce pressure on potable water resources in urban and peri-urban areas. They developed a cost-effective treatment system that combines a sequence of physical filtration through ceramic media, quartz gravel, hollow fibre membranes, and final ultraviolet (UV) disinfection. Three types of greywater were evaluated—kitchen, sink, and bathroom—and treatment effectiveness was measured before and after processing, focusing on parameters such as turbidity, total coliforms, Biochemical Oxygen Demand (BOD_5), and chemical oxygen demand (COD). The treatment system demonstrated an efficiency exceeding 60% for all parameters, enabling greywater from sinks, after passing through the system, to meet international quality standards for domestic irrigation and gardening purposes.

8. INTER-INSTITUTIONAL AND PARTICIPATORY GOVERNANCE MODELS IN WATER MANAGEMENT AS DECENTRALISATION POLICIES AND COMMUNITY-BASED RESOURCE MANAGEMENT

A group of researchers, including Shahana Bilalova from Leuphana Universität Lüneburg (Germany), Jens Newig, and Sergio Villamayor-Tomás from the Universitat Autònoma de Barcelona, conducted a study as part of the European project NEWAVE (*Next Water Governance*), which aims to renew and strengthen water governance approaches through empirical evidence (Bilalova et al., 2024). In a systematic review of 165 studies comprising 223 empirical cases published between 1985 and 2020, the researchers examined how different paradigms of water governance relate to institutional characteristics, specific water-related problems, and sustainability outcomes. They classified issue categories—such as agricultural aquifer overexploitation or surface water pollution—and analysed their associations with paradigms like Integrated Water Resources Management (IWRM), participatory/cooperative governance, and community-based management, as outlined in the Table 4.

Table 4. Principal Water Governance Paradigms.

Governance Paradigm	General Description	Domain or Context of Application	Key Strengths	Potential Limitations
Integrated Water Resources Management (IWRM)	Coordinated and equitable management of water across sectors, users, and scales.	Public policy, national planning	Holistic vision, promotes equity and systemic sustainability	May be bureaucratic and difficult to implement; risk of fragmentation
Participatory and Collaborative Governance	Actively involves citizens and local actors in decision-making.	Municipalities, river basins, consultative processes	Enhances legitimacy and social acceptance; fosters transparency and accountability	Risk of symbolic participation; requires genuine political will
Community-Based Management	Direct administration of water by local or Indigenous communities.	Rural areas, Indigenous communities	Local resilience, contextual adaptation, traditional knowledge use	May lack technical and financial resources; limited operational scale
Market-Based Approaches	Utilisation of pricing, privatisation, or concessions as allocation and efficiency mechanisms.	Urban and commercial sectors	Incentivises efficient use; may attract private investment	Risk of social exclusion; prioritisation of profit over universal access
Polycentric Models	Distribution of authority among multiple autonomous actors and levels of government.	Complex or decentralised regions	Encourages innovation, diverse solutions, institutional adaptability	Coordination challenges; potential overlap or jurisdictional conflicts
Deregulation or Regulatory Reforms	Reduction of state role to allow decentralised or self-regulated solutions.	Economic reforms, liberalised sectors	Administrative agility, local empowerment	May weaken environmental and social oversight
Technology and Data-Driven Approaches	Use of digital platforms, sensors or AI for automated management and monitoring.	Smart cities, IoT networks	Improves operational efficiency, enables real-time response, accurate data	Requires high initial investment; technological dependence and digital divide risks

One of the central findings of the study is that while paradigms such as IWRM, citizen participation, and community-based management tend to be associated with better sustainability outcomes, these results are highly context-dependent. There are no universal solutions. For example, a community-based approach may be highly successful in certain rural regions but ineffective in complex urban settings. Similarly, a participatory system may yield positive outcomes when political will exists, but fail if limited to symbolic or non-decisive involvement. Moreover, the study reveals a frequent gap between declared paradigms and actual practices. It is common to encounter studies or projects labelled as "integrated" or "participatory" whose execution contradicts these principles—e.g. through the exclusion of key actors, centralised decision-making, or lack of cross-sectoral coordination. This highlights the fact that the mere adoption of a governance label does not guarantee its effective implementation. The study also points out that many cases lack systematic outcome evaluation. The majority of reviewed articles focus on institutional processes without clearly assessing their effects on environmental indicators (e.g. water quality, ecosystem conservation), social indicators (e.g. equity, access), or economic aspects (e.g. efficiency, costs). This hinders comparative analysis and limits collective learning across contexts.

Researchers from UTE and FLACSO (Ecuador), alongside the University of Saskatchewan (Canada) and Universidad de los Hemisferios, argue that traditional water governance models—grounded in technocratic hierarchies—fail to achieve equity or sustainability in cities of the Global South. In response, they propose participatory river governance through a citizen science approach that integrates local knowledge in processes of valuation, diagnosis, and urban river management (Alvarado-Arias et al., 2025). They have also developed a theoretical-methodological framework combining the theory of hydro-social territories with mixed participatory techniques. Specifically, they employed participatory mapping and spatial questionnaires (PPGIS) to collect both positive and negative social values associated with the Santa Clara, San Pedro, Pita, and San Nicolás rivers in Sangolquí (Quito). Citizens' perceptions of beauty, recreation, spiritual well-being, heritage, and life-supporting functions were mapped, along with perceived threats such as flooding, insecurity, and pollution. A Maximum Entropy (MaxEnt) model was then applied to generate predictive spatial distribution maps of these values, as shown in the Figure 3 and summarised in the Table 5.

Figure 3. Study Distribution within a Selected Area in Sangolquí.

Table 5. Methodological Practices Employed.

Dimension	Description	Key Details
Cultural and Institutional	Identifies a hybrid dynamic in Latin America, where formal European-type structures coexist with Indigenous traditional knowledge and practices.	Institutional structures replicate Western models, while local control and symbolic territorial meaning persist.
Governance Paradigms	Emphasis on participatory and collaborative approaches that promote citizen inclusion and local knowledge recognition.	Approaches that revalue the concept of "caring for water" through citizen engagement and collective action.
Methodological Practices	Mixed data collection and analysis methods were used to integrate citizen science with environmental modelling.	Includes PPGIS for social values, GIS analysis of biophysical variables, and MaxEnt modelling validated via AUC (0.75–0.96).

9. CASE STUDIES OF SMART WATER CITIES

In a global context where ageing water distribution networks and significant resource losses pose increasing challenges to cities, the experience of Singapore stands out as an early and functional example of the application of smart technologies for water management. The case documented in this study presents the implementation of a Smart Water Grid, known as *WaterWiSe*, designed to provide real-time monitoring, advanced analytics, and automated detection of leaks and anomalies in the city's potable water supply network (Allen et al., 2012). The system was developed by Visenti Pte Ltd, in collaboration with the Singapore-MIT Alliance for Research and Technology (SMART) and the Massachusetts Institute of Technology (MIT), with the objective of enhancing operational efficiency, reducing non-revenue water losses, and enabling immediate responses to infrastructure issues. The deployment of this smart grid initially took place in Singapore's urban area, where local authorities—particularly the Public Utilities Board (PUB)—were already seeking to modernise the system through advanced technological approaches. The technological foundation of the *WaterWiSe* system integrates hydraulic and water quality sensors strategically installed throughout the pipeline network. These sensors collect real-time data on key parameters such as pressure, flow rate, and water quality conditions, which are then continuously transmitted via wireless networks to analytics servers. This architecture enables active, uninterrupted monitoring of the entire network. The collected data are processed by computational models simulating the hydraulic behaviour of the system and employing anomaly detection algorithms. These algorithms are designed to identify irregular patterns potentially indicating leaks, pipe bursts, suboptimal pressure, or deterioration in water quality. Based on these analyses, automated alerts are generated, allowing a rapid response from maintenance authorities. The integration of sensors with wireless transmission capabilities, real-time processing, and the use of computational algorithms are foundational to the current Internet of Things (IoT) approach applied to water. In this regard, *WaterWiSe* can be considered a direct precursor of modern smart water resource management systems. While it does not explicitly refer to the term "AI", the use of advanced data analysis and detection algorithms constitutes a functional application of artificial intelligence in hydraulic networks. In terms of outcomes, the project enabled the early detection of incipient leaks that previously required weeks to identify using conventional methods. Furthermore, it improved pressure monitoring capabilities across the network, reducing incidents of excessive pressure that contribute to premature pipe wear. The platform also facilitated faster and more accurate decision-making by system operators, resulting in lower operational costs, increased supply reliability, and improved service quality for end users (Allen et al., 2012).

Figure 4 presents a layered architectural framework of a smart water grid as implemented in advanced urban water management systems. The figure delineates the hierarchical configuration of such a grid across four interdependent layers. At the base lies the physical infrastructure layer, comprising distributed sensors that monitor pressure, flow rate, and water quality in real time. Above this, the connectivity layer facilitates data transmission through low-power wide-area network (LPWAN) technologies such as LoRaWAN and NB-IoT. The third tier, the analytics layer, integrates hydraulic modelling techniques and artificial intelligence algorithms for anomaly detection, leak localisation, and consumption pattern analysis. At the top, the decision-making and governance layer encompasses visualisation dashboards, automated alert systems, and citizen engagement tools that support responsive and participatory water management. This architectural synthesis is informed by empirical case studies such as the *WaterWiSe* initiative in Singapore (Allen et al., 2012) and the *PUMAGUA* programme in Mexico, providing a generalisable model for the implementation of smart water grids in metropolitan environments.

Figure 4. Layered Architecture of a Smart Water Grid: Sensor Networks, Data Transmission, AI-Based Analytics, and Decision-Making Modules.

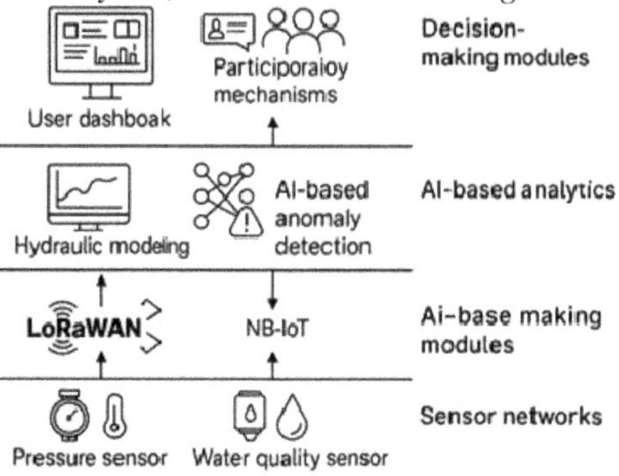

At a time when cities face growing challenges related to climate change, population growth, and infrastructure pressures, the article "Exploring Big Data Applications in Sustainable Urban Infrastructure: A Review" offers a comprehensive overview of how Big Data technology can enhance urban sustainability. The central focus lies on key urban infrastructure sectors—transport, energy, water, waste management, and green spaces—and how the capture and analysis of large volumes of data from sensors, IoT devices, satellite imagery, and administrative records contribute to more informed and efficient decision-making (Ogunkan & Ogunkan, 2025). The authors first define Big Data as a set of information characterised by high variety, volume, velocity, and veracity. These attributes enable near real-time monitoring of urban systems, which is essential for detecting inefficiencies, anticipating issues, and optimising resource use. Notable examples include traffic sensors feeding predictive congestion models, smart energy grids adjusting distribution in response to demand, and waste management systems optimising collection routes using live data. Urban water management is a significant focus within the review. Although the article does not delve into a specific leakage detection technology, it highlights the use of bidirectional IoT sensor networks and Big Data platforms to detect anomalies in water consumption and quality. These tools enable operators to monitor pressure, flow, and contaminants, as well as automate preventive responses, directly contributing to water efficiency and infrastructure resilience. Similarly, in energy and waste management, the article emphasises the role of advanced analytics (machine learning) in classifying electricity consumption patterns, forecasting peaks, reducing losses, optimising waste collection routes, and encouraging recycling behaviours through smart notifications. An important section of the study addresses the challenges and limitations of implementing such systems: technical difficulties such as interoperability between IoT devices and platforms, high processing and storage requirements, and ethical concerns related to data privacy, equity, and digital divides. To mitigate these risks, the authors propose data governance frameworks based on transparency, citizen participation, and open standards (Ogunkan & Ogunkan, 2025). In conclusion, the article posits that the use of Big Data, supported by IoT and artificial intelligence algorithms, is transforming practices such as prefetching, predictive maintenance, evidence-based urban planning, and rapid emergency response. This comprehensive approach fosters more efficient, sustainable, and resilient city management, aligned with the Sustainable Development Goals (SDGs), particularly those concerning urban infrastructure (SDG 9), sustainable cities (SDG 11), and water management (SDG 6).

In 2008, the Water Management, Use and Reuse Programme (*PUMAGUA*) of the National Autonomous University of Mexico (UNAM) emerged as a comprehensive initiative to transform water use at University City, the country's largest university campus. It was developed in response to a diagnostic report identifying critical leaks (up to 50% losses in a 54 km network), low potable water consumption efficiency, and the absence of real-time monitoring (González-Villareal et al., 2018). This smart water network—Smart Water Management (SWM)—integrates sensors within the hydraulic infrastructure for continuous monitoring of both quantity (flow meters in buildings and wells) and quality (residual chlorine, pH, turbidity, and temperature). Information is centralised on a real-time digital platform, the UNAM Water Observatory, which facilitates consumption tracking, anomaly and leakage detection, and both operational and behavioural decision-making. The application of this technology since 2008 has led to remarkable outcomes: potable water consumption on campus was reduced by 25–30%, even as the daily population increased from 135,000 to 180,000 individuals. Leakage rates were halved, with losses reduced from 50 L/s to 25 L/s. The programme also improved water quality through the installation of disinfection plants (sodium hypochlorite), monitoring at 20 points and 56 cisterns, and campus-wide installation of safe water dispensers, reducing plastic bottle usage. Today, real-time readings, measurement systems, and a modern network ensure reliable and safe potable water across the entire campus. A key element of PUMAGUA's success is its participatory approach, involving more than 1,300 community members, 15 analytical groups, students and academics who generate proposals, and trained staff responsible for operating and maintaining the system. This coordinated participation has fostered an institutional culture focused on water efficiency and sustainability. Moreover, PUMAGUA has extended its results beyond the original campus, replicating its models at other UNAM sites such as Juriquilla and FES Aragón, and piloting urban projects in low-income areas. It has also contributed to academic initiatives such as the National Wetlands Inventory, evidencing a strong link between operational management and institutional knowledge. In summary, PUMAGUA's SWM technology comprises automatic meters, continuous quality sensors, online monitoring stations, and a digital management platform. Together, these elements have delivered tangible savings, enhanced water quality, and built a well-informed, service-oriented community committed to sustainable water provision. This emblematic case demonstrates that, within a university setting, the implementation of smart water technologies can yield concrete benefits: reduced losses, financial savings, cultural reinforcement, and replicability. It stands as an international reference in intelligent and participatory water management (González-Villareal et al., 2018).

10. CONCLUSIONS

The convergence of digital technologies with water management strategies, as explored throughout this document, reveals a profound transformation in the way water resources are monitored, utilised, and conserved across various contexts—from agricultural fields to urban infrastructures. The integration of intelligent systems such as IoT-based platforms, machine learning algorithms, wireless sensor networks, and decentralised treatment technologies signifies a paradigm shift from reactive and manual approaches to proactive, predictive, and automated water governance models.

The implementation of smart irrigation systems, particularly in precision agriculture, stands as a salient example of this transformation. The deployment of real-time soil moisture sensors, automated control units, and data-driven decision models such as GesCoN or MPC (Model Predictive Control) has led to significant enhancements in Water Use Efficiency (WUE). Studies conducted in Penn State, India, and elsewhere demonstrate that these systems not only reduce water consumption by up to 40% compared to traditional evapotranspiration-based methods, but also improve crop yields and system resilience (Zhang et al., 2022; Sreelatha Reddy et al., 2024). The affordability of these systems, as demonstrated by prototypes costing under $1,000 USD, renders them accessible to small and medium-scale farmers, enhancing their replicability in diverse agricultural settings.

Parallel advancements in leak detection and predictive maintenance showcase the critical role of AI and IoT in mitigating water losses in domestic and urban networks. The development of smart meters incorporating microcontrollers like ESP32, flow sensors (YF S201), and cloud-integrated platforms such as UBIDOTS has enabled households to remotely monitor consumption patterns, detect anomalies, and receive real-time alerts via mobile interfaces (León Lazo & Macancela Sumba, 2024). Such systems not only improve operational transparency and consumer empowerment but also significantly reduce losses due to silent leaks or billing inaccuracies.

From an infrastructural perspective, modular wastewater treatment plants represent a key innovation in decentralised water management. The utilisation of simulation tools such as GPS-X in diagnosing and resolving inefficiencies in biological treatment processes—as exemplified in the IIT Jammu case—demonstrates the value of model-based design in enhancing plant performance and compliance with environmental discharge standards (Srivastava et al., 2024). Moreover, the capacity to adaptively reconfigure hydraulic retention times and aeration regimes underscores the importance of operational flexibility in small-scale treatment systems.

Greywater reuse technologies, addressed through both systematic reviews and experimental implementations, further reinforce the feasibility of sustainable water recovery in regions suffering from hydric stress. The filtration-disinfection hybrid systems proposed by researchers in Vietnam and Malaysia achieved removal efficiencies exceeding 60% for turbidity, BOD, and microbial contaminants, making them viable for non-potable applications such as domestic irrigation (Ngo et al., 2024).

Smart city initiatives illustrate the broader systemic impacts of intelligent water management. Singapore's *WaterWiSe* project and Mexico's *PUMAGUA* programme have demonstrated the benefits of integrating sensor networks with real-time data processing and automated response mechanisms. These initiatives have successfully reduced non-revenue water, optimised hydraulic pressure, improved service reliability, and fostered a participatory culture of water conservation (Allen et al., 2012; González-Villareal et al., 2018).

Despite these advancements, several technical and institutional challenges remain. The deployment of such technologies often encounters barriers related to interoperability, data privacy, maintenance costs, and skill gaps among users and operators. Addressing these limitations will require robust governance frameworks, inclusive policy design, and capacity-building programmes tailored to local needs.

In conclusion, the smart water systems analysed herein provide compelling evidence of the efficacy and necessity of digital transformation in water management. Their scalability, cost-effectiveness, and adaptability make them indispensable tools in the global effort to achieve sustainable development goals, particularly SDG 6 (Clean Water and Sanitation), SDG 9 (Industry, Innovation, and Infrastructure), and SDG 11 (Sustainable Cities and Communities). The integration of real-time monitoring, predictive analytics, and participatory governance mechanisms stands as a cornerstone for building resilient and intelligent water infrastructures in the face of twenty-first-century environmental and demographic challenges.

REFERENCES

Allen, A., Chua, S., & Lee, H. (2012). Case study: A smart water grid in Singapore. *Water Practice & Technology*, *7*(4), 1–8. DOI: 10.2166/wpt.2012.089

Alvarado-Arias, N., Soria-Delgado, J., Staines, J., & Moya-Almeida, V. (2025). Towards Participatory River Governance Through Citizen Science. *Water (Basel)*, *17*(9), 1358. DOI: 10.3390/w17091358

Ayala, G. C., Macías, C. L., Rúelas, A. L., García, J. M., Enríquez, A. M., Meza, H. C., & Beltrán, J. F. (2011). Diseño de un prototipo didáctico para la implementación de redes de sensores inalámbricos basados en el protocolo Zigbee. *Ra Ximhai*, *7*(3), 3. Advance online publication. DOI: 10.35197/rx.07.03.2011.01.gc

Banda, T. D., & Kumarasamy, M. (2024). Artificial Neural Network (ANN)-Based Water Quality Index (WQI) for Assessing Spatiotemporal Trends in Surface Water Quality—A Case Study of South African River Basins. *Water (Basel)*, *16*(11), 1485. DOI: 10.3390/w16111485

Bilalova, S., Newig, J., & Villamayor-Tomas, S. (2024). *Toward Sustainable Water Governance?* Taking Stock of Paradigms, Practices, and Sustainability Outcomes., DOI: 10.1002/wat2.1762

Bwambale, E., Abagale, F. K., & Anornu, G. K. (2022). Smart irrigation monitoring and control strategies for improving water use efficiency in precision agriculture: A review. *Agricultural Water Management*, *260*, 107324. DOI: 10.1016/j.agwat.2021.107324

Denicia Carral, C., Yáñez García, G. J., Ballinas Hernández, A. L., & Minquiz Xolo, G. M. (2024). Prediction of water quality through dissolved oxygen saturation using data mining: A case study of Puebla, Mexico. *International Journal of Combinatorial Optimization Problems and Informatics*, *15*(5), 228–236. DOI: 10.61467/2007.1558.2024.v15i5.583

Flores-Iwasaki, M., Guadalupe, G. A., Pachas-Caycho, M., Chapa-Gonza, S., Mori-Zabarburú, R. C., & Guerrero-Abad, J. C. (2025). Internet of Things (IoT) Sensors for Water Quality Monitoring in Aquaculture Systems: A Systematic Review and Bibliometric Analysis. *AgriEngineering*, *7*(3), 3. Advance online publication. DOI: 10.3390/agriengineering7030078

González-Villareal, F., Lartigue, C., Hidalgo, J., & Hernández, B. (2018). (PDF) Tecnología SWM de México para la gestión eficiente del agua en universidades: El caso de PUMAGUA, UNAM, Ciudad de México. Retrieved July 4, 2025, from https://www.researchgate.net/publication/329775317_Mexico_SWM_technology_for_efficient_water_management_in_universities_the_case_of_PUMAGUA_UNAM_Mexico_City

Guezouli, L., Guezouli, L., & Bentahrour, A. (2024). (PDF) IoT and AI for Real-time Water Monitoring and Leak Detection. *Journal of Renewable Energies*, *27*(2), 243–281. DOI: 10.54966/jreen.v27i2.1210

Kunt, Y. E. (2025). Development of a Smart Autonomous Irrigation System Using Iot and AI (arXiv:2506.11835). arXiv. https://doi.org//arXiv.2506.11835DOI: 10.48550

Lamrini, M., Ben Mahria, B., Chkouri, M. Y., & Touhafi, A. (2024). Towards Reliability in Smart Water Sensing Technology: Evaluating Classical Machine Learning Models for Outlier Detection. *Sensors (Basel)*, *24*(13), 4084. DOI: 10.3390/s24134084 PMID: 39000863

Lee, S., & Kim, B. (2023). Machine Learning Model for Leak Detection Using Water Pipeline Vibration Sensor. *Sensors (Basel)*, *23*(21), 8935. DOI: 10.3390/s23218935 PMID: 37960635

Lei, Z., Xie, Y., & Ji, X. (2025). Design and implementation of smart iot water Meter based on LoRa. EITCE '24: En Proceedings of the 2024 8th International Conference on Electronic Information Technology and Computer Engineering (pp. 1447-1451). Association for Computing Machinery. DOI: 10.1145/3711129.3711371

León Lazo, R. I., & Macancela Sumba, J. G. (2024). Construcción de un medidor de agua inteligente mediante Arduino para reducir las pérdidas en la distribución de agua. https://dspace.ucacue.edu.ec/handle/ucacue/16769

Liopa-Tsakalidi, A., Thomopoulos, V., Barouchas, P., Boursianis, A. D., & Goudos, S. K. (2024). A LoRaWAN-based IoT platform for smart irrigation in olive groves. *Smart Agricultural Technology*, *9*, 100673. DOI: 10.1016/j.atech.2024.100673

Mohd Yussof, N. A., & Ho, H. W. (2022). Review of Water Leak Detection Methods in Smart Building Applications. *Buildings (Basel, Switzerland)*, *12*(10), 1535. DOI: 10.3390/buildings12101535

Ogunkan, D. V., & Ogunkan, S. K. (2025). Exploring big data applications in sustainable urban infrastructure: A review. *Urban Governance*, *5*(1), 54–68. DOI: 10.1016/j.ugj.2025.02.003

Otamendi, U., Maiza, M., Olaizola, I. G., Sierra, B., Flores, M., & Quartulli, M. (2024). Integrated Water Resource Management in the Segura Hydrographic Basin: An Artificial Intelligence Approach. *Journal of Environmental Management*, *370*, 122526. DOI: 10.1016/j.jenvman.2024.122526 PMID: 39357444

Rajitha, A. K. A., Nagpal, A., Kalra, R., Maan, P., Kumar, A., & Abdul-Zahra, D. S. (2024). Machine Learning and AI-Driven Water Quality Monitoring and Treatment. 3rd International Conference on Applied Research and Engineering (ICARAE2023). E3S Web of Conferences. Volume 505, 2024. DOI: 10.1051/e3sconf/202450503012

Ramírez-Hernández, U. A., Trejo-Macotela, F. R., & Robles-Camarillo, D. (2025). Intelligent system for management and optimization of residential water consumption: Master's thesis summary. International Journal of Combinatorial Optimization Problems and Informatics, 16(1), 226–236. DOI: 10.61467/2007.1558.2025.v16i1.906

Reddy, S., Harivardhagini, & Sreelakshmi. (2024). IoT and Cloud Based Sustainable Smart Irrigation System. International Conference on Renewable Energy, Green Computing and Sustainable Development (ICREGCSD 2023). Volume 472. DOI: 10.1051/e3sconf/202447201026

Rodríguez, A. (2024). Medidor inteligente de agua | Telcel Empresas. https://www.telcel.com/empresas/tendencias/notas/funcion-de-medidor-inteligente-de-agua

Ruiz-Vanoye, J. A., Díaz-Parra, O., Ramos-Fernández, J. C., Trejo-Macotela, F. R., & Xicoténcatl-Pérez, J. M. (2023). Editorial: A brief panorama of water smart cities. *International Journal of Combinatorial Optimization Problems and Informatics*, *14*(1), 1. DOI: 10.61467/2007.1558.2023.v14i1.332

Shaikh, I. N., & Ahammed, M. M. (2020). Quantity and quality characteristics of greywater: A review. *Journal of Environmental Management*, *261*, 110266. DOI: 10.1016/j.jenvman.2020.110266 PMID: 32148323

Singh, Y., & Walingo, T. (2024). Smart Water Quality Monitoring with IoT Wireless Sensor Networks. *Sensors (Basel)*, *24*(9), 9. Advance online publication. DOI: 10.3390/s24092871 PMID: 38732981

Sloat, S. (2025, mayo 1). Farmers are using IoT to take the guesswork out of growing. Business Insider. https://www.businessinsider.com/iot-technology-precision-agriculture-transforming-farming-2025-5

Srivastava, S., Brar, S. K., Rao, S., & Kumar, P. (2024). Assessing operational issues in a modular sewage treatment plant and providing remedies via comprehensive modeling and simulation through GPS-X. *Journal of Water Process Engineering*, *57*, 104678. DOI: 10.1016/j.jwpe.2023.104678

Touil, S., Richa, A., Fizir, M., & Gómez, S. (2022). A review on smart irrigation management strategies and their effect on water savings and crop yield. https://onlinelibrary.wiley.com/doi/10.1002/ird.2735

Xia, W., Chen, X., & Song, C. (2022). A framework of blockchain technology in intelligent water management. *Frontiers in Environmental Science*, *10*, 909606. Advance online publication. DOI: 10.3389/fenvs.2022.909606

Zevallos Apaza, A. A., Onque Gárate, S. S., Canaza Cuadros, A. E. J., & Choqueneira Ccasa, P. M. (2022). Predictive model of water potability through a decision tree in Artificial Intelligence. *Revista Innovación y Software*, *3*(2), 121–131. DOI: 10.48168/innosoft.s9.a72

Zhang, X., He, L., Gioia, F. D., Choi, D., Elia, A., & Heinemann, P. (2022). LoRaWAN based internet of things (IoT) system for precision irrigation in plasticulture fresh-market tomato. *Smart Agricultural Technology*, *2*, 100053. DOI: 10.1016/j.atech.2022.100053

Chapter 6
Safe Cities and Smart Government for Transparency, Equity, and Resilience

Francisco R. Trejo-Macotela
https://orcid.org/0000-0003-2133-3456
Universidad Politécnica de Pachuca, Mexico

ABSTRACT

This chapter critically explores the transformation of urban safety paradigms in response to accelerating urbanisation, complex systemic risks, and emerging technologies. It examines the integration of intelligent surveillance systems, predictive crime analytics, and advanced emergency management platforms, underpinned by artificial intelligence, the Internet of Things (IoT), and multisectoral data fusion. Emphasis is placed on the ethical and governance imperatives surrounding algorithmic transparency, digital equity, and cyber resilience. The analysis demonstrates that safe cities must move beyond reactive models towards anticipatory, inclusive frameworks that embed technological innovation within democratic, human-centred urban governance. The chapter concludes by identifying future challenges—including neuro-rights, post-quantum security, and digital exclusion—and advocates for a holistic, ethically grounded vision of urban resilience.

1. INTRODUCTION

The twenty-first century marks an era of profound and accelerated urban transformation, where unprecedented demographic expansion, escalating environmental

DOI: 10.4018/979-8-3373-5535-1.ch006

crises, and the proliferation of complex, multidimensional threats are redefining the paradigms of urban governance. In this evolving landscape, the imperative to design and maintain safe, resilient, and inclusive cities has transitioned from a policy aspiration to an existential necessity. The demographic forecast articulated by the United Nations (2019), which anticipates that nearly 70% of the global population will reside in urban areas by 2050, underscores the urgency of this transformation. This projected urban concentration entails not only a substantial increase in the density of inhabitants but also a magnified demand on essential public services, transportation systems, healthcare infrastructure, energy supply chains, and security mechanisms. Consequently, the challenges of urban safety are becoming increasingly entangled with issues of environmental sustainability, technological dependency, social equity, and institutional preparedness.

Urban safety, historically construed through the lens of crime prevention and physical protection, now encompasses a vastly more intricate matrix of vulnerabilities. These include, but are not limited to, the growing threat of cyberattacks on critical infrastructure (Oliha et al., 2024), the public health ramifications of environmental degradation, the structural fragility exposed by extreme weather events, and the sociopolitical instability precipitated by rapid and uneven urbanisation. Furthermore, events such as the COVID-19 pandemic have laid bare the fragility of conventional public health systems, revealing the inadequacy of existing frameworks in addressing transboundary crises (OECD, 2020; Allam & Jones, 2021). The confluence of these dynamics necessitates a radical rethinking of urban safety strategies—ones that are data-driven, technologically integrated, and rooted in a holistic understanding of systemic interdependencies.

In this context, the deployment of intelligent technologies ceases to be optional or experimental; it emerges as a core pillar of contemporary urban planning. The convergence of the Internet of Things (IoT), artificial intelligence (AI), big data analytics, and digital twin simulations represents a paradigm shift in the capacity of cities to perceive, analyse, and respond to emerging risks in real time (Lim et al., 2020). These tools enable predictive governance mechanisms that are no longer confined to post-incident reactions but are increasingly oriented towards preemptive and adaptive responses. Whether through early wildfire detection in peri-urban areas, AI-enabled crime pattern recognition, or dynamic environmental quality monitoring, technological integration is reshaping the operational and strategic contours of urban safety.

Yet, as this digital transformation accelerates, it also exposes new vulnerabilities, ethical dilemmas, and equity challenges. The need for comprehensive governance frameworks—anchored in principles of transparency, accountability, and inclusiveness—is more pressing than ever. Urban safety in the digital age is no longer merely a matter of defending physical spaces; it involves safeguarding human dignity, digital rights, and the environmental viability of our cities. As such, the concept of a "safe city" must be redefined to reflect this broader, multidimensional vision—one that prioritises technological innovation, institutional integrity, and social justice in equal measure.

1.1. Global Context: Multifaceted Threats and Urban Transformations

Over the past two decades, cities have undergone a remarkable transformation, not only in scale but also in the nature and complexity of the risks they face. In addition to long-recognised and, to some extent, managed traditional threats – such as street crime, natural disasters (earthquakes, volcanic eruptions, etc.), or industrial accidents – there now exists a growing array of digital, environmental, and health-related challenges that demand innovative and coordinated responses.

In the digital domain, cyberattacks targeting critical infrastructure – such as power grids, water supply systems, public transport, or emergency services – have become a persistent and high-impact threat, capable of paralysing entire cities and endangering lives (Oliha et al., 2024). These attacks are not solely focused on data theft, but also aim at the deliberate disruption of essential services, thereby necessitating robust and proactive urban cybersecurity.

Simultaneously, severe environmental pollution has emerged as a silent public health crisis in many metropolises. Poor air quality, waste accumulation, and noise pollution directly impact citizens' health, requiring technological solutions for monitoring and mitigation. Uncontrolled urban fires and, more recently, public health crises such as the COVID-19 pandemic have exposed cities' vulnerability to events that transcend geographical borders and traditional health systems (OECD, 2020; Allam & Jones, 2021). The pandemic, in particular, underscored the need for resilient healthcare infrastructure, real-time epidemiological monitoring capabilities, and effective public communication systems.

This complex transition towards a more diversified and dynamic risk landscape has significantly accelerated the adoption of smart technologies. The Internet of Things (IoT), with its networks of interconnected sensors; artificial intelligence (AI) for predictive analysis; big data for processing massive volumes of information; and digital twins for simulation and modelling have become indispensable tools. These technologies enable cities to monitor and anticipate risks in real time, transforming emergency management from reactive to predictive. For instance, numerous cities are integrating sensor networks in urban forests and urban-rural interfaces to detect wildfires in their early stages, using AI to predict their spread. Similarly, air quality sensors are deployed across urban grids to identify pollution sources, and machine learning models are used to detect crime patterns and allocate police resources more efficiently (Oliha et al., 2024; Lim et al., 2020).

Moreover, extreme weather events – such as sudden floods, prolonged heatwaves, and increasingly intense hurricanes – exacerbated by global climate change, have drastically increased the need for robust early warning systems, adaptive green infrastructure (such as floodable parks or green roofs that mitigate the heat island effect), and data-driven emergency management platforms that allow for coordinated and effective disaster responses (UNDRR, 2022). This includes everything from population evacuations to aid distribution and post-disaster recovery.

On the other hand, increasing urbanisation has not only generated environmental and physical safety challenges but has also highlighted profound inequalities in access to safe and quality services, particularly in informal settlements, marginalised neighbourhoods, or historically underserved communities. This social and ethical challenge compels cities to rethink the very concept of urban safety, considering not only crime prevention or disaster protection, but also equity, inclusion, and the safeguarding of fundamental rights for all inhabitants, regardless of socioeconomic background or geographical location. In this sense, safety is a universal right.

Figure 1 provides a conceptual map of the multifaceted components constituting urban safety in contemporary cities. It illustrates how digital infrastructure, environmental resilience, social equity, public health, and governance interlink to shape a holistic model of urban risk governance.

Figure 1. Interconnected Dimensions of Urban Safety in the Digital Era.

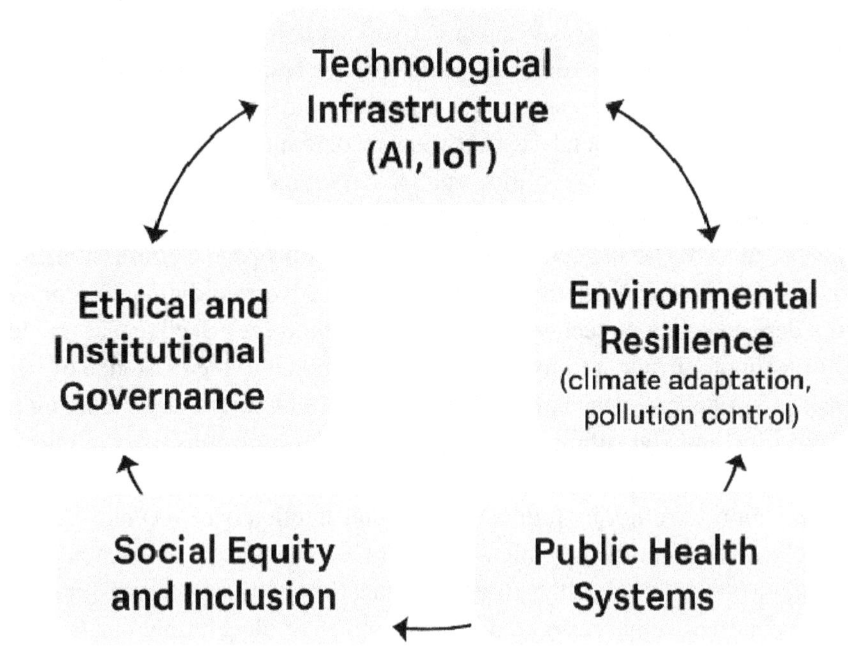

1.2. Towards a Comprehensive Definition of a Safe City in the Digital Age

The concept of a safe city has undergone a remarkable and significant evolution, expanding beyond traditional interpretations. In the past, the notion was primarily associated with police surveillance, crime control, and the physical protection of people and property, often through reactive means. However, today, a safe city is understood as a complex and multifaceted ecosystem. It is a dynamic environment that synergistically integrates resilient physical infrastructure, intelligent and interconnected technological networks, active and empowered citizen participation, and robust legal frameworks that not only protect physical safety but also safeguard digital rights and individual privacy (EIU, 2021; UNESCO, 2020).

This expanded definition entails the strategic implementation of digital platforms and advanced monitoring systems to gain real-time situational awareness of the urban environment. These platforms enable the anticipation of incidents (from criminal activity to disaster risk), the efficient coordination of multisectoral responses across different agencies (police, fire brigades, medical services, disaster management), and the empowerment of citizens through information and participation tools. Leading global cities such as Singapore, Barcelona, and New York have clearly demonstrated that the intelligent integration of sensor networks, predictive analytics algorithms, and accessible mobile applications can yield tangible results: significantly reducing emergency response times, enhancing the efficiency and transparency of police operations, and strengthening social trust between citizens and institutions. For example, predictive analytics can assist in the strategic deployment of patrols in areas with higher probabilities of incidents, while citizen apps enable the immediate reporting of risk situations, triggering coordinated responses (European Commission, 2022).

It is essential to recognise that security in these advanced digital environments does not depend solely on technology. On the contrary, the effectiveness and legitimacy of technological solutions are intrinsically linked to the existence of ethical and transparent governance. This means that the use of surveillance technologies, data collection, and algorithmic applications must be subject to strict public scrutiny and clear regulatory frameworks. Accordingly, global institutions such as the European Union (through its proposed Artificial Intelligence Act) and UNESCO have developed regulatory and ethical frameworks that promote the responsible use of surveillance technologies, the rigorous protection of personal data (preventing misuse or unauthorised access), and the prevention of algorithmic discrimination (ensuring that AI systems do not perpetuate or amplify pre-existing social biases, particularly in sensitive areas such as justice or security) (European Commission, 2022; UNESCO, 2020).

In conclusion, a safe city in the digital age is far more than a city merely protected from external threats. Fundamentally, it is a city that guarantees dignity, rights, and comprehensive well-being for all its inhabitants. This is achieved through an ecosystem of integrated, sustainable, and crucially, human-centred technological solutions, where technology serves as a facilitator in building more just, inclusive, and resilient communities. This aligns with the definition proposed by Ruiz-Vanoye & Díaz-Parra (2022), which characterises a safe city as a community using technology to reduce crime likelihood and foster a comfortable environment. The vision is of cities that not only withstand challenges but thrive despite them, offering a safe and high-quality living environment for each of their citizens.

The evolving notion of urban safety demands a systemic comparison between traditional approaches and the emerging smart city paradigms. Table 1 below contrasts key elements of both models, highlighting the technological, ethical, and governance transitions shaping twenty-first-century urban resilience.

Table 1. Comparative Dimensions of Traditional vs. Smart Urban Safety Approaches.

Dimension	Traditional Urban Safety	Smart Urban Safety Framework
Main Focus	Crime prevention and physical protection	Integrated risk governance and resilience
Technologies Used	CCTV, police patrols	AI, IoT, digital twins, predictive analytics
Response Mode	Reactive	Predictive and proactive
Data Governance	Fragmented, limited integration	Multisectoral data fusion with ethical oversight
Citizen Role	Passive recipients	Active sensors and co-producers of safety
Ethical Considerations	Rarely addressed	Central (privacy, algorithmic bias, inclusion)

2. INTELLIGENT SURVEILLANCE SYSTEMS: AN EVOLVING ECOSYSTEM

In the contemporary configuration of smart urban environments, intelligent surveillance systems have assumed a pivotal role in redefining the operational frameworks of urban safety, risk mitigation, and crisis response. Far removed from the passive and often limited monitoring capabilities of traditional closed-circuit television (CCTV), today's surveillance architecture constitutes an intricate, multilayered ecosystem comprising real-time data acquisition, advanced analytics, and dynamic interoperability across sectors. This profound transformation is underpinned by the exponential advancement of both hardware—namely, high-resolution sensors, embedded systems, and edge-computing units—and software, particularly artificial intelligence (AI) algorithms capable of pattern recognition, anomaly detection, and contextual analysis. Such systems are no longer confined to observation alone; they have evolved into proactive instruments of decision support, predictive modelling, and automated intervention.

The fusion of the Internet of Things (IoT), machine learning, and geospatial analytics has enabled the development of a distributed surveillance infrastructure that mirrors the complexity of urban life. These technologies facilitate the seamless integration of heterogeneous data streams—from video feeds and acoustic sensors to environmental monitors and citizen-generated alerts—thereby constructing a situational awareness framework that is both granular and comprehensive. For instance, facial recognition algorithms, though ethically contentious, are increasingly embedded in urban surveillance grids for the identification of persons of interest, while environmental sensors concurrently monitor hazardous gas levels or seismic vibrations to pre-empt infrastructural collapse (Oliha et al., 2024; Smith & Miller, 2021).

Nevertheless, this techno-centric expansion is not without significant ethical, legal, and societal implications. The deployment of pervasive surveillance mechanisms must be scrutinised under the lens of data protection, algorithmic transparency, and civil liberties, particularly in contexts where disproportionate surveillance may exacerbate existing inequalities or reinforce discriminatory practices (Leslie, 2020). Hence, the evolution of intelligent surveillance systems must be accompanied by stringent regulatory oversight and inclusive policy frameworks. Ultimately, the true efficacy of such systems lies not merely in their technical sophistication, but in their capacity to harmonise public safety with democratic values, accountability, and human dignity.

2.1. IoT Devices and Advanced Sensors: The Eyes and Ears of the Smart City

The mass deployment of Internet of Things (IoT) systems is marking a watershed moment in urban surveillance (Sharma et al., 2024). By integrating an extensive network of interconnected sensors, intelligent cameras, and embedded technologies in everyday elements—such as vehicles, street lighting, and traffic signals—a surveillance infrastructure is being constructed that enables collaborative, real-time monitoring, far beyond what human capabilities alone could achieve.

- **AI-Enabled Cameras and Facial Recognition**:

Intelligent cameras equipped with artificial intelligence have become the cornerstone of many modern surveillance systems. These cameras do not merely record video but are capable of processing and analysing imagery in real time, detecting objects, suspicious activities, crowd densities, and even unusual movement patterns. Among these capabilities, facial recognition technologies have advanced remarkably over recent decades, achieving impressive accuracy under ideal conditions. However, their large-scale deployment in urban environments brings with it serious and complex ethical and human rights implications. Numerous academic studies and civil society reports have demonstrated that many facial recognition implementations may exhibit racial and gender biases, with significantly lower accuracy rates for racial minorities and women, thereby exacerbating existing inequalities and perpetuating racial or social profiling (Leslie, 2020; Smith & Miller, 2021). For instance, some studies have found that facial recognition software may have an error rate up to ten times higher for dark-skinned women than for white men. This algorithmic bias is not inherent to the technology itself but reflects the training datasets used, which frequently lack sufficient diversity.

The case of London serves as a clear example of these tensions. The Metropolitan Police have expanded the use of retrospective facial recognition (RFR), involving the scanning of existing CCTV footage databases to identify individuals, rather than conducting live scans on the streets. While law enforcement authorities argue that it is a vital tool in combating serious crime, its implementation has provoked strong criticism due to its impact on citizens' privacy and the potential for misuse. Concerns have been intensified by the absence of comprehensive and transparent data impact assessments, raising serious questions about how personal data is managed and the risks of intrusive mass surveillance (United Kingdom WIRED, 2021). The debate surrounding facial recognition is not solely focused on efficacy but centres on the delicate balance between security and individual freedoms, as well as the need for ethical governance and stringent regulations (IEEE Public Safety Technology, 2025).

- **Advanced Environmental Sensors**:

Beyond cameras, the urban IoT network is complemented by a wide array of environmental sensors. In addition to traditional devices designed to measure air quality (particulate matter levels, pollutant gases) and noise pollution – which already enable the generation of risk maps and public alerts – more specialised sensors with significantly enhanced capabilities are being introduced. These include sensors that detect unusual vibrations in structures (bridges, buildings, tunnels), which may indicate material fatigue or seismic damage; sensors that identify the presence of hazardous chemicals in the air or water, which are crucial for the early detection of industrial leaks or chemical attacks; and sensors that monitor structural anomalies in real time. Such systems allow for the issuance of preventive alerts that can drastically reduce risks related to infrastructure collapse, undetected pollution, or critical failures, thereby protecting lives and property (Oliha et al., 2024). For instance, in cities with high seismic activity, sensors embedded in buildings can provide structural integrity data following an earthquake, expediting safety assessments.

- **Collaborative Detection and Sensor Networks**:

The true power of intelligent surveillance systems lies in the interconnection and collaboration of multiple devices. These are not isolated sensors but rather intelligent networks sharing data in real time. This interconnection may include cameras installed in emergency vehicles (ambulances, police cars, fire engines) transmitting live footage to command centres; adaptive traffic lights that not only regulate vehicle flow but also integrate cameras or environmental sensors; and even wearable devices (such as smartwatches or wristbands) that could, in the future, contribute to fall detection among the elderly or the monitoring of vital signs during emergencies. This technological convergence enables the construction of distributed sensor networks that drastically improve spatial and temporal coverage, as well as responsiveness to any type of incident. By fusing data from diverse sources, surveillance becomes more dynamic, contextualised, and holistic, allowing authorities to obtain a comprehensive view of a critical situation, ranging from a security incident to a natural disaster.

The backbone of intelligent surveillance systems lies in the diversity of sensors deployed across urban infrastructures. As demonstrated by Campero-Jurado et al. (2019), embedded IoT systems leveraging Vehicle-to-Everything (V2X) technologies enhance real-time communication and decision-making in intelligent urban environments. This complements the chapter's discussion on integrated sensor networks and real-time data flow in intelligent surveillance. Table 2 outlines the types of sensors used and their specific contributions to public safety.

Table 2. Typology of Urban Sensors and Their Safety Functions.

Sensor Type	Monitored Variables	Safety Applications
Air Quality Sensors	PM2.5, NO_2, CO, O_3	Pollution alerts, respiratory health risk management
Structural Vibration Sensors	Seismic activity, material fatigue	Early warnings of potential infrastructure collapse
Acoustic Sensors (ShotSpotter)	Gunshots, loud anomalies	Rapid firearm incident localisation
Facial Recognition Cameras	Biometric facial patterns	Identification of suspects (subject to ethical constraints)
Thermal Sensors	Temperature variations	Fire detection, body heat detection in rescue operations

2.2. Video and Audio Analysis: The Intelligence Behind Raw Data

The vast amount of data generated by IoT devices would be rendered useless without advanced analytical capabilities. It is in this realm that artificial intelligence applied to video and audio analysis plays a pivotal role, offering significant opportunities for enhancing safety, yet also raising regulatory and ethical challenges that require careful consideration.

Figure 2 outlines the functional architecture of an intelligent surveillance system, highlighting the integration of IoT sensors, data analytics platforms, and command centres. This layered configuration underpins real-time monitoring, predictive modelling, and automated emergency response.

Figure 2. Architecture of an AI-Enabled Surveillance Ecosystem.

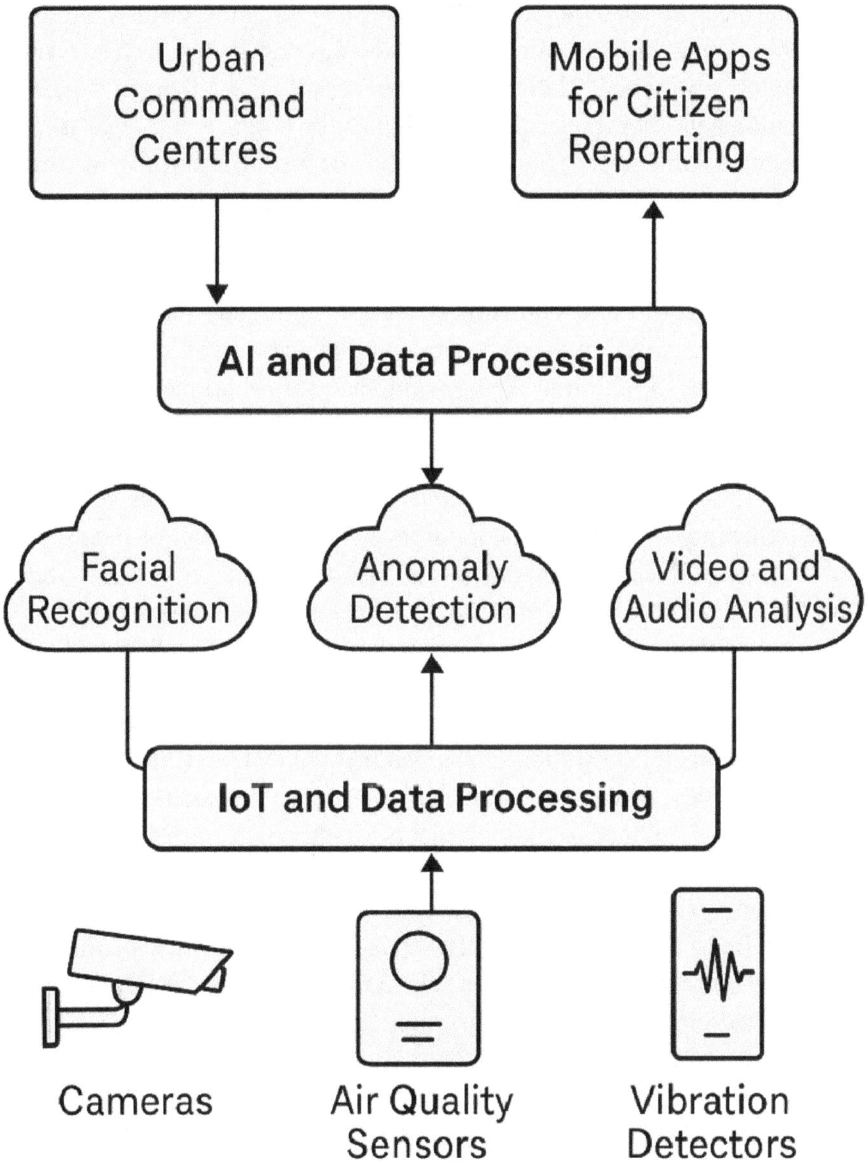

- **Deepfake Detection and Generative Watermarking**: With the relentless proliferation of AI-generated manipulated multimedia content – commonly referred to as "deepfakes" (highly realistic yet falsified images, videos, or audio) – the dissemination of disinformation and identity spoofing have become serious threats to public safety and information integrity. In response, countermeasure technologies such as invisible digital watermarking for both video and audio content are being actively developed. These watermarks are imperceptibly embedded digital codes that certify the authenticity and origin of multimedia files, enhancing traceability for forensic and legal investigations and helping to curb the spread of disinformation and fake news that may destabilise society (IEEE Public Safety Technology, 2025). Moreover, methods are being explored to embed these watermarks directly into the output of generative AI models – a technique known as generative watermarking.
- **Intelligent Audio and Gunshot Detection**: Solutions such as ShotSpotter utilise strategically deployed acoustic microphone networks in urban areas to detect gunfire in real time. The system analyses sound patterns to differentiate gunshots from other urban noises and triangulates the precise location of the event. The underlying premise is that this allows law enforcement to respond more swiftly to firearm-related incidents. However, the effectiveness and reliability of such technologies have been the subject of intense debate and scrutiny. Recent investigations and critical analyses reveal that over 80% of alerts generated by systems like ShotSpotter may be false positives—that is, sounds incorrectly identified as gunfire ("What is ShotSpotter?", 2024). These may include fireworks, car backfires, banging noises, or even industrial sounds. Such false positives can lead to unnecessary police deployments that, unfortunately, disproportionately affect vulnerable communities and racial minorities, where these systems tend to be implemented more densely (ShotSpotter Wikipedia, 2024; "What is ShotSpotter?", 2024; Calhoun et al., 2021). This biased deployment can result in over-policing in these areas, exacerbating existing tensions, increasing unwarranted police encounters, and undermining community trust. The debate hinges on whether the benefits of rapid detection outweigh the social and ethical costs of false alarms and intensified surveillance in certain communities.

The evolution of intelligent surveillance systems—from basic IoT devices to AI-based video and audio analysis—presents vast potential for improving urban safety and emergency management. However, this technological progress must be accompanied by a robust ethical and regulatory framework that transparently and proactively addresses issues of privacy, algorithmic bias, and civil rights implications.

Only then can we build truly safe cities that are also just, equitable, and respectful of the dignity of all their inhabitants.

3. EMERGENCY MANAGEMENT PLATFORMS: ORCHESTRATING THE INTELLIGENT RESPONSE

In the contemporary landscape of urban risk governance, emergency management has undergone a paradigmatic transformation—evolving from a traditionally reactive model into an integrated, intelligence-driven ecosystem enabled by digital platforms and advanced coordination tools. The increasing frequency, complexity, and unpredictability of urban emergencies—ranging from natural disasters and technological accidents to public health crises and security threats—has exposed the limitations of conventional response mechanisms. In response, the emergence of specialised emergency management platforms has enabled a fundamental restructuring of urban resilience strategies. These platforms function as strategic command infrastructures that consolidate data, coordinate resources, and execute multilateral actions across agencies, thereby enabling cities to transition from fragmented decision-making to coherent, real-time orchestration of crisis response (SafetyCulture Content Team, 2024; Veoci, n.d.).

Such platforms are characterised by a high degree of interoperability and configurability, allowing them to integrate heterogeneous data streams from IoT sensor networks, emergency call systems, social media inputs, and citizen reports. Leveraging artificial intelligence, geospatial analytics, and cloud-based communication, they facilitate the automation and optimisation of critical tasks such as resource allocation, emergency planning, risk forecasting, and post-event analysis. Platforms like SafetyCulture, Veoci, and E-Plan exemplify this technological shift by providing multifunctional environments where emergency teams can not only manage operations, but also simulate scenarios, train personnel, and systematically evaluate performance outcomes (Veoci, n.d.).

Moreover, the role of citizens has been profoundly redefined within this framework. Emergency platforms now enable public participation through mobile applications that empower individuals to report incidents, receive alerts, and engage in collective safety efforts. In this manner, the population becomes an active node in the safety network, contributing to real-time situational awareness and enhancing the granularity of information available to response teams (Irwin et al., 2024).

Nevertheless, this digitalisation must be accompanied by robust governance mechanisms to ensure data security, ethical usage, and inclusivity. A technologically advanced emergency response system must not only optimise operational efficiency but also uphold the principles of transparency, equity, and human dignity—particularly in times of acute vulnerability. In this regard, emergency management platforms represent not merely a technical innovation, but a strategic axis for fostering truly resilient, just, and intelligent urban systems.

3.1. Specialised Software: The Brain of Coordinated Response

The backbone of modern emergency management lies in specialised software that provides advanced functionalities for efficient coordination, data-driven decision-making, and agile response. Leading tools in the market such as SafetyCulture, Veoci, and E-Plan illustrate the diversity and sophistication of these solutions, each with its distinct strengths (SafetyCulture Content Team, 2024; FEMA, n.d.; Veoci, n.d.).

- **SafetyCulture (formerly iAuditor)**:

This mobile and web platform has gained significant traction for its capacity to standardise protocols and procedures during emergency situations. SafetyCulture enables first response teams and crisis management organisations to create customisable digital inspection checklists that guide users through critical steps during an incident. This ensures that essential tasks—such as equipment checks or area evacuations—are not overlooked. The platform also facilitates online training for personnel and volunteers, ensuring that all stakeholders are well-prepared and up-to-date with the latest protocols. Its real-time response coordination feature allows for task assignment, progress tracking, and instant communication among team members, even when geographically dispersed. In 2024, SafetyCulture was recognised as one of the top emergency management tools, largely for its ability to enhance data-driven decision-making. By digitising incident records and damage assessments, the platform enables managers to analyse patterns, identify bottlenecks, and optimise future responses. Its adoption extends beyond public safety into industry and construction, underscoring its versatility in high-risk environments (SafetyCulture Content Team, 2024).

- **Veoci: The Virtual Emergency Operations Centre (EOC)**:

Veoci has positioned itself as a comprehensive platform functioning as a fully virtual Emergency Operations Centre. It is especially popular in complex environments such as universities, hospitals, large corporations, and public utilities, where coordination is paramount. The platform offers a complete suite of tools covering the full emergency management cycle:

- **Planning**: Facilitates the creation and storage of detailed emergency plans, contact lists, available resources, and communication protocols.
- **Drills**: Enables the execution of realistic simulations in which teams can practise responses in a virtual environment, identify weaknesses, and improve coordination without real-world risk.
- **Operational Coordination**: During real incidents, Veoci centralises information, allowing incident commanders to view resource status, team locations, situational maps, and real-time reports—thus optimising personnel and equipment deployment.
- **Mass Notifications**: Its capability to send mass or targeted alerts to key personnel, the community, or specific stakeholder groups ensures that critical information is disseminated rapidly, enhancing safety and reducing uncertainty.
- **Post-Event Analysis**: Following an emergency, Veoci supports comprehensive post-incident assessments by collecting and analysing data, thus enhancing future resilience. Its flexibility and adaptability were evident during the California wildfires of January 2025, where it was used to coordinate the evacuation of thousands, the deployment of firefighters, and the management of temporary shelters—demonstrating its effectiveness in large-scale disaster scenarios (Veoci, n.d.).

- **E-Plan: A Pillar for Chemical Emergencies**:

E-Plan is a specialised tool that has become indispensable for managing chemical and hazardous material emergencies. Widely used by fire departments and emergency response agencies in the United States, this platform houses detailed databases on chemical risks, including information about hazardous substances stored in industrial and commercial facilities, their properties, associated risks, and mitigation procedures. It also integrates safety codes, specialised guides, and material safety data sheets (MSDS), delivering critical information in seconds to teams responding to toxic spills or releases. Its free access makes it an invaluable resource, especially for small- and medium-sized cities lacking the capacity to develop proprietary hazardous materials databases, thereby enhancing public safety by ensuring responders have the knowledge required to manage extremely dangerous situations safely and effectively (FEMA, n.d.).

Emergency response platforms offer advanced and diverse functionalities tailored to the complex nature of contemporary urban crises. Table 3 synthesises the comparative features of three prominent platforms discussed in this chapter.

Table 3. Core Functionalities of Leading Emergency Management Platforms.

Platform	Core Functionalities	Specialised Use Cases
SafetyCulture	Custom digital checklists, remote coordination, training modules	Industrial safety, infrastructure inspection
Veoci	Virtual EOC, resource tracking, scenario simulation, mass alerts	Large-scale evacuations, universities, healthcare
E-Plan	Chemical substance databases, response protocols, regulatory integration	Hazardous material response, small municipalities

(Sources: SafetyCulture Content Team, 2024; Veoci, n.d.; FEMA, n.d.)

Interoperability is a key success factor for these platforms. The use of open APIs (Application Programming Interfaces) is crucial to enable seamless communication and data exchange among police, healthcare, transportation, emergency services, and other governmental agencies. This multi-layered real-time coordination capability enables a truly unified and efficient response to any incident, from a traffic accident to a large-scale terrorist attack.

3.2. Citizen Participation: The Active Role of Citizens as Sensors

In the era of smart cities, the public has become an active and vital sensor in emergency management. Citizens are no longer passive recipients of information; rather, they can actively contribute to early detection and the provision of crucial data, thereby enhancing situational awareness for authorities.

- **Alert and Citizen Reporting Applications**: Mobile applications such as CrisisGo exemplify how technology empowers citizens to act in risk scenarios. These apps include functionalities such as geolocated panic buttons, which allow users to send silent or direct alerts to authorities with precise location data in cases of personal emergency (e.g., assault, medical incident, or harassment). Silent alerts can be distributed to response teams or predefined contacts using low-energy communication technologies such as LoRaWAN, ensuring communication even in areas with limited connectivity. The apps also facilitate immediate communication with emergency teams via instant messaging or calls. CrisisGo has proven particularly effective in educational contexts. In 2020, it recorded 486,000 alerts and 48 million critical messages across schools in the United States, highlighting its essential role in ensuring school safety and crisis communication (Irwin et al., 2024; CrisisGo, n.d.). The ability to report minor incidents, such as water leaks or power outages, further contributes to improved everyday urban management.

- **Social Media Monitoring**: Social networks have become invaluable and spontaneous sources of real-time information during emergencies. Active monitoring of platforms such as X (formerly Twitter), Facebook, or Instagram allows public safety and emergency management agencies to rapidly detect incidents such as flash floods (through user-shared images and videos), civil disturbances (via eyewitness reports), or medical emergencies (via help requests)—often even before emergency services receive calls. Natural language processing algorithms and sentiment analysis can filter noise and extract relevant information, enabling rapid, targeted action. This real-time crowdsourcing of information complements sensor and camera data, offering a human and contextualised perspective of unfolding events.

3.3. Automation with AI and Drones: Enhancing Response Capabilities

The integration of artificial intelligence (AI) and the use of drones are elevating emergency management to a new level of automation and efficiency, augmenting human capabilities and accelerating response times.

- **Rapid Response Drones**: Drones (unmanned aerial vehicles) have established themselves as invaluable tools in emergency management, especially in scenarios that are difficult to access or pose high risks to personnel. They have proven highly effective in various applications:
    - **Defibrillator Delivery**: In remote or hard-to-reach areas, drones equipped with automated external defibrillators (AEDs) can reach cardiac arrest victims much faster than land-based ambulances, significantly increasing survival chances.
    - **Structural Damage Assessment**: After disasters such as earthquakes, tsunamis, or explosions, drones equipped with high-resolution cameras and LIDAR sensors can swiftly survey affected areas to assess structural damage in buildings and infrastructure, identifying hazardous zones and guiding search and rescue operations.
    - **Search and Rescue**: Equipped with thermal cameras, drones can locate trapped or injured individuals in debris, forested areas, or bodies of water—even in low-visibility conditions.
    - **Fire Monitoring**: Drones provide real-time aerial views of forest or urban fires, helping firefighters understand fire extent, wind direction, and resource deployment. Their use is growing in European and Asian cities that are investing in emergency drone fleets, recognising their life-saving potential and operational efficiency.

- **AI for Automated Resource Allocation**: In crisis scenarios, the ability to allocate the right resources (patrols, ambulances, technical teams, firefighters) to the right location at the right time is critical—and can mean the difference between life and death. AI plays a transformative role in this domain. AI algorithms can process real-time data on emergency locations, incident severity (using sensor data, citizen reports, or video analysis), the availability and capacity of nearby response units, and traffic conditions. With this data, AI can recommend or even autonomously execute the optimal allocation of resources, minimising response times and maximising efficiency. This alleviates human teams from complex coordination tasks, allowing them to focus on direct intervention.
- **Advanced AI in EOC Platforms**: The integration of advanced AI into Emergency Operations Centre (EOC) platforms represents the next evolutionary step. These AI capabilities extend beyond resource allocation and include decision-support systems that analyse vast amounts of historical and real-time data to forecast crisis evolution, recommend mitigation strategies, or identify vulnerabilities. According to reports by FEMA (United States Federal Emergency Management Agency), AI implementation in emergency management can reduce response times by up to 30%. This is achieved by automating incident classification, optimising communication, forecasting resource demand, and providing actionable information for decision-making—ultimately resulting in lives saved and damage reduced.

In summary, emergency management platforms—empowered by specialised software, active citizen participation, and intelligent automation through AI and drones—are creating a more robust, proactive, and efficient urban safety ecosystem. This enables cities not only to respond more effectively to crises but also to be fundamentally more resilient in the face of future challenges.

4. PREDICTIVE CRIME ANALYSIS: ANTICIPATING URBAN SECURITY IN THE DIGITAL ERA

The emergence of predictive crime analysis marks a pivotal shift in the strategic management of urban security, transforming traditional paradigms that were historically reactive into frameworks characterised by anticipatory intelligence and data-driven foresight. In the context of increasingly complex, heterogeneous, and dynamic urban environments, the ability to anticipate potential criminal activity, identify emerging patterns, and deploy preventive measures in a timely and efficient manner has become an indispensable component of contemporary public safety governance. This transformation is underpinned by the integration of artificial intelligence (AI), machine learning (ML), and advanced geospatial analysis, which collectively enable the processing of vast volumes of structured and unstructured data to detect non-obvious correlations and probabilistic risk zones (Sundharakumar et al., 2024; Vasuki et al., 2024).

Predictive crime analysis is not solely concerned with forecasting isolated criminal events; rather, it constitutes a broader epistemological framework that seeks to model the spatiotemporal dynamics of crime as an emergent property of urban complexity. By incorporating multifactorial datasets—ranging from historical crime statistics and socioeconomic indicators to environmental variables and mobility flows—advanced algorithms can generate highly granular and context-sensitive forecasts that inform strategic decision-making at both the operational and policy levels. This enables the proactive allocation of police patrols, the strategic design of urban interventions, and the tailoring of community-based prevention programmes aimed at mitigating underlying risk factors (Mohler et al., 2015).

Nevertheless, the deployment of predictive policing technologies raises profound ethical, legal, and social concerns. Issues such as algorithmic bias, the reinforcement of structural inequalities, and the risk of unjustified surveillance in historically marginalised communities must be critically examined through transparent auditing mechanisms and regulatory safeguards (Lum & Isaac, 2016). Furthermore, the protection of individual privacy and the responsible use of personal data necessitate the adoption of privacy-preserving methodologies such as differential privacy and federated learning, as outlined by Tera et al. (2024) and Dwork & Roth (2014). Moreover, optimisation approaches for anticipating urban expansion, such as the SVM (Support Vector Machine) model enhanced by SHAP (SHapley Additive exPlanations) values for predicting urban growth in Mexican cities, demonstrate how machine learning methods can inform proactive, data-driven urban planning strategies (Llamas-Valenzuela et al., 2025).

Thus, predictive crime analysis represents not merely a technological innovation but a normative challenge: how to harness the predictive power of AI in ways that are both effective and equitable. Only through a careful balance between analytical precision, institutional accountability, and civic trust can predictive systems truly contribute to a safer and more just urban future.

Machine Learning plays a foundational role in predictive crime analysis. Table 4 provides an overview of commonly implemented models, their strengths, and specific urban safety applications.

Table 4. Main Predictive Crime Analysis Models and Their Characteristics.

ML Model	Key Features	Urban Safety Applications
Deep Neural Networks	Processes non-linear and complex spatial-temporal patterns	Forecasting crime hotspots with high spatial accuracy
Random Forest	Ensemble-based, integrates socioeconomic variables	Reduces false positives and improves context sensitivity
Support Vector Machines	Effective with smaller, structured datasets	Classifying crime typologies

(Based on: Sundharakumar et al., 2024; Vasuki et al., 2024)

4.1. Machine Learning Models: The Foundation of Criminal Forecasting

At the core of predictive crime analysis lie Machine Learning (ML) models. These sophisticated algorithms are capable of identifying intricate relationships and hidden patterns within extensive datasets, thereby transforming how law enforcement agencies anticipate and respond to criminal activity. Unlike traditional statistical methods, ML integrates and processes multiple data sources simultaneously, enabling a far more granular and dynamic understanding of the urban environment.

Data sources utilised by these models are remarkably diverse and encompass:

- **Historical police records**: Including crime type, location, time, day of the week, and modus operandi.
- **Socioeconomic indicators**: Such as poverty rates, unemployment levels, educational attainment, population density, and income distribution, which often correlate with specific types of criminal activity.
- **Weather conditions**: Factors such as temperature, humidity, and precipitation, which may influence criminal behaviour by affecting public presence or visibility.
- **Urban mobility data**: Information regarding vehicular and pedestrian flows and public transport usage, indicating high-density areas or potential escape routes.
- **Geographical information**: Physical environment characteristics, such as the presence of parks, bars, retail outlets, surveillance cameras, or lighting infrastructure.

The efficacy of such models has been demonstrated through multiple case studies. For instance, Sundharakumar et al. (2024) deployed deep neural networks—an advanced form of deep learning algorithm inspired by the human brain—to predict crime outbreaks in specific urban districts. This method enabled the processing of highly complex spatial and temporal patterns, achieving an impressive 85% accuracy in identifying future crime "hotspots." In essence, the system reliably forecasted where and when criminal activity was most likely to surge.

Figure 3 delineates the typical workflow of predictive crime analysis based on machine learning. It visualises the data flow from diverse sources through model training to the generation of actionable intelligence for strategic deployment.

Figure 3. Predictive Crime Analysis Workflow Using Machine Learning (Sundhar-akumar et al., 2024); Vasuki et al. (2024)).

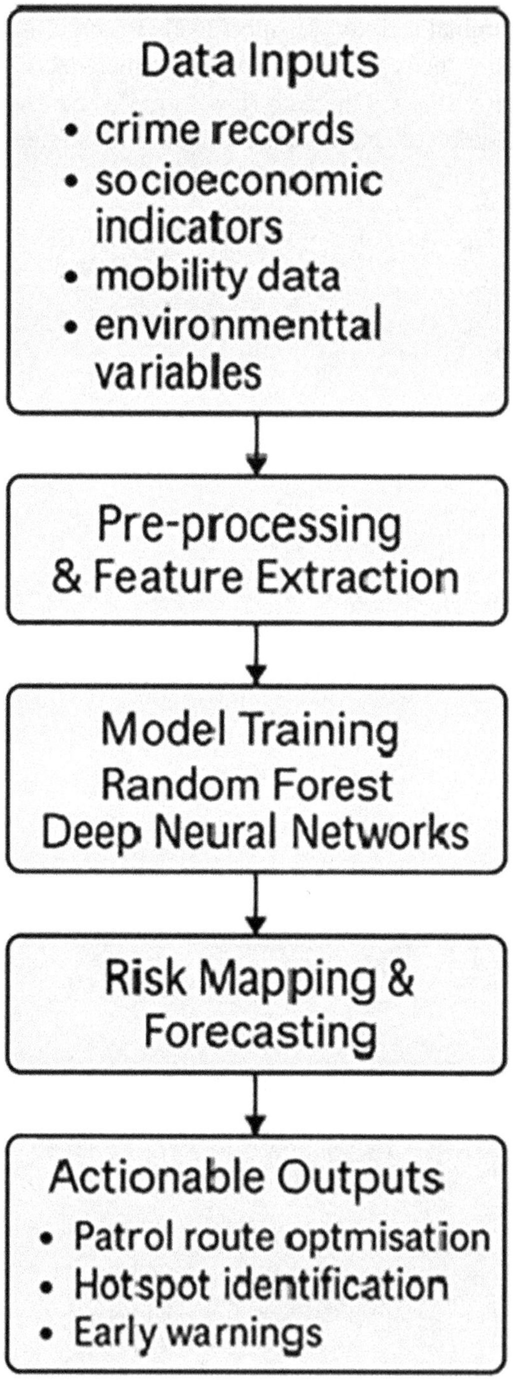

Conversely, Vasuki et al. (2024) adopted a different approach by developing Random Forest models (an ensemble algorithm combining multiple decision trees) for crime prediction. Their key innovation was the integration of detailed socioeconomic data—poverty, unemployment, and education levels—into the analysis of criminal patterns in Medellín, Colombia. The inclusion of social variables, often disregarded by models based solely on police data, was instrumental in contextualising criminal activity and reducing false positives by 12%. This reduction is crucial, as it minimises the unnecessary deployment of police resources to low-risk areas, thus avoiding the stigmatisation and potential harassment of innocent communities.

Beyond accuracy, the deployment of such systems entails a fundamental concern: the protection of personal data privacy. To address this, developers and regulators are increasingly incorporating privacy-preserving techniques such as differential privacy and federated encryption.

- **Differential Privacy** (Dwork & Roth, 2014) is a cryptographic technique that introduces controlled randomness or "noise" into datasets, such that general patterns can be discerned while individual-specific information remains indecipherable. This enables the training of ML models and statistical analysis on large datasets without compromising personal or sensitive data.
- **Federated Learning**, on the other hand, allows ML models to be trained locally (e.g., within police databases or on officers' mobile devices) without transferring raw data to a central server. Only the training parameters and aggregated outcomes are shared centrally to construct a more robust global model. This approach adheres strictly to regulations such as the EU General Data Protection Regulation (GDPR) and similar national frameworks, including the Personal Data Protection Laws in various Latin American jurisdictions (Arenas-Ramiro, 2022). These techniques ensure that the predictive power of ML is harnessed without infringing on citizens' fundamental privacy rights.

4.2. Proactive Prevention: From Analysis to Strategic Action

The true value of predictive analysis lies in its capacity to design and implement proactive prevention strategies, thereby shifting police response from reactive to anticipatory.

One of the most prominent and debated applications is predictive patrolling. This method dynamically optimises police patrol routes and schedules based on crime heat maps (hotspots) generated by ML models. The aim is to deploy officers at locations and times where crimes are statistically more likely to occur, thereby maximising deterrence and response capacity. In Chicago, the PredPol (Predictive

Policing) model was an early pioneer, with initial studies suggesting a 7% reduction in certain crime categories in deployment areas (Mohler et al., 2015). However, predictive patrolling has also attracted substantial criticism due to potential geographic and socioeconomic biases. Scholars such as Lum and Isaac (2016) have argued that models trained on historical crime and arrest data may unintentionally stigmatise and disproportionately represent certain neighbourhoods—particularly those comprising vulnerable or minority communities. This may lead to a "vicious cycle" wherein increased police presence results in more arrests, which then feed the model and reinforce further surveillance of the same areas. Ongoing algorithmic transparency and auditing are essential to mitigate such risks.

Another significant innovation contributing to proactive prevention is the use of virtual simulations with Augmented Reality (AR) to train law enforcement and emergency response personnel. Unlike traditional training methods, AR enables agents to experience realistic and dynamic scenarios without the costs, dangers, or logistical constraints of physical drills. In the context of proactive prevention and the transition from analytical insights to strategic implementation, the comprehensive report authored by the National Urban Security Technology Laboratory and DAGER Technology, LLC (2024) provides a critical evaluation of augmented reality (AR) training systems tailored for first responders. By systematically surveying the current market landscape, the document elucidates the operational benefits, technical capabilities, and deployment challenges associated with AR platforms in emergency preparedness and response scenarios. Its findings underscore the potential of immersive technologies not only to enhance situational awareness and decision-making under duress but also to bridge the gap between theoretical readiness and practical field application. Such contributions are instrumental in fostering evidence-based strategies aimed at reinforcing anticipatory capacities within civil protection frameworks, thereby aligning technological innovation with strategic foresight in security-oriented domains. This not only enhances operational efficiency but also improves the safety of officers and citizens alike by fostering more coordinated and effective responses.

4.3. Combating Cybercrime: Safeguarding Urban Digital Infrastructure

With the exponential increase in digitalisation across all facets of urban life, cybercrime has emerged as a central and pervasive threat to the resilience and functioning of smart cities. The reliance on interconnected systems to manage essential services (water, electricity, transport), communication infrastructure, and municipal governance renders cities attractive targets for cyberattacks. In response, two primary lines of action have gained prominence: the regulation of illicit content and the fortification of security architecture.

Firstly, the rise of technologies such as deepfakes has introduced novel legal and ethical challenges. Illicit deepfakes—used for identity theft, defamation, fraud, or disinformation—have prompted governments to implement new regulations to protect citizens and information integrity. For instance, Spain's Penal Code since 2022 includes specific sanctions for identity fraud committed using artificial intelligence, prescribing prison sentences of up to three years. This legislative measure aims to deter malicious use of deepfakes and establish a legal framework to prosecute offenders (Boletín Oficial del Estado, 2022). It sets a significant precedent for other jurisdictions, underscoring the need for legal adaptation to rapidly evolving technologies.

Secondly, to shield urban digital infrastructure from cyberattacks, advanced security architectures such as the Zero Trust model are being actively promoted. Unlike traditional perimeter-based security models—which trust internal actors and distrust external ones—Zero Trust adheres to the principle of "never trust, always verify." Under this paradigm, no entity (user, device, or application) is inherently trusted, regardless of its network location. Every access attempt to municipal network resources must be continually authenticated and authorised. Implementation of Zero Trust entails:

- **Continuous identity verification**: Users and devices must be authenticated and authorised for each resource access attempt, even if already within the network.
- **Network segmentation**: Municipal networks are divided into small, isolated segments. This containment strategy prevents lateral movement by attackers who breach one segment.
- **Principle of least privilege**: Users are granted only the minimum permissions necessary for their tasks, thereby reducing the attack surface (Rose et al., 2020).

By adopting such architectures, cities can build far more resilient digital environments, impeding attacker mobility and safeguarding sensitive data and critical infrastructure from disruptions or breaches. Predictive analysis, combined with robust cybersecurity, thus constitutes a foundational pillar for ensuring multidimensional security in the cities of the future.

5. INTEGRATION OF MULTISECTORAL DATA: THE BACKBONE OF THE RESILIENT CITY

In the context of increasingly interconnected and vulnerable urban systems, the integration of multisectoral data has emerged as a foundational pillar in the construction of truly resilient cities. Urban resilience, understood as the capacity of cities to absorb, adapt to, and recover from a wide array of disruptions—ranging from environmental shocks and public health crises to security threats and infrastructure failures—cannot be realised without the systematic consolidation and analysis of data originating from diverse domains. Public safety, healthcare, environmental monitoring, transport, energy distribution, and social services generate vast and heterogeneous datasets which, when effectively integrated, enable an unparalleled level of situational awareness and proactive governance.

The shift from siloed information systems to integrated urban data architectures facilitates not only cross-sectoral coordination but also the predictive management of risks and resources. Unified platforms, such as Urban Operations Centres (UOCs), function as the central nervous system of the smart city, assimilating real-time data flows and translating them into actionable intelligence through dynamic dashboards, predictive models, and geospatial simulations. Such platforms, as exemplified by Barcelona's Superblocks and Singapore's Smart Nation initiative, illustrate how the cross-referencing of traffic patterns, environmental quality metrics, public health indicators, and emergency service data can substantially reduce response times, optimise mobility, and enhance safety outcomes (Nieuwenhuijsen, 2024; Du et al., 2024).

Furthermore, the success of data integration efforts hinges on the establishment of common standards, interoperability frameworks, and robust governance mechanisms. Open protocols such as FIWARE and NGSI-LD facilitate semantic compatibility among heterogeneous devices and systems, preventing the formation of data silos and fostering the development of modular, adaptive digital ecosystems. Equally critical are ethical considerations relating to data privacy, cybersecurity, and algorithmic accountability, particularly in contexts involving biometric surveillance or sensitive health information. Hence, the intelligent integration of multisectoral data is not merely a technical challenge, but a multidimensional endeavour requiring institutional coordination, public trust, and regulatory foresight. Only through such integrated intelligence can cities move beyond fragmented management toward a holistic model of sustainable and equitable urban resilience.

5.1. Unified Platforms: Urban Operations Centres

At the heart of this data integration lie Urban Operations Centres (UOCs). These are not merely control rooms; they function as neurological coordination hubs that centralise a continuous stream of real-time data, transforming it into actionable intelligence for swift and effective decision-making. UOCs act as the "brain" of the smart city, enabling urban managers to attain an unprecedented level of situational awareness.

- **Barcelona Example – Superblocks**: The city of Barcelona has implemented an ambitious urban transformation project known as the Superblocks. Beyond its urbanistic impact on creating public spaces and reducing traffic, this model exemplifies the integration of multisectoral data to enhance both safety and quality of life. The Superblocks system integrates real-time information from a dense network of traffic sensors (monitoring speed, volume, and direction of vehicles), road incident data (records of accidents and their causes), air quality sensors (measuring pollutants and particulates), and pedestrian activity metrics (flows of people in public spaces). This amalgamation of information is centralised in a UOC, enabling the analysis of the interaction between urban design and city behaviour. A study conducted by the Ajuntament de Barcelona (Nieuwenhuijsen et al., 2024) revealed that following the implementation of these optimised zones, a significant 40% reduction in road incidents was observed within the Superblock perimeters. This improvement not only translates into fewer accidents and injuries but also a reduction in congestion and pollution, contributing to a safer and more liveable city. The key to this success lies in the cross-referencing of data to identify critical points and evaluate the impact of interventions. Figure 4 presents a schematic representation of how Urban Operations Centres aggregate multisectoral data to deliver integrated and real-time intelligence. It underscores the importance of interoperability across urban systems.

Figure 4. Urban Operations Centre (UOC) Data Integration Model.

- **Smart Nation Singapore – The Vanguard of Cross-Sectoral Integration**: Singapore is globally recognised as a benchmark in smart city implementation, and its Smart Nation initiative represents a paradigm of large-scale data integration. Its cross-sectoral command does not operate in a single domain but unifies signals from a broad array of services and agencies:
  - **Transport**: Real-time traffic flow data, public transport usage, smart parking systems, and road surveillance cameras.
  - **Hospitals and Health Services**: Information on bed availability, medical resources, patient flows, and epidemiological alerts.

- o **Emergency Services**: Data from fire brigades, ambulance services, and police, including unit locations, response times, and incident types.
- o **Law Enforcement**: Information on criminal incidents, crime patterns, and personnel deployment.

This centralisation of information within a common, interoperable platform has enabled Singapore to reduce emergency response times in urban settings by an impressive 25% (Du et al., 2024). In the case of a serious accident, fire, or public health crisis, diverse services can coordinate seamlessly, dispatching the appropriate resources to the precise location with unprecedented efficiency. The interconnection of data allows, for example, a traffic accident alert to automatically trigger the mobilisation of ambulances and police units, while simultaneously notifying hospitals of potential casualties—all within seconds.

These unified platforms do not merely collect data; they transform it using interactive geospatial dashboards that visualise information via three-dimensional city maps. They incorporate AI algorithms to detect anomalies, identify emerging patterns, and conduct predictive analysis. Heat maps reveal zones of high incident concentration (e.g. crime, accidents, pollution hotspots). In addition, they employ simulation models to anticipate how risk scenarios might unfold (e.g. the spread of a fire or the dispersion of a crowd), optimising evacuation routes and resource deployment accordingly to ensure a proactive and effective response.

5.2. Standards and Governance: The Architecture of Digital Trust

Interoperability, security, and reliability within digitalised urban environments cannot be achieved without the establishment of robust standards and a trustworthy, transparent data governance framework. These elements are vital to the development of a resilient and ethically sound digital infrastructure.

- **Post-Quantum Cryptography: Protection Against Future Threats**: The impending advent of quantum computing poses a significant threat to current encryption methods. The algorithms that presently safeguard our communications and sensitive data could be rendered obsolete by the immense computational power of quantum machines. In anticipation of this challenge, major cities and nations are investing in post-quantum cryptography (PQC). PQC comprises new cryptographic algorithms resistant to quantum attacks, ensuring the long-term security of information. Cities such as New York and London are leading the way by testing and beginning to deploy PQC protocols to safeguard sensitive communications, from public safety networks to municipal financial transactions (IBM, 2024; NIST, 2023). This proactive stance is essential to protect critical infrastructure and citizens' data in a future where quantum computing could potentially compromise current encryption standards.

- **Ethical Framework – The EU AI Act: Regulating AI for Responsible Use**: The European Union's Artificial Intelligence Act represents a pioneering regulatory framework that seeks to establish clear and ethical standards for the use of AI, particularly in high-risk domains such as urban surveillance systems. The Act directly addresses the use of biometric data in public cameras, imposing strict limitations. For example, it prohibits mass surveillance systems in public spaces without explicit consent—a crucial safeguard for privacy and civil liberties. Furthermore, it mandates that AI systems employed in urban security and management undergo periodic, rigorous audits to assess performance, detect bias, ensure transparency, and uphold accountability. This framework fosters a culture of responsibility, aiming to prevent the misuse of AI technologies and promote their use for public good rather than indiscriminate monitoring (European Parliament, 2021).
- **FIWARE and NGSI-LD: Enabling IoT Data Interoperability**: For data from myriad sensors and platforms to communicate and be understood coherently, open and standardised protocols are indispensable. FIWARE and NGSI-LD are key examples. FIWARE is an open-source suite of software components that facilitates the development of smart applications and data management. NGSI-LD (Next Generation Service Interface – Linked Data) is a data model and API that enables seamless interoperability among IoT devices and urban data platforms, regardless of manufacturer or vendor. These open standards are critical as they promote interoperable urban ecosystems, avoiding the formation of "data silos" and allowing information to flow freely among various city services and applications. This not only reduces integration costs but also fosters innovation by enabling third-party developers to build new applications and services atop existing data infrastructures (FIWARE Foundation, 2023).

5.3. Mobility and Road Safety: A Pillar of Urban Security

Safe and efficient mobility constitutes an essential component of any smart and resilient city. Technological advances in this domain are not only aimed at optimising traffic flow but also at drastically reducing accidents and protecting all road users.

- **V2X (Vehicle-to-Everything): The Future of Road Communication**: V2X technology is central to the next generation of mobility. It enables autonomous and semi-autonomous vehicles to exchange real-time data not only with each other (V2V – Vehicle-to-Vehicle) but also with a variety of external elements (V2I – Vehicle-to-Infrastructure, V2P – Vehicle-to-Pedestrian, V2N – Vehicle-to-Network). This multidirectional communication encompasses:

- o **Traffic Lights**: Vehicles receive information on signal phase changes, allowing them to adjust speed to avoid abrupt braking and reduce collisions.
- o **Road Infrastructure**: Sensors on bridges can alert vehicles to ice or wet conditions, while roadside devices can report accidents or congestion.
- o **Pedestrians and Cyclists**: Vehicles can detect and receive alerts from pedestrians or cyclists equipped with smart devices, significantly reducing collision risk.
- o **Network (Cloud)**: Vehicles access real-time traffic data, weather updates, or emergency alerts from a central server.

An innovative V2X pilot programme in Tokyo demonstrated a promising 30% reduction in minor collisions during its initial phase (Shladover, 2020). This technology has the potential to create a significantly safer road environment by enhancing situational awareness and issuing early warnings of hazards.

- **Structural Batteries in EVs: Optimising Emergency Vehicles**: Structural batteries represent a cutting-edge innovation in electric vehicle (EV) design. Unlike conventional batteries, which are separate modules added to the vehicle chassis, structural batteries are integrated directly into the frame or body of the vehicle. This integration provides multiple advantages:
  - o **Weight reduction**: Eliminating traditional battery casings significantly lowers the overall vehicle weight.
  - o **Space optimisation**: Integration permits more efficient use of interior space.
  - o **Enhanced structural integrity**: The battery contributes to the vehicle's structural rigidity, improving crash safety.
  - o **Increased agility and efficiency**: Reduced weight and optimised mass distribution enhance energy efficiency and manoeuvrability.

For emergency service vehicles (ambulances, police cars, electric fire engines), these innovations are transformative (Danzi et al., 2021). A lighter, more agile vehicle can reach incident sites more swiftly, navigate dense urban environments more easily, and carry more equipment without compromising performance. This translates directly into faster response times and more effective operations, ultimately improving public safety.

These innovations in mobility, together with real-time traffic data analytics and predictive driving pattern analysis, enable a shift towards preventive and significantly safer mobility. The smart city, through the integration of such components, becomes a dynamic and adaptive system capable of responding intelligently and resiliently to the challenges of urban life.

6. CHALLENGES AND FUTURE TRENDS: NAVIGATING THE NEXT DECADE OF SAFE CITIES

As cities transition into the second quarter of the twenty-first century, the pursuit of urban safety must confront a rapidly evolving constellation of risks, technological innovations, and ethical dilemmas that transcend conventional governance frameworks. The vision of a smart and secure city, while increasingly anchored in tangible technological achievements, is simultaneously shadowed by emerging threats inherent to hyperconnectivity, digital dependence, and sociotechnical asymmetries. In this context, ensuring the long-term viability of safe cities necessitates a dual approach: one that is both anticipatory—capable of forecasting and mitigating future vulnerabilities—and adaptive—able to respond dynamically to evolving social, environmental, and technological landscapes.

Foremost among the emerging challenges is the intensification of cyber vulnerabilities affecting critical urban infrastructure. As essential services—such as energy distribution, water supply, healthcare, and transport—become increasingly digitised and interconnected, they are rendered susceptible to sophisticated cyberattacks, including those perpetrated by state-sponsored actors with the capacity to inflict large-scale disruption and societal harm (Oliha et al., 2024). Moreover, this threat is magnified by the systemic interdependence of urban systems, wherein a failure in one domain may cascade into others, compounding the risk and complexity of urban crises.

Parallel to technological risk is the spectre of digital exclusion. The unequal distribution of access to smart technologies, particularly among elderly populations, economically marginalised groups, and communities lacking digital literacy or infrastructure, poses a significant barrier to inclusive urban safety. When emergency alerts, public services, and safety applications rely exclusively on digital interfaces, entire segments of the population may be rendered invisible to the smart city apparatus, exacerbating their vulnerability and undermining the democratic ethos of resilience (Ahmad et al., 2022).

Furthermore, the advent of neurotechnologies introduces a new frontier of ethical and legal concern. Devices that interface directly with human cognition raise fundamental questions regarding mental privacy, cognitive liberty, and the potential for coercive manipulation. Regulatory frameworks for neuro-rights, as exemplified by recent developments in Spain, illustrate the urgent need for anticipatory legislation to safeguard the most intimate domains of human autonomy (Ligthart et al., 2023).

Thus, the trajectory of safe cities over the next decade will depend not solely on the sophistication of technological systems, but on society's collective ability to govern innovation responsibly. Only through integrative, ethical, and inclusive strategies can cities navigate the uncertainties of the digital age while preserving human dignity, equity, and environmental sustainability.

6.1. Emerging Risks: The Shadow of Hyperconnectivity

The increasing reliance on technology in urban management introduces unprecedented vulnerabilities that demand urgent attention from policymakers and technologists.

- **State-Sponsored Cyberattacks on Critical Infrastructure**: With the deep digitalisation of urban systems, a city's critical infrastructure – including power grids supplying homes and hospitals, transport systems mobilising millions, and water networks ensuring public health and life – has become a high-value target for malicious actors. These include not only sophisticated cybercriminal groups but increasingly also state-backed entities. Such cyberattacks do not merely seek disruption but may aim at sabotage, espionage, or large-scale data manipulation. According to Oliha et al. (2024), sophisticated cyberattacks pose a real and escalating threat to public safety, with the potential to paralyse essential services, incite social chaos, and endanger citizens' lives. A successful attack on the power grid could leave an entire metropolis without electricity for days, impacting hospitals, communications, and supply chains. A targeted assault on a transport system could cause massive breakdowns or, in the case of autonomous vehicles, directly endanger lives. The interconnected nature of smart city systems means a vulnerability in one sector can cascade into others, magnifying the impact. This necessitates massive investment in resilient cybersecurity, the establishment of rapid incident response teams, and international cooperation to trace and neutralise such threats.
- **Digital Exclusion of Vulnerable Groups**: Despite the promises of smart technologies for enhanced safety, there is an inherent risk that these developments could widen existing social inequalities. Population ageing in many societies and persistent socioeconomic disparities result in significant gaps in access to and use of intelligent safety systems. Groups such as the elderly – who may be less familiar with new technologies or face physical and cogni-

tive barriers – or low-income communities lacking reliable internet access or smart devices, are at considerable risk of being excluded from technologies that enhance urban resilience and security. For instance, if early warning systems or incident reporting platforms rely exclusively on mobile applications, those without smartphones or internet access may not receive vital information during emergencies. This not only limits their ability to benefit from safety improvements but also exacerbates their vulnerability in crisis situations. Urban policies must therefore prioritise digital inclusion, ensuring that technological solutions are accessible, intuitive, and accompanied by training and support programmes, as well as non-digital alternatives where required (Ahmad et al., 2022).

- **Neuro-Rights at Risk: The New Ethical and Legal Frontier**: The proliferation of neurotechnologies – devices and interfaces that interact directly with brain activity – presents a novel and complex category of risks related to privacy and individual autonomy. These technologies include brain-computer interfaces (BCIs), which enable device control through thought; neurostimulation devices for enhancing cognitive performance or treating neurological conditions; and advanced systems capable of decoding neural patterns. While they hold transformative potential for medicine and care, they also raise profound concerns regarding neuro-rights. There is an urgent need to protect mental privacy (the non-intrusion or unauthorised reading of thoughts or neural data), cognitive identity (the right to one's own identity and thoughts without external manipulation), free will (preventing neurological coercion), equal access (ensuring these technologies do not deepen health or capability divides), and safeguards against algorithmic bias in neural data interpretation. Spain has been a pioneering country in this debate, with progress since 2023 in developing conceptual frameworks and legislative discussions on how to incorporate these rights into its legal system, thereby setting a significant global precedent (Ligthart et al., 2023; Gómez-Rodríguez, 2022; Ligthart et al., 2023; Universitat Oberta de Catalunya, 2024; Institutodeinnovaciondigital.ar, 2025). The regulation of neuro-rights is an emerging but vital field to ensure that future urban security does not compromise the very essence of humanity.

6.2. Key Innovations (2025–2030): Horizon of Opportunities

Despite the challenges, the forthcoming half-decade promises a proliferation of technological innovations poised to redefine urban safety and resilience.

- **Multi-Functional Robots for Rescue and Security**: Autonomous robots are rapidly evolving from niche tools into multifunctional allies in safety maintenance and emergency response. During 2025–2030, the proliferation of autonomous units capable of executing complex and hazardous tasks is expected, thereby reducing risks for human first responders. These units may:
    - **Extinguish fires**: Specialised robots equipped with water cannons or extinguishing agents could access burning buildings or high-risk zones inaccessible to human firefighters.
    - **Provide medical assistance**: First aid robots could reach injured persons in otherwise inaccessible areas, assess their condition, provide basic life support, or deliver critical medication.
    - **Perform rescue operations**: Drones and ground robots fitted with thermal cameras, ground-penetrating radar, and sensitive microphones could search for victims under rubble or in hazardous environments. One example is the SPROUT robot, designed to penetrate collapsed structures due to its flexible architecture and manoeuvrability in confined spaces, locating victims and transmitting their exact coordinates to rescue teams (Wahl, 2025).
    - **Patrol and monitor**: In cities such as Dubai, patrol robots are already being deployed. The "Patrol Unit M01" exemplifies how robots may conduct routine surveillance, respond to minor alerts, and collect data in public spaces, thereby allowing human officers to focus on more complex tasks (Redacción, 2025; LeoTronics Robotics, 2022; Solmaz et al., 2024). These robots may be equipped with environmental sensors, high-definition cameras, and communication systems, thereby enhancing surveillance coverage.
- **Global Protection of Neuro-Rights**: As neurotechnologies become more widespread, the need to safeguard the human mind becomes imperative. The trend for 2025–2030 involves active exploration of a global treaty or the adaptation of international instruments (such as the Universal Declaration of Human Rights or cybersecurity treaties) to protect mental privacy, cognitive autonomy, and non-discrimination in the use and interpretation of neural data. This could entail the creation of legal frameworks regulating the development and deployment of BCIs, prohibiting their coercive use or unauthorised extraction of cerebral data. Countries and international bodies are collaborating to establish a consensus on these fundamental rights, seeking to prevent a future where technology might manipulate human will or identity. The ongoing discussions in Spain are a clear example of this global endeavour to anticipate the ethical challenges of neurotechnology (Gómez-

Rodríguez, 2022; Ligthart et al., 2023; Universitat Oberta de Catalunya, 2024; Institutodeinnovaciondigital.ar, 2025).

6.3. Sustainability and Resilience: The Fusion of Green and Digital

The cities of the future will not only be intelligent but inherently sustainable and resilient. This vision integrates technology with ecological principles and circular economy practices.

- **Green Infrastructure and Osmotic Energy**: Green infrastructure is a key component of urban resilience. The integration of green roofs, living walls, and permeable urban parks not only enhances aesthetics and biodiversity but also mitigates the heat island effect, manages stormwater, improves air quality, and may serve as natural barriers or evacuation corridors. Complementarily, osmotic energy (also known as blue energy) is emerging as an innovative source of renewable energy. This technology harnesses the salinity gradient between freshwater and seawater to generate electricity. The concept involves integrating osmotic energy systems within urban infrastructure – for instance, where rivers meet the sea or in water treatment plants – to directly power command centres, sensor networks, and other critical components of the smart city. This not only strengthens security by providing a resilient, independent power source for surveillance and emergency infrastructure, but also promotes urban sustainability by reducing fossil fuel dependency and minimising the city's carbon footprint.
- **Digital and Ecological Resilience: A Holistic Approach**: True resilience in a smart city is a fusion of digital robustness and ecological awareness. This involves:
  - **Edge computing architectures**: Rather than relying on a single centralised data centre, edge computing processes data closer to its source (within the sensors, cameras, or IoT devices themselves). This reduces latency, enhances response speed, and – crucially – increases resilience by distributing processing power, thus avoiding single points of failure (e.g., in the event of a massive cyberattack or a natural disaster impacting a central data facility). Should one node fail, the remainder of the network may continue to operate.
  - **Renewable energy sources in data centres**: The data centres powering smart cities are major energy consumers. Integrating solar panels, wind energy, or geothermal systems to power these facilities reduces

environmental impact while enhancing energy autonomy and resilience, decreasing reliance on potentially vulnerable power grids.

- **Circular economy principles for urban smart hardware lifecycle**: The production and disposal of vast quantities of sensors, cameras, and IoT devices pose a significant environmental burden. The circular economy aims to mitigate this impact by designing hardware to be durable, repairable, reusable, and recyclable. This involves using sustainable materials, standardising components to facilitate repairs, implementing efficient recycling programmes for end-of-life devices, and considering environmental impact from the design phase. By adopting these principles, cities construct not only a safer and more resilient digital infrastructure but also one that is ecologically responsible, laying the groundwork for a truly sustainable urban future.

Sustainability is a critical pillar of smart safety ecosystems. Table 5 presents key strategies integrating environmental sustainability and digital resilience in urban planning.

Table 5. Integration of Ecological and Digital Resilience Strategies in Safe Cities.

Strategy	Technological/Ecological Basis	Urban Safety Benefits
Edge Computing	Local data processing in IoT nodes	Reduced latency and increased operational resilience
Green Infrastructure	Urban parks, green roofs, living walls	Stormwater control, heat island mitigation
Structural Batteries in EVs	Lightweight, energy-efficient vehicle architecture	Enhanced emergency vehicle performance
Circular IoT Economy	Reusable, repairable sensor ecosystems	Reduced environmental impact and long-term system viability

In sum, the evolution of safe cities is an ongoing process that demands continuous vigilance toward emerging risks and a proactive outlook on innovation. The 2025–2030 period will be crucial for consolidating a model in which technology and ethics converge to create urban environments that not only protect their inhabitants but also enable them to thrive in a more secure, equitable, and sustainable future.

7. CONCLUSION

The transformation of urban safety in the digital age represents one of the most significant reconfigurations of twenty-first-century governance. As cities expand in complexity, scale, and interdependence, the very notion of safety must be re-conceptualised—not as a fixed state but as a dynamic, adaptive process grounded in technological innovation, cross-sectoral coordination, and normative reflection. This chapter has critically examined the technological architectures, operational paradigms, and governance frameworks that define the evolving landscape of safe cities, offering a comprehensive synthesis of the challenges, enablers, and prospects of intelligent urban security.

7.1. Reconceptualising Urban Safety in the Age of Complexity

The contemporary urban environment is no longer shaped merely by physical infrastructure and static risk factors; rather, it is defined by intricate networks of sociotechnical systems operating in constant flux. In this context, safety must be understood as an emergent property of resilience—the capacity of a city to anticipate, absorb, respond to, and recover from multiple, concurrent disruptions. The emergence of intelligent surveillance systems, emergency management platforms, and predictive analytics tools signifies a decisive shift away from reactive modalities toward pre-emptive, evidence-based governance. However, this shift is not without epistemological and ethical tension. The question is no longer whether technology can deliver safer cities, but how such technologies are deployed, who governs their application, and to what ends.

7.2. The Central Role of Integrated Digital Infrastructure

A salient conclusion drawn from this analysis is the indispensable role of integrated digital infrastructure in constructing effective safety ecosystems. The deployment of interoperable platforms capable of aggregating multisectoral data—from environmental sensors and health systems to transport networks and law enforcement—has proven essential for fostering real-time situational awareness. Urban Operation Centres (UOCs), intelligent command dashboards, and data fusion frameworks allow for coordinated response strategies that transcend administrative silos. These infrastructures not only enable rapid detection and resolution of incidents but also facilitate long-term planning through the use of digital twins and predictive modelling.

Moreover, the integration of public participation mechanisms—such as citizen-reporting apps and community-based risk mapping tools—repositions the population from passive recipients to active co-producers of urban safety. This participatory model not only enhances the responsiveness and granularity of emergency systems but also reinforces civic trust and democratic legitimacy in safety governance.

7.3. Navigating the Ethical and Governance Landscape

Despite the demonstrable benefits of intelligent safety systems, the findings underscore the urgent need for robust governance frameworks that can mitigate the risks associated with algorithmic surveillance, data centralisation, and digital exclusion. The proliferation of biometric identification tools and predictive policing software, for instance, raises serious concerns regarding discrimination, over-policing, and infringements on individual privacy. Without adequate transparency, accountability, and oversight, these tools risk replicating and amplifying structural inequalities.

The development of neurotechnologies and the deployment of AI systems capable of cognitive analysis introduce even more complex ethical dilemmas. As explored in the chapter, mental privacy and cognitive liberty are emerging human rights frontiers that require anticipatory regulation. In this regard, regulatory initiatives such as Spain's pioneering framework on neuro-rights should serve as guiding references for global urban policy-makers.

In addition, the reliance on digital infrastructures renders cities increasingly vulnerable to cyber threats. From ransomware attacks on critical public services to the disruption of emergency platforms through denial-of-service attacks, cyber risk is now a core dimension of urban safety. Therefore, cybersecurity must be conceived not as an auxiliary measure but as a foundational layer in the design and operation of urban safety architectures.

7.4. Strategic Priorities for Future Urban Resilience

To chart a viable path forward, this chapter proposes several strategic priorities for advancing the safe city agenda in the coming decade:

1. **Institutional Integration and Interoperability**: Cities must foster institutional ecosystems that support seamless data and operational interoperability across public, private, and civil society stakeholders.
2. **Ethical AI Governance**: The design and deployment of AI-driven safety systems must be subjected to rigorous ethical assessment, with mechanisms for algorithmic auditing, human oversight, and redress for affected individuals or communities.
3. **Inclusive Digital Participation**: Urban safety platforms should be designed with accessibility and inclusiveness in mind, ensuring that digitally marginalised groups are not excluded from emergency services, alerts, and participatory mechanisms.

4. **Cybersecurity-by-Design**: Cyber risk must be integrated at every stage of system development and policy planning, ensuring that urban infrastructures are resilient to internal and external digital threats.
5. **Scenario-Based Simulation and Training**: Investment in advanced simulation environments, including virtual reality and digital twins, can enhance the preparedness of emergency services and improve inter-agency coordination during complex crises.

The Table 6 below summarises the interrelationship between the main technological pillars of urban safety and their associated governance imperatives.

Table 6. Technological Pillars of Urban Safety and Their Corresponding Governance Imperatives.

Technological Pillar	Function	Governance Imperatives
Intelligent Surveillance	Real-time threat detection and forensic analysis	Data protection, algorithmic transparency
Emergency Management Platforms	Incident coordination and resource deployment	Inter-agency interoperability, user accountability
Predictive Crime Analytics	Anticipation of spatiotemporal risk zones	Bias mitigation, judicial oversight
Multisectoral Data Integration	Systemic risk forecasting and resilience planning	Open standards, privacy-by-design, inclusive access
Neurotechnology & AI Systems	Cognitive analysis and behavioural inference	Mental privacy, ethical frameworks, public scrutiny

7.5. Concluding Reflections

In conclusion, the vision of a safe city cannot be reduced to a technologically enhanced space governed by surveillance and automation. Rather, it must be conceived as a complex sociotechnical ecosystem that embeds technological innovation within a framework of democratic governance, ethical integrity, and human dignity. Urban safety is not merely the absence of risk, but the presence of robust institutions, inclusive processes, and adaptive capabilities that together constitute a resilient and just urban order.

The journey towards truly safe and intelligent cities is ongoing, contingent on continuous innovation, critical reflection, and sustained collaboration between technologists, policy-makers, urban planners, and the communities they serve. Only by aligning technological progress with normative commitments to equity, privacy, and collective well-being can cities thrive amidst the profound transformations of the digital era.

REFERENCES

Ahmad, K., Maabreh, M., Ghaly, M., Khan, K., Qadir, J., & Al-Fuqaha, A. (2022). Developing future human-centered smart cities: Critical analysis of smart city security, data management, and ethical challenges. *Computer Science Review*, *43*, 100452. DOI: 10.1016/j.cosrev.2021.100452

Allam, Z., & Jones, D. S. (2021). Future (post-COVID) digital, smart and sustainable cities in the wake of 6G: Digital twins, immersive realities and new urban economies. *Land Use Policy*, *101*, 105201. DOI: 10.1016/j.landusepol.2020.105201

Arenas-Ramiro, M. (2022). Data protection in Latin America (pp. 140–159). Edward Elgar Publishing eBooks. DOI: 10.4337/9781786438515.00013

Boletín Oficial del Estado. (2022, October 13). Ley Orgánica 10/2022, de garantía integral de la libertad sexual. Gobierno de España. https://www.boe.es/buscar/doc.php?id=BOE-A-2022-17325

Calhoun, R. B., Dunson, C., Johnson, M. L., Lamkin, S. R., Lewis, W. R., Showen, R. L., Sompel, M. A., & Wollman, L. P. (2021). Precision and accuracy of acoustic gunshot location in an urban environment. arXiv. https://doi.org//arXiv.2108.07377DOI: 10.48550

Campero-Jurado, I., Quintanar Gómez, J., Vargas-Buitrón, O. D., Trejo-Macotela, F. R., Robles-Camarillo, D., & Simancas-Acevedo, E. (2019). Embedded system based on IoT and V2X for Smart Cities. *International Journal of Combinatorial Optimization Problems and Informatics*, *10*(3), 50–58. https://ijcopi.org/ojs/article/view/128

CrisisGo. (n.d.). CrisisGo safety platform overview. CrisisGo Inc. https://www.crisisgo.com/

Danzi, F., Salgado, R. M., Oliveira, J. E., Arteiro, A., Camanho, P. P., & Braga, M. H. (2021). Structural Batteries: A Review. *Molecules (Basel, Switzerland)*, *26*(8), 2203. DOI: 10.3390/molecules26082203 PMID: 33920481

Du, Y. F., Sun, T., & Huang, Y. (2024). A Comprehensive Review of Smart City Initiatives in Singapore Technological Advancements and Urban Planning from 2015 to 2023. DOI: 10.31219/osf.io/yqfsv

Dwork, C., & Roth, A. (2014). The algorithmic foundations of differential privacy. Foundations and Trends® in Theoretical Computer Science, 9(3–4), 211–407. DOI: 10.1561/0400000042

Economist Intelligence Unit (EIU). (2021). Safe Cities Index 2021. The Economist. https://safecities.economist.com

European Commission. (2022). Artificial Intelligence Act Proposal. https://digital-strategy.ec.europa.eu/en/policies/european-approach-artificial-intelligence

European Parliament. (2021). Artificial Intelligence Act. European Union. https://eur-lex.europa.eu/legal-content/EN/TXT/?uri=CELEX%3A52021PC0206

Federal Emergency Management Agency (FEMA). (n.d.). Emergency response plan. Ready.gov. Retrieved 7 August 2025, from https://www.ready.gov/business/emergency-plans/emergency-response-plan

FIWARE Foundation. (2023). FIWARE: Open source platform for the smart digital future. FIWARE Foundation. https://www.fiware.org/

Gómez-Rodríguez, J. M. (2022). Inteligencia artificial y neuroderechos. Retos y perspectivas. Cuestiones Constitucionales. *Cuestiones Constitucionales*, *1*(46), 93–119. DOI: 10.22201/iij.24484881e.2022.46.17049

IEEE Public Safety Technology. (2025). AI and ethical considerations in public safety technologies. IEEE. https://publicsafety.ieee.org/

Institutodeinnovaciondigital.ar. (2025). Informe sobre la protección de los neuro-derechos. Instituto de Innovación Digital. https://www.institutodeinnovaciondigital.ar/neuroderechos

Irwin, V., Wang, K., Cui, J., & Thompson, A. (2024, July). Report on Indicators of School Crime and Safety: 2023 (NCES 2024-145/NCJ 309126). National Center for Education Statistics, U.S. Department of Education, and Bureau of Justice Statistics, Office of Justice Programs. Retrieved 7 August 2025, from https://nces.ed.gov/pubs2024/2024145.pdf

LeoTronics Robotics. (2022). Patrol robot M01: Features and capabilities. LeoTronics Robotics. https://www.leotronics.eu/

Leslie, D. (2020). Understanding bias in facial recognition technologies. arXiv. https://doi.org//arXiv.2010.07023DOI: 10.48550

Ligthart, S., Ienca, M., Meynen, G., Molnár-Gábor, F., Andorno, R., Bublitz, C., Catley, P. F., Claydon, L., Douglas, T., Fins, J. J., Goering, S., Haselager, W. F. G., Jotterand, F., Lavazza, A., McCay, A., Wajnerman Paz, A., Rainey, S., Ryberg, J., & Kellmeyer, P. (2023). Minding rights: Mapping ethical and legal foundations of "neurorights." Cambridge Quarterly of Healthcare Ethics, 1–21. https://doi.org//arXiv.2302.06281DOI: 10.48550

Lim, K. Y. H., Zheng, P., Zheng, P., & Chen, C.-H. (2020). A state-of-the-art survey of Digital Twin: Techniques, engineering product lifecycle management and business innovation perspectives. *Journal of Intelligent Manufacturing, 31*(6), 1313–1337. DOI: 10.1007/s10845-019-01512-w

Llamas-Valenzuela, A. C., de la Rosa, J. I., Moreno-Chávez, G., Gonzales-Ramírez, E., Villa, J., & Celaya-Padilla, J. M. (2025). Predicting urban expansion in Zacatecas-Guadalupe cities: A support vector machine approach enhanced by SHAP values. *International Journal of Combinatorial Optimization Problems and Informatics, 16*(1), 75–89. DOI: 10.61467/2007.1558.2025.v16i1.500

Lum, K., & Isaac, W. (2016). To predict and serve? *Significance, 13*(5), 14–19. DOI: 10.1111/j.1740-9713.2016.00960.x

Mohler, G., Short, M. B., Malinowski, S., Johnson, M. E., Tita, G. E., Bertozzi, A. L., & Brantingham, P. J. (2015). Randomized Controlled Field Trials of Predictive Policing. *Journal of the American Statistical Association, 110*(512), 1399–1411. DOI: 10.1080/01621459.2015.1077710

National Urban Security Technology Laboratory & DAGER Technology, LLC. (2024, January). Augmented reality (AR) training systems for first responders: Market survey report (SAVER-T-MSR-45) [PDF]. Science and Technology Directorate, U.S. Department of Homeland Security. Retrieved from https://www.dhs.gov/sites/default/files/2024-02/24_02_16_st_artrainingsystemsmsr_0.pdf

Nieuwenhuijsen, M., de Nazelle, A., Cirach Pradas, M., Daher, C., Dzhambov, A. M., Echave, C., Gössling, S., Iungman, T., Khreis, H., Kirby, N., Khomenko, S., Leth, U., Lorenz, F., Matkovic, V., Müller, J., Palència, L., Pereira Barboza, E., Pérez, K., Tatah, L., & Mueller, N. (2024). The Superblock model: A review of an innovative urban model for sustainability, liveability, health and well-being. *Environmental Research, 251*(Part 1), 118550. DOI: 10.1016/j.envres.2024.118550 PMID: 38432569

NIST. (2023). Post-quantum cryptography standardization. National Institute of Standards and Technology. https://csrc.nist.gov/projects/post-quantum-cryptography

OECD. (2020). Smart Cities and Inclusive Growth: Building on the outcomes of the OECD Roundtable. https://www.oecd.org/cfe/cities/smart-cities.htm

Oliha, J. S., Biu, P. W., & Chimezie, O. (2024). Securing the smart city: A review of cybersecurity challenges and strategies. Open Access Research Journal of Multidisciplinary Studies, 7(1), 094–101. DOI: 10.53022/oarjms.2024.7.1.0013

Redacción. (2025, 8 June). Así es el nuevo robot urbano diseñado para la Policía de Dubai. El Correo del Golfo. Retrieved 7 August 2025, from https://www.elcorreo.ae/articulo/emiratos-arabes/asi-es-nuevo-robot-urbano-disenado-policia-dubai/

Rose, S., Borchert, O., Mitchell, S., & Connelly, S. (2020). Zero trust architecture (NIST Special Publication 800-207). National Institute of Standards and Technology. DOI: 10.6028/NIST.SP.800-207

Ruiz-Vanoye, J. A., & Díaz-Parra, O. (2022). Editorial comments about safe cities. *International Journal of Combinatorial Optimization Problems and Informatics*, *13*(3), 1. Advance online publication. DOI: 10.61467/2007.1558.2022.v13i3.314

SafetyCulture Content Team. (2024). Top emergency management tools in 2024. SafetyCulture. https://safetyculture.com/topics/emergency-management/

Sharma, S., Sharma, S. K., Sahu, A. K., & Sharma, A. (2024). Internet of Things (IoT) and Smart Cities. *Deleted Journal*, *2*(08), 2526–2531. DOI: 10.47392/IRJAEM.2024.0365

Shladover, S. E. (2020). Connected and automated vehicle systems: Introduction and overview. *Journal of Intelligent Transport Systems*, *22*(3), 190–200. DOI: 10.1080/15472450.2017.1336053

ShotSpotter Wikipedia. (2024). ShotSpotter. In Wikipedia. https://en.wikipedia.org/wiki/ShotSpotter

Smith, M., & Miller, S. (2021). The ethical application of biometric facial recognition technology. *AI & Society*, •••, 1–9. DOI: 10.1007/s00146-021-01199-9 PMID: 33867693

Solmaz, S., Innerwinkler, P., Wójcik, M., Tong, K., Politi, E., Dimitrakopoulos, G., Purucker, P., Höß, A., Schuller, B. W., & John, R. (2024). Robust Robotic Search and Rescue in Harsh Environments: An Example and Open Challenges. DOI: 10.1109/ROSE62198.2024.10591144

Sundharakumar, K. B., Bhalaji, N., & Mirunalini, P. (2024). Spatio Temporal Modelling of Repeat Crimes and Hotspots Prediction Using Recurrent Deep Neural Networks. DOI: 10.1109/ICITIIT61487.2024.10580830

Tera, T., Kelvin, K., & Tobiloba, B. (2024). Privacy Preserving Machine Learning Algorithms Using Local Information Privacy. https://doi.org/DOI: 10.31234/osf.io/x5mc4

UNDRR. (2022). Global Assessment Report on Disaster Risk Reduction 2022. United Nations Office for Disaster Risk Reduction. https://www.undrr.org/gar2022

UNESCO. (2020). Recommendation on the Ethics of Artificial Intelligence. https://unesdoc.unesco.org/ark:/48223/pf0000379920

United Nations. (2019). World Urbanization Prospects: The 2018 Revision. https://population.un.org/wup

Vasuki, M., Victoire, T. A., & Seventhi, S. (2024). *Forecasting Criminal Activity Using Machine Learning Approaches.* International Journal of Innovative Science and Research Technology., DOI: 10.38124/ijisrt/IJISRT24MAY645

Veoci. (n.d.). Veoci emergency management platform overview. Veoci Inc. https://veoci.com/

Wahl, H. (2025, 2 April). A flexible robot can help emergency responders search through rubble. MIT News. Massachusetts Institute of Technology. Retrieved from https://news.mit.edu/2025/sprout-flexible-robot-help-emergency-responders-search-rubble-0402

What is ShotSpotter? Controversial gunshot-detection technology facing increasing scrutiny. (2024, 20 May). Boston.com. Retrieved 7 August 2025, from https://www.boston.com/news/local-news/2024/05/20/what-is-shotspotter-controversial-gunshot-detection-technology-facing-increasing-scrutiny/

Chapter 7
Smart Cities as Open Governance Laboratories:
Multidisciplinary Approach From Engineering

Mario Oscar Ordaz Oliver
https://orcid.org/0000-0002-9302-0988
Tecnológico Nacional de México, Pachuca, Mexico

Evelin Gutiérrez
https://orcid.org/0000-0001-7610-9318
Universidad Politécnica de Pachuca, Mexico

Jesús Patricio Ordaz
https://orcid.org/0000-0002-5055-2183
Universidad Autónoma del Estado de Hidalgo, Mexico

Javier Hernández Pérez
https://orcid.org/0000-0003-0371-4255
Universidad Politécnica de Pachuca, Mexico

Amadeo Manuel Hernández Hernández
https://orcid.org/0009-0004-1266-0759
Tecnológico Nacional de México, Pachuca, Mexico

Justo Fabián Montiel Hernández
Universidad Autónoma del Estado de Hidalgo, Mexico

ABSTRACT

This chapter addresses smart cities not simply as a technological deployment, but as a space where different branches of engineering complement each other. It analyzes some of the contributions of mechanical, mechatronic, electrical, electronic, computational, and chemical engineering, highlighting how each of them, from its perspective, integrates innovative and preferred factors to make a city more efficient, safe, and, above all, tailored to its inhabitants. It also presents some specific examples of the implementation and management of smart cities and governments, such as Barcelona, Singapore, New York, and Amsterdam. The text details some of the actions these places have taken to become smart. It analyzes how the knowledge

DOI: 10.4018/979-8-3373-5535-1.ch007

contributed by different branches of engineering articulates with the Internet of Things, electrical grids, and the mechatronic design of smart sensor networks to give rise to innovative systems.

1. INTRODUCTION

When we hear the phrase “Smart City,” many people immediately think of a complex city due to its use of technology. However, many people fail to imagine the diversity of aspects associated with this concept, and it can be worrying for those unfamiliar with using modern equipment, even as simple as a cell phone. A Smart City is not only the result of the use of technology, but also a new form of urban management. It is a governance model where information circulates openly and transparently, harnessing the potential offered by Information and Communication Technologies (TIC) (Serra et al., 2014). The implementation of the Smart City model enables new forms of collaboration between governments, engineers, academics, and citizens in general, as they can share decision-making within a framework of open governance. Thanks to these changes, cities can be formed in which people experience greater satisfaction with their quality of life, facilitating processes and allowing access to a greater number of resources.

Today, most people live in cities, and in a world marked by accelerated urbanization, the worsening climate crisis, and the growing demand for efficient services, it is necessary to redesign the way urban environments function. The emergence of Smart Cities represents a robust response to these challenges, offering more integrated models focused on people's needs.

In the Smart City model, development is people-oriented and supported by TICs, enabling rapid transformation of various aspects of everyday life, including:

- More efficient public services, such as energy, water supply, health services, public safety, and education, can be managed to some extent with digital technologies.
- Urban planning allows for controlled expansion, respecting the environment and ensuring the ability to provide services to all. It also considers the creation of green spaces, planning for the implementation of efficient transportation, and optimizing mobility through strategic routes.
- Smart mobility, which includes the integration of public transportation and traffic monitoring systems, where priority can be given to vehicles such as school buses, healthcare vehicles, and security vehicles such as police and firefighters.

- Data and information management, using sensors distributed throughout the city, the Internet of Things (IoT), big data, and digital platforms, which enable decisions based on data captured in real time.
- Citizen participation, which can be achieved through the use of user-friendly digital platforms that allow citizens to report problems, provide feedback, and, ideally, collaborate in making important decisions. Citizen participation through digital platforms also benefits people with reduced mobility.
- Sustainability, which consists of promoting practices that allow the use of resources, while ensuring their availability.

In summary, a Smart City uses large amounts of data collected through sensors, cameras, and other electronic devices, allowing it to manage services and resources and solve everyday problems, making people's lives easier, while at the same time taking care of resources and improving the style and quality of life (Tiwari et al., 2021).

Actually, governments constantly face a large number of challenges, such as those related to health, security, education, migration, and resource provision, among others. They must provide efficient and accessible public services for all citizens. The work of today's governments is possible when they improve their means of communication and can implement transparent public management. To address current challenges and move toward building a Smart City, it is necessary to implement the use of TICs. The application of these technologies allows for the optimization of various tasks, such as the management of human, material, and financial resources. Also, it allows for efficient planning of their future use.

The implementation of technology for data management and protection is also a crucial aspect of effectively managing a Smart City. Safeguarding medical and public safety information, environmental monitoring in overcrowded and polluted cities, and managing population records have become crucial due to population growth and the new information emerging from increased migration.

Population growth, expanded access to education and health services, and the growing demand for resources, among other factors, make the management of complex databases essential, something that cannot be ignored in modern urban planning today.

One of the first steps in facilitating a contemporary city's transition to a Smart City is the digitalization of public services. Examples of this type of service include internet portals, through which many citizens willing to use technology can save time and facilitate procedures such as obtaining personal documents or even paying for services, which previously could only be done through public servants at counters. This type of action reduces the workload for staff at various institutions and also makes it easier for many people to complete procedures from the comfort of their homes (Bouskela et al., 2016).

Some authors have mentioned that the development of Smart Cities is centered on five main axes, including infrastructure, technology, economy, environment, and people. For this reason, a Smart City can be understood as a dynamic system, in which each component is interrelated through data, intelligent processes, and decisions that can be made collaboratively.

Managing a Smart City requires a diverse group of professionals capable of applying theory to real-life situations, providing solutions to the new challenges that arise in society. The work of these science professionals encompasses the design of new products, machinery, industrial processes, and information manipulation through the use of technological tools, ensuring efficiency, functionality, user satisfaction, and environmental protection. Specifically, engineers from various disciplines are responsible for planning, supervising, and executing the construction of buildings, roads, transportation systems, information management, energy management, and other areas, ensuring safety and comfort in the daily lives of many people.

Another essential function is the implementation of methods for the extraction, transformation, and use of raw materials, geared toward the production of essential goods, all with a growing commitment to environmental protection. An additional challenge facing engineers today is the generation of energy through clean, renewable, and sustainable sources, as part of their responsibility to improve the quality of life. In other words, those involved in various branches of engineering must work together, making decisive contributions to social well-being in areas such as healthcare, security, energy supply, education, financial systems, and modern urban infrastructure (Wickert & Lewis, 2013).

In this context, innovation, the result of work across different areas of science, gives rise to a new form of governance, allowing citizens to become active players in the functioning of their environment through their ongoing collaboration.

This chapter will address the notion of Smart Cities from a multidisciplinary perspective focused on engineering. Concrete examples will be presented of how disciplines such as mechanical, mechatronic, electrical, computer systems, and chemical engineering contribute their knowledge to the construction of more sustainable, automated, and safe urban environments that enable citizen collaboration.

Throughout the text, various aspects related to Smart Cities will be explored, including the design of urban infrastructure equipped with sensors for data collection and real-time monitoring, the automation of services and public spaces for ease of use, as well as environmental monitoring to ensure people's quality of life, and the implementation of smart grids that promote more efficient and sustainable energy use, thereby contributing to combating global environmental problems.

2. BACKGROUND

2.1 Smart Urban Infrastructure: Contribution of Mechanical Engineering

Mechanical engineering deals with the design, development, and evaluation of complex mechanical systems, which may include electric generators, motors, turbines, air conditioning equipment, industrial machinery, and automated devices. The work of mechanical engineers is fundamental to the development of Smart Cities, where energy efficiency, service automation, and sustainable infrastructure are key elements for improving living standards (US Dept of Labor, 2000; Smith, 2020).

By integrating mechanical systems with TIC and leveraging the information generated, it is possible to strengthen smart governance models that enable informed and transparent decision-making regarding the environment. In the Smart City landscape, urban infrastructure ceases to be merely a physical element and becomes part of a collaborative, interconnected, and adaptable system.

Among the contributions of mechanical and electrical engineering to the development of smart systems, the implementation of heating, ventilation, and air conditioning (HVAC) systems monitored through the Internet of Things (IoT) stands out. When these types of systems are not monitored continuously and in real time, they consume considerable amounts of energy, causing considerable economic waste and contributing to environmental impact, mainly when the energy sources are not environmentally friendly (Dhanalakshmi et al., 2020).

Dhanalakshmi et al. (2020) designed an HVAC system incorporating a dust sensor to monitor particulate matter ($PM_{2.5}$), a temperature sensor, and a sensor to measure carbon dioxide (CO_2), this system was implemented and evaluated within a laboratory. The integration of this type of systems into open urban monitoring platforms opens the possibility of achieving a reduction in energy consumption, while at the same time reducing the pollution associated with the energy sources currently used. They also allow the generation of data that can be used by authorities, citizens, and the scientific community to search for the problem generated.

Among the main applications of the IoT is the management of smart grids. When these systems are combined, they allow for more efficient management of energy consumption, for example, in HVAC systems. Serra et al. (2014) developed an HVAC system integrated into a smart grid; through this integration, they achieved dynamic energy consumption management. Their system allows remote interaction with the equipment, adjustment of the comfort temperature, and real-time visualization of energy consumption from different devices. Among the most important effects for the authors is the reduction in energy consumption costs. Their system works by measuring temperature at different points using a wireless sensor network (WSN).

The information is periodically sent to a central device (gateway), where they implemented an energy scheduling algorithm. This algorithm selects a combination of HVAC modules that should be turned on or off to maintain the temperature within a user-defined range, while also minimizing energy costs. Once the decisions are made, they are sent to programmable electric current regulators (actuators), which turn the HVAC modules on or off (Serra et al., 2014).

In addition to representing a step forward in terms of efficiency and sustainability, this type of development contributes to a more participatory form of energy governance by providing citizens with direct access to both information and decision-making.

Working with HVAC systems represents a key tool for advancing the transformation of traditional cities into Smart Cities, where special attention is paid to improving energy efficiency. Choi et al. (2017) worked on a project called Zero Energy Building (ZEB) to combat two major problems: climate change, which can be addressed by reducing greenhouse gas emissions, and resource depletion through optimal energy use. This research group's project was tested in a senior care facility. To monitor air quality, they used sensors for temperature, humidity, carbon dioxide (CO_2), carbon monoxide (CO), dust and particulate matter, formaldehyde, volatile organic compounds (VOCs), and methane (CH_4). The developed system enabled a 13.7% reduction in energy consumption, demonstrating its viability and highlighting the potential of using the Internet of Things to continuously work on sustainability and improve well-bcing in smart urban environments.

Another notable work on HVAC systems is the one conducted by Rajith et al. (2018), designed for use in corporate buildings. Their system provides real-time thermal information from sensors and collects user feedback, all using an Internet of Things-based architecture. Highlights of this work include the researchers' use of predictive models based on artificial neural networks and optimization of HVAC control using mixed linear programming (MLP). Furthermore, one advantage is that their system does not require constant user feedback; when data is lacking, the system assumes comfortable conditions. In their implementation, they achieved a 20% to 40% reduction in energy consumption. The research conducted by this group demonstrates that integrating artificial intelligence, the IoT, and strategies that respond to user demand makes it possible to make better use of energy and reduce waste without compromising thermal comfort. This is essential to pave the way for smart, sustainable urban infrastructures capable of meeting the real needs of users.

The collaborative work of engineering fields such as mechanical and electrical engineering in the design and implementation of modern HVAC systems that incorporate the use of TIC drives the development of more efficient and sustainable cities, where people feel more welcome and engaged in a more participatory urban environment. The integration of IoT technologies, optimization techniques, and smart grids into these systems exemplifies how urban infrastructure can be transformed into a continuous source of data useful for decision-making.

2.2 Urban Automation: Contributions of Mechatronics

Mechatronics engineering emerges from the integration of mechanical engineering, electronics, computer science, and control systems. Currently, mechatronics engineering is one of the most influential areas in the engineering field. In Mexico, this program is offered at various universities, demonstrating its relevance and the growing demand for professionals capable of modernizing cities through knowledge.

Within the tasks of mechatronics engineering professionals, the opportunity to offer innovative solutions aimed at reducing energy consumption, mitigating environmental impact, and improving the efficiency of industrial processes, transportation systems, automated devices, and smart technologies applied in different sectors stands out (Peter, 2024; Ryalat et al., 2024). In this sense, mechatronic engineering can contribute significantly to the development of Smart Cities, especially in areas such as transport optimization, efficient energy distribution, improved emergency response, and automated infrastructure maintenance, thus ensuring an improvement in people's quality of life (Cassandras, 2017).

Among the contributions of Mechatronics Engineering, we can mention various works reported in the literature, whose main objective is process automation. For example, the development of intelligent transportation systems (ITS) is a key factor in improving urban mobility, as it reduces traffic congestion and improves the efficiency of public transportation. The reported works are aimed at monitoring and controlling vehicle movement in a Smart City. Among these are those that describe intelligent traffic light control systems, which prioritize the passage of emergency vehicles. This innovation is especially useful when caring for people who require medical care or are in risky situations and need the support of trained personnel, such as police officers or firefighters. Various studies highlight that even a few minutes can be decisive in saving a life.

Researchers Lee and Chiu (2020) worked on the design and implementation of an intelligent vehicular traffic control system, whose main objective is to facilitate urban mobility by prioritizing, among other things, the passage of emergency vehicles (ambulance, firefighters, police) and public transport. In addition, this system supports various applications typical of Smart Cities, such as adaptive traffic light control, the promotion of efficient-ecological driving, and the dissemination of messages to nearby drivers. This was achieved through integration with the infrastructure (V2X: vehicle to Everything), which allows vehicles to share information from their sensors, cameras, and internal systems with other vehicles, nearby pedestrians, road infrastructure, and systems installed in Smart Cities through wireless data connectivity.

The system they describe was built from three subsystems. An RSU (Roadsite Unit) subsystem that connects directly to the traffic light controller, an OBU (On-Board Unit) that is the subsystem inside the vehicle and enables communication between the vehicle and the road infrastructure, and finally a Cloud Center responsible for coordinating, storing, and analyzing data.

In addition to the solutions proposed for traffic management, progress in electromobility, primarily in the design of smart charging systems for electric vehicles (EVs), can also contribute to reducing fossil fuel consumption and the carbon footprint (Nayak, 2019). In the development of Smart Cities, these systems, in addition to being efficient, must be safe and adequately integrated into the urban electricity grid, avoiding overloads and enabling proper management of energy consumption.

The increasing number of electric vehicles in different cities around the world makes it necessary to improve battery charging systems. This represents not only a considerable expense for urban infrastructure but also an interesting challenge for some researchers specializing in the subject. Haghbin et al. (2012) consider that an alternative to solve the economic problem posed by EV charging is the use of onboard batteries. However, achieving efficient battery design can be complex, as factors such as weight and space occupied within the vehicle, cost, charging time, useful life, and the environmental impact they can generate must be addressed. These researchers designed a high-power, bidirectional integrated battery charger. One of its main advantages is that it uses components already present in the vehicle, including the motor and inverter of the drive system. This proposal, in addition to reducing the costs and complexity of the system, would also represent a significant step toward more efficient, compact, and sustainable electric mobility.

In this same approach to innovation applied to urban transportation, the incorporation of the IoT represents a key element to strengthen the intelligence and connectivity of mobility systems. The IoT allows everyday objects, such as vehicles, to connect and interact with each other and with the network, regardless of the hardware or software platforms used. A smart vehicle is one equipped with sensors and devices capable of collecting data in real time, both from the environment and from the vehicle itself. Thanks to this, modern vehicles can communicate through different interfaces, such as vehicle-to-infrastructure (V2I), vehicle-to-vehicle (V2V), vehicle-to-cloud (V2C), and vehicle-to-everything (V2X). This form of expanded connectivity allows for the optimization of transportation routes, improved road safety, and the integration of smart vehicles with other urban systems (Khattak et al., 2019).

Khattak et al. (2019) developed a proof of concept applied to an emergency vehicle, where the IoT was used to transmit the ambulance's location, the patient's vital signs, and the case's criticality level in real time to a cloud platform. The system, programmed in Java SE and Android, analyzed this information to suggest the nearest hospital to users. This system also allows for advance hospital management, ensuring admission and notification of medical personnel. This approach demonstrates that vehicular connectivity can improve coordination between emergency transport and hospital infrastructure, reducing care times and optimizing the response to a critical situation.

Another contribution of mechatronics engineering to the development of Smart Cities is the design of urban assistance robots. These robots can facilitate various tasks, such as cleaning, surveillance, and even caring for people with reduced mobility. Grigorescu et al. (2019) indicate that a Smart City is a dynamic concept that continuously evolves as a result of urban technological innovations and their management. These researchers highlight the importance of health in Smart Cities and present as a case study a medical screening kiosk based on an autonomous robotic platform, designed to integrate into the urban environment. The system is structured in five functional layers, both for the robotic platform and the application, and incorporates innovative technologies such as biometric sensors, wireless connectivity, human-machine interface, local processing, and remote monitoring. Its design minimizes human intervention, and due to the system's versatility, it can be adapted to other key areas such as security, education, or tourism.

Taken together, advances in automation and robotics aimed at improving urban environments, driven by mechatronics engineering, have the potential to transform the way Smart Cities are designed, managed, and experienced. From efficient mobility, automated healthcare, traffic control, electromobility, and urban assistance, engineering, and especially mechatronics engineering, integrate complex technologies to offer practical solutions to social needs, improving their quality of life in various aspects.

The population growth experienced in recent decades has driven the search for effective mechanisms to manage information and provide care in multiple areas, such as education, healthcare, and security, among others. However, birth rates are currently trending downward in several countries, which, in the long term, could lead to personnel shortages in key sectors. In the new scenario emerging in different countries, the incorporation of robots in cities will cease to be a complementary option and become a strategic and necessary solution, capable of ensuring the continuity of essential services and the efficient functioning of urban life.

2.3 Contributions of Chemical Sciences to the Development of Smart Cities

Chemistry-related disciplines play a fundamental role in the development of Smart Cities, for example, by providing solutions for monitoring, controlling, and improving environmental quality, chemical safety, and urban sustainability.

Among the main contributions of chemical sciences to urban development is the implementation of advanced sensors capable of detecting pollutants even at very low concentrations. The integration of chemistry with digital technologies allows us to more effectively address current urban challenges. Chemistry is also linked to the development of new functional and environmentally friendly materials. It also allows for the identification of materials that pose a risk to health and ecosystems. In other words, it allows for the creation of safer and healthier urban environments.

Among the elements that are a fundamental part of a Smart City are water management systems, essential today due to pollution and the effects of climate change. Another key aspect in a Smart City environment is the reduction of energy consumption, which can be addressed from different perspectives, such as that related to infrastructure, where the use of innovative materials in construction allows for reduced energy consumption in buildings. Likewise, chemistry plays an important role in the development of lightweight and resistant materials for the manufacture of safe vehicles, thus contributing to the reduction of fossil fuel use, one of the main causes of environmental pollution.

Despite the great benefits of the transition from a conventional city to a Smart City, there are some disadvantages, including the high demand for raw materials, many of them critical and non-renewable. Rapid urbanization and industrial development have led to a significant decline in natural resources, generating considerable economic, social, and environmental impacts. To address this problem, chemistry can implement strategies such as the 4Rs: reduce, reuse, recycle, and replace, promoting a more efficient and sustainable use of resources. In sectors such as construction, urban mobility, and water management, chemistry is becoming a fundamental science, as it provides knowledge for the development of new materials that allow us to move toward more sustainable urban environments (Woinaroschy, 2016).

Pollution reduction is one of the crucial aspects that must be achieved in the development of Smart Cities; aspects such as good air quality impact how people perceive their quality of life. Dutta et al. (2017) developed a low-cost air quality monitoring system (AirSense). This system allows for the collection of environmental data in both indoor and outdoor spaces. It also enables strategic citizen participation, making it possible to obtain frequent and spatially diverse data without requiring complex infrastructure. The proposed device is based on a portable device connected to smartphones via Bluetooth. It is built on the Arduino Pro Mini hardware platform, which is an attractive alternative for the creation of low-cost, portable devices. This microcontroller acts as an interface between the air quality sensors and the communication module. To keep costs low, they use two sensors: the MQ-135, which allows the identification of gases such as ammonia (NH_3), sulfur dioxide (SO_2), nitrogen oxides (NO_X), benzene (C_6H_6), carbon monoxide (CO), and volatile organic compounds; and the MQ-7, which specializes in the detection of carbon monoxide (CO). The device proposed by this research team allows for both individual and collective monitoring, which is useful for obtaining information that can be used to generate air quality maps that facilitate decision-making, such as choosing less polluted routes or scheduling outdoor activities. Its low cost and small size contrast with traditional environmental monitoring systems.

In conjunction with other engineering disciplines, chemical sciences play an essential role in the development of Smart Cities, helping to balance technological progress with environmental sustainability. Its ability to generate innovative solutions in areas such as environmental monitoring, resource management, and chemical safety enables it to respond to current and future urban challenges. The integration of this discipline with branches such as computer science and artificial intelligence drives the creation of more sustainable urban environments.

2.4 Smart Grids and Sustainable Urban Energy: The Role of Electrical, Electronic, and Computer Engineering

In the context of Smart Cities, smart grids represent one of the critical sectors with the greatest impact on the urban environment. This self-sufficient electrical infrastructure is designed to quickly detect and resolve problems within the electrical system, reducing the need for manual intervention and ensuring a sustainable, reliable, secure, and high-quality energy supply. Through remote monitoring, energy demand prediction, and real-time data management, smart grids enable more efficient control of energy generation, distribution, and consumption. These electrical grids also incorporate storage technologies, two-way communication, cyber protection, and automation, facilitating the integration of renewable energy and immediate response to failures or overloads. These capabilities make electrical grids an essential component for sustainable urban governance, enabling more informed decisions and the active participation of various stakeholders in the management of the electrical system (Bayindir et al., 2016).

Electrical engineering and computer science, working together, play a fundamental role in the design, implementation, and operation of smart electricity systems. These disciplines provide the technical knowledge and tools necessary to achieve the integration of advanced technologies, from the design of transmission and distribution systems to the development of algorithms for the intelligent analysis of energy data. While electrical engineers transform traditional infrastructure to support new energy sources, computer specialists create real-time monitoring and control platforms and implement artificial intelligence to predict consumption patterns and optimize decision-making. This interdisciplinary collaboration allows for reducing energy losses, improving resource efficiency, and advancing toward more effective automation of the urban electricity system.

Additionally, electronic engineering is essential for the development of Smart Cities geared toward sustainability. This discipline, in addition to fostering innovation, enables the redesign of existing processes through the incorporation of advanced electronic technologies. In particular, the implementation of systems based on robotics and the Internet of Things (IoT) facilitates the creation of prototypes and practical solutions that enable more efficient and automated energy management. The synergy between electronic engineering and computer science enables the development of platforms capable of monitoring, controlling, and optimizing critical processes in smart urban infrastructures (Budrin et al., 2020).

Tiwari et al. (2021) point out that the application of machine learning algorithms represents a significant advance in the evolution of smart grids toward more robust and predictive systems. These techniques allow for the analysis of large volumes of data collected by sensors distributed throughout the network, facilitating the prediction of system stability under dynamic consumption conditions. Machine learning-based models can anticipate critical configurations that would put the grid at risk, allowing action to be taken before failures occur. This automated approach not only reduces the risk of outages but also strengthens the reliability and sustainability of urban electrical systems. Progress toward transforming traditional cities into Smart Cities requires the ability to understand, manipulate, and apply large volumes of data, with the goal of improving the functioning of urban infrastructure and people's quality of life.

A tangible example of the impact of these technologies can be found in the intelligent management of public lighting, where collaboration between engineering firms has enabled significant innovations. Through the use of wireless sensor networks (WSNs), distributed systems have been developed capable of autonomously controlling the switching on, off, and dimming of luminaires, adapting to factors such as the presence of pedestrians or vehicles, environmental conditions, and scheduled schedules. In this area, Viani et al. (2016) implemented a smart public lighting system in urban areas of Trento, Italy, with more than 700 lamps that demonstrated their ability to generate significant energy savings, confirming its viability as an effective and sustainable alternative within the framework of Smart Cities.

Together, electrical, electronic, and computer engineering not only drive the modernization of urban energy infrastructure but also strengthen data-driven governance, technological participation, and commitment to sustainability goals. These disciplines, working in a coordinated manner, enable cities to respond more agilely and effectively to the challenges of urban growth and the transition to cleaner energy systems.

3. GLOBAL PATHWAYS TOWARD SMART CITIES: TECHNOLOGY, GOVERNANCE, AND CITIZEN PARTICIPATION

The development of Smart Cities is a gradual process that depends both on available economic and social resources and on the commitment of the people who drive them and, ultimately, constitute their very reason for being. Moving forward in this direction requires not only the application of existing knowledge but also a permanent willingness to learn and continuously improve. The transition toward these types of cities should be considered a short-term project in different parts of the world, primarily due to demographic changes and associated environmental challenges, such as resource scarcity and heavy dependence on fossil fuels. The need to advance the transformation of conventional cities into Smart Cities is also linked to the evolution that society has undergone over the years; changes in sectors such as education, healthcare, and the economy, among others, mean that managing large volumes of data and information can no longer be carried out using traditional methods, making it essential to adopt new ways of organizing, processing, and analyzing information. In this context, financial support from governments is essential to address critical sectors such as infrastructure, education, mobility, health, and security, without which effective and equitable urban transformation is impossible.

In different parts of the world, Smart Cities have ceased to be a simple technological aspiration to become scenarios where engineering acts as a bridge between the physical, digital, and social spheres. However, this depends largely on their economic potential. One of the key sectors for achieving this goal is health. Strengthening the health system is one of the most sensitive and important aspects in the development of these cities. Currently, quality medical care depends largely on specialized personnel; however, this sector can be affected or collapse due to high demand. Therefore, the use of advanced technologies can facilitate this, supported by ICTs. For example, it is possible to maintain electronic medical records and use cloud platforms that allow the management of large volumes of medical information, facilitating faster diagnoses and better-informed decisions. More efficient information management also enables proper management by the responsible authorities. A city that invests in digital health will be better prepared to face the various demographic and social challenges, offering its population a more well-being environment.

Hayat (2016) indicates that many cities have begun their transformation into Smart Cities; however, it is difficult to simultaneously meet all the conditions that define this term, mainly because it evolves rapidly and continuously. Among the regions and cities that have made progress in building Smart Cities are:

- Barcelona (Spain), which received the European Capital of Innovation award in 2014. The city project was structured around five key pillars: open data, sustainable urban growth, social innovation, partnerships between public, private, and academic actors, and TIC-based smart services. As an essential part of these strategies, Smart City Barcelona is conceived as a collaborative movement that integrates the business sector, academic institutions, government authorities, and citizens, working together to promote projects that strengthen the city's competitive profile and foster its urban development. Implemented initiatives include geospatial mapping, open data sharing between public and private organizations, and citizens, smart traffic lights, green buildings, smart parking, an urban operating system with a wide network of sensors and citizen service kiosks, open government, a smart bus network, and remote assistance for the elderly (Hayat, 2016; Capdevila & Zarlenga, 2015; Bakıcı et al., 2013). In this city, a platform called Sentilo was designed by telecommunications engineers as open-source software that links information from urban sensors through standardized APIs. This solution, far from being confined to the administration, opened the door for residents, groups, and companies to directly access raw data from sensor networks and, based on this, identify solutions to real-world problems. This idea led to the emergence of Smart Citizen, a set of open environmental sensors that allows citizens to compare official information using citizen science methods (Anthopoulos et al., 2022). This is not the only example in Spain: the community network Guifi.net, expanded beyond Catalonia and based on open source hardware, demonstrates that engineering can expand society's scope for action. Added to this is the superblock system, where sensors embedded in the pavement work hand in hand with Barcelona's Decidim platform. In a participatory process, 68% of the proposals favored expanding green areas rather than allocating more space for parking; a result that reinforces the idea that open standards like FIWARE not only optimize infrastructure but can also transform it into digital commons (Capdevila & Zarlenga, 2015).

- Singapore, located in Asia, has advanced toward a Smart City through various initiatives in health, living, mobility, and digital services. In the healthcare sector, patient care is being improved, mobility for older adults is supported through robotics, some applications are being leveraged to promote healthy habits, and home health is being monitored. In the living sector, applications are being used to strengthen communication between the municipality and citizens and to optimize housing conditions. In the mobility sector, access to public transportation is being facilitated, urban mobility is being analyzed, and research into autonomous mobility is being promoted. Finally, in the services sector, digital platforms are being offered to access public services, manage finances, and conduct electronic transactions (Hayat, 2016; Bhati et al., 2017; Cavada et al., 2019).

- Rio de Janeiro (Brazil) is among the cities that have moved from conventional to smart. Its strategies include improving transportation and urban infrastructure, creating the open data system Rio Datamine, and implementing Knowledge Squares and digital centers in vulnerable areas, which have enabled digital literacy among citizens in vulnerable areas (Hayat, 2016). These actions are complemented by citizen participation and real-time management initiatives, such as the Rio Agora platform, the 1746 Citizen Service Center, and especially the Rio Operations Center, which coordinates emergency response, manages traffic, and supports the organization of major events through an integrated urban monitoring system (Gaffney & Robertson, 2018).
- New York, one of the most populous cities in the world, has faced several challenges in waste management, air quality, water use, mobility, connectivity, and public spaces. To advance its transformation into a Smart City, it has implemented a system that transports garbage to recycling and energy plants, promotes recycling, and separates organic waste. It also installed smart "Big Belly" containers with sensors and solar compactors that optimize collection. Regarding air quality, it has monitored air quality for years, identifying sources of pollution and reducing sulfur dioxide emissions, while promoting cleaner municipal vehicles and natural gas heating. Regarding water use, it uses automated systems to measure consumption and encourages the use of gray water and rainwater harvesting. Through the LinkNYC program, it installed thousands of free Wi-Fi hotspots and access to digital services, improving connectivity. Public lighting was upgraded with LED lights that form a smart network to collect real-time data on traffic, pollution, and safety, saving energy and reducing emissions. Smart benches with mobile charging and data collection capabilities have been installed in public spaces to improve park management. For mobility, it implemented Traffic Signal Priority, which favors the passage of buses, installed cameras to control speed in school zones, and promoted the use of public bicycles with Citibike (Shah et al., 2019).
- Amsterdam, the idea for City Data Commons was born as something more than a centralized database. Initially, according to its promoters, it was a practical response to the need to share information without putting people's privacy at risk. The data engineers involved designed a set of ethical protocols that, in addition to anonymizing records, allow users to modify their consent at any time; all in compliance with the General Data Protection Regulation (GDPR) (Nasijuk et al., 2022). This is no small detail: this framework made it possible for the Johan Cruyff Arena to implement a microgrid capable of storing solar energy in second-life batteries from electric vehicles. The result did not stop at efficiency numbers; through an app, residents can check how much energy they have contributed to generating and how much they have

collectively saved, a kind of social measurement tool for electrical engineering (Gracias et al., 2023). Interestingly, a project involving autonomous boats equipped with water quality sensors emerged at the same time. These boats publish their measurements on Amsterdam Open Data. However, in their initial months, most initiatives (82%) focused on efficiency, neglecting equity criteria. This trend led several municipal governments to adjust their funding rules, prioritizing inclusive proposals, such as the installation of sensors in parking spaces reserved for people with disabilities (New et al., 2017).

- In Chennai, India, the Transparent Chennai experience showed that technology can be quite useful in solving problems and highlighting them without sugarcoating the numbers. They used geographic information system (GIS) tools to map the location and number of public restrooms, and what they found was astonishing, as they determined that only 714 facilities were in a condition to serve an estimated 8 to 10 million inhabitants. The disparity was even more serious, given that in informal settlements, there were more than a thousand people per restroom (1,056, to be exact); in formal areas, the ratio was one for every sixty (Sadoway & Shekhar, 2014). While this may seem like an infrastructure problem, in practice it was linked to public health risks and, in particular, to women's safety. To better document this, collaborative mapping platforms allowed citizens to add information on specific shortcomings, combining technical data with personal accounts. This was followed by participatory design workshops focused on pedestrian mobility. This led to the official commitment to redesign 12 km of streets in Nanganallur. Interestingly, the process didn't focus on imposing a "laboratory" solution, but rather on strengthening the civic intelligence that already existed, connecting it with technical tools that made visible what had previously remained obscure.
- In the Mirafiori Sud district of Turin, the MiraMap tool became more than just a technological experiment. It was the result of a collaborative effort between software engineers and the community, seeking a way to communicate problems and proposals without leaving anyone behind. The platform combined the geolocalized social network First Life with a business process management system (BPM), but what was interesting was how it adapted to local constraints. For example, reports could be sent via SMS, and small Arduino devices automatically translated them into emails for users without internet access. Thus, a neighbor could report a pothole or suggest an improvement from a basic phone, and the message would reach the administrative system with an objectively established response time. Interactive maps were updated with colored markers to show the status of each case (De Filippi et al., 2016). In the first phase, 63 reports were received (47 about problems and 16 with

proposals), a modest but sufficient number to catalyze a 110% increase in funding for social projects. This jump was likely due not only to technology, but to the fact that the communication was designed for everyone, including older adults and people with limited digital resources.

- In Salatiga, Indonesia, the idea of becoming a Smart City faced obstacles that are rarely acknowledged in official plans. Although a fairly comprehensive protocol existed, the reality was different: there was no data center or command center to efficiently coordinate information. They even lacked high-capacity internet networks, which are an indispensable requirement for any IoT initiative. Limited budgets explained part of the problem, but not all (Ilhami et al., 2022). What is more relevant in this scenario is the combination of talent shortages and wasted resources: only three ICT engineers served the entire city, while 86 computer institutes remained underutilized, largely disconnected from the local strategy. The consequence was that many projects were put on hold or only partially implemented. Importantly, this case highlights something deeper: open governance is not sustained solely by good ideas or ambitious plans; It requires a balanced ecosystem where infrastructure, human capital, and financing work in a coordinated manner, because the absence of any of these elements ultimately affects the others. In other words, intention alone is not enough; technical and administrative capacity must accompany the strategic vision.

University campuses sometimes function as small urban laboratories, where technologies can be tested before being applied to an entire city. At EPFL in Lausanne, energy engineers installed microgrids connected to solar panels, but the interesting thing is not just the infrastructure: students actively participate, suggesting optimal consumption schedules through interactive dashboards. This Smart City application has not only enabled energy optimization but has also contributed to reducing the carbon footprint (Gassmann et al., 2019). At NUS, autonomous shuttles have not been limited to transporting people; they are linked to mechatronic systems and applications that enable real-time ratings, offering an effective way to measure how collective participation can improve urban mobility performance (Gracias et al., 2023). Before being implemented in entire cities, these experiments allow for the evaluation of complex technologies such as VANET-WSN networks, used for communication between vehicles and infrastructure, while minimizing risks. It is important to note that the real value of these campuses is not only in the devices or algorithms, but in how they facilitate interaction with real users, revealing behavioral patterns and practical challenges that would be difficult to capture in larger urban environments (Mahmood, 2018).

In summary, the cases studied show that interoperability through open standards is key to preventing urban systems from fragmenting. It is worth highlighting that standards such as HyperCat in the United Kingdom or models such as City Data Commons not only organize data: they also make information accessible to those who would normally be excluded, through SMS, dashboards, or interactive maps (New et al., 2017). Chennai, for example, demonstrated how integrating local knowledge with GIS can generate more inclusive decisions, while Salatiga showed that even the most ambitious plans fail if technical and administrative capacity is not properly applied. Interestingly, as Anthopoulos et al. (2022) point out, Smart Cities function as subdomains within smart governments: ethical frameworks for algorithms, including the prohibition of bias in facial recognition, are as important as physical sensors (Löfgren & Webster, 2020). In other words, engineering creates the technical foundation necessary for urban democracy laboratories, but their success depends on how innovation is linked to collective intelligence and genuine citizen participation.

CONCLUSION

This chapter provides a clear and coherent overview of engineering practice and the open governance dynamics that shape smart cities. Its main contribution lies in consolidating an interpretive framework where technological development is translated into direct inputs for public decision-making and citizen participation processes. It comprehensively addresses the contributions of mechanical engineering (particularly in thermal and HVAC systems), mechatronics in urban automation and robotics, chemical sciences in environmental monitoring and materials, and electrical, electronic, and computational engineering in the construction of smart grids, distributed sensors, and data analysis platforms.

This interdisciplinary synthesis not only summarizes relevant findings and projects but also articulates a working hypothesis: cities can operate as "open laboratories" in which technological instrumentation, data processing, and governance architectures provide feedback to produce more efficient, transparent, and socially responsible urban decisions.

From a methodological and objective perspective, the chapter fulfills its purpose of showing how engineering transforms physical inputs and hardware (such as sensors, actuators, microgrids, and autonomous vehicles) into information capital that can be used by public administrations and communities.

The selected case studies (Barcelona, Singapore, New York, Amsterdam, Rio de Janeiro, Chennai, and university experiences) serve as diverse examples, demonstrating different degrees of technological maturity and socio-political integration.

These cases allow us to deduce replicable patterns: interoperability through open standards, the existence of platforms that generalize access to data, and the ability to integrate predictive models into the city's operational processes are determining factors for a technical intervention to culminate in effective governance.

In terms of projected impact, the proposals analyzed suggest concrete paths for applying engineering solutions to public policies: the use of HVAC and pollutant measurement as inputs for local environmental quality policies, the integration of V2X and platforms in the prioritization of emergency fleets, and the use of microgrids and second-life batteries for local energy policies. These applications demonstrate how engineering can enable real-time response capabilities and accountability mechanisms, for example when platforms such as Sentilo or City Data Commons allow citizens to compare official data with community measurements. In practical terms, this implies that engineers not only design smart systems but also configure the traceability and verifiability of urban decisions, which is a key aspect for the legitimacy of open governance processes.

This chapter presents a robust and multidisciplinary conceptual framework useful for researchers and policymakers and also establishes an operational overview of technologies and cases that can guide concrete technical decisions. It also defines the characteristics that establish the capacity for its practical application, which is mediated by contextual factors recognized in the chapter itself: availability of financing, institutional capacity, digital literacy, and regulatory frameworks. Furthermore, the chapter establishes an operational link between technology and reflection, but does so with a certain sense of urgency: it is not enough to describe and implement sensors, algorithms, or architectures; it is necessary to design assessment tools that capture the real complexity of the city. These tools must combine performance measurements (network response, service stability, energy efficiency) with indicators that make social dynamics visible (who has access, how it is used, and who is excluded) and with criteria that allow for the evaluation of the governance of public decisions.

Finally, the chapter offers solutions that can be applied in practice, supported by a conceptual framework that links infrastructure, data management, and democratic processes. For this proposal to move from paper to reality, it is essential that empirical evaluations take center stage, applying them in diverse settings where not only technical performance can be assessed, but also its social impact and its capacity to strengthen governance.

REFERENCES

Anthopoulos, L., Sirakoulis, K., & Reddick, C. G. (2022). Conceptualizing smart government: Interrelations and reciprocities with smart city. *Digital Government: Research and Practice*, *2*(4), 1–28. DOI: 10.1145/346506

Bakıcı, T., Almirall, E., & Wareham, J. (2013). A smart city initiative: The case of Barcelona. *Journal of the Knowledge Economy*, *4*(2), 135–148. DOI: 10.1007/s13132-012-0084-9

Bayindir, R., Colak, I., Fulli, G., & Demirtas, K. (2016). Smart grid technologies and applications. *Renewable & Sustainable Energy Reviews*, *66*, 499–516. DOI: 10.1016/j.rser.2016.08.002

Bhati, A., Hansen, M., & Chan, C. M. (2017). Energy conservation through smart homes in a smart city: A lesson for Singapore households. *Energy Policy*, *104*, 230–239. DOI: 10.1016/j.enpol.2017.01.032

Bouskela, M., Casseb, M., Bassi, S., De Luca, C., & Facchina, M. (2016). *La ruta hacia las Smart Cities: migrando de una gestión tradicional a la ciudad inteligente. Banco interamericano de Desarrollo*. BID.

Budrin, A. G., Budrina, E. V., Lebedeva, A. S., Rogavichene, L. I., & Abdullah, M. (2020). Electronic Engineering as a Factor of Sustainable Development for Smart City. In 2020 IEEE Conference of Russian Young Researchers in Electrical and Electronic Engineering (EIConRus) (pp. 1637-1642). IEEE. DOI: DOI: 10.1109/EIConRus49466.2020.9038943

Capdevila, I., & Zarlenga, M. I. (2015). Smart city or smart citizens? The Barcelona case. *Journal of Strategy and Management*, *8*(3), 266–282. DOI: 10.1108/JSMA-03-2015-0030

Cassandras, C. G. (2017). Automating mobility in smart cities. *Annual Reviews in Control*, *2017*, 1–8. DOI: 10.1016/j.arcontrol.2017.10.001

Cavada, M., Tight, M. R., & Rogers, C. D. (2019). A smart city case study of Singapore-Is Singapore truly smart? In *Smart city emergence* (pp. 295–314). Elsevier. DOI: 10.1016/B978-0-12-816169-2.00014-6

Choi, M. I., Cho, K., Hwang, J. Y., Park, L. W., Jang, K. H., Park, S., & Park, S. (2017). Design and implementation of IoT-based HVAC system for future zero energy building. In 2017 IEEE International Conference on Pervasive Computing and Communications Workshops (PerCom Workshops) (pp. 605-610). IEEE. DOI: DOI: 10.1109/PERCOMW.2017.7917631

De Filippi, F., Coscia, C., Boella, G., Antonini, A., Calafiore, A., Cantini, A., Guido, R., Salaroglio, C., Sanasi, L., & Schifanella, C. (2016). MiraMap: A We-government tool for smart peripheries in Smart Cities. *IEEE Access : Practical Innovations, Open Solutions*, *4*, 3824–3843. DOI: 10.1109/ACCESS.2016.2548558

Dhanalakshmi, S., Poongothai, M., & Sharma, K. (2020). IoT based indoor air quality and smart energy management for HVAC system. *Procedia Computer Science*, *171*, 1800–1809. DOI: 10.1016/j.procs.2020.04.193

Dutta, J., Chowdhury, C., Roy, S., Middya, A. I., & Gazi, F. (2017). Towards smart city: sensing air quality in city based on opportunistic crowd-sensing. In *Proceedings of the 18th international conference on distributed computing and networking* (pp. 1-6). DOI: 10.1145/3007748.3018286

Gaffney, C., & Robertson, C. (2018). Smarter than smart: Rio de Janeiro's flawed emergence as a smart city. *Journal of Urban Technology*, *25*(3), 47–64. DOI: 10.1080/10630732.2015.1102423

Gassmann, O., Böhm, J., & Palmié, M. (2019). Smart cities. In *Smart cities* (pp. 25–66). Emerald Publishing Limited., DOI: 10.1108/978-1-78769-613-620191009

Gracias, J. S., Parnell, G. S., Specking, E., Pohl, E. A., & Buchanan, R. (2023). Smart cities—A structured literature review. *Smart Cities*, *6*(4), 1719–1743. DOI: 10.3390/smartcities6040080

Grigorescu, S. D., Argatu, F. C., Paturca, S. V., Cepisca, C., Seritan, G. C., Adochiei, F. C., & Enache, B. (2019). Robotic platform with medical applications in the smart city environment. In 2019 11th International Symposium on Advanced Topics in Electrical Engineering (ATEE) (pp. 1-6). IEEE. DOI: DOI: 10.1109/ATEE.2019.8724993

Haghbin, S., Lundmark, S., Alakula, M., & Carlson, O. (2012). Grid-connected integrated battery chargers in vehicle applications: Review and new solution. *IEEE Transactions on Industrial Electronics*, *60*(2), 459–473. DOI: 10.1109/TIE.2012.2187414

Hayat, P. (2016). Smart cities: A global perspective. *India Quarterly*, *72*(2), 177–191. DOI: 10.1177/0974928416637930

Ilhami, R., Marlovia, E., & Achmad, W. (2022). Smart government policy implementation for smart city concept realization. *International Journal of Health Sciences*, *6*(S5), 8379–8389. DOI: 10.53730/ijhs.v6nS5.11753

Khattak, H. A., Farman, H., Jan, B., & Din, I. U. (2019). Toward integrating vehicular clouds with IoT for smart city services. *IEEE Network*, *33*(2), 65–71. DOI: 10.1109/MNET.2019.1800236

Lee, W. H., & Chiu, C. Y. (2020). Design and implementation of a smart traffic signal control system for smart city applications. *Sensors (Basel)*, *20*(2), 508. DOI: 10.3390/s20020508 PMID: 31963229

Löfgren, K., & Webster, C. W. R. (2020). The value of Big Data in government: The case of 'smart cities'. *Big Data & Society*, *7*(1), 1–14. DOI: 10.1177/2053951720912775

Mahmood, Z. Mahmood, & Wheeler. (2018). Smart Cities. Springer.

Nayak, S. K. (2019). *Electric vehicle charging topologies, control schemes for smart city application. In 2019 IEEE transportation electrification conference (ITEC-India).* IEEE.

New, J., Castro, D., & Beckwith, M. (2017). *How national governments can help smart cities succeed.* Center for Data Innovation.

Peter, O., Pradhan, A., & Mbohwa, C. (2024). Smart Mechatronics: Innovating Sustainable Solutions for the Future. In Proceedings 5th African international conference industrial engineering & operations management (pp. 1037-1047).

Rajith, A., Soki, S., & Hiroshi, M. (2018). Real-time optimized HVAC control system on top of an IoT framework. In 2018 Third international conference on fog and mobile edge computing (FMEC) (pp. 181-186). IEEE. DOI: 10.1109/FMEC.2018.8364062

Ryalat, M., Franco, E., Elmoaqet, H., Almtireen, N., & Al-Refai, G. (2024). The integration of advanced mechatronic systems into Industry 4.0 for smart manufacturing. *Sustainability (Basel)*, *16*(19), 8504. DOI: 10.3390/su16198504

Sadoway, D., & Shekhar, S. (2014). (Re) prioritizing citizens in 'smart cities' governance: Examples of smart citizenship form India. *Journal of Community Informatics*, *10*(3). Advance online publication. DOI: 10.15353/joci.v10i3.3447

Serra, J., Pubill, D., Antonopoulos, A., & Verikoukis, C. (2014). Smart HVAC control in IoT: Energy consumption minimization with user comfort constraints. *TheScientificWorldJournal*, *2014*(1), 1–11. DOI: 10.1155/2014/161874 PMID: 25054163

Shah, J., Kothari, J., & Doshi, N. (2019). A survey of smart city infrastructure via case study on New York. *Procedia Computer Science*, *160*, 702–705. DOI: 10.1016/j.procs.2019.11.024

Smith, J. (2020). The Future of Smart Cities: Integrating Mechanical Systems with IoT. *American Journal Of Mechanical Engineering And Technology*, *1*(6), 8–15.

Tiwari, S., Jain, A., Ahmed, N. M. O. S., Charu, , Alkwai, L. M., Dafhalla, A. K. Y., & Hamad, S. A. S. (2021). Machine learning-based model for prediction of power consumption in smart grid-smart way towards smart city. *Expert Systems: International Journal of Knowledge Engineering and Neural Networks*, *39*(5), e12832. DOI: 10.1111/exsy.12832

US Dept of Labor. (2000). *Occupational outlook handbook.* JIST Publishing.

Viani, F., Polo, A., Robol, F., Giarola, E., & Ferro, A. (2016). Experimental validation of a wireless distributed system for smart public lighting management. In 2016 IEEE International Smart Cities Conference (ISC2) (pp. 1-6). IEEE. DOI: DOI: 10.1109/ISC2.2016.7580852

Wickert, J., & Lewis, K. (2013). An introduction to mechanical engineering. Cengage learning.

Woinaroschy, A. (2016). Smart cities will need chemistry. Acta Marisiensis. *Seria Technologica*, *13*(1), 5.

Chapter 8
Future Perspectives and Innovative Governance Models:
Digital Innovation for Future Governance

Miguel Ruiz Jaimes
https://orcid.org/0000-0002-2585-9896
Universidad Politécnica del Estado de Morelos, Mexico

Angel Israel Daza Castillo
El Centro Nacional de Investigación y Desarrollo Tecnológico (CENIDET), Mexico

Yadira Toledo Navarro
Universidad Politécnica del Estado de Morelos, Mexico

Jazmín Rodríguez Flores
https://orcid.org/0000-0002-3313-0325
Universidad Politécnica de Pachuca, Mexico

Ana Lidia Barcenas Cortés
https://orcid.org/0000-0001-7281-1409
Instituto Tecnológico de Tláhuac III, Mexico

José Efrén Marmolejo Valle
https://orcid.org/0000-0002-7191-4489
Universidad Autónoma de Guerrero, Mexico

ABSTRACT

This chapter, per the authors, explores the evolving landscape of public governance in the digital era, emphasizing the integration of emerging technologies, citizen participation, and innovative institutional models. It outlines short-, medium-, and long-term trends shaping digital governance, including artificial intelligence, blockchain, and predictive analytics. Through real-world examples and comparative case studies, the chapter highlights the transition from traditional bureaucratic systems to collaborative, technology-enabled models. It also presents forward-looking public

DOI: 10.4018/979-8-3373-5535-1.ch008

policy recommendations centered on transparency, adaptability, and inclusivity, with an emphasis on multistakeholder collaboration and digital literacy. The chapter concludes with critical reflections on ethical governance, social inclusion, and the challenges posed by accelerated technological change, offering a roadmap for building resilient, citizen-centric institutions.

1. INTRODUCTION

Public governance is changing quickly because digital technologies are now used everywhere. Old ways of running government, which rely on strict hierarchies, top-down sharing of information, and rigid rules, are not working well anymore in today's connected world. New ways of governing are coming up, focusing on teamwork, shared responsibility, flexibility, and putting people at the center.

This shift is not just about technology, but also about a new way of thinking. The Digital Era Governance model, proposed by Dunleavy et al. (2006), marks a move from traditional government systems to more connected, digital-focused processes. Today, openness, responsiveness, and data-driven decision-making are key. Governments are no longer just service providers they are spaces for citizen participation and shared responsibility among various actors.

The move from rigid government control to collaborative design reflects how agile thinking is reshaping public administration. According to De Luna et al. (2014), Agile Governance in ICT helps agencies become more flexible, develop solutions in stages, and focus on user needs. Inspired by agile software methods, this approach values adaptability and stakeholder involvement. Public organizations now need to work in real time, test quickly, and adjust as citizens' needs evolve.

Technology has made services more efficient and has also created new ways of governing. Schneider et al. (2020) introduced the idea of Modular Politics, where governance is like a computer system that is spread out. In this model, different parts such as citizens, nongovernmental organizations, and public agencies work independently but follow common rules and use open systems. This approach makes the system stronger, helps avoid delays in decisionmaking, and allows governments to react faster to emergencies or public needs.

At the center of this chapter is the belief that the future of governance depends on combining innovation, technology, and citizen involvement. Simply putting old processes online isn't enough; public institutions must be redesigned to align digital tools with democratic values. This requires rethinking decision-making, participation, and how trust is built in data-driven systems. Governance today is no longer linear it's a dynamic system that evolves. Like computer networks, the goal isn't perfect central control, but collaboration and adaptability. People, empowered by technology, are now both the drivers and guardians of democratic innovation.

2. SHORT, MEDIUM, AND LONG-TERM TRENDS IN DIGITAL GOVERNANCE

2.1 Short-Term Projections

Digital government has transformed the relationship between citizens and the state, making interaction with public institutions less bureaucratic and more accessible (Ramírez et al, 2024). The adoption of digital government has opened up a world of possibilities for improving the provision of public services, as well as resource management and communication between the government and society (Alcudia & Venancio, 2023), therefore, the implementation of digital technologies has allowed governments to respond more effectively to the citizens' needs, thereby improving transparency and accountability (Zendejas, 2024).

In Latin America, countries like Uruguay, implemented a citizen service window offering over two thousand digital procedures, as outlined in decree 353/2023, by the Agency for Electronic Government and Information and Knowledge Society, meanwhile, Chile developed a digital procedures portal where people can complete processes for temporary and permanent residency, document verification, and more. In Colombia, they've launched a single window for procedures and services, enabling citizens to handle everything from document requests to tax payments without needing to be physically present (Ramírez et al, 2024; CEPAL, 2021).

On the other hand, Morales (2021), mentions that the Mexican standard NOM-151-SCFI-2016, establishes the rules that companies and/or organizations in Mexico must follow to ensure the protection of digital documents. Currently, some basic services such as tax payments, passport renewal, driver's licenses, and birth certificates have largely evolved, as they can now be requested, paid for, and downloaded online, without the need to visit a physical office (2024).

These advancements lead to greater inclusion and transparency. However, this progress is not enough yet; given that digital infrastructure, resistance to change from officials, and some important cybersecurity aspects are obstacles that need to be addressed as soon as possible (OECD, 2020).

Trends for the next three years

In the coming years, the trend is for digital government to focus on personalized and automated services, as artificial intelligence and digital government will play a major role. This includes advanced chatbots that resolve complex queries without human intervention (Segovia, 2025; Dominguez-Tabera, 2024), similarly, the utilization of facial biometrics for face identification in web applications and on mobile devices (Galindo et al. 2025).

In addition, the development of virtual assistants in legal fields and the creation of intelligent platforms capable of involving citizens in decision-making regarding security and justice will help to improve crime prevention, and optimize court cases, processing them quickly, automatically evaluating evidence, and suggesting sentences based on projected data and the context of the case.

Finally, the development of a public resource monitoring platform, where real-time data on government expenditures or contract awards can be processed, allowing for the detection of irregularities and alerting authorities to potential fraud or acts of corruption (Castelán & Aceves, 2024; Silos et al, 2023).

2.2 Medium-Term Trends

AI Integration in Data Analysis for Public Policy

The integration of Artificial Intelligence (AI) into data analysis processes for public policy marks a significant advancement. It greatly enhances governments' ability to make better, more efficient, and citizen-focused decisions. By leveraging AI, public administrations can examine vast volumes of data, identify patterns and trends, predict outcomes, and optimize resource allocation, leading to the creation of more effective policies and overall improvement in services (Zendejas, 2024).

AI offers various applications for data analysis in the public sector, such as:

- **Information Observation:** When machine learning algorithms and data science are applied, they streamline the review and synthesis of extremely significant volumes of information. This is crucial for formulating laws, reports, and databases, enabling technical teams to make more informed decisions (Sánchez et al, 2021).
- **Decision Making:** AI systems predict outcomes and optimize decision-making by automating complex tasks. This is particularly useful for digital governance, where AI and big data are redefining the paradigms of political communication. (De la Garza & Gómez, 2024).
- **Optimizing Administrative Processes:** The implementation of AI proves practical for automating repetitive tasks, and helps processes to be optimal (Sandoya & Mawyin, 2025).
- **Advanced Citizen Attention:** Chatbots, an AI tool, streamline citizen services by acting as virtual assistants for inquiries, procedures, and resolving doubts, thereby enhancing the citizen experience. AI applied in government services offers greater efficiency and better use of time, allowing employees to foster improved relationships with citizens. (Ocaña et al, 2021).

- **Fraud Detection:** AI identifies anomalies in large volumes of data, which detects irregularities and contributes to data transparency in public management. (Sandoya & Mawyin, 2025; Silos et al, 2023).
- **Data Governance:** For AI to truly thrive in the public sector, it's absolutely crucial to implement an integrated data governance strategy. This approach ensures the quality, security, and accessibility of information (Zendejas, 2024; Salvador, 2021).

Chatbots are computer programs that simulate human-like conversations, allowing the public to interact with government services in a closer, more accessible, and efficient way. (Domínguez-Tabera et al, 2024). Conversational AI utilizes technologies like Natural Language Processing (NLP) to respond intelligently to user queries. (Gordon, 2023).

Conversational Chatbots in Social Services offer:

- **Information and Orientation:** Chatbots answer frequently asked questions about procedures. A great example of this was during the COVID-19 pandemic, where chatbots were instrumental in disseminating government information and regulations. (Peña et al, 2022).
- **Greater Accessibility:** Chatbots are always available and accessible from various devices, effectively eliminating geographical and time barriers. This makes it much easier to access information and services, especially for vulnerable populations. (Minguijon & Serrano-Martínez, 2022).
- **Collection for Continuous Improvement:** Chatbots generate important data on citizen needs, which allows social service agencies to identify areas for improvement. However, it's crucial to consider data privacy and the responsibility for decisions made by these systems (Arguelles & Amaro, 2023).

Impact Assessment of Automated Decisions

Algorithmic Impact Assessment (AIA) is an emerging accountability tool for organizations that develop and implement automated decision-making support systems. Its purpose is to identify the harms caused by these algorithmic systems and to ensure that appropriate measures are taken to mitigate them. (Ashar et al., 2025).

Impact Assessment includes key aspects, which are:

- **Risk Identification:** It's essential to foresee potential risks and harms from AI, even in self-learning and deep learning systems. This involves considering the sources of risk and negligence, as well as the areas where these systems have effects. (Aguirre-Sala, 2022).

- **Ethical Impact Assessments (EIA):** It's important to evaluate the ethical implications of AI systems. EIAs identify both positive and negative impacts at early stages to protect the benefits of AI and avoid its disadvantages. (Mittelstadt et al., 2023).
- **Stakeholder Participation:** A crucial aspect of Algorithmic Impact Assessment (AIA) is co-creation, where external perspectives shouldn't be overlooked in decision-making. It's vital to ensure that those who will experience the impact are represented in the process of defining it, considering social, technological, legal, and political aspects (Mbuy et al., 2022). Impact assessment is an essential mechanism that ensures AI systems are accountable, promoting their ethical and beneficial development and use for society.

2.3 Long-Term Scenarios

Autonomous Adaptive Government (Government 5.0)

When we talk about Autonomous Adaptive Government, it symbolizes an evolution in public administration where technology, especially Artificial Intelligence (AI), is integrated and managed to create government systems that are more resilient and highly efficient for citizens. This model shows us that public administrations need to be proactive, capable of anticipating challenges and adapting to constant change. (Díaz-Parra et al, 2022).

Government 5.0, the adaptive model we're discussing, highlights the interconnection between cyberspace and physical space to solve large-scale social and economic problems. This involves utilizing advanced technologies like mixed reality, the Internet of Things (IoT), robotics, and AI to create personalized, evidence-based solutions. (Travez-Tipan, & Villafuerte-Garzon, 2023). Adaptability is a cornerstone that allows policies and services to dynamically integrate with changes in population needs and emerging challenges. (Minguijon & Serrano-Martinez, 2022).

Predictive Governance Models with real-time analysis use AI, big data, and other advanced technologies to process large volumes of data from diverse sources. They identify patterns, predict future trends, and generate policy recommendations instantaneously.

This is represented in various areas:

- **Epidemic Prevention and Public Health:** Real-time analysis of health data (such as climate data, reported citizen cases, and people's mobility) allows governments to anticipate disease outbreaks, identify at-risk groups, and proactively and efficiently offer medical resources, as was seen during COVID-19. (Dominguez-Tabera, 2024; Peña et al, 2022).

- **Citizen Safety:** By monitoring patterns considered criminal, predictive models help security forces prevent crimes before they occur.
- **Smart Urban Administration:** Connected sensors throughout the city collect data on traffic, air quality, energy consumption, and the use of public spaces. A predictive governance model can analyze this data in real time to optimize traffic flow, anticipate infrastructure maintenance needs, or identify high-probability areas for incidents for early intervention.
- **Natural Disaster Management:** The study of real-time meteorological and geological data, combined with predictive models, allows governments to anticipate natural phenomena, assess their impact, and manage evacuations more quickly and effectively. Adaptability and resilience are fundamental in these scenarios. (Minguijon & Serrano-Martinez, 2022).

For these models to be effective, robust data and AI governance is fundamental. This ensures the privacy, reliability, and quality of data. This involves establishing normative frameworks and continuously monitoring the performance of these models to prevent biases and guarantee equitable and just results. (Salvador, 2021).

Benefits:

- **Traffic Management:** Sensors and cameras collect real-time data on vehicle flow. Predictive models can anticipate congestion based on historical patterns, special events, or weather conditions. This allows authorities to dynamically adjust traffic lights or suggest alternative routes.
- **Optimization of Urban Services:** Real-time analysis of data on energy usage, water consumption, or waste generation optimizes urban infrastructure, resource planning, and the implementation of more sustainable policies.

On the other hand, the government metaverse symbolizes a transformative interaction between the State and citizens, particularly in the provision of public services. By establishing virtual spaces for citizen deliberation, the metaverse has the potential to transform civic participation, government transparency, and administrative efficiency. These are environments where citizens can interact with avatars of officials, access public information intuitively, participate in consultations and debates, and even experience proposed policies before their implementation. (González-Sanmiguel, 2025).

The concept of the metaverse implies hyper-space-temporality, sustainability through its internal cycles, interoperability, and heterogeneity (Moya-Martínez, 2024). These characteristics are essential for its potential in public administration. A timeline graphic illustrates the different technological phases that have transformed the relationship between government and citizens, highlighting the potential of the government metaverse.

3. INNOVATIVE GOVERNANCE MODELS

Over the past two decades, the paradigm of public governance has undergone profound transformations, driven by technological advances, shifting social dynamics, and the urgent need to build trust in institutions. This chapter explores innovative models of governance from distributed decision-making to participatory ecosystems in smart cities by integrating practical examples and real-world cases.

3.1 From Centralized Power to Distributed Decision-Making

Concept of Distributed Governance

Governance has traditionally relied on hierarchical structures, where the flow of information and decisions move vertically. In contrast, distributed governance proposes a decentralized model in which multiple actors, including citizens, organizations, and both public and private institutions—share power and responsibility in decision-making processes.

In computational terms, distributed governance parallels distributed systems in computer science: there are interconnected nodes (actors), each capable of processing, validating, and generating decisions independently, without relying on a single central authority. This architecture mitigates bottlenecks and enhances the resilience of political and administrative systems.

One of the most emblematic cases of distributed governance is the use of blockchain technology in participatory processes. Blockchain is a form of Distributed Ledger Technology (DLT) that enables transaction validation without intermediaries, fostering trust through cryptography and consensus mechanisms among multiple nodes.

Case Study: In cities like Seoul (South Korea) and Zug (Switzerland), blockchain-based platforms have been implemented for participatory budgeting. Citizens are empowered to propose projects and vote securely. Each vote becomes a recorded blockchain transaction, resistant to tampering, ensuring transparency and trust.

- Benefits of Blockchain in Civic Participation
- Vote traceability
- Prevention of electoral manipulation
- Participant anonymity
- Reduction in auditing costs

Numerical Example: Consider a municipality with 10,000 voters. In a traditional voting system, the average cost of organization, staffing, and auditing may total around $50,000 USD. With blockchain, operational costs can be reduced by 40–60%, as votes are automatically validated

Table 1. Cost Comparison: Traditional Voting vs. Blockchain-Based Voting

Aspect	Traditional System	Blockchain System
Staffing Costs	$20,000	$8,000
Auditing	$15,000	$5,000
Infrastructure	$15,000	$10,000
Total	**$50,000**	**$23,000**

3.2 Experimental and Agile Government

Government Innovation Labs

Experimental innovation is a methodology that applies agile principles common in software development to the design of public policies. This is where government innovation laboratories (GovLabs) emerge: interdisciplinary spaces for prototyping solutions before scaling them.

As in agile programming, work is done in short iterations (sprints), pilot tests are conducted, and feedback from real users (in this case, citizens or civil servants) is integrated throughout the process.

Case: The Governance Lab (GovLab), based at New York University, has established itself as one of the leading research and action centers dedicated to governmental innovation. Its mission is to transform how governments tackle public problems, promoting more collaborative, transparent, and evidence-based models. Through initiatives such as Open Data 500, Smarter Crowdsourcing, and Data Stewards, GovLab facilitates the design of policies that incorporate citizen knowledge and real-time data analysis.

GovLab operates as a think-and-do tank, combining academic research with practical implementation. It collaborates with governments, civil society organizations, and companies to develop solutions based on open data, collective intelligence, and civic technology. Its projects include platforms such as DataCollaboratives.org, CrowdLaw and The Living Library. These initiatives foster the responsible exchange of data and enable citizen participation in policymaking.

Examples of Application:

- In the Responsible Data for Children project, GovLab worked with thousands of sensitive datasets to improve mental health services in Uganda.
- In its virtual community's report, GovLab analyzed more than 15,000 users across 15 countries, conducting interviews with 50 group leaders and 26 international experts to understand the social impact of online groups.
- The Open Data 500 initiative has cataloged hundreds of companies that leverage open data to generate both public and economic value.

Case: MindLab, founded in Denmark in 2002, was the first intra-ministerial government innovation lab in Europe, and one of the global pioneers in applying user-centered design methodologies in the public sector. It operated until 2018, and its legacy lives on through the Danish Design Centre, which has adopted many of its practices. Unlike traditional approaches to public policy design, MindLab promoted co-creation among citizens, civil servants, and experts, with the goal of redesigning public services based on the real experience of users. Its structure included three ministries: Education, Employment, and Economy, allowing for cross-sectoral collaboration and the breaking of bureaucratic silos.

Example: One of MindLab's most representative impacts was the redesign of the social assistance application process. Using interviews, direct observation, and co-creation sessions with users and officials, friction points were identified that were invisible from the institutional perspective. The result was a simplified process that reduced processing times by 30%, improving both administrative efficiency and citizen experience.

Although MindLab closed in 2018, its influence has spread globally. Similar labs have been established in cities such as Mexico City, Helsinki, Singapore, and Washington D.C., inspired by its model. In Denmark, many municipalities and government agencies continue to use its methods—even if not explicitly labeled "Design Thinking."

MindLab didn't just redesign services, it redesigned how the government thinks, listens, and acts. Its legacy is an invitation to rethink governance as an open, empathetic, and experimental process.

Practical Example: Imagine that in Denmark, a person in vulnerable circumstances needs to apply for housing assistance. Prior to MindLab's intervention, the process was highly bureaucratic, with an average duration of 90 days from submission of documentation to receiving a response.

Main issues identified included:

- Excessive duplication of forms, each required by different departments.
- A requirement to submit physical documents, even when digital government databases already hold them.

- Slow communication between responsible ministries (Labor, Social Affairs, Finance).
- Limited understanding of the process from the citizen's perspective, leading to frustration and mistrust.

3.3 Smart Cities and Participatory Ecosystems

Smart cities represent one of the most significant urban transformations of the 21st century. It's not just about embedding sensors or digital networks into urban space but about rethinking how cities can use technology to address social, economic, and environmental challenges in a participatory and sustainable way.

Medellín as an Urban Laboratory

Smart cities represent one of the most significant urban transformations of the 21st century. It is not merely about incorporating sensors, digital networks, or technological infrastructure into urban space, but about redefining the city model: a city that uses technology as a tool to address social, economic, and environmental problems in a participatory, inclusive, and sustainable way. This approach implies open governance, where citizens are not mere recipients of services, but active participants in decision-making, public policy design, and the creation of innovative solutions. Urban intelligence does not reside solely in devices, but in the ability to articulate collective knowledge, open data, and political will to improve quality of life.

The transformation of Medellín (Colombia) is an emblematic case of how a city can become an urban laboratory. For decades, Medellín faced high levels of violence, inequality, and social fragmentation. However, beginning in the 2000s, the city undertook a process of social fabric reconstruction based on two fundamental pillars: technology and citizen participation.

Medellín not only adopted digital tools but redefined its urban development model with a smart city vision that integrates innovation, inclusion, and sustainability. This transformation has been internationally recognized, positioning Medellín as one of the most innovative cities in Latin America.

Key Initiatives

- Medellín Smart City: Implementation of IoT sensors for traffic management, public safety, and environmental monitoring. Examples include the CITRA system for smart mobility and EPM's smart water system using IoT technology.
- Ruta N: Innovation center that connects the ecosystem of science, technology, and innovation. It has mobilized over 139 billion Colombian pesos in capital, created 14,223 jobs, and strengthened more than 2,100 STI-based businesses.

- Mi Medellín: Digital citizen participation platform that allows residents to submit ideas, vote on projects, and co-create urban solutions. This tool has been key to democratizing urban planning and strengthening local governance.

Transformative Results

- Reduction in homicides: Medellín achieved a reduction of more than 80% in homicides over two decades, thanks to integrated policies in security, social urbanism, and technology.
- Growth of the digital economy: The city has attracted more than 1 billion U.S. dollars in foreign investment, consolidating its position as a regional tech hub.
- Co-designed urban projects: From parks to transportation systems like the Metrocable, many projects have been co-created with the community, integrating participatory design and territorial approaches.

Innovation and Participation Ecosystem

Medellín has developed a participatory ecosystem that connects academia, government, businesses, and citizens. This quadruple helix model has enabled innovation to become not an isolated process, but a collective dynamic that responds to the real challenges of the territory.

The city has implemented more than 50 smart city initiatives, including the Neutral Network for digital connectivity, the ICT Laboratory for territorial renewal, and the Smart City Master Plan, which positions Medellín as one of the three smartest cities in Latin America.

Government as Platform: Civic-Digital Ecosystems

The notion of Government as a Platform (GaaP) represents a paradigmatic shift in how the State interacts with society. Rather than being the sole provider of public services, the government becomes an enabling infrastructure, offering APIs, open data, regulatory frameworks, and digital environments so that third parties—businesses, civil society organizations, universities, and citizens—can co-create public solutions.

This model draws inspiration from technology platforms like Amazon Web Services (AWS), which do not offer final products but instead provide modular infrastructure upon which others build applications, services, and experiences. In a governmental context, this means the State provides the digital foundations for innovation to occur in a distributed, collaborative, and scalable manner.

Emblematic Examples

- o United Kingdom – Government Digital Service (GDS): GDS has been a pioneer in implementing the GaaP model. Through its GOV.UK platform, it offers a set of reusable components, such as authentication systems (One Login), payment gateways (GOV.UK Pay), and user-centered design guides. This has enabled multiple government agencies to develop coherent, secure, and citizen-centered services.
- o Brazil – Participa.br and Brasil Participativo: Brazil has developed platforms like Participa.br and Brasil Participativo, which allow citizens to propose, vote on, and debate laws, public policies, and participatory budgets. These digital tools have been key in strengthening deliberative democracy and institutional transparency.

Advantages of the GaaP Model

- Cost savings: By reusing digital components (such as APIs, identity systems, or payment modules), duplicated efforts are avoided and public spending on technology development is reduced.
- Greater citizen participation: Open platforms enable citizens to directly engage in the creation, evaluation, and improvement of public services, strengthening democratic legitimacy.
- Accelerated innovation: By opening the governmental ecosystem to developers, startups, and civil organizations, agile solutions tailored to local contexts and with high social impact are encouraged.

Civic-Digital Ecosystems

The GaaP model is not limited to technological infrastructure. It also involves the creation of collaborative ecosystems, where the government acts as a facilitator, not a controller. This requires:

- Open standards and interoperability
- Shared governance between public and private actors
- Data protection and digital security
- Institutional capacity to adopt agile methodologies

Comparison between Traditional Models vs. Innovative Governance Models

To understand the magnitude of the changes, the following comparative table is presented.

Table 2. Traditional Models vs. Innovative Governance Models

Characteristic	Traditional Model	Innovative Model
Decision-making	Hierarchical, centralized	Distributed, collaborative
Citizen role	Service recipient	Policy co-creator
Technologies	Closed, legacy systems	Blockchain, APIs, platforms
Policy management	Long-term planning	Iterative, experimental
Transparency	Limited, periodic reports	Open data, real-time
Innovation speed	Slow	High, with rapid prototyping
Costs	High, rigid structures	Reduced through digitization
Notable examples	Classical bureaucracy	GovLabs, GaaP, Smart Cities

Governance models represent a paradigm shift that goes beyond mere digitization of processes. They involve a structural redesign of how power, participation, and public value creation are conceived. Moreover, understanding these approaches is essential, since technology has become the infrastructure supporting sectors such as democracy, state efficiency, and citizen trust.

4. POLICY RECOMMENDATIONS FOR A TECHNOLOGY-DRIVEN AND CITIZEN-CENTRIC GOVERNMENT

Throughout human history, humankind has demonstrated its ability to anticipate challenges, adapt to changing circumstances, and build systems of government that foster coexistence, progress, and social justice. However, in the last three decades, rapid technological development, the complexity of crises, and the disproportionate interdependence of societies have posed new challenges to public institutions. Formulating public policies no longer involves addressing existing issues, but also anticipating realities that are not yet fully visible.

For a government that needs to promote technology and focus on citizens, policies must be implemented around transparency, citizen participation, efficiency, and accessibility in the provision of public services. Thus, in specific terms, additionally essential are investment in digital infrastructure, the promotion of digital literacy among the population, the protection of personal data through the use of encryption, and the stimulation of technological innovation in public administration.

In this context, it is essential to redefine how public policies are constructed, implemented, and evaluated. Reaction is not enough; It takes anticipation. It's not enough to have rigid rules; it takes flexibility. It's not enough to make decisions in the dark; it takes transparency. And it's not enough to govern from a single institution; it takes collaboration. Below, we explore five guiding principles that, together, can guide the design of more resilient, responsible, and effective policies: proactivity, adaptability, transparency, inter-institutional collaboration, and ethical and technological assessment.

4.1 Principles for Designing Future-Ready Policies

In a digital government that focuses on citizens, transparency and accountability should not just be seen as routine tasks but as important basics that help build and keep public confidence in the government. Using e-government systems has shown to be a good way to make information more accessible, limit unnecessary choices in decisions, and encourage people to actively watch over how government works.

These digital tools also allow for real-time tracking of how well institutions are doing and help include citizens more effectively in decision-making. Setyarto et al. (2025) say that e-government improves how quickly and efficiently government work gets done and makes corruption seem less likely by removing unnecessary steps and simplifying official processes. This research shows the need for creating forward-thinking public policies that include transparency, accountability, and shared efforts from the start, as these are key to dealing with new challenges in the digital age.

4.2 Multistakeholder Collaboration

Numerous policies recommend measures to promote technology- and citizen-based governance by encouraging multi-level and multi-sector collaboration, particularly within the triple helix between governments, academia, and civil society. These recommendations emphasize the integration of information and communication technologies (ICTs) to strengthen participatory governance and jointly develop public policies.

Triple Helix (government–academia–civil society).

The original Triple Helix model (Etzkowitz and Leydesdorff, 1995) has been the subject of multiple reformulations that seek to adapt it to contexts where innovation transcends the technological-market dimension. Particularly in Latin America, a variant is emerging that reconfigures the vertices of the triangle and replaces industry with a centrally organized civil society. This reformulation responds to:

a) Criticism of economism in innovation policies
b) Recognition of non-academic knowledge
c) The demand for more inclusive development models

In the socialized Triple Helix model, each actor plays specific roles that, when articulated, generate collaborative dynamics for social innovation. Universities adopt a transformative role that transcends the mere production of academic knowledge, shifting toward participatory action research, where scientific knowledge is built in dialogue with local knowledge. For its part, organized civil society assumes a leading role in identifying local problems, co-producing solutions, and assessing social impact. In this framework, the government abandons its traditional role as central planner to become a facilitator of deliberative spaces, an articulator of public policies, and a provider of resources with a territorial focus.

These structures operate as interfaces that mediate between diverse institutional logics, enabling the fluid circulation of knowledge and resources.

Example: Public policies co-created with digital participation platforms

Digital participation platforms play a fundamental role in the joint development of public policies, as they enhance citizen participation and promote collaborative governance. These platforms facilitate the integration of diverse stakeholder contributions, resulting in more inclusive and effective policy outcomes. The following describes the essential elements of how digital platforms contribute to the development of various public policies. We explore how digital platforms are redefining the relationship between the state and civil society, with an emphasis on urban mobility and participatory budgeting.

Sustainable Mobility Plan in Bogotá (Colombia)

The Bogotá Mayor's Office developed the Bogotá Abierta platform to co-design its 2020-2024 Mobility Plan. Through open digital consultations, hybrid workshops, and monitoring tools, projects to expand bike paths and improve public transportation were prioritized. In 2021, key results include a 30% increase in bicycle use and a 15% reduction in CO_2 emissions on intervened corridors.

Participatory Budgeting in Madrid: Expanding Information Based on the Decide Madrid Platform

In 2015, the digital citizen participation platform "Decide Madrid" was created in Madrid, which included participatory budgeting processes. This platform allowed citizens to choose how to spend the city's municipal budget. A total of €50 million was allocated annually: €15 million for popular initiative projects, and €35 million for district-level projects. This platform allowed residents to propose their own projects and then vote on them: in 2022, €30 million of the budget was allocated to community urban gardens and school renovations (Peña-López, 2023). The platform is recognized by the ONU as a model of inclusiveness and has been replicated in cities such as Paris and Buenos Aires.

4.3 Digital Literacy and Inclusion as Cornerstones

Digital literacy and inclusion become crucial aspects for implementing programs that develop digital skills in citizens of all ages. Digital literacy is critically important for older adults. Since they may have difficulty adapting to new technologies, plans designed to improve digital literacy among adults can improve their quality of life, well-being, and social cohesion. It is also crucial to take into account the specificities of the context in which older adults live and work, such as language barriers, socioeconomic status, and prior experience using technology.

Promoting digital citizenship skills.

It is also important that these programs provide equitable access to the Internet, connected devices, and ongoing technical support. The way of training must be changed and not limited to offering technology classes, empowering digital citizens to strengthen their daily activities, in this way promoting meaningful social participation, in addition to their personal needs and motivations (White, 2023).

The path to a truly technology-driven, citizen-centered government is not just a matter of implementing digital platforms. It is a profound reconfiguration of the relationship between state and society. The public policies we have described, ranging from transparency and initiative to cross-sector cooperation and digital literacy, should not be viewed as isolated recommendations, but as interconnected elements of a single social framework. Technology, in and of itself, is merely a tool; its true value is revealed when it becomes a means of participation, a catalyst for equity, and a guarantee of trust.

Digital literacy programs for older adults.

The entire world faces the challenge of bridging the digital divide. The lack of connectivity particularly affects older adults with limited economic resources. That is why digital literacy programs are important for bridging the digital and cognitive divide in countries, especially now that the population is aging and technology is a part of our lives. With these programs, training older adults toward digital citizenship can enable them to participate more actively in society and access the information they need.

In Latin America, initiatives such as Digital Literacy for Older Adults in Peru and the Ibirapita Plan in Uruguay seek to equip older adults with digital skills. These initiatives aim to improve social inclusion and combat isolation through technology (Sunkel & Ullmann, 2019).

Key skills in Digital Literacy:

- Basic device functions: Even simple tasks such as turning a device on and off and using apps can be a challenge for many older adults.
- Internet Navigation: Being able to search for information and use social media online can be vital to staying connected in a meaningful way.
- Safety and Security: Understanding what privacy and protection measures one can take can help someone defend themselves. Most people can protect themselves against online scams and misinformation.

Challenges Faced:

- Cognitive and Physical Barriers: Older adults often experience cognitive decline, lack of familiarity with technology, and physical limitations.
- Access to Resources: Lack of access to digital devices and internet access impede learning opportunities. (Xu et al., 2024)

The path to a truly technology-driven and citizen-centered government is not just a matter of implementing digital platforms. It is a profound reconfiguration of the relationship between the state and society. The public policies we have described, ranging from transparency and initiative to cross-sector cooperation and digital literacy, should not be seen as isolated recommendations, but as interconnected elements of a single social framework. Technology, in and of itself, is only a tool; its true value is revealed when it becomes a means for participation, a catalyst for equity, and a guarantee of trust.

5. CHALLENGES AND CRITICAL REFLECTIONS

Currently, technological development has enabled governance models to have opportunities for growth through the implementation of new technologies characterized by accelerated technological change. Digital transformation, driven by technologies such as artificial intelligence (AI), automation and big data, has generated new opportunities, but also social and technological gaps. Innovative governance involves developing new regulatory, ethical and operational structures to respond with agility to emerging risks, ensuring responsible implementation of technologies.

Risks and technological gaps

The variety of emerging technologies has generated a digital divide between developed and developing countries, as well as between different sectors within societies. This gap not only implies inequality in access to digital infrastructure and services, but also in the capacity to generate local innovation and adopt advanced technological solutions. The World Economic Forum study (2023), Figure 1 shows that while Europe and North America reach digitization levels above 80%, regions such as Africa and Latin America barely exceed 40%. This generates a risk of technological exclusion, affecting economic development, education, and access to digital health services.

Figure 1. Technological Development Index by Region (estimate). Source: Own elaboration based on data from the World Economic Forum (2023).

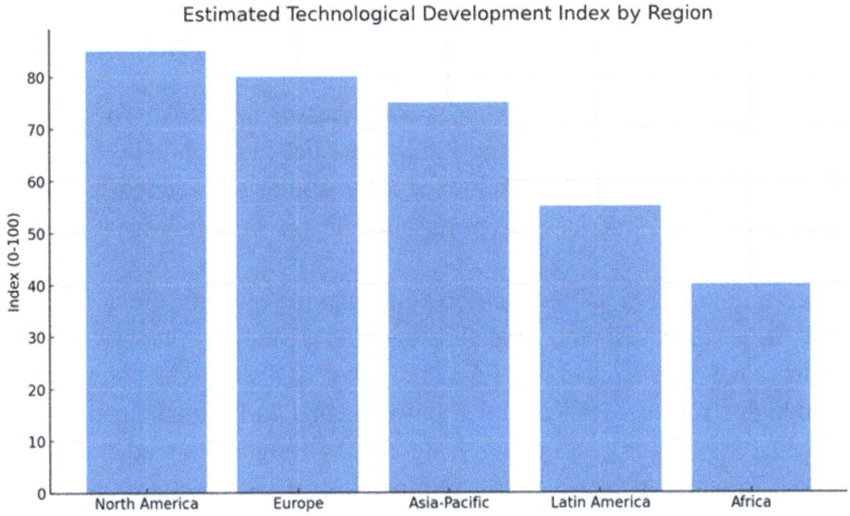

In addition to the differences mentioned between regions, structural risks are identified, such as the automation of work. According to the OECD (2021), 14% of current jobs are at high risk of being automated, and another 32% could be significantly transformed. The lack of labor reconversion policies and digital training aggravates this scenario, especially in informal economies.

Tension between algorithmic efficiency and human rights

One of the most significant problems in contemporary technological governance is the tension between algorithmic efficiency and the protection of human rights. Automated decisions, used in sectors such as justice, security, marketing or labor recruitment, optimize processes, but may reproduce or even amplify structural biases.

Agile governance

World Economic Forum (WEF) and OECD highlight the need for agile regulatory models that combine:

- Approaches such as the FAST Government (Flatter, Agile, Streamlined, Tech enabled) model promote flatter, flexible, technology and data-driven public structures.
- The OECD proposes principles such as regulatory iteration, continuous learning, and shared design between government, business and civil society.
- Tension between algorithmic efficiency and human rights

In today's technological governance there is tension between algorithmic efficiency and the protection of human rights. Automated decisions, used in sectors such as justice, security, marketing or labor recruitment, optimize processes, but may reproduce or even amplify structural biases. Some examples of these are:

- The COMPAS system for criminal risk assessment (USA) (Angwin et al., 2016), this system uses an algorithm to predict the probability of criminal recidivism in various states, however some studies showed that it had racial biases: African Americans were misclassified as high risk more often than whites.
- Rekognition is a facial recognition system from Amazon Buolamwini, J., & Gebru, T. (2018) which is a facial recognition technology that was sold to law enforcement agencies in the U.S. Studies by MIT and ACLU showed that it had high error rates, especially with women and dark-skinned people.
- Predictive Policing, a system with algorithms designed to predict high-crime areas. Research revealed that it reinforced policing practices on racialized and poor communities.

The above examples not only indicate some kind of bias in the way they operate but also violate human rights.

Collaborative and resilient governance

Finland, which has always been a reference in education, has developed courses that promote artificial intelligence based on citizen training, data ethics, and open innovation. The "Elements of AI" course, offered free of charge, has been completed by more than 10% of the Finnish population, showing how digital inclusion can form a central part of governance (Ministry of Economic Affairs and Employment of Finland, 2021).

Measuring efficiency

The WEF estimates the following quantitative results:

- US $5.8 billion in administrative efficiency from government digitalization.
- US $1.1 trillion in cost savings from increased transparency and reduced corruption

These indicators refer to long-term and global value. The report also highlights that these benefits depend on the institutional maturity and level of digital connectivity of the country

As for the successful implementation of case studies they can be described as outlined in World Economic Forum (2023):

- Azerbaijan (e-visa): public implementation with external technical support, reduced administrative time and costs.
- Rwanda (IremboGov): integrated national platform built with public-private collaboration, saving millions in service time.
- Sweden: regulatory sandbox for autonomous vehicle testing in Göteborg, in collaboration between government, academia and private companies

6. CONCLUSIONS

The way we run our governments needs a major change that goes beyond just using technology to fix old systems. New approaches, such as agile government, more shared decision-making, and digital communities where citizens have a bigger say, are helping policies work better, faster, and more fairly for everyone. In the coming years, we can expect more automation and personalized services. Over the next few years, AI will help make better decisions and handle data more efficiently. Looking further ahead, we might see governments that can change and adapt quickly, use predictions to plan better, and even operate in virtual spaces like the metaverse.

These changes need to follow important ideas like being open and honest, taking responsibility, being flexible, and having ethics in check. People's involvement is not something that can be left out anymore—it is essential for creating policies that can handle the future. To deal with new challenges, governments should put money into better digital systems, make sure everyone has access to technology, work together with different groups, and keep learning over time. The way governments operate is changing from a system where decisions are made by a few to a more open and teamwork-based approach, where technology helps people have more power instead of limiting them.

7. REFERENCES

Aguirre-Sala, J. (2022). Modelos y buenas prácticas evaluativas para detectar impactos, riesgos y daños de la inteligencia artificial. Paakat. *Revista de Tecnología y Sociedad, 12*(23). Advance online publication. DOI: 10.32870/Pk.a12n23.742

Alcaldía Mayor de Bogotá, D. C. (2021). Plan de movilidad sostenible y segura de Bogotá: Metodología de participación ciudadana [Documento técnico]. Secretaría Distrital de Movilidad. https://www.movilidadbogota.gov.co/web/plan_de_movilidad_sostenible_y_segura

Alcudia, D., & Venancio, A. (2023). Aproximación a la gobernanza digital en Iberoamérica. *Revista de Direito da Cidade, 15*(2), 1–20.

Angwin, J., Larson, J., Mattu, S., & Kirchner, L. (2016, mayo 23). Machine bias: There's software used across the country to predict future criminals. And it's biased against blacks. ProPublica. https://www.propublica.org/article/machine-bias-risk-assessments-in-criminal-sentencing

Arguelles, E., & Amaro, M. (2023). Chatbots y COVID-19: Ética, responsabilidad y acceso a la información en México. Revista Jurídicas UNAM, 34(1), 55–72. https://revistas.juridicas.unam.mx/index.php/derecho-informacion/article/view/17472/17922

Ashar, A., Ginena, K., Cipollone, M., Barreto, R., & Cramer, H. (2025). Algorithmic impact assessments and accountability: The co-construction of impacts. In *Proceedings of the 2021 ACM Conference on Fairness, Accountability, and Transparency (FAccT '21)* (pp. 123–134). ACM. https://doi.org/DOI: 10.1145/3442188.3445935

Buolamwini, J., & Gebru, T. (2018). Gender shades: Intersectional accuracy disparities in commercial gender classification. In Proceedings of Machine Learning Research (Vol. 81, pp. 1–15). http://proceedings.mlr.press/v81/buolamwini18a/buolamwini18a.pdf

Castelán, M., & Aceves, M. (2024). El principio de equivalencia funcional en los títulos de crédito electrónicos. Revista Saberes Administrativos, 5, 8–16. https://www.uv.mx/iiesca/files/2025/02/02SA2024-02.pdf

De la Garza, D., & Gómez, C. (2024). Inteligencia artificial y big data: Nuevos paradigmas de la comunicación política y la gobernanza digital. *Más Poder Local*, (56), 9–26. DOI: 10.56151/maspoderlocal.214

De Luna, A. J. H., Costa, C. P., & de Moura, H. P. (2014). Gobernanza ágil en tecnologías de la información y la comunicación: Cambio de paradigmas. arXiv. https://arxiv.org/abs/1411.2458

Díaz-Parra, O., Fuentes-Penna, A., Barrera-Cámara, R., Trejo-Macotela, F., Ramos-Fernández, J., Ruiz-Vanoye, J., Ochoa, A., & Rodríguez-Flores, J. (2022). Educación inteligente y tendencias futuras. *International Journal of Combinatorial Optimization Problems and Informatics, 13*(1), 65–74. https://ijcopi.org/ojs/article/view/294

Dominguez-Tabera, M., González-Mosqueda, M., Martínez-Tapía, K., Simancas-Acevedo, E., León-Olivares, E., & Robles-Camarillo, D. (2024). The application of artificial intelligence for the design of a virtual assistant (chatbot) as an innovative approach in user service: Social Security Center No. 102. *International Journal of Combinatorial Optimization Problems and Informatics, 15*(4), 149–162. DOI: 10.61467/2007.1558.2024.v15i4.484

Dunleavy, P., Margetts, H., Bastow, S., & Tinkler, J. (2006). *Digital era governance: IT corporations, the state, and e-government.* Oxford University Press. DOI: 10.1093/acprof:oso/9780199296194.001.0001

Etzkowitz, H., & Leydesdorff, L. (1995). The triple helix of university–industry–government relations: A laboratory for knowledge-based economic development. EASST Review, 14(1), 14–19. https://www.leydesdorff.net/th12/th12.pdf

Galindo, C., Ortíz, R., & Villegas, J. (2025). Prototipo de autenticación de doble factor basado en reconocimiento facial para email. Revista Pistas Educativas, (149), 1–15. https://pistaseducativas.celaya.tecnm.mx/index.php/pistas/article/view/3834

González-Sanmiguel, N. (2025). El metaverso en la configuración de la administración pública. *DICERE: Revista de Derecho y Estudios Internacionales, 2*(1), 100–117. DOI: 10.33324/dicere.v2i1.896

Gordon, R. (2023). Chatbots e inteligencia artificial: Aportes, innovaciones y aplicación en el desarrollo de sistemas de información empresarial. *Visión Antataura, 7*(1), 1–15. DOI: 10.48204/j.vian.v7n1.a3930

Government Digital Service. (2015, marzo 29). Government as a platform: The next phase of digital transformation. GDS Blog. https://gds.blog.gov.uk/2015/03/29/government-as-a-platform-the-next-phase-of-digital-transformation/

GovLab. (n.d.). About The GovLab. The Governance Lab. https://www.thegovlab.org/about.html

Mbuy, H., O'Neil, M., & Theodosiou, M. (2022). Algorithmic impact assessment for an ethical use of AI in SMEs. In *Proceedings of the 35th British HCI and Doctoral Consortium 2022* (pp. 1–8). https://doi.org/DOI: 10.14236/ewic/HCI2022.34

Minguijon, J., & Serrano-Martinez, C. (2022). La inteligencia artificial en los servicios sociales: Estado de la cuestión y posibles desarrollos futuros. *Cuadernos de Trabajo Social, 35*(2), 319–329. DOI: 10.5209/cuts.78747

Minguijon, J., & Serrano-Martinez, C. (2022). La inteligencia artificial en los servicios sociales: Estado de la cuestión y posibles desarrollos futuros. *Cuadernos de Trabajo Social, 35*(2), 319–329. DOI: 10.5209/cuts.78747

Ministry of Economic Affairs and Employment of Finland. (2021). Finland's artificial intelligence program. https://tem.fi/en/artificial-intelligence

Mittelstadt, B., Floridi, L., & Taddeo, M. (2023). A systematic review of artificial intelligence impact assessments. *Artificial Intelligence Review, 42*(5), 1021–1056. DOI: 10.1007/s10462-023-10420-8

Morales, M. (2021). Firmas digitales en México: conceptos, oportunidades y desafíos. En Jornadas de Divulgación – TopTamaulipas 2021 (pp. 9–18). https://ccc.inaoep.mx/~mmorales/divulg/JD05.pdf

Moya-Martínez, J. (2024). Metaverso: Amenazas internacionales y cooperación en la digitalización. Barataria. *Revista Castellano-Manchega de Ciencias Sociales,* (35), 1–20. DOI: 10.20932/barataria.v0i35.687

Moya-Martínez, J. (2024). Metaverso: Amenazas internacionales y cooperación en la digitalización. Barataria. *Revista Castellano-Manchega de Ciencias Sociales,* (35), 1–20. DOI: 10.20932/barataria.v0i35.687

Ocaña, Y., Valenzuela-Fernández, L., Vera, M., & Lozano, R. (2021). Inteligencia artificial (IA) aplicada a la gestión pública. *Revista Venezolana de Gerencia, 26*(94), 25–40. DOI: 10.52080/rvgv26n94.14

Organisation for Economic Co-operation and Development. (2020). *The OECD digital government policy framework: Six dimensions of a digital government (OECD Public Governance Policy Papers, No. 2)*. OECD Publishing., DOI: 10.1787/f64fed2a-

Organisation for Economic Co-operation and Development. (2021). The impact of AI on the labour market. OECD. https://www.oecd.org/employment/impact-of-ai-on-jobs.htm

Peña, J., Giraldo, S., Arango, C., & Bucheli, V. (2022). Un chatbot para asistir a las necesidades de información en tiempos de COVID-19. *Revista Ingeniería y Competitividad, 24*(1), 1–15. DOI: 10.25100/iyc.v24i1.11004

Peña, J., Giraldo, S., Arango, C., & Bucheli, V. (2022). Un chatbot para asistir a las necesidades de información en tiempos de COVID-19. *Revista Ingeniería y Competitividad, 24*(1), 1–15. DOI: 10.25100/iyc.v24i1.11004

Peña-López, I. (2023). *Crowdlaw: Casos de participación legislativa digital*. Editorial UOC.

Ramírez, J., Neri-Suárez, M., & Torres, M. (2024). Automatización de la auditoría fiscal en las PYMES mediante un algoritmo secuencial para extracción de comprobantes fiscales: Un enfoque en la economía digital. *International Journal of Combinatorial Optimization Problems and Informatics, 15*(5), 146–154. DOI: 10.61467/2007.1558.2024.v15i5.565

Salvador, M. (2021). Inteligencia artificial y gobernanza de datos en las administraciones públicas: Reflexiones y evidencias para su desarrollo. *Gestión y Análisis de Políticas Públicas*, (26), 20–32. DOI: 10.24965/gapp.i26.10855

Salvador, M. (2021). Inteligencia artificial y gobernanza de datos en las administraciones públicas: Reflexiones y evidencias para su desarrollo. *Gestión y Análisis de Políticas Públicas*, (26), 20–32. DOI: 10.24965/gapp.i26.10855

Sánchez, R., González, F., & Ortiz, T. (2021). *Uso responsable de la IA para las políticas públicas: Manual de ciencia de datos*. Banco Interamericano de Desarrollo., DOI: 10.18235/0002876

Sandoya, L., & Mawyin, M. (2025). La inteligencia artificial y su impacto en la gestión pública. *LATAM Revista Latinoamericana de Ciencias Sociales y Humanidades, 6*(1), 710–718. DOI: 10.56712/latam.v6i1.3373

Schneider, N., De Filippi, P., & Frey, S. (2020). Modular politics: Toward a governance layer for online communities. arXiv. https://arxiv.org/abs/2005.13701

Segovia, N., & Guzmán, A. (2025). Evaluación de un chatbot basado en aprendizaje supervisado: Impacto en la satisfacción y propuestas de mejora. Revista Electrónica de Tecnología Educativa, (92), e3849. DOI: 10.21556/edutec.2025.92.3849

Setyarto, D. B., Alimuddin, A., Mulyaningsih, M., & Judijanto, L. (2025). The role of e-government in increasing transparency and accountability of public administration in the digital era. *Edelweiss Applied Science and Technology, 9*(2), 1771–1783. DOI: 10.55214/25768484.v9i2.4908

Silos, J., Ramírez-Hernández, U. A., Reyes-Hernández, Y., Ortiz-Suarez, L. A., Gómez-Pérez, L. J., Cruz-Rojano, D., Trejo-Macotela, F. R., & Robles-Camarillo, D. (2023). Analysis of the feasibility of smart contracts in Mexico's legal and social framework: A study on the future of trade agreements. *International Journal of Combinatorial Optimization Problems and Informatics*, *14*(3), 71–90. DOI: 10.61467/2007.1558.2023.v14i3.404

Sunkel, G., & Ullmann, H. (2019). Older adults in the digital age in Latin America: Bridging the digital age divide. *CEPAL Review*, *127*(127), 215–236. DOI: 10.18356/e9ed7f26-en

The GovLab. (n.d.). The GovLab. https://thegovlab.org/

Travez-Tipan, A., & Villafuerte-Garzon, C. (2023). Industria 5.0, revisión del pasado y futuro de la producción y la industria. *Ciencia Latina Revista Científica Multidisciplinar*, *7*(1), 1059–1070. DOI: 10.37811/cl_rcm.v7i1.4457

White, Z. M. (2023). Re-envisioning digital equity and connection literacy for older adults. *North Carolina Medical Journal*, *84*(2). Advance online publication. DOI: 10.18043/001c.73013 PMID: 39302329

World Economic Forum. (2023). The global public impact of GovTech: A $9.8 trillion opportunity (Global Technology Governance Report). World Economic Forum. https://www.weforum.org/publications/the-global-public-impact-of-govtech/

Xu, L., Lam, Y. Y., Ng, D. T. K., Peng, P., Suen, W. L., Lee, C. S., & Chu, S. K. W. (2024). Digital literacy education for older adults: A scoping review. *Proceedings of the Association for Information Science and Technology*, *61*(1), 691–696. DOI: 10.1002/pra2.1081

Zendejas, R. (2024). Ciberpolítica: Estrategias de gobernanza para el empoderamiento de la ciudadanía digital. Ediciones Universidad de Xalapa. https://www.researchgate.net/publication/390137588_CIBERPOLITICA_Y_GOBERNANZA_Estrategias_de_gobernanza_para_el_empoderamiento_de_la_Ciudadania_Digital

Zendejas, R. (2024). *Ciberpolítica: Estrategias de gobernanza para el empoderamiento de la ciudadanía digital*. Ediciones Universidad de Xalapa.

Chapter 9
Cybersecurity, Data Protection, and Ethics in Digital Government:
Emotional Stability and Institutional Trust in the Age of Artificial Intelligence

Miguel Ruiz Jaimes
https://orcid.org/0000-0002-2585-9896
Universidad Politécnica del Estado de Morelos, Mexico

Yadira Toledo Navarro
Universidad Politécnica del Estado de Morelos, Mexico

Marco Antonio García Márquez
https://orcid.org/0000-0002-0644-4839
Universidad Politécnica de Pachuca, Mexico

José Efrén Marmolejo Valle
https://orcid.org/0000-0002-7191-4489
Universidad Autónoma de Guerrero, Mexico

Manuel Erazo Valadez
https://orcid.org/0009-0005-2530-8532
El Centro Nacional de Investigación y Desarrollo Tecnológico (CENIDET), Mexico

Angel Israel Daza-Castillo
El Centro Nacional de Investigación y Desarrollo Tecnológico (CENIDET), Mexico

Tlaloc Humberto Vergara Morales
https://orcid.org/0009-0008-3823-5784
El Centro Nacional de Investigación y Desarrollo Tecnológico (CENIDET), Mexico

ABSTRACT

This chapter explores the intersection of cybersecurity, data protection, and digital ethics in government, emphasizing how secure and transparent digital environments

DOI: 10.4018/979-8-3373-5535-1.ch009

influence citizen trust and emotional well-being. Building on the conceptual model of synthetic happiness, it argues that digital security is not only a technical requirement but a foundation for institutional legitimacy in AI-driven societies. The discussion incorporates international legal frameworks such as GDPR, NIST CSF, and ISO 27001, along with national laws like Mexico's LGPDPPSO, to illustrate challenges in harmonizing cross-border data policies. It also analyzes ethical considerations surrounding algorithmic bias, AI transparency, and surveillance, presenting best practices including explainable AI, blockchain-based accountability, and citizen participation platforms. Through a multidisciplinary approach, the chapter proposes strategic recommendations for governments to build inclusive, ethical, and emotionally resilient digital ecosystems.

1. INTRODUCTION

In a society that is becoming more reliant on automated systems and digital platforms, cybersecurity is no longer just a technical issue it's a key part of emotional well-being and social stability. Ruiz-Vanoye et al. (2025) introduced the idea of Synthetic Happiness, organized through a hierarchical pyramid. The first level Digital Security and Stability forms the foundation of the emotional ecosystem. This level includes data privacy, strong encryption, protection against cyberattacks, and reliable digital environments. These factors allow citizens to use public services, healthcare, and education managed by AI without fear or uncertainty.

Government digitalization has brought many benefits, such as better efficiency, automation, and easier access to services. However, it has also created new opportunities for attacks: identity theft, ransomware targeting public platforms, and manipulation of election data are just a few threats that directly affect the digital citizen's sense of security. The model proposed by Ruiz-Vanoye et al. (2025) suggests that if the first level security fails, the higher levels of emotional well-being will collapse. That's why government strategies should be based on the principle of "security by design. "

The use of artificial intelligence in government processes raises ethical questions about data use, automated decision-making, and algorithmic discrimination. Ruiz-Vanoye et al. (2025) emphasize that emotional wellbeing depends not just on technology, but on how it is managed. Ethics in AI such as algorithm transparency, decision traceability, and protection against bias becomes a key factor that strengthens the credibility of institutions and the sense of fairness felt by citizens.

Based on the work of Ruiz-Vanoye et al. (2025), who believe cybersecurity is a key part of how emotions influence societies that depend a lot on AI, new global research backs up this idea. Silva et al. (2024) studied more than 3,000 public digital platforms and found that many still don't have strong safety rules, reliable certificates, or protection against known security problems. This issue isn't just about keeping personal information safe it can also affect the emotional well-being of groups and reduce people's trust in government. Because of this, when governments try to move toward digital changes, they need a well-planned security strategy that covers both the technical aspects and the ethical responsibility to follow clear and open standards.

2. POLICIES AND REGULATORY FRAMEWORKS FOR INFORMATION PROTECTION

2.1. International and National Data Protection Laws

Contemporary Regulatory Landscape

The protection of personal data around the world has undergone a radical transformation in recent decades, moving from a secondary issue on political agendas to a fundamental pillar of contemporary digital law. This evolution responds to the growing digitization of public administration and the pressing need to protect citizens' privacy in an environment where personal data is an invaluable strategic asset.

The European Union's General Data Protection Regulation (GDPR), in force since May 2018, marked an unprecedented milestone in global data protection regulation. Its influence transcends European borders, establishing standards that have been adopted and adapted by numerous jurisdictions worldwide. The European Commission has pointed out that EU data protection rules empower citizens and are adapted to the digital age, demonstrating the effectiveness of this regulatory framework in the current context (Klinger et al., 2023).

On the other hand, Negri-Ribalta et al. (2024) mention that the European Union's General Data Protection Regulation (GDPR) establishes a series of requirements that organizations must comply with. However, these requirements are complex to implement due to their legal nature or because they are sometimes imprecise.

For Ghosh et al. (2025), artificial intelligence (AI) has revolutionized the ways in which humans conduct transactions, make decisions, and participate in social environments, with applications in important sectors such as health, banking, and criminal justice. AI systems may offer fully efficiency, but they pose significant threats and ethical issues, gaps in accountability, and algorithmic biases. The challenge for AI-driven governments is to establish governance structures that effectively manage the changing threats posed by increasingly complex and autonomous AI systems (Ghosh et al., 2025).

Mexican Regulatory Framework

Mexico has developed a dual data protection system that reflects the complexity of Mexican federalism. Article 16 of the Political Constitution of the United Mexican States establishes that every person has the right to the protection of their personal data, to access, rectify, and cancel it, as well as to express their opposition. This constitutional basis is implemented through two main regulatory instruments: the Federal Law on the Protection of Personal Data Held by Private Parties (LFPDPPP) and the General Law on the Protection of Personal Data Held by Obligated Subjects (LGPDPPSO) (De Datos, 2010; Lostal Martínez, 2024).

The duality of Mexican regulations has unique characteristics that distinguish it from other regulatory models. While the LFPDPPP regulates the processing of data by private entities, the LGPDPPSO integrates the handling of personal information by public bodies. This distinction is fundamental to understanding the scope and implications of data protection in the Mexican governmental context (De Datos, 2010; LGPDPPSO, 2025).

Mexican legislation establishes specific requirements for data breach notifications and data protection measures, creating a framework of responsibility that requires government entities to implement technical, administrative, and physical safeguards to ensure the integrity of personal information (Gómez Sánchez, 2020).

Impact on Government Digital Platforms

The reform and implementation of robust regulatory frameworks has led to several specific changes in the design and operation of government digital platforms, requiring the redefinition of technological architectures and the incorporation of privacy by design and privacy by default strategies.

These modifications range from the reconfiguration of databases to the implementation of explicit consent mechanisms for the processing of personal data. Online transaction platforms, transparency portals, and citizen participation systems have had to adapt to comply with international data protection standards, which has presented both opportunities and challenges for the modernization of the state (Bade & Tomomewo, 2024).

Interoperability between government systems has become more complex due to the need to ensure that information exchanges comply with the principles of purpose, proportionality, and temporality established by data protection regulations. This situation has led to the development of new technologies and methodologies for the secure exchange of information between public entities (Lostal Martínez, 2024).

2.2. Institutional Cybersecurity Policies

Evolution of Internal Policies

Government organizations have recognized that cybersecurity cannot be addressed solely from a technological perspective, but requires a comprehensive approach that incorporates organizational, procedural, and cultural elements. This understanding has led to the development of increasingly sophisticated institutional policies that seek to minimize cyber risks on multiple fronts.

The development of effective internal policies requires a deep understanding of the specific threats faced by government institutions. These threats range from attacks by state actors to incidents caused by internal negligence. The diversity of attack vectors has forced organizations to develop multidimensional policy frameworks that address both technical and human aspects of information security.

International Reference Guidelines

ISO 27001: The Global Standard

The ISO 27001 standard has established itself as the de facto standard for information security management at the international level. ISO/IEC 27001 helps organizations become risk aware and proactively identify and address weaknesses, promoting a holistic approach to information security that includes the assessment of people, policies, and technology. The implementation of ISO 27001 in government entities involves the adoption of an Information Security Management System (ISMS) that establishes systematic processes for identifying, assessing, and addressing security risks. This process-based approach allows organizations to develop adaptive response capabilities to emerging threats (ThamaraiSelvan & Dr Arun, 2025).

NIST Cybersecurity Framework: Flexibility and Practicality

The National Institute of Standards and Technology Cybersecurity Framework (NIST CSF) is a set of guidelines for all organizations to manage and reduce cybersecurity risks. Its voluntary nature and focus on practical methodologies have made it an especially useful tool for government organizations seeking to implement cybersecurity measures gradually and, in a manner, tailored to their specific resources (Bernardo et al., 2025).

The NIST CSF organizes cybersecurity activities into five main functions: Identify, Protect, Detect, Respond, and Recover. This structure provides a conceptual framework that facilitates communication between different organizational levels and allows for the establishment of clear performance metrics to evaluate the effectiveness of the measures implemented (Bernardo et al., 2025; White & Sjelin, 2022).

Spain's National Security Scheme (ENS)

In Spain, the ENS represents a particularly relevant model for public administrations, as it was specifically designed for the government sector. Its focus on information classification and the proportionality of security measures provides a practical framework for organizations with limited resources and specific regulatory compliance needs (Normas ISO, 2007).

Integration and Complementarity of Frameworks

White & Sjelin (2022) y Alshar'e (2023) mention that practical experience has shown that successful implementation of cybersecurity policies does not involve adopting a single framework exclusively, but rather intelligent integration with elements from different standards. The NIST CSF is designed as a guide, while ISO 27001 is designed as a standard, with the NIST CSF serving as an instruction manual and ISO 27001 as a test requiring certain measures.

This complementarity allows government organizations to develop hybrid approaches that leverage the flexibility of NIST CSF for strategic planning and the rigor of ISO 27001 for operational implementation. The result is a more robust policy framework that is adaptable to the specific needs of each institution (Bernardo et al., 2025; White & Sjelin, 2022).

2.3. Interoperability and Legal Harmonization Challenges

Cross-Border Data Governance Initiatives

The transnational nature of digital data has created an urgent need to develop governance frameworks that transcend national borders. Cross-border initiatives face complex challenges related to digital sovereignty, jurisdictional competition, and the harmonization of technical and legal standards.

The exponential technological advances seen in recent decades, particularly the use of big data and digital services, enhanced by the new dynamics imposed by the health emergency resulting from the pandemic, have put a lot of pressure on personal data protection regulation. This pressure has accelerated the need for international cooperation to develop coherent governance frameworks (Oselame Graf & Muller Bitencourt, 2024).

Regional initiatives, such as the Pacific Alliance's Digital Governance Framework or the information exchange agreements between USMCA countries, exemplify efforts to create secure digital spaces that facilitate intergovernmental collaboration without compromising personal data protection (Bade & Tomomewo, 2024).

Regulatory Difficulties Between Public Entities

In (Bade & Tomomewo, 2024), regulatory fragmentation represents one of the main obstacles to the effective implementation of data protection policies in the public sector. This fragmentation manifests itself in multiple dimensions: vertical (between different levels of government), horizontal (between different sectors and entities), and temporal (due to the asymmetric evolution of regulations).

Differences in state and municipal regulatory frameworks have created significant operational complexities for the exchange of information between public entities. These differences not only affect operational efficiency but can also create security vulnerabilities when data transits between systems with different levels of protection (Nurbojatmiko et al., 2025).

The lack of uniform technical standards exacerbates these difficulties, creating barriers to interoperability that go beyond purely legal differences. The adoption of different technologies, incompatible communication protocols, and divergent security criteria creates fragmented ecosystems that hinder the implementation of coherent data protection policies (Ghosh et al., 2025).

Towards Effective Harmonization

Effective legal harmonization requires a multidimensional approach that addresses both substantive and procedural aspects. Harmonization efforts must consider not only regulatory uniformity, but also technical compatibility, functional equivalence, and reciprocity in the mutual recognition of protection standards.

International experience suggests that successful harmonization requires robust institutional mechanisms for inter-jurisdictional coordination, exchange of best practices, and resolution of regulatory conflicts. These mechanisms must be flexible enough to adapt to local particularities while maintaining minimum standards of protection (Catoira et al., 2025; Esteves & Rodríguez-Doncel, 2024)

Table 1. Comparative table of data protection laws in certain regions.

Region / Country	Main Regulation	Year of Enforcement	Main Characteristics	Control Authority
European Union	GDPR	2018	Extraterritoriality, explicit consent, right to be forgotten	National authorities + CEPD
Mexico	LGPDPPSO / LFPDPPP	2017 / 2010 / 2025	Dual (public/private), ARCO rights	INAI
United States	Sectoral (CCPA, HIPAA)	Variable	Sectoral approach, self-regulation	CPPA (California)
Brazil	LGPD	2020	Inspired by GDPR, broad legal bases.	ANPD
Argentina	PDPA	2000 (reformed in 2018)	Traditional approach, recently updated	AAIP
Canada	PIPEDA	2000	Privacy principles, limited enforcement	OPC
Singapore	PDPA	2012 (reformed in 2020)	Responsible innovation, regulatory sandbox	PDPC
United Kingdom	UK GDPR + DPA 2018	2021	Post-Brexit, similar to GDPR	ICO

(Akoh Atadoga et al., 2024; Alkhedhairy, 2025; Alshar'e, 2023; Pillai et al., 2025; Renuka et al., 2025)

Comparative Analysis of Regulatory Trends

The influence of the GDPR is evident in the most recent regulations, which have adopted concepts such as extraterritoriality, explicit consent, and expanded digital rights. However, each jurisdiction has adapted these principles to its specific local contexts (Akoh Atadoga et al., 2024; Tikkinen-Piri et al., 2018).

The trend toward sectoral specialization is particularly notable in jurisdictions such as the United States, where the absence of comprehensive federal law has led to a patchwork of sector-specific regulations. This approach contrasts with the more comprehensive approach adopted by the European Union and replicated by countries such as Brazil and Mexico (Bouraffa & Hui, 2025; Pantanowitz et al., 2024).

Final Considerations

Data protection in the context of digital government represents a multifaceted challenge that requires the convergence of legal, technical, and organizational expertise. Experience accumulated over the last few decades shows that the most effective regulatory frameworks are those that manage to balance the protection of fundamental rights with the need for modernization and efficiency in each state (Navaratna & Deepak Saxena, 2025).

The successful implementation of data protection policies cannot be approached as a purely technical or legal exercise, but requires a holistic approach that considers the human, organizational, and cultural dimensions of information security. International frameworks such as ISO 27001 and NIST CSF provide valuable structures, but their effectiveness depends on their intelligent adaptation to the specific contexts of each organization (Alshar'e, 2023).

The future of data protection in digital government will depend on the ability of institutions to develop adaptive frameworks that can evolve alongside the technological landscape and citizen expectations. This evolution will require ongoing investments in training, technology, and organizational culture, as well as robust mechanisms for inter-jurisdictional cooperation and the exchange of best practices.

3. BEST PRACTICES FOR TRANSPARENCY AND CITIZEN PARTICIPATION

The relationship between government and citizens is undergoing a significant transformation in the digital age. The demand for greater transparency, effective accountability, and channels for meaningful participation has driven the adoption of new technologies and governance paradigms. More than a trend, open government has consolidated itself into a management model that seeks to strengthen democracy through cooperation and access to information (Ramírez-Alujas and Dassen, 2014). This model is based on the idea that open government is essential for citizens to monitor the actions of their representatives and participate in public life in an informed manner (Sandoval-Almazán, 2015).

The following examines three technological pillars identified as essential for achieving the objectives of open government: open government data platforms, digital citizen participation tools, and the use of blockchain for public integrity. Best practices that are redefining the social contract in the 21st century are explored through specific case studies and an analysis of their mechanisms.

3.1 Open Government Data Platforms

Open data platforms are digital infrastructures that publish government sector information in standardized, accessible, machine-processable, and freely usable formats. Governments aim to transform their vast repositories of government information, which until now have been generally opaque, into a public good that can foster economic innovation, academic research, and, above all, citizen oversight (Barros, 2012). Therefore, open data principles ensure that information is not only accessible but also reusable, ensuring that it acquires useful value when analyzed by third parties to develop new valuable services or applications (Santos Pinacho et al., 2022).

Case: National Transparency Platform (Mexico)

The emblematic case of the implementation of these platforms is the National Transparency Platform of Mexico (PNT). Created by the General Law on Transparency and Access to Public Information of 2015, the PNT centralizes in a single portal all the information that Obligated Subjects at the three levels of government (federal, state, and municipal) are required to publish (Rojas Flores, 2020). In terms of design, it seeks to mitigate information fragmentation and allow the exercise of the right of access to information. The platform is composed of four main systems: information requests, transparency obligations, review resources, and communication between the guarantor body and the obligated subjects.

In Mexico, with the National Public Service (PNT), much has been achieved towards the function of the standardization and availability of public information, so that journalists, academics and civil society organizations can carry out investigations of public spending, contracts and institutional performance that before demanded a complex set of procedures scattered (Jasso López, 2023).

Use of Open Data in Citizen Oversight

Thanks to the data from citizens in punishing bad actions, the full power of platforms such as the National Public Service (PNT) is received. PNT information has also been utilized in data journalism and contributed to the revelation of corruption and unethical spending. Civil society uses information of public contracting to follow invitations to tender and to identify irregularities, such as the award of contracts to ghost bidders such as non-existing companies or non-observance of norms (Bello Jiménez, 2025).

But the PNT is threatened. Information may be partial or outdated, and the quality and granularity of the data are generally low (Sandoval-Almazán, 2019). In addition, there is still a distance between the availability of data and the use of data available to the public, indicates the importance of promoting greater data literacy and digital literacy (Estrada Zamora and Vargas-Hernández, 2018). By contrast, the existence of a central repository such as the PNT in itself is a key practice that serves as an infrastructure for democratic control and oversight.

3.2. Digital Participation Tools

If open data is the basement of transparency, digital participation tools fill it up with active citizens. These tools, known as civic tech, do not just offer information consultations, but also spaces for citizens to articulate, discuss, and venture to collectively decide in community matters) Villanueva et al., 2016). Their influence lies in their ability to increase participation by overcoming the geographical and temporal limitations of traditional mechanisms.

Example: Decide Madrid and the Consul Platform

Decide Madrid is one of the most recognized digital participation initiatives in the world. Launched by Madrid City Council in 2015, the platform allows citizens to propose, debate, and vote on how a portion of the municipal budget is spent (participatory budgeting), as well as submit city-wide policy proposals that, if they receive sufficient support, are then submitted to a popular vote.

The success of Decide Madrid is largely due to its underlying software, Consul, an open-source tool that the government made available to any other public administration for use and adaptation. Currently, Consul is used by more than 180 institutions in 35 countries, forming a global network of participatory democracy. The platform incorporates various functions, as shown in Table 2, making it a crucial tool for citizen participation.

Table 2. Digital Participation Platforms: Functions and Adoption

Feature	Decide Madrid (Spain)	Consul (Open Source Software)	Pleno Ciudadano (México)
Main Functions	Participatory budgeting, citizen proposals, debates, voting, collaborative legislation.	Framework for implementing Decide Madrid and other custom features.	Dialogue between legislators and citizens, proposals, follow-up on initiatives.
Decision Mechanism	Direct voting by citizens on budgets and projects.	Flexible and adaptable to the mechanisms of each institution.	Influence the legislative agenda through direct interaction.
Adoption Level	Consolidated platform at the municipal level with high participation.	Adopted by over 180 cities and organizations worldwide.	Civil society initiative with limited reach and adoption.
Documented Impact	Implementation of hundreds of citizen projects. Direct influence on the budget.	It has facilitated similar processes in cities such as Paris, Turin and Buenos Aires.	It has generated specific dialogues, but with a less clear systemic impact.

3.3. Blockchain for accountability

The use of blockchain technology is one of the most promising avenues for transparency and the fight against corruption. A blockchain is a distributed, cryptographically secure digital ledger whose main characteristic is its immutability: once a transaction is recorded in the database, it cannot be modified or deleted (Moya & Rivera, 2024). This quality makes it an exceptionally powerful tool for ensuring the integrity of public records and strengthening accounting performance.

One of the sectors most susceptible to corruption on a global scale is public procurement. Common practices include opacity in bidding procedures, document tampering, and improper payments. Blockchain offers a radical solution to these problems. Every step of the public procurement process, from the announcement of the call and the submission of bids to the decision on the contract and payments, must be recorded on a blockchain. This will create a single, transparent, and auditable record for all involved parties (government agencies, bidding companies, law firms, oversight bodies, and the public).

The potential of blockchain is being explored in pilot projects around the world. For example, by creating an immutable record of bids, manipulation is prevented after submission. By linking payments to the verifiable delivery of goods or services through smart contracts, budget execution is automated and made transparent.

Advantages: Immutability, Auditability, and Trust

The benefits of using blockchain technology for accounting are clear and revolutionary:

- Immutability - Cryptographic security guarantees that even an internal bad actor cannot modify the history of transactions, which rules out the discoveries of a corrupt activity.
- Auditability: Oversight bodies and citizens may continuously and remotely audit the process rather than resort to post-process expensive and often ineffective reviews. This is more proactive oversight rather than reactive auditing.
- Trust: The technology creates a system of trust as trust in the honesty of the system instead of trust in the good faith of the officers. This decreases injustice and encourages an honourable society in public service.

While the potential uses of blockchain technology in public sector is immense, the applications are limited due to challenges including technical complexity, the requirement for clearly defined regulatory framework, the compatibility with legacy system and scalability. Nevertheless its ability to promote verifiable trust ecosystems renders it one of the presenting best practices for the tamper proof testing.

4. DIGITAL TOOLS FOR ACCOUNTABILITY AND E-SOCIETY INTERACTION

After the pandemic that struck in 2019, most of the companies began working from home, clearly revealing that this new way of operating would require tools to facilitate tasks in a virtual environment such as meetings, discussions, evaluations, supervision, and more. Today, many of those companies have returned to their previous ways of working, for one reason or another. Whether that shift is ultimately a good or bad decision is up for debate, but what that period undeniably demonstrated to many organizations is that the adoption of digital tools and platforms brings significant advantages not only for employees, but also for the people they serve. In this chapter, we will briefly explore some of the ways these tools are being used, especially within public service.

4.1. Mobile Applications for Complaints and Oversight

In the Mexican government, digital tools for processing documents and filing complaints have already been implemented for some time now. A clear example of this is the government's own website (Gob.mx). However, for a while, its functionality was fairly limited it primarily focused on streamlining the processing of just a few key documents, such as the CURP or a birth certificate, to name a couple. It wasn't until more recently that a wider range of features and services began to be introduced. One concrete example of how these tools have been applied is the

CDMX mobile app, a smartphone application available for Android, iPhone, and Huawei devices. The app clearly outlines its capabilities on the website of the Digital Agency for Public Innovation (ADIP, 2022): it allows users to digitally process documents such as a driver's license, access taxi services, view a calendar of events happening in the city, and connect with public services such as the police or emergency medical assistance. It also provides information about the weather, cars restricted from circulation, the location of hotels or free public Wi-Fi, and even enables users to report corruption or file civic complaints.

On the other hand, the government's main website (Gob, 2025) has evolved over time into a more robust and user-friendly platform. It primarily serves to make it easier for citizens to complete a variety of official procedures without needing to be physically present at government offices. In addition, it helps keep people informed about those same procedures, as well as about public events, social programs, and current news. The site even provides region-specific information, offering updates and resources tailored to each individual state. It is worth highlighting that this very same portal has seen significant improvements in recent years. This progress may be attributed to the government's initiatives to enhance its digital platforms, as well as to the introduction of new technologies such as the integration of biometric data in digital form, managed directly by the government. Setting aside the controversy surrounding this implementation, these technological advancements are closely tied to decisions made by the government itself; in other words, by the public institutions and their strategic goals. After all, the adoption and use of these new tools is ultimately driven by the specific needs and objectives of each organization, whether aimed at improving processes for their employees or delivering better services to the public.

4.2. AI-Based Monitoring Tools

The use of artificial intelligence has grown rapidly in recent years, some might even say at a disproportionate pace. In fact, AI has become so prominent that it is sometimes used as a marketing tool to promote products or services that may not actually need it, or that are unable to take full advantage of its potential. However, in situations involving massive amounts of data where manual processing by a person would be overwhelming AI and other technological solutions truly stand out in a positive light. For instance, wouldn't it be more effective to manage complaints, public spending, or even electoral behavior using AI-powered systems that offer greater flexibility and speed?

Gómez-Magadán et al. (2023) developed a framework using BERT embeddings, semantic clustering, and classification models to analyze complaints submitted to a public agency. Their system made it possible to detect latent patterns in real time, reduce redundant categories by 27%, and improve classification efficiency by over

32%. Similarly, Gao et al. (2023) applied natural language processing (NLP) combined with systematic anomaly detection to analyze official databases of financial complaints. Their approach integrated classification techniques with quantitative analysis to uncover irregularities.

In the social media space, Preotiuc-Pietro, Gaman, and Aletras (2019) used neural and linguistic models to automatically identify complaints on Twitter, achieving an F1 score of up to 0.79. Later, Jin and Aletras (2020) employed Transformer-based models to detect complaints in social media posts, reaching a macro-F1 score of approximately 0.87.

In the political arena, Sernani et al. (2025) examined the digital campaigns for the 2024 European Parliament elections in Italy. They used machine learning to analyze social media interactions such as comments, likes, shares, and images to measure the popularity of specific posts and assess how that popularity correlated with election results.

Of course, the implementation of such powerful and still relatively unexplored technology inevitably generates some concern. Even without these tools, processes like these are already complex and difficult to manage. Nonetheless, this hasn't stopped those with a deeper understanding of AI from offering valuable insights, recommendations, and warnings about potential challenges. For example, Deepak et al. (2023) mapped five areas of the electoral process such as voter registration, polling station location, biometric authentication, and election monitoring to analyze the opportunities and risks of using AI. Likewise, Cerina and Rouméas (2025) explored the use of machine-learning-powered survey techniques (like multilevel regression with poststratification, or MrP), while addressing important concerns related to privacy, autonomy, strategy, and manipulation.

4.3. Social Media and Civic Engagement

After all, even though the vast amounts of data used to understand human behavior can be treated as just that "data" they still represent personal information about individuals. And many people often feel uneasy about the mass use of their data, even when it is argued that such use may ultimately lead to benefits for them.

Morley et al. (2020) offer a critical review of tools and methods aimed at translating ethical principles in AI such as beneficence, fairness, and transparency into concrete design practices. While the focus is largely on machine learning, their insights are also relevant to network monitoring systems. They highlight significant gaps and propose a design approach called "Ethics as a Service." The following year, they expanded on this idea in their study Ethics as a Service: A Pragmatic Operationalisation of AI Ethics, where they developed the concept further with the goal of making ethics more practical and actionable within research labs and design workflows. This work discusses major challenges such as excessive flexibility or superficial ethics sometimes referred to as "ethics washing" and how to overcome them. Similarly, in Operationalising AI Ethics: Barriers, Enablers and Next Steps, Floridi et al. (2021) conducted a qualitative study among AI practitioners to identify the real-world difficulties of implementing ethics in their projects. They outlined key barriers, such as lack of expertise and insufficient institutional support, as well as motivation for ethical implementation and the need for tools that are both accessible and actionable.

Without a doubt, when implementing these kinds of tools in areas where large volumes of sensitive information are involved, it becomes especially important to place a stronger emphasis on ethics and on the proper protection of that data. Not only is this essential to prevent the misuse of such information, but also to preserve the trust of the individuals who provide access to it in the first place.

5. CYBERSECURITY PROTOCOLS AND RISK MANAGEMENT IN PUBLIC INSTITUTIONS

5.1. Incident Response and SOCs in Government

Introduction

In the current context, public institutions face increasing threats in cyberspace that compromise the confidentiality, integrity, and availability of government information. As digital services have become an indispensable tool for public management and citizen service, ensuring the security of these environments has become a strategic priority. This section addresses the fundamental role of Security Operations Centers (SOC) in incident response, highlighting best practices and policies most suitable for the public sector.

Importance of Incident Response in the Public Sector

Cyber incident response in public entities involves not only technical aspects but also an institutional responsibility towards citizens. Data breaches, ransomware, and denial-of-service (DDoS) attacks have the potential to paralyze critical services and undermine public trust. In this regard, response time is crucial. The implementation of well-defined response protocols allows damage mitigation, operation recovery, and strengthening of the security posture.

According to the U.S. National Institute of Standards and Technology (NIST), an effective incident response process must include four phases: preparation, detection and analysis, containment and eradication, and recovery (NIST, 2012). This methodology has been widely adopted by the public sector worldwide and constitutes an essential normative reference.

Figure 1. Incident Response Phases. NIST Special Publication 800-61 Rev. 2 - Computer Security Incident Handling Guide (2012)

The Role of the SOC in the Government Ecosystem

A Security Operations Center (SOC) is a specialized unit responsible for monitoring, analyzing, and acting against cybersecurity threats in real time. In the governmental sphere, the SOC operates as a central node for coordinating the security of multiple entities within the organizational structure, facilitating an integrated and coordinated response.

Public sector SOCs have specific functions including:

- **Continuous Monitoring:** Uninterrupted surveillance of technological assets, networks, and systems using intrusion detection tools (IDS/IPS), behavior analysis, and event correlation.
- **Incident Management:** Identification and classification of incidents based on severity, activating tiered response procedures.
- **Forensic Analysis:** Detailed investigation of incidents to identify attack vectors, actors involved, and exploited vulnerabilities.
- **Threat Intelligence:** Collection and analysis of information on emerging threats from internal and external sources.
- **Interagency Coordination:** Effective communication with other public sector agencies, ensuring timely information flow during emergencies.

Figure 2. SOC Operational Flow

The structure of the SOC may vary depending on the scope, size of the institution, and its maturity in cybersecurity. In countries with centralized strategies, national SOCs have been established to cover multiple public agencies under the direction of a superior information technology authority.

Figure 3. SOC Tools and Technical Capabilities

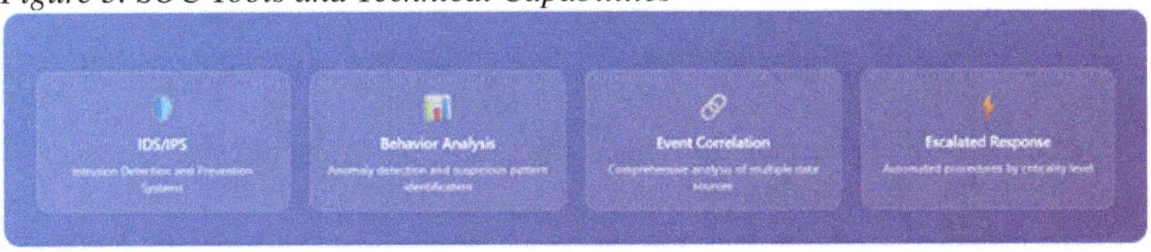

Best Practices for Incident Management

To ensure an effective government SOC, operations must be based on recognized standards and a series of best practices:

1. **Development of a National Incident Response Plan**

Establishing a national framework regulating responses to cyber incidents allows different government levels to act coherently and in coordination. This plan should include:

- o Standardized reporting procedures.
- o Severity levels for incidents.
- o Secure communication channels among entities.
- o Rulesfor responsible information disclosure.

This type of planning prevents improvised responses and reduces the institutional impact of crises.

2. **Ongoing Training and Drills**

Regular staff training is key to maintaining a high level of preparedness. In addition, conducting drills allows testing the effectiveness of protocols and fosters team collaboration. According to ENISA (2022), cyber crisis exercises strengthen institutional resilience and promote a prevention-oriented organizational culture.

3. **Implementation of Automation Tools**

The use of SIEM (Security Information and Event Management) and SOAR (Security Orchestration, Automation and Response) platforms facilitates event correlation, alert prioritization, and automation of repetitive tasks. These technologies allow analysts to focus on critical incidents and reduce average response time.

4. **Post-Incident Assessments and Continuous Improvement**

Every incident should become a learning opportunity. Conducting post-mortem reports (lessons learned) helps identify process failures, improve controls, and strengthen cybersecurity posture. This continuous improvement cycle is essential to maintain SOC effectiveness.

Relevant Cases in Latin America

In recent years, several Latin American countries have made progress in creating national SOCs with jurisdiction over the public sector. For example:

- **Mexico:** The National Digital Strategy promoted the creation of the National Cyber Incident Response Center (CERT-MX), which serves as a focal point for the protection of critical infrastructures.
- **Chile:** Through the Government's Computer Security Incident Response Team (CSIRT), a coordination model was implemented with State entities, especially during contingencies.
- **Colombia:** The Police Cyber Center leads incident management in public entities, in close collaboration with the Ministry of Defense and civil agencies.

These examples reflect a progressive effort by governments to establish an organized and professional defense against growing threats.

Real Case: Attack on Mexico's Ministry of Economy (2020)

In February 2020, the Ministry of Economy suffered a cyberattack that affected its internal servers, suspending processes such as trademarks, patents, and foreign trade. Although the agency activated contingency protocols, full service restoration took several days.

This case revealed three common weaknesses:

- Lack of continuous monitoring and early warning systems.
- Insufficient staff preparation for cyber incidents.
- Dependence on outdated systems with inadequate backup.

The main lesson was that having policies is not enough; their effective execution requires resources, training, and institutional leadership.

Current Challenges and Future Outlook

Despite progress, there are still significant challenges in implementing effective SOCs in the public sector:

- **Shortage of Specialized Talent:** The lack of trained cybersecurity professionals limits SOC growth and affects operational continuity.
- **Limited Budget:** Budget constraints often prevent the adoption of advanced technologies and the hiring of qualified personnel.
- **Institutional Fragmentation:** The absence of clear governance and cross-cutting policies complicates coordination among public agencies.

To overcome these obstacles, a state vision that prioritizes cybersecurity as an essential component of national sovereignty is necessary. Investment in training, promotion of stable regulatory frameworks, and international cooperation become indispensable strategies.

6 ETHICS, ALGORITHMIC SURVEILLANCE AND CITIZEN TRUST

6.1. Algorithmic Bias in Public Services

The popularity of algorithmic systems in public services has generated numerous ethical and social challenges, among which is the risk of bias that may result in unfair or discriminatory decisions. Algorithms can reproduce or even amplify existing social inequalities, as they learn patterns based on historical data that often contain structures of discrimination, exclusion, or unequal access to opportunities (Bouraffa & Hui, 2025; Ghosh et al., 2025).

An illustrative example of this is what happens with educational scholarship allocation systems. Algorithms trained on socioeconomic data may incorporate biases that penalize groups historically subject to discrimination, reducing their chances of accessing financial support. This perpetuates existing inequality gaps instead of helping to close them (Navaratna & Deepak Saxena, 2025).

Algorithmic systems have also started to be used in the field of public security through crime prediction systems, which has sparked significant criticism regarding their use. Tools employed to predict areas with high crime rates or individuals with a higher likelihood of recidivism can display bias against specific communities, ethnic minorities, or economically disadvantaged groups. Studies show how these types of algorithms often concentrate surveillance in poor or Black communities, even when crime rates do not justify such focused attention. This not only undermines principles of justice but may also deepen public distrust toward government institutions (Ghosh et al., 2025).

The primary danger of algorithmic discrimination lies in the fact that many systems operate as black boxes, and there is excessive trust in their supposed technological objectivity. When someone is excluded from public assistance or subjected to increased surveillance, it is often difficult to determine which data or criteria influenced that decision, making it challenging to review or correct potential errors (Alshar'e, 2023).

Addressing algorithmic bias is not merely a technical issue but also an ethical and social commitment. Public institutions have the duty to audit and monitor the functioning of these systems, establish mechanisms for transparency, and provide clear explanations about automated decisions to ensure that algorithms do not reproduce or worsen existing inequalities (Renuka et al., 2025; ThamaraiSelvan M & Ambikapathy, 2025).

6.2. Explainability and AI Transparency

The incorporation of artificial intelligence (AI) systems into public services has created the need to ensure that automated decisions are easily understandable for citizens. The concept of explainability has become an important element to reduce the risk of decisions that could endanger fundamental rights and generate distrust toward public institutions (Renuka et al., 2025; ThamaraiSelvan M & Ambikapathy, 2025).

Explainability means that AI systems should be able to clearly and accessibly explain how and why a specific outcome or prediction was reached. This does not imply providing a detailed technical description of how the algorithms work but rather translating complex processes into information that is easily understood by people who are not technology experts. For example, in the healthcare sector, AI models used to determine how medical resources are allocated must be able to explain the factors considered in their decision-making, to avoid perceptions of arbitrariness or bias (Pantanowitz et al., 2024).

As a response to this need, tools and models of explainable artificial intelligence (XAI) have emerged, such as LIME or SHAP, which help identify which variables had the greatest influence on a prediction. However, their implementation in the public sector faces significant challenges, as there is an obligation to ensure transparency while also maintaining a balance with the protection of sensitive data and system security (Negri-Ribalta et al., 2024).

Furthermore, the right to receive explanations about automated decisions is increasingly becoming an ethical principle and, in some cases, a legal one, especially within frameworks like the European Union's General Data Protection Regulation (GDPR), which recognizes the right of individuals to obtain meaningful information about the logic underlying automated decisions (Pantanowitz et al., 2024; Renuka et al., 2025).

Ensuring explainability is not merely a technical challenge but is also an essential component for democratic legitimacy and the protection of human rights in this digital age. Achieving this requires clear regulations, training within public institutions, and a people-centered approach that considers both the benefits and the risks associated with automation in the governmental sector (ThamaraiSelvan M & Ambikapathy, 2025).

6.3. Surveillance Technologies vs Civil Liberties

The use of technologies in the governmental sector is experiencing rapid growth, driven by technological advancements and security concerns. Tools such as facial recognition, real-time geolocation, and the analysis of large volumes of data generated by social media enable public institutions to carry out functions like migration control or epidemiological monitoring. However, these technologies raise serious ethical and legal questions, especially regarding the protection of civil liberties and individuals' privacy (Graf & Bitencourt, 2024; White & Sjelin, 2022).

Facial recognition has been implemented in airports, transportation hubs, and public spaces to identify individuals sought by law enforcement or to prevent potential threats. Nevertheless, various studies have shown that these systems can produce higher false positive rates for people belonging to Black, Asian, or Latino communities, which increases the risk of discrimination and unjustified detections (Graf & Bitencourt, 2024; Tikkinen-Piri et al., 2018).

Geolocation has been used to track population or individual movements and was crucial in situations like the COVID-19 pandemic. However, it has also sparked concern due to its indiscriminate use and the lack of clear mechanisms to limit access to and use of this information. International organizations have warned that the mass storage of location data can lead to excessive surveillance and restrict fundamental rights, such as freedom of movement (White & Sjelin, 2022).

The analysis of data from social media has become another significant tool for governments, both to anticipate social movements and to detect security risks. While it can provide valuable information for public administration, it also poses ethical dilemmas regarding the surveillance of public opinion and the potential restriction of freedom of expression if used for political or repressive purposes (Oselame Graf & Muller Bitencourt, 2024).

The main challenge lies in balancing the legitimate need for governmental security and efficiency with respect for civil liberties. This involves applying principles such as proportionality, necessity, and legitimate purpose in the use of surveillance technologies, as well as establishing clear regulatory frameworks and accountability mechanisms to prevent abuses and protect citizens' trust (Tikkinen-Piri et al., 2018; White & Sjelin, 2022).

7. CONCLUSIONS AND STRATEGIC RECOMMENDATIONS

In a time when governments rely more on data and algorithms, cybersecurity, data privacy, and digital ethics are not something they can ignore—they are crucial for survival. This chapter shows how digital trust, the credibility of institutions, and even people's emotional health are closely connected to strong cybersecurity systems and the responsible use of new technologies like artificial intelligence. It's not just about technical protection; it's about the basic agreement between citizens and their governments that shapes society.

The model created by Ruiz-Vanoye et al. (2025) shows that digital security is the base of a pyramid for emotional well-being. It explains that when there are security problems, they don't just affect systems they also harm people. People often feel fear, frustration, and become less involved in society when there are data breaches, unfair algorithms, or not enough transparency. Because of this, cybersecurity should not be considered alone. Instead, it should be a key part of building strong, healthy democracies.

From a regulatory point of view, international standards like GDPR and ISO 27001, as well as national laws such as Mexico's LGPDPPSO, provide good examples to follow. But the main difficulty is in putting these rules into action and making sure they work together smoothly. When regulations are too scattered or too strict, it becomes harder for digital platforms to connect securely. Because of this, governments need to work on making laws more consistent across different countries while still allowing room for local rules and new challenges.

Ethics shouldn't be something we think about later. When machines make decisions, watch people through algorithms, or provide public services with AI, we need more than just accuracy we also need to care about what's right and fair.

Transparency, explainability, and getting citizens' consent are not just good ideas anymorethey are things governments must do. If they don't, people won't trust them. A government that can't explain how it uses algorithms may become secretive, hard to hold accountable, and lose the support of the people it's supposed to help.

In terms of strategy, governments should focus on these key steps:

1. Create policies that put people first in cybersecurity, covering both the technical aspects and the feelings people have about trust online.

2. Set up strong cyber response teams across different sectors, such as Security Operations Centers, and keep training programs going that follow top international standards like NIST CSF.
3. Check on the ethics of AI systems and make sure there is always someone watching when important decisions are made that affect people's rights.
4. Put money into programs that explain AI and teach people how to use technology, so everyone can better understand and keep up with new advancements.
5. Work together with other countries to agree on rules, share information, and act as a team to deal with cyber threats that affect multiple nations.

Lastly, digital transformation should be based on human values. The aim isn't just to make services faster or more efficient, but to build environments that are fair, safe, and emotionally supportive. Technology should support public service values, not take their place. As we use more algorithms to make decisions, we need to make sure every digital rule or tool shows respect for people's worth, clear government actions, and fair leadership.

In the end, it's not just about keeping systems running it's about keeping people safe.

8. REFERENCES

ADIP. (2022). App CDMX. https://www.adip.cdmx.gob.mx/app-cdmx

Alkhedhairy, M. A. (2025). Balancing Privacy and Risk: A Critical Analysis of Personal Data Use as Governed by Saudi Insurance Law. *Laws*, *14*(4), 47. DOI: 10.3390/laws14040047

Alshar'e, M. (2023). Cyber Security Framework Selection: Comparision Of Nist And Iso27001. *Applied Computing Journal*, 245–255. https://doi.org/DOI: 10.52098/acj.202364

Astudillo Moya, M., & Porras Rivera, R. (2024). Corruption in Public Finance and Open Government in Mexico. IntechOpen. https://doi.org/DOI: 10.5772/intechopen.1007196

Atadoga, A., Farayola, O. A., Ayinla, B. S., Amoo, O. O., Abrahams, T. O., & Osasona, F. (2024). A COMPARATIVE REVIEW OF DATA ENCRYPTION METHODS IN THE USA AND EUROPE. *Computer Science & IT Research Journal*, *5*(2), 447–460. DOI: 10.51594/csitrj.v5i2.815

Bade, S. O., & Tomomewo, O. S. (2024). A review of governance strategies, policy measures, and regulatory framework for hydrogen energy in the United States. *International Journal of Hydrogen Energy*, *78*, 1363–1381. DOI: 10.1016/j.ijhydene.2024.06.338

Barros, A. (2012). Datos abiertos: ¿Qué son y cuál es su utilidad? En A. Hofmann, A. Ramírez-Alujas, & J. A. Bojórquez (Coords.), La promesa del gobierno abierto. licensed under a Creative Commons Reconocimiento - NoComercial - Compartir Igual 3.0 Unported License. Retriev July 20, 2025 from https://biblio.juridicas.unam.mx/bjv/detalle-libro/5182-la-promesa-del-gobierno-abierto

Bello Jiménez, A. J. (2025). Inteligencia artificial, el eslabón entre bases de datos y combate a la corrupción. Caso México. *Revista Especializada en Investigación Jurídica*, *9*(16), 1–20. Advance online publication. DOI: 10.20983/reij.2025.1.6

Bernardo, L., Malta, S., & Magalhães, J. (2025). An Evaluation Framework for Cybersecurity Maturity Aligned with the NIST CSF. *Electronics (Basel)*, *14*(7), 1364. DOI: 10.3390/electronics14071364

Bouraffa, T., & Hui, K.-L. (2025). Regulating Information and Network Security: Review and Challenges. *ACM Computing Surveys*, *57*(5), 1–38. DOI: 10.1145/3711124

Catoira, A. A., Balaguer Callejón, F., Cotino Hueso, L., Hernández Ramos, M., Presno Linera, M., Rebollo Delgado, L., & Tudela Aranda, J. (2025). Encuesta sobre Inteligencia artificial y Derechos fundamentales. *Teoría y Realidad Constitucional*, *55*(55), 11–86. DOI: 10.5944/trc.55.2025.45027

Cerina, R., & Rouméas, É. (2025). The democratic ethics of artificially intelligent polling. *AI & Society*, *40*(5), 3209–3223. DOI: 10.1007/s00146-024-02150-4

De Datos, L. F. D. P. (2010). Ley Federal de Protección de Datos Personales en Posesión de los Particulares. *Diario Oficial de la Federación*, *5*, •••. https://www.diputados.gob.mx/LeyesBiblio/pdf/LFPDPPP.pdf

de Gobierno de Chile, C. S. I. R. T. (2023). *Informe Anual de Gestión 2022*. https://csirt.gob.cl/documents/4395/16RSC23-00010-01.pdf

ENISA. (2022). *Cyber Crisis Management: Exercise Handbook*. European Union Agency for Cybersecurity. https://www.enisa.europa.eu/publications/best-practices-for-cyber-crisis-management

Esteves, B., & Rodríguez-Doncel, V. (2024). Analysis of ontologies and policy languages to represent information flows in GDPR. *Semantic Web*, *15*(3), 709–743. DOI: 10.3233/SW-223009

Floridi, L., Morley, J., Kinsey, L., & Elhalal, A. (2021). Operationalising AI ethics: Barriers, enablers and next steps. *AI & Society*, *36*, 415–436. DOI: 10.1007/s00146-021-01308-8

Gao, P., Sun, N., Wang, X., Yang, C., & Zitikis, R. (2023). NLP-based detection of systematic anomalies among the narratives of consumer complaints. arXiv:2308.11138. https://arxiv.org/abs/2308.11138

Ghosh, A., Saini, A., & Barad, H. (2025). Artificial intelligence in governance: Recent trends,risks, challenges, innovative frameworks and future directions. *AI & Society*. Advance online publication. DOI: 10.1007/s00146-025-02312-y

GOB. (2025). Gobierno de Mexico. https://www.gob.mx/index.xhtml

Gómez Sánchez, M. A. (2020). La protección de datos personales en México. *Revista Mexicana de Ciencias Penales*, *3*(10), 47–58. DOI: 10.57042/rmcp.v3i10.97

Graf, O. J., & Bitencourt, M. C. (2024). Digital government and the handling of sensitive data in the execution of public policies: Challenges and possibilities. *Araucaria*, *56*(56), 139–154. DOI: 10.12795/araucaria.2024.i56.06

Instituto Nacional de Estándares y Tecnología (NIST). (2012). *Computer Security Incident Handling Guide* (SP 800-61 Revision 2). U.S. Department of Commerce. https://nvlpubs.nist.gov/nistpubs/SpecialPublications/NIST.SP.800-61r2.pdf

Jasso López, L. C. (2023). Vigilar al vigilante: Transparencia y rendición de cuentas sobre las tecnologías de vigilancia pública en México. *Revista Estudios en Derecho a la Información*, (15), 31–53. DOI: 10.22201/iij.25940082e.2023.15.17470

Jin, M., & Aletras, N. (2020). Complaint Identification in Social Media with Transformer Networks. arXiv:2010.10910. https://arxiv.org/abs/2010.10910 DOI: 10.18653/v1/2020.coling-main.157

Klinger, E., Wiesmaier, A., & Heinemann, A. (2023). *A Review of existing GDPR Solutions for Citizens and SMEs*. https://doi.org/https://doi.org/10.48550/arXiv.2302.03581

LGPDPPSO. https://www.diputados.gob.mx/LeyesBiblio/pdf/LGPDPPSO.pdf (2025). https://www.diputados.gob.mx/LeyesBiblio/pdf/LGPDPPSO.pdf

Lostal Martínez, F. R. (2024). *The Impact of Artificial Intelligence on Mexico's Logistics Sector: Challenges and Opportunities* (pp. 95–114). https://doi.org/DOI: 10.1007/978-3-031-71993-6_7

Morley, J., Floridi, L., Kinsey, L., & Elhalal, A. (2020). From What to How: An Initial Review of Publicly Available AI Ethics Tools, Methods and Research to Translate Principles into Practices. *Science and Engineering Ethics*, *26*(3), 2141–2168. DOI: 10.1007/s11948-019-00165-5 PMID: 31828533

Navaratna, A. R., & Deepak Saxena. (2025). From policy to practice in digital governance: A three-level analysis of citizen-centric applications. *JeDEM - EJournal of EDemocracy and Open Government, 17*(1), 33–64. https://doi.org/DOI: 10.29379/jedem.v17i1.906

Negri-Ribalta, C., Lombard-Platet, M., & Salinesi, C. (2024). Understanding the GDPR from a requirements engineering perspective—A systematic mapping study on regulatory data protection requirements. *Requirements Engineering*, *29*(4), 523–549. DOI: 10.1007/s00766-024-00423-4

Normas, I. S. O. (2007). Esquema Nacional de Seguridad. *Normas ISO*. https://www.normas-iso.com/esquema-nacional-de-seguridad/

Nurbojatmiko, N., Karimiyah, M. S. K., Asnadi, N. M., & Anisyah, R. (2025). ISO 27001 As Information Security Solution In Society 5.0 Era: Systematic Literature Review. *Sinkron*, *9*(1), 484–492. DOI: 10.33395/sinkron.v9i1.14448

Pantanowitz, L., Hanna, M., Pantanowitz, J., Lennerz, J., Henricks, W. H., Shen, P., Quinn, B., Bennet, S., & Rashidi, H. H. (2024). Regulatory Aspects of Artificial Intelligence and Machine Learning. *Modern Pathology*, *37*(12), 100609. DOI: 10.1016/j.modpat.2024.100609 PMID: 39260776

Pillai, R., Islam, M., Sreejith, S., & Al-Malkawi, H. A. (2025). Comparative analysis of environmental, social and governance (ESG) ratings: Do sectors and regions differ? *The Journal of Management and Governance*, *29*(1), 69–109. DOI: 10.1007/s10997-023-09692-7

Preotiuc-Pietro, D., Gaman, M., & Aletras, N. (2019). Automatically Identifying Complaints in Social Media. arXiv:1906.03890. https://arxiv.org/abs/2308.11138 DOI: 10.18653/v1/P19-1495

Ramírez-Alujas, Á. V., & Dassen, N. (2014). Vientos de cambio: el avance de las políticas de Gobierno Abierto en América Latina y el Caribe. Banco Interamericano de Desarrollo. Retriev July 20, 2025 from https://short-link.me/196zA

Renuka, O. RadhaKrishnan, N., Priya, B. S., Jhansy, A., & Ezekiel, S. (2025). Data Privacy and Protection. In *Emerging Threats and Countermeasures in Cybersecurity* (pp. 433–465). Wiley. https://doi.org/DOI: 10.1002/9781394230600.ch19

Rojas Flores, G. (2020). Plataformas digitales: mecanismos de acceso a la información en lo subnacional (Veracruz 2000-2018). Revista de Estudios de Políticas Públicas, 6(2), 99-115. ISSN edición web: 0719-6296 DOI: 10.5354/0719-6296.2020.58242

Ruiz-Vanoye, J. A., Fuentes-Penna, A., Barrera-Cámara, R. A., Díaz-Parra, O., Trejo-Macotela, F. R., Gómez-Pérez, L. J., Aguilar-Ortiz, J., Ruiz-Jaimes, M. Á., Domínguez Mayorga, C. R., & Toledo-Navarro, Y. (2025). Digital Security and Stability as a Foundation for Emotional Well-Being in an AI-Driven Society. *International Journal of Combinatorial Optimization Problems and Informatics*, *16*(1), 14–37. DOI: 10.61467/2007.1558.2025.v16i1.932

Sandoval-Almazán, R. (2015). Gobierno abierto y transparencia: Construyendo un marco conceptual. *Convergencia*, *22*(68), 203–227. https://www.researchgate.net/publication/321893741_Gobierno_abierto_y_transparencia_construyendo_un_marco_conceptual. DOI: 10.29101/crcs.v0i68.2958

Sandoval-Almazán, R. (2019). Gobierno abierto y transparencia en México: Estudio longitudinal 2015-2018. *Innovar (Universidad Nacional de Colombia)*, *29*(74), 115–131. DOI: 10.15446/innovar.v29n74.82097

Santos Pinacho, M., Rentería-Gaeta, R., & García García, L. M. (2022). La Política Nacional de Datos Abiertos como instrumento para la consolidación de un Gobierno Abierto en México. *Encrucijada Revista Electrónica Del Centro De Estudios En Administración Pública*, (40), 34–57. DOI: 10.22201/fcpys.20071949e.2022.40.81278

Sernani, P., Cossiri, A., Di Cosimo, G., & Frontoni, E. (2025). Analyzing Digital Political Campaigning Through Machine Learning: An Exploratory Study for the Italian Campaign for European Union Parliament Election in 2024. *Computers, 14*(4), 126. DOI: 10.3390/computers14040126

Silva, J. M., Ribeiro, D., Ramos, L. F., & Fonte, V. (2024). *A worldwide overview on the information security posture of online public services*. En Bui, T. X. & Sprague, R. H. (Eds.), *Proceedings of the 57th Hawaii International Conference on System Sciences* (pp. 1881–1890). Disponible en SSRN: https://ssrn.com/abstract=4577703

ThamaraiSelvan M, & Ambikapathy, A. (2025). Literature Review And *Identification Of Research Gaps In Cybersecurity Risk Management. IAPQR Transactions, 89–95.* https://www.researchgate.net/publication/392831911_LITERATURE_REVIEW_AND_IDENTIFICATION_OF_RESEARCH_GAPS_IN_CYBERSECURITY_RISK_MANAGEMENT

Tikkinen-Piri, C., Rohunen, A., & Markkula, J. (2018). EU General Data Protection Regulation: Changes and implications for personal data collecting companies. *Computer Law & Security Review, 34*(1), 134–153. DOI: 10.1016/j.clsr.2017.05.015

Villanueva, E., Andrea, M. C., & Edith, F. G. Sandra, & Martínez Bermeo, José Roberto. (2016). La participación digital en la construcción de la e-democracia y ciudadanía digital. RIDE. Revista Iberoamericana para la Investigación y el Desarrollo Educativo, 7(13), 126-146. ISSN 2007-7467. Retriev July 20, 2025 from https://www.scielo.org.mx/scielo.php?script=sci_arttext&pid=S2007-74672016000200126&lng=es&tlng=es

White, G. B., & Sjelin, N. (2022). The NIST Cybersecurity Framework. In *Research Anthology on Business Aspects of Cybersecurity* (pp. 39–55). IGI Global., DOI: 10.4018/978-1-6684-3698-1.ch003

Compilation of References

AAIP. (2025). Agencia de Acceso a la Información Pública Retrieved May 14, 2025 from https://portal.transparencia.gob.ar/

Abdulsaheb, J. A., Nafea, R. M., Al-Jawher, W. A. M., & Hayyawi, M. L. (2024). IoT Based Smart Parking System. *Journal Port Science Research*, *7*(3), 196–203. DOI: 10.36371/port.2024.3.1

ADIP. (2022). App CDMX. https://www.adip.cdmx.gob.mx/app-cdmx

African Development Bank. (2025a). Kenya Data Portal. Retrieved June 26, 2025 from https://kenya.opendataforafrica.org

African Development Bank. (2025b). Nigeria Data Portal. Retrieved June 29, 2025 from https://nigeria.opendataforafrica.org/

agesic. (2025). Plataforma de Participación Ciudadana Digital. Retrieved July 3, 2025 from https://plataformaparticipacionciudadana.gub.uy/

AGID. (2025a). dati.gov.it i dati aperti della pubblica amministrazione. Retrieved June 15, 2025 from https://www.dati.gov.it/

AGID. (2025b). Yucca Smart Data Platform Smart Data Platform. Retrieved June 16. 2025 from https://developers.italia.it/en/software/d5da261d-68f6-4c81-9ba8-6f2984515c85.html

Aguirre-Sala, J. (2022). Modelos y buenas prácticas evaluativas para detectar impactos, riesgos y daños de la inteligencia artificial. Paakat. *Revista de Tecnología y Sociedad*, *12*(23). Advance online publication. DOI: 10.32870/Pk.a12n23.742

Agustí i Hernàndez, C. (2022). Promoting platforms for bottom-up participatory governance: a policy instrument approach through the facilitation of strategic smart city governance. In Vacca, J. R. (Ed.), *Smart Cities Policies and Financing* (pp. 297–304). Elsevier. https://doi.org/https://doi.org/10.1016/B978-0-12-819130-9.00043-7

Ahmad, K., Maabreh, M., Ghaly, M., Khan, K., Qadir, J., & Al-Fuqaha, A. (2022). Developing future human-centered smart cities: Critical analysis of smart city security, data management, and ethical challenges. *Computer Science Review*, *43*, 100452. DOI: 10.1016/j.cosrev.2021.100452

Ajuntament de Barcelona. (2022). Informe Smart City Barcelona 2022. https://ajuntament.barcelona.cat

Ajuntament de Barcelona. (2024). Participa Barcelona: Inteligencia artificial para la participación ciudadana. Barcelona City Council, Digital Innovation Report.

Akhter Shareef, M., Kumar, V., Kumar, U., & Akhter Hasin, A. (2009). Diffusion of Innovation and Capability Theory in the Context of E-Government. In Dwivedi, Y. K., Lal, B., Williams, M. D., Schneberger, S. L., & Wade, M. (Eds.), *Handbook of Research on Contemporary Theoretical Models in Information Systems* (pp. 193–211). IGI Global Scientific Publishing. DOI: 10.4018/978-1-60566-659-4.ch011

Alavikia, Z., & Shabro, M. (2022). A comprehensive layered approach to implementing IoT technologies in smart grid. *Digital Communications and Networks*, *8*(4), 506–520. DOI: 10.1016/j.dcan.2022.01.002

Al-Besher, A., & Kumar, K. (2022). Use of artificial intelligence to enhance e-government services. *Measurement. Sensors*, *24*, 100484. https://doi.org/https://doi.org/10.1016/j.measen.2022.100484

Albino, V., Berardi, U., & Dangelico, R. M. (2015). Smart Cities: Definitions, Dimensions, Performance, and Initiatives. *Journal of Urban Technology*, *22*(1), 3–21. DOI: 10.1080/10630732.2014.942092

Alcaldía Mayor de Bogotá, D. C. (2021). Plan de movilidad sostenible y segura de Bogotá: Metodología de participación ciudadana [Documento técnico]. Secretaría Distrital de Movilidad. https://www.movilidadbogota.gov.co/web/plan_de_movilidad_sostenible_y_segura

Alcudia, D., & Venancio, A. (2023). Aproximación a la gobernanza digital en Iberoamérica. *Revista de Direito da Cidade*, *15*(2), 1–20.

Alex Bazigu and Johnson Mwebaze. (2025). A framework for IoT-enabled smart manufacturing for energy and resource optimization. arXiv. /arXiv.2502.03040. DOI: 10.48550

Alkhedhairy, M. A. (2025). Balancing Privacy and Risk: A Critical Analysis of Personal Data Use as Governed by Saudi Insurance Law. *Laws*, *14*(4), 47. DOI: 10.3390/laws14040047

Allam, Z., & Jones, D. S. (2021). Future (post-COVID) digital, smart and sustainable cities in the wake of 6G: Digital twins, immersive realities and new urban economies. *Land Use Policy*, *101*, 105201. DOI: 10.1016/j.landusepol.2020.105201

Allam, Z., & Newman, P. (2018). Redefining the Smart City: Culture, metabolism and governance. *Smart Cities*, *1*(1), 4–25. DOI: 10.3390/smartcities1010002

Allen, J. G., Loo, J., & Luna Campoverde, J. L. (2025). Governing intelligence: Singapore's evolving AI governance framework. 1. DOI: 10.1017/cfl.2024.12

Allen, A., Chua, S., & Lee, H. (2012). Case study: A smart water grid in Singapore. *Water Practice & Technology*, *7*(4), 1–8. DOI: 10.2166/wpt.2012.089

Alotaibi, E. M., Issa, H., & Codesso, M. (2025). Blockchain-based conceptual model for enhanced transparency in government records: A design science research approach. *International Journal of Information Management Data Insights*, *5*(1), 100304. https://doi.org/https://doi.org/10.1016/j.jjimei.2024.100304

Alshar'e, M. (2023). Cyber Security Framework Selection: Comparision Of Nist And Iso27001. *Applied Computing Journal*, 245–255. https://doi.org/DOI: 10.52098/acj.202364

Alvarado-Arias, N., Soria-Delgado, J., Staines, J., & Moya-Almeida, V. (2025). Towards Participatory River Governance Through Citizen Science. *Water (Basel)*, *17*(9), 1358. DOI: 10.3390/w17091358

Aman, S., & Jan, M. (2022). Are we moving towards a managerial model of e-governance? building a case for citizen centric e-participation in khyber pakhtunkhwa, pakistan. *Biological and Clinical Sciences Research Journal*, *3*(1), 500–523. DOI: 10.47264/idea.jhsms/3.1.35

Ambientum.com. (2025). Línea Verde. In (Version May 5, 2025) https://play.google.com/store/apps/details?id=lineaVerde.App

ANDRONICEANU, A., Georgescu, I., & Kinnunen, J. (2022). "public administration digitalization and corruption in the eu member states. a comparative and correlative research analysis". Transylvanian Review of Administrative Sciences, (65E), 5-22. DOI: 10.24193/tras.65E.1

Angelidou, M. (2014). Smart city policies: A spatial approach. *Cities (London, England)*, *41*, S3–S11. DOI: 10.1016/j.cities.2014.06.007

Angelidou, M. (2017). The Role of Smart City Characteristics in the Plans of Fifteen Cities. *Journal of Urban Technology*, *24*(4), 3–28. DOI: 10.1080/10630732.2017.1348880

Angwin, J., Larson, J., Mattu, S., & Kirchner, L. (2016, mayo 23). Machine bias: There's software used across the country to predict future criminals. And it's biased against blacks. ProPublica. https://www.propublica.org/article/machine-bias-risk-assessments-in-criminal-sentencing

Anthopoulos, L., Sirakoulis, K., & Reddick, C. G. (2022). Conceptualizing smart government: Interrelations and reciprocities with smart city. *Digital Government: Research and Practice*, *2*(4), 1–28. DOI: 10.1145/346506

Ardielli, E. (2015). Public administration transparency in e-government at local level of czech government. *The International Journal of Management Science and Business Administration*, *2*(8), 24–33. DOI: 10.18775/ijmsba.1849-5664-5419.2014.28.1003

Arenas-Ramiro, M. (2022). Data protection in Latin America (pp. 140–159). Edward Elgar Publishing eBooks. DOI: 10.4337/9781786438515.00013

Arguelles, E., & Amaro, M. (2023). Chatbots y COVID-19: Ética, responsabilidad y acceso a la información en México. Revista Jurídicas UNAM, 34(1), 55–72. https://revistas.juridicas.unam.mx/index.php/derecho-informacion/article/view/17472/17922

Ashar, A., Ginena, K., Cipollone, M., Barreto, R., & Cramer, H. (2025). Algorithmic impact assessments and accountability: The co-construction of impacts. In *Proceedings of the 2021 ACM Conference on Fairness, Accountability, and Transparency (FAccT '21)* (pp. 123–134). ACM. https://doi.org/DOI: 10.1145/3442188.3445935

Ashraf, M. J. (2020). Precision policing: a way forward to reduce crime. https://www.hsdl.org/?abstract&did=839420

Astudillo Moya, M., & Porras Rivera, R. (2024). Corruption in Public Finance and Open Government in Mexico. IntechOpen. https://doi.org/DOI: 10.5772/intechopen.1007196

Atadoga, A., Farayola, O. A., Ayinla, B. S., Amoo, O. O., Abrahams, T. O., & Osasona, F. (2024). A COMPARATIVE REVIEW OF DATA ENCRYPTION METHODS IN THE USA AND EUROPE. *Computer Science & IT Research Journal*, *5*(2), 447–460. DOI: 10.51594/csitrj.v5i2.815

Attard, M., & Balbontin, C. (2024). Workshop 6 report: Micromobility movement in urban transport. Recherche En Matière d'économie Des Transports. DOI: 10.1016/j.retrec.2023.101399

Australian Energy Market Operator (AEMO). (2023). DER Integration Projects – Flexible Export Test. https://aemo.com.au/en/initiatives/major-programs/der-program/flexible-exports

Authors, F. (2024). Transparency and accountability in AI systems. *Frontiers in Human Dynamics*, *6*, 1421273. DOI: 10.3389/fhumd.2024.1421273

Ayala, G. C., Macías, C. L., Rúelas, A. L., García, J. M., Enríquez, A. M., Meza, H. C., & Beltrán, J. F. (2011). Diseño de un prototipo didáctico para la implementación de redes de sensores inalámbricos basados en el protocolo Zigbee. *Ra Ximhai*, *7*(3), 3. Advance online publication. DOI: 10.35197/rx.07.03.2011.01.gc

Ayello, M. F., & Lopes, Y. (2023). Interoperability based on IEC 61850 standard: Systematic literature review, certification method proposal, and case study. *Electric Power Systems Research*, *220*, 109355. DOI: 10.1016/j.epsr.2023.109355

Bade, S. O., & Tomomewo, O. S. (2024). A review of governance strategies, policy measures, and regulatory framework for hydrogen energy in the United States. *International Journal of Hydrogen Energy*, *78*, 1363–1381. DOI: 10.1016/j.ijhydene.2024.06.338

Bakıcı, T., Almirall, E., & Wareham, J. (2013). A smart city initiative: The case of Barcelona. *Journal of the Knowledge Economy*, *4*(2), 135–148. DOI: 10.1007/s13132-012-0084-9

Banda, T. D., & Kumarasamy, M. (2024). Artificial Neural Network (ANN)-Based Water Quality Index (WQI) for Assessing Spatiotemporal Trends in Surface Water Quality—A Case Study of South African River Basins. *Water (Basel)*, *16*(11), 1485. DOI: 10.3390/w16111485

Barone, G., Buonomano, A., Forzano, C., Palombo, A., & Russo, G. (2023). The role of energy communities in electricity grid balancing: A flexible tool for smart grid power distribution optimization. *Renewable & Sustainable Energy Reviews*, *187*, 113742. DOI: 10.1016/j.rser.2023.113742

Barros, A. (2012). Datos abiertos: ¿Qué son y cuál es su utilidad? En A. Hofmann, A. Ramírez-Alujas, & J. A. Bojórquez (Coords.), La promesa del gobierno abierto. licensed under a Creative Commons Reconocimiento - NoComercial - Compartir Igual 3.0 Unported License. Retriev July 20, 2025 from https://biblio.juridicas.unam.mx/bjv/detalle-libro/5182-la-promesa-del-gobierno-abierto

Batty, M. (2018). Digital twins. *Environment and Planning. B, Urban Analytics and City Science*, *45*(5), 817–820. DOI: 10.1177/2399808318796416

Batty, M. (2024). *The Computable City: Histories, Technologies, Stories, Predictions. MIT Press*. MIT Press., DOI: 10.7551/mitpress/14099.001.0001

Batty, M., Axhausen, K. W., Giannotti, F., Pozdnoukhov, A., Bazzani, A., Wachowicz, M., & Portugali, Y. (2012). Smart cities of the future. *The European Physical Journal. Special Topics, 214*(1), 481–518. DOI: 10.1140/epjst/e2012-01703-3

Bayindir, R., Colak, I., Fulli, G., & Demirtas, K. (2016). Smart grid technologies and applications. *Renewable & Sustainable Energy Reviews, 66*, 499–516. DOI: 10.1016/j.rser.2016.08.002

Beatley, T. (2016). *Handbook of Biophilic City Planning and Design*. Island Press. DOI: 10.5822/978-1-61091-621-9

Beer, S. (1972). *Brain of the firm*. Allen Lane.

Bello Jiménez, A. J. (2025). Inteligencia artificial, el eslabón entre bases de datos y combate a la corrupción. Caso México. *Revista Especializada en Investigación Jurídica, 9*(16), 1–20. Advance online publication. DOI: 10.20983/reij.2025.1.6

Benitez Eyzaguirre, L. (2021). Blockchain para la transparencia, gestión pública y colaboración. Teknokultura. *Revista de Cultura Digital y Movimientos Sociales, 18*(1), 23–32. DOI: 10.5209/tekn.71514

Bernardo, L., Malta, S., & Magalhães, J. (2025). An Evaluation Framework for Cybersecurity Maturity Aligned with the NIST CSF. *Electronics (Basel), 14*(7), 1364. DOI: 10.3390/electronics14071364

Bhati, A., Hansen, M., & Chan, C. M. (2017). Energy conservation through smart homes in a smart city: A lesson for Singapore households. *Energy Policy, 104*, 230–239. DOI: 10.1016/j.enpol.2017.01.032

Bienert, R. (2023). Standardizing Demand-Side Management: The OpenADR Standard. In Demand-Side Management (Ch. 5). Wiley. DOI: 10.1002/9781119899457.ch5

Bilalova, S., Newig, J., & Villamayor-Tomas, S. (2024). *Toward Sustainable Water Governance?* Taking Stock of Paradigms, Practices, and Sustainability Outcomes., DOI: 10.1002/wat2.1762

Billi, M., Delgado, V., Jiménez, G., Morales, B., Neira, C., Silva, M., & Urquiza, A. (2020). Gobernanza policéntrica para la resiliencia al cambio climático: Análisis legislativo comparado y ley marco de cambio en chile. *Estudios Públicos*, (160), 7–53. DOI: 10.38178/07183089/1028191015

Bishr, A. (2019). Dubai: A City Powered by Blockchain. *Innovations: Technology, Governance, Globalization, 12*(3-4), 4–8. DOI: 10.1162/inov_a_00271

BOE. (2013, December 10). Ley de transparencia, acceso a la información pública y buen gobierno. Retrieved June 11, 2025 from https://www.boe.es/eli/es/l/2013/12/09/19

Boletín Oficial del Estado. (2022, October 13). Ley Orgánica 10/2022, de garantía integral de la libertad sexual. Gobierno de España. https://www.boe.es/buscar/doc.php?id=BOE-A-2022-17325

Bonilla Gutiérrez, J. C. (2025). Las plataformas digitales como herramientas anticorrupción: democracia, tecnología y transparencia en la era digital. Universita Ciencia, 13(36). https://doi.org/https://doi.org/10.5281/zenodo.15121040

Boudou, M. (2023). Digital divide, e-government and trust in public service: The key role of educational inequalities. *Frontiers in Sociology*, *8*, 1140416. DOI: 10.3389/fsoc.2023.1140416 PMID: 36895333

Bouraffa, T., & Hui, K.-L. (2025). Regulating Information and Network Security: Review and Challenges. *ACM Computing Surveys*, *57*(5), 1–38. DOI: 10.1145/3711124

Bouskela, M., Casseb, M., Bassi, S., De Luca, C., & Facchina, M. (2016). *La ruta hacia las Smart Cities: migrando de una gestión tradicional a la ciudad inteligente. Banco interamericano de Desarrollo*. BID.

Bryson, J. J., Diamantis, M. E., & Grant, T. D. (2017). Of, for, and by the people: The legal lacuna of synthetic persons. *Artificial Intelligence and Law*, *25*(3), 273–291. DOI: 10.1007/s10506-017-9214-9

Budrin, A. G., Budrina, E. V., Lebedeva, A. S., Rogavichene, L. I., & Abdullah, M. (2020). Electronic Engineering as a Factor of Sustainable Development for Smart City. In 2020 IEEE Conference of Russian Young Researchers in Electrical and Electronic Engineering (EIConRus) (pp. 1637-1642). IEEE. DOI: DOI: 10.1109/EIConRus49466.2020.9038943

Buolamwini, J., & Gebru, T. (2018). Gender shades: Intersectional accuracy disparities in commercial gender classification. In Proceedings of Machine Learning Research (Vol. 81, pp. 1–15). http://proceedings.mlr.press/v81/buolamwini18a/buolamwini18a.pdf

Burczyk, S., Kozłowski, M., & Kułaszka, A. (2022). LTE and NB-IoT performance estimation based on indicators measured by the radio module. *Electronics (Basel)*, *11*(18), 2892. DOI: 10.3390/electronics11182892

Bwambale, E., Abagale, F. K., & Anornu, G. K. (2022). Smart irrigation monitoring and control strategies for improving water use efficiency in precision agriculture: A review. *Agricultural Water Management*, *260*, 107324. DOI: 10.1016/j.agwat.2021.107324

California, I. S. O. (2023). Duck Curve Management: Smart Grid Tools and Challenges. https://www.caiso.com

Callon, M. (1986). Some elements of a sociology of translation: Domestication of the scallops and the fishermen of St Brieuc Bay. In Law, J. (Ed.), *Power, action and belief: A new sociology of knowledge?* (pp. 196–233). Routledge.

Campana, P., Censi, R., Ruggieri, R., & Amendola, C. (2025). Smart Grids and Sustainability: The Impact of Digital..... *Energies*, *18*(9), 2149. Advance online publication. DOI: 10.3390/en18092149

Campero-Jurado, I., Quintanar Gómez, J., Vargas-Buitrón, O. D., Trejo-Macotela, F. R., Robles-Camarillo, D., & Simancas-Acevedo, E. (2019). Embedded system based on IoT and V2X for Smart Cities. *International Journal of Combinatorial Optimization Problems and Informatics*, *10*(3), 50–58. https://ijcopi.org/ojs/article/view/128

Canal del Congreso. (2025, June 30). Senado aprueba Ley de Telecomunicaciones. Retrieved July 4, 2025 from https://www.canaldelcongreso.gob.mx/noticia/senado-aprueba-ley-de-telecomunicaciones#:~:text=Al%20respecto%2C%20la%20nueva%20normativa,Registro%20de%20Poblaci%C3%B3n%20(CURP)

Capdevila, I., & Zarlenga, M. I. (2015). Smart city or smart citizens? The Barcelona case. *Journal of Strategy and Management*, *8*(3), 266–282. DOI: 10.1108/JSMA-03-2015-0030

Cardozo, N. (2024). Las crisis en la literatura de políticas públicas. *Análisis Plural*, (8). Advance online publication. DOI: 10.31391/4291h136

Cardullo, A., Di Feliciantonio, C., & Kitchin, R. (2019). *The right to the smart city*. Emerald Publishing Limited., DOI: 10.1108/9781787691391

Cardullo, P., & Kitchin, R. (2025). Provincialising platform citizenship: Citizen participation in and through civic platforms. *Digital Geography and Society*, *8*, 100123. DOI: 10.1016/j.diggeo.2025.100123

Cassandras, C. G. (2017). Automating mobility in smart cities. *Annual Reviews in Control*, *2017*, 1–8. DOI: 10.1016/j.arcontrol.2017.10.001

Castelán, M., & Aceves, M. (2024). El principio de equivalencia funcional en los títulos de crédito electrónicos. Revista Saberes Administrativos, 5, 8–16. https://www.uv.mx/iiesca/files/2025/02/02SA2024-02.pdf

Castillo Jiménez, E. (2024, November 8). La desaparición del INAI amenaza con dejar 15 000 millones de datos en el limbo. El País. https://elpais.com/mexico/2024-11-09/la-desaparicion-del-inai-amenaza-con-dejar-15000-millones-de-datos-en-el-limbo.html

Castillo Jiménez, E. (2025, July 1). Claudia Sheinbaum, sobre la Ley de Telecomunicaciones: "No hay censura, ni espionaje". El Paiss, Mexico. https://elpais.com/mexico/2025-07-01/claudia-sheinbaum-sobre-la-ley-de-telecomunicaciones-no-hay-censura-ni-espionaje.html?utm_source=chatgpt.com

Catoira, A. A., Balaguer Callejón, F., Cotino Hueso, L., Hernández Ramos, M., Presno Linera, M., Rebollo Delgado, L., & Tudela Aranda, J. (2025). Encuesta sobre Inteligencia artificial y Derechos fundamentales. *Teoría y Realidad Constitucional, 55*(55), 11–86. DOI: 10.5944/trc.55.2025.45027

Cavada, M., Tight, M. R., & Rogers, C. D. (2019). A smart city case study of Singapore-Is Singapore truly smart? In *Smart city emergence* (pp. 295–314). Elsevier. DOI: 10.1016/B978-0-12-816169-2.00014-6

CEER. (2025). 3rd CEER Report on Power Losses. https://www.ceer.eu/publication/3rd-ceer-report-on-power-losses

CEPA. (2024). Principles of Effective Governance for Sustainable Development Retrieved June 22, 2025 from https://www.un.org/ssr/sites/www.un.org.ssr/files/news_articles/_principles_of_effective_governance_for_sustainable_development.pdf

Cerina, R., & Rouméas, É. (2025). The democratic ethics of artificially intelligent polling. *AI & Society, 40*(5), 3209–3223. DOI: 10.1007/s00146-024-02150-4

Cerrillo, I., & Martínez, A. (2023). *Ciudades inteligentes y derechos digitales. De las Smart Cities a las Ciudades integradoras. Propuestas socio-jurídicas para una administración local del s. XXI.* Dykinson., DOI: 10.14679/2245

Change.org. (2025). Change.org. Retrieved July 3, 2025 from http://change.org

Chatfield, A. and Brajawidagda, U. (2013). Political will and strategic use of youtube to advancing government transparency: an analysis of jakarta government-generated youtube videos., 26-37. DOI: 10.1007/978-3-642-40358-3_3

Chintapalli, S., Arzamasov, V., & Monti, A. (2024). From prototype to interoperable DERs: A Hardware-in-the-Loop interoperability approach. *2024 IEEE International Conference on Industrial Cyber-Physical Systems (ICPS)*, 1–6. DOI: 10.1109/ICPS61098.2024.10662284

Choi, M. I., Cho, K., Hwang, J. Y., Park, L. W., Jang, K. H., Park, S., & Park, S. (2017). Design and implementation of IoT-based HVAC system for future zero energy building. In 2017 IEEE International Conference on Pervasive Computing and Communications Workshops (PerCom Workshops) (pp. 605-610). IEEE. DOI: DOI: 10.1109/PERCOMW.2017.7917631

Choo, M., Choi, Y., Yoon, H., Bae, S., & Yoon, D. (2023). Citizen engagement in smart city planning: The case of living labs in south korea. *Urban Planning*, *8*(2). Advance online publication. DOI: 10.17645/up.v8i2.6416

Cho, W., & Melisa, W. D. (2021). Citizen Coproduction and Social Media Communication: Delivering a Municipal Government's Urban Services through Digital Participation. *Administrative Sciences*, *11*(2), 59.

Chung, C.-S. (2015). The Introduction of e-Government in Korea: Development Journey, Outcomes and Future. Gestion et management public, 3(4), 107-122. DOI: 10.3917/gmp.034.0107

Citizens Foundation. (2025). Your Priorities. Retrieved June 2, 2025 from yrpri.org/domain/3

City of Boston Digital Service. (2025). BOS:311. In (Version 6.4.24) https://play.google.com/store/apps/details?id=gov.cityofboston.citizensconnect

Ciudadanía Inteligente. (2025). Chileleaks de la ciudadania inteligente. Retrieved July 5, 2025 from https://chileleaks.org

CLAD. (2016). Carta Iberoamericana de Gobierno Abierto. Bogotá, Colombia Retrieved from https://segib.org/es/publicacion/declaracion-de-la-xvii-conferencia-de-ministros-de-administracion-publica-y-reforma-del-estado/

Colab. (2025a). Colab. In (Version 7.6.11) https://play.google.com/store/apps/details?id=thirtyideas.colab_android&hl=pt_BR

Colab. (2025b, July 4). Colab a rede social paa cidadania. Retrieved July 4, 2025 from https://app.colab.re/

Combaz, A., Mas, D., Sanders, N., & Victor, M. (2025). Applications of Artificial Intelligence Tools to Enhance Legislative Engagement: Case Studies from Make.Org and MAPLE.

Congreso de la Unión. (2025a, March 20). Ley General de Protección de Datos Personales en Posesión de Sujetos Obligados. Diario Oficial de la Federación. https://www.diputados.gob.mx/LeyesBiblio/pdf/LGTAIP.pdf

Congreso de la Unión. (2025b). Ley General de Transparencia y Acceso a la Información Pública. Diario Oficial de la Federación. https://www.diputados.gob.mx/LeyesBiblio/ref/lgtaip/LGTAIP_orig_20mar25.pdf

Congreso de la Unión. (2025c). Ley General de Transparencia y Acceso a la Información Pública: Artículo 3, Fracción VIII. Diario Oficial de la Federación. https://www.diputados.gob.mx/LeyesBiblio/ref/lgtaip/LGTAIP_orig_20mar25.pdf

Controladoria-Geral da União. (2025, June 10). Portal da Transparência. Retrieved June 29, 2025 from https://portaldatransparencia.gov.br/

Cordella, A., & Paletti, A. (2018). Icts and value creation in public sector: Manufacturing logic vs service logic. *Information Polity*, *23*(2), 125–141. DOI: 10.3233/IP-170061

Cowley, R., Joss, S., & Dayot, Y. (2018). The smart city and Its publics: Insights from across six UK cities. *Urban Research & Practice*, *11*(1), 53–77. DOI: 10.1080/17535069.2017.1293150

CPLT. (2025). Portal de Transparencia. Retrieved June 30, 2025 from https://www.portaltransparencia.cl/PortalPdT/

CrisisGo. (n.d.). CrisisGo safety platform overview. CrisisGo Inc. https://www.crisisgo.com/

Cruz-Meléndez, C., Jiménez Canseco, J. M., & Martínez Gutiérrez, R. (2024). La implementación de chatbots en gobiernos municipales mexicanos. Exploración y diagnóstico de uso. *Revista Mexicana de Análisis Político y Administración Pública*, *13*(26), 119–153. DOI: 10.15174/remap.v13i26.441

da Costa Peixoto, A. (2015). Instrumentos da Democracia Participativa: Um estudo sobre o Participa.br e o Dialoga Brasil Universidade de Brasília]. Brasília, DF. https://bdm.unb.br/bitstream/10483/12701/1/2015_AbnerdaCostaPeixoto.pdf

Dabhade, V., Shah, R., & Nikam, D. (2024). Smart street lighting using IoT. *International Research Journal of Modernization in Engineering Technology and Science*. Advance online publication. DOI: 10.56726/IRJMETS50033

Danaher, J., Hogan, M. J., Noone, C., Kennedy, R., Behan, A., De Paor, A., Felzmann, H., Haklay, M., Khoo, S.-M., Morison, J., Murphy, M. H., O'Brolchain, N., Schafer, B., & Shankar, K. (2017). Algorithmic governance: Developing a research agenda through the power of collective intelligence. *Big Data & Society*, *4*(2), 1–21. DOI: 10.1177/2053951717726554

Danzi, F., Salgado, R. M., Oliveira, J. E., Arteiro, A., Camanho, P. P., & Braga, M. H. (2021). Structural Batteries: A Review. *Molecules (Basel, Switzerland)*, *26*(8), 2203. DOI: 10.3390/molecules26082203 PMID: 33920481

De Datos, L. F. D. P. (2010). Ley Federal de Protección de Datos Personales en Posesión de los Particulares. *Diario Oficial de la Federación*, *5*, •••. https://www.diputados.gob.mx/LeyesBiblio/pdf/LFPDPPP.pdf

De Filippi, F., Coscia, C., Boella, G., Antonini, A., Calafiore, A., Cantini, A., Guido, R., Salaroglio, C., Sanasi, L., & Schifanella, C. (2016). MiraMap: A We-government tool for smart peripheries in Smart Cities. *IEEE Access : Practical Innovations, Open Solutions*, *4*, 3824–3843. DOI: 10.1109/ACCESS.2016.2548558

de Gobierno de Chile, C. S. I. R. T. (2023). *Informe Anual de Gestión 2022*. https://csirt.gob.cl/documents/4395/16RSC23-00010-01.pdf

De la Garza, D., & Gómez, C. (2024). Inteligencia artificial y big data: Nuevos paradigmas de la comunicación política y la gobernanza digital. *Más Poder Local*, (56), 9–26. DOI: 10.56151/maspoderlocal.214

De Luna, A. J. H., Costa, C. P., & de Moura, H. P. (2014). Gobernanza ágil en tecnologías de la información y la comunicación: Cambio de paradigmas. arXiv. https://arxiv.org/abs/1411.2458

Dei, H. (2024). The role of big data in ensuring transparency and accountability of public authorities. *Health Leadership and Quality of Life*, *3*, 421. DOI: 10.56294/hl2024.421

Deloitte. (2023). The benefits of demand response in network modernization: economic and operational perspectives. https://www2.deloitte.com

Democrcia en Red. (2025). democraciaOS: Public Consultation. Retrieved July 3, 2025 from https://www.democraciaos.org/consultadigital

Denicia Carral, C., Yáñez García, G. J., Ballinas Hernández, A. L., & Minquiz Xolo, G. M. (2024). Prediction of water quality through dissolved oxygen saturation using data mining: A case study of Puebla, Mexico. *International Journal of Combinatorial Optimization Problems and Informatics*, *15*(5), 228–236. DOI: 10.61467/2007.1558.2024.v15i5.583

Dhanalakshmi, S., Poongothai, M., & Sharma, K. (2020). IoT based indoor air quality and smart energy management for HVAC system. *Procedia Computer Science, 171*, 1800–1809. DOI: 10.1016/j.procs.2020.04.193

Díaz-Parra, O., Fuentes-Penna, A., Barrera-Cámara, R., Trejo-Macotela, F., Ramos-Fernández, J., Ruiz-Vanoye, J., Ochoa, A., & Rodríguez-Flores, J. (2022). Educación inteligente y tendencias futuras. *International Journal of Combinatorial Optimization Problems and Informatics, 13*(1), 65–74. https://ijcopi.org/ojs/article/view/294

Dilip, D. (2024). *Exploring the Symbiotic Relationship between Digital Transformation.* Infrastructure, Service Delivery, and Governance for Smart Sustainable Cities., DOI: 10.3390/smartcities7020034

DINUM. (2025). The French public data platform. Retrieved June 2, 2025 from https://www.data.gouv.fr

Dominguez-Tabera, M., González-Mosqueda, M., Martínez-Tapía, K., Simancas-Acevedo, E., León-Olivares, E., & Robles-Camarillo, D. (2024). The application of artificial intelligence for the design of a virtual assistant (chatbot) as an innovative approach in user service: Social Security Center No. 102. *International Journal of Combinatorial Optimization Problems and Informatics, 15*(4), 149–162. DOI: 10.61467/2007.1558.2024.v15i4.484

Dunleavy, P., Margetts, H., Bastow, S., & Tinkler, J. (2006). *Digital era governance: IT corporations, the state, and e-government.* Oxford University Press. DOI: 10.1093/acprof:oso/9780199296194.001.0001

Dutch government. (2025). National Data Portal of the Dutch government. Retrieved June 16, 2025 from https://data.overheid.nl/

Dutta, J., Chowdhury, C., Roy, S., Middya, A. I., & Gazi, F. (2017). Towards smart city: sensing air quality in city based on opportunistic crowd-sensing. In *Proceedings of the 18th international conference on distributed computing and networking* (pp. 1-6). DOI: 10.1145/3007748.3018286

Du, Y. F., Sun, T., & Huang, Y. (2024). A Comprehensive Review of Smart City Initiatives in Singapore Technological Advancements and Urban Planning from 2015 to 2023. DOI: 10.31219/osf.io/yqfsv

Dwork, C., & Roth, A. (2014). The algorithmic foundations of differential privacy. Foundations and Trends® in Theoretical Computer Science, 9(3–4), 211–407. DOI: 10.1561/0400000042

Dzvinchuk, D., Borshch, H., Tsygylyk, N., Dobosh, Z., & Dziubynska, O. (2022). Public management for sustainable development: Current challenges and future trends. *Cuestiones Políticas*, *40*(73), 741–753. DOI: 10.46398/cuestpol.4073.42

Economist Intelligence Unit (EIU). (2021). Safe Cities Index 2021. The Economist. https://safecities.economist.com

Ejjami, R. (2024). Public administration 5.0: Enhancing governance and public services with smart technologies. *International Journal for Multidisciplinary Research*, *6*(4), 26086. Advance online publication. DOI: 10.36948/ijfmr.2024.v06i04.26086

ENISA. (2022). *Cyber Crisis Management: Exercise Handbook*. European Union Agency for Cybersecurity. https://www.enisa.europa.eu/publications/best-practices-for-cyber-crisis-management

Esteves, B., & Rodríguez-Doncel, V. (2024). Analysis of ontologies and policy languages to represent information flows in GDPR. *Semantic Web*, *15*(3), 709–743. DOI: 10.3233/SW-223009

Estrada, E., Maciel, R., Ortíz Zezzatti, C. A. O., Bernabe-Loranca, B., Oliva, D., & Larios, V. (2018). Smart City Visualisation Tool for the Open Data Georeferenced Analysis Utilizing Machine Learning. *International Journal of Combinatorial Optimization Problems and Informatics*, *9*(2), 25–40.

Etzkowitz, H., & Leydesdorff, L. (1995). The triple helix of university–industry–government relations: A laboratory for knowledge-based economic development. EASST Review, 14(1), 14–19. https://www.leydesdorff.net/th12/th12.pdf

EU Commission. (2024). Estonia 2024 Digital Decade Country Report. Retrieved July 5,2025 from https://digital-strategy.ec.europa.eu/en/factpages/estonia-2024-digital-decade-country-report

European Commission, Joint Research Centre. (2022). Explicit demand response for small end-users and independent aggregators: Status, context, enablers and barriers (EUR 31190 EN). Publications Office of the European Union. DOI: 10.2760/625919

European Commission. (2018). General Data Protection Regulation (GDPR). https://eur-lex.europa.eu/eli/reg/2016/679/oj

European Commission. (2022). Artificial Intelligence Act Proposal. https://digital-strategy.ec.europa.eu/en/policies/european-approach-artificial-intelligence

European Commission. (2023). *Artificial intelligence in education: Generative models and participatory learning*. Publications Office of the European Union.

European Commission. (n.d.). Smart cities and communities. Retrieved from https://digital-strategy.ec.europa.eu/en/policies/smart-cities-and-communities

European Environment Agency. (2022). Air quality in Europe — 2022 report. https://www.eea.europa.eu/publications/air-quality-in-europe-2022

European Parliament. (2021). Artificial Intelligence Act. European Union. https://eur-lex.europa.eu/legal-content/EN/TXT/?uri=CELEX%3A52021PC0206

European Union Agency for Cybersecurity (ENISA). (2023). Cybersecurity for Smart Grids: Threat Landscape 2023. https://www.enisa.europa.eu (2023).

European Union Agency for Cybersecurity. (2023). *ENISA Threat Landscape 2023.* https://www.enisa.europa.eu

European Union. (2025). eGovernment Benchmark Report 2025: On track for user-friendly online public services. Luxembourg: Publications Office of the European Union. DOI: 10.2759/0837457

EXPANSIÓN. (2015, September 7). Pleno ciudadano. Retrieved June 19, 2025 from https://expansion.mx/nacional/2015/09/07/pleno-ciudadano-una-app-para-vigilar-a-los-legisladores-mexicanos

Ezeigweneme, C. A., Nwasike, C. N., Adefemi, A. O., Adegbite, B. O., & Gidiagba, J. O. (2024). Smart Grids in Industrial Paradigms: A Review of the Progress, Benefits, and Implications of Maintenance. *Journal of Engineering Science and Technology*, *5*(1), 1–20. DOI: 10.51594/estj/v5i1.719

Fagnant, D. J., & Kockelman, K. (2015). Preparing a nation for autonomous vehicles: Opportunities, barriers and policy recommendations. *Transportation Research Part A, Policy and Practice*, *77*, 167–181. DOI: 10.1016/j.tra.2015.04.003

Fagundes, V. S. Jonice de Oliveira. (2017). Análise da Plataforma de Participação Social: Participação do Cidadão e Organizações na Elaboração de Políticas Públicas. XXXVII Congresso da Sociedade Brasileira de Computação, São Paulo.

Fan, C., Xu, J., Natarajan, B. Y., & Mostafavi, A. (2023). Interpretable machine learning learns complex interactions of urban features to understand socio-economic inequality. *Computer-Aided Civil and Infrastructure Engineering*, *38*(14), 2013–2029. Advance online publication. DOI: 10.1111/mice.12972

FEDER. (2025). Osoigo, El portal de los políticos que escuchan. Fondo Europeo de Desarrollo Regional. Retrieved July 4, 2025 from https://www.osoigo.com/

Federal Electricity Commission (CFE). (2022). Operational continuity report after instability events 23/06/2022. https://www.cfe.mx

Federal Emergency Management Agency (FEMA). (n.d.). Emergency response plan. Ready.gov. Retrieved 7 August 2025, from https://www.ready.gov/business/emergency-plans/emergency-response-plan

Feng, S., Chen, L., Sun, R., Feng, Z., Li, J., Khan, M. S., & Jing, Y. (2019). The Distribution and Accessibility of Urban Parks in Beijing, China: Implications of Social Equity. *International Journal of Environmental Research and Public Health, 16*(24), 4894. DOI: 10.3390/ijerph16244894 PMID: 31817222

Fernández-Añez, V., Güell, J., & Giffinger, R. (2018). Smart city implementation and discourses: An integrated conceptual model. the case of vienna. *Cities (London, England), 78*, 4–16. DOI: 10.1016/j.cities.2017.12.004

Fernández, J. (2021). La gobernanza inteligente de las metrópolis y la participación ciudadana. *Información Comercial Española*, (920). Advance online publication. DOI: 10.32796/ice.2021.920.7178

Fernandez-Monge, F., Barns, S., Kattel, R., & Bria, F. (2023). Reclaiming data for improved city governance: Barcelona's New Data Deal. *Urban Studies (Edinburgh, Scotland)*. Advance online publication. DOI: 10.1177/00420980231204835

Fiorucci, E., Musolino, A., Ferri, M., Pacioni, A., & Luiso, M. (2025). Driving sustainable development with PMU systems in distribution grids. *Sustainability, 17*(12), 5280. DOI: 10.3390/su17125280

FIWARE Foundation. (2023). FIWARE: Open source platform for the smart digital future. FIWARE Foundation. https://www.fiware.org/

Flood, D. (2023). #kalasatama: Discursive Views of the Helsinki Landscape Through the Virtual Window. *Philosophy of the City Journal, 1*(1), 112–126. DOI: 10.21827/potcj.1.1.40448

Flores-Iwasaki, M., Guadalupe, G. A., Pachas-Caycho, M., Chapa-Gonza, S., Mori-Zabarburú, R. C., & Guerrero-Abad, J. C. (2025). Internet of Things (IoT) Sensors for Water Quality Monitoring in Aquaculture Systems: A Systematic Review and Bibliometric Analysis. *AgriEngineering, 7*(3), 3. Advance online publication. DOI: 10.3390/agriengineering7030078

Floridi, L., Cowls, J., Beltrametti, M., Chatila, R., Chazerand, P., Dignum, V., Luetge, C., Madelin, R., Pagallo, U., Rossi, F., Schafer, B., Valcke, P., & Vayena, E. (2018). AI4People—An ethical framework for a good AI society. *Minds and Machines, 28*(4), 689–707. DOI: 10.1007/s11023-018-9482-5 PMID: 30930541

Floridi, L., Morley, J., Kinsey, L., & Elhalal, A. (2021). Operationalising AI ethics: Barriers, enablers and next steps. *AI & Society*, *36*, 415–436. DOI: 10.1007/s00146-021-01308-8

Flynn, M., & Gathright, J. (2025, April 1). Transparency law slashed by D.C. Council as lawmakers want more privacy. Retrieved July 7, 2025 from https://www.washingtonpost.com/dc-md-va/2025/04/01/dc-vote-closed-meetings-council/

Franco, I. (2021). Las smart cities en la agenda del planeamiento y la gobernanza urbana en américa latina. *Cuadernos de Geografia*, *30*(2), 280–296. DOI: 10.15446/rcdg.v30n2.89479

Fuentes-Penna, A., Gómez Cárdenas, R., Hernández González, O. D., González Ibarra, J., Cuesta Gómez, E., Morales Prado, W. L., & Vera Jiménez, M. A. (2023). Smart Cities facing the growth of poverty. *International Journal of Combinatorial Optimization Problems and Informatics*, *14*(3), 1–2. DOI: 10.61467/2007.1558.2023.v14i3.371

Fuentes-Penna, A., Ruiz-Vanoye, J. A., Gómez-Cárdenas, R., Salgado Ramírez, J. C., Trejo-Macotela, F. R., Díaz-Parra, O., Poblano Verastegui, A., & Rentería Torres, P. L. (2023). Mexico and PRONACES towards to become a smart city. *International Journal of Combinatorial Optimization Problems and Informatics*, *14*(3), 31–41. DOI: 10.61467/2007.1558.2023.v14i3.387

Fu, M., & Li, Y. (2025). Optimizing Sustainable Community Spatial Layouts and Public Service Facility Accessibility: A GIS and Machine Learning Approach. *Applied and Computational Engineering*, *129*(1), 103–108. DOI: 10.54254/2755-2721/2025.20489

Fu, Z., Novan, K., & Smith, A. (2024). Do time-of-use prices deliver energy savings at the right time? *Journal of Environmental Economics and Management*, *128*, 103054. DOI: 10.1016/j.jeem.2024.103054

Gaffney, C., & Robertson, C. (2018). Smarter than smart: Rio de Janeiro's flawed emergence as a smart city. *Journal of Urban Technology*, *25*(3), 47–64. DOI: 10.1080/10630732.2015.1102423

Gajjar, V., & Sharma, U. (2022). Relevance of Urban Ecosystem Services for Sustaining Urban Ecology in Cities-A Case Study of Ahmedabad City. In Piselli, C., Altan, H., Balaban, O., & Kremer, P. (Eds.), *Innovating Strategies and Solutions for Urban Performance and Regeneration. Advances in Science, Technology & Innovation*. Springer., DOI: 10.1007/978-3-030-98187-7_18

Galindo, C., Ortíz, R., & Villegas, J. (2025). Prototipo de autenticación de doble factor basado en reconocimiento facial para email. Revista Pistas Educativas, (149), 1–15. https://pistaseducativas.celaya.tecnm.mx/index.php/pistas/article/view/3834

Galushi, L., & Malatji, T. (2022). Digital public administration and inclusive governance at the south african local government, in depth analysis of e-government and service delivery in musina local municipality. *Academic Journal of Interdisciplinary Studies*, *11*(6), 116. DOI: 10.36941/ajis-2022-0154

Gao, P., Sun, N., Wang, X., Yang, C., & Zitikis, R. (2023). NLP-based detection of systematic anomalies among the narratives of consumer complaints. arXiv:2308.11138. https://arxiv.org/abs/2308.11138

Gassmann, O., Böhm, J., & Palmié, M. (2019). Smart cities. In *Smart cities* (pp. 25–66). Emerald Publishing Limited., DOI: 10.1108/978-1-78769-613-620191009

Geman, H., Hamida, S. B., & Roncoroni, A. (2023). Distributed energy resources flexibility as volumetric options. *Frontiers of Mathematical Finance*, *2*(3–4), 247–330. DOI: 10.3934/fmf.2023018

Ghosh, A., Saini, A., & Barad, H. (2025). Artificial intelligence in governance: Recent trends,risks, challenges, innovative frameworks and future directions. *AI & Society*. Advance online publication. DOI: 10.1007/s00146-025-02312-y

Gibbons, M., Limoges, C., Nowotny, H., Schwartzman, S., Scott, P., & Trow, M. (1994). *The new production of knowledge: The dynamics of science and research in contemporary societies*. SAGE Publications.

Gil-Garcia, J. R., Pardo, T. A., & Nam, T. (2015). What makes a city smart? Identifying core components and proposing an integrative and comprehensive conceptualization. *Information Polity*, *20*(1), 61–87. DOI: 10.3233/IP-150354

GOB. (2025). Gobierno de Mexico. https://www.gob.mx/index.xhtml

Gobierno de Argentina. (2025). Datos Argentina. Retrieved June 30, 2025 from https://datos.gob.ar/

Gobierno de Chile. (2025). Datos.Gob, el portal de datos abiertos del Estado. Retrieved June 20, 2025 from https://datos.gob.cl/

Gobierno de España, & Pública. (2025). Open data initiative of the Government of Spain. Retrieved June 15, 2025 from https://datos.gob.es/es

Gobierno de México. (2025a). Datos abiertos de Mexico. Retrieved June 28, 2025 from https://historico.datos.gob.mx

Gobierno de México. (2025b). Sistema Integral de Denuncias Ciudadanas (SIDEC). Retrieved May 25, 2025 from https://sidec.buengobierno.gob.mx/

Gobierno del Paraguay. (2025). Portal Unificado de Acceso a la Información Pública. Retrieved May 24, 2025 from https://informacionpublica.paraguay.gov.py/#!/

Gómez Sánchez, M. A. (2020). La protección de datos personales en México. *Revista Mexicana de Ciencias Penales*, *3*(10), 47–58. DOI: 10.57042/rmcp.v3i10.97

Gómez-Rodríguez, J. M. (2022). Inteligencia artificial y neuroderechos. Retos y perspectivas. Cuestiones Constitucionales. *Cuestiones Constitucionales*, *1*(46), 93–119. DOI: 10.22201/iij.24484881e.2022.46.17049

González-Sanmiguel, N. (2025). El metaverso en la configuración de la administración pública. *DICERE: Revista de Derecho y Estudios Internacionales*, *2*(1), 100–117. DOI: 10.33324/dicere.v2i1.896

González-Villareal, F., Lartigue, C., Hidalgo, J., & Hernández, B. (2018). (PDF) Tecnología SWM de México para la gestión eficiente del agua en universidades: El caso de PUMAGUA, UNAM, Ciudad de México. Retrieved July 4, 2025, from https://www.researchgate.net/publication/329775317_Mexico_SWM_technology_for_efficient_water_management_in_universities_the_case_of_PUMAGUA_UNAM_Mexico_City

Gordon, R. (2023). Chatbots e inteligencia artificial: Aportes, innovaciones y aplicación en el desarrollo de sistemas de información empresarial. *Visión Antataura*, *7*(1), 1–15. DOI: 10.48204/j.vian.v7n1.a3930

Government Digital Service. (2015, marzo 29). Government as a platform: The next phase of digital transformation. GDS Blog. https://gds.blog.gov.uk/2015/03/29/government-as-a-platform-the-next-phase-of-digital-transformation/

Government of Bangladesh. (2025, June 29). Bangladesh National Portal. Retrieved June 29, 2025 from https://bangladesh.gov.bd/index.php

Government of India. (2025). Open Government Data (OGD) Platform India. Retrieved June 30, 2025 from https://www.data.gov.in/

Government of Japan. (2025). e-Gov Data Portal. Retrieved June 30, 2025 from https://data.e-gov.go.jp/info/en

Government of Singapore. (2025, April 3). Kaki Chatbot Retrieved July 1, 2025 from https://www.oneservice.gov.sg/kaki

Government of the Republic of Korea. (2018). End-of-Term Self-Assessment Report 2016–2018 [Government Report](Open Government Partnership, Issue. https://www.opengovpartnership.org/documents/south-korea-end-of-term-self-assessment-report-2016-2018/

GovLab. (n.d.). About The GovLab. The Governance Lab. https://www.thegovlab.org/about.html

Gracias, J. S., Parnell, G. S., Specking, E., Pohl, E. A., & Buchanan, R. (2023). Smart cities—A structured literature review. *Smart Cities*, *6*(4), 1719–1743. DOI: 10.3390/smartcities6040080

Graf, O. J., & Bitencourt, M. C. (2024). Digital government and the handling of sensitive data in the execution of public policies: Challenges and possibilities. *Araucaria*, *56*(56), 139–154. DOI: 10.12795/araucaria.2024.i56.06

Grigorescu, S. D., Argatu, F. C., Paturca, S. V., Cepisca, C., Seritan, G. C., Adochiei, F. C., & Enache, B. (2019). Robotic platform with medical applications in the smart city environment. In 2019 11th International Symposium on Advanced Topics in Electrical Engineering (ATEE) (pp. 1-6). IEEE. DOI: DOI: 10.1109/ATEE.2019.8724993

Grimmelikhuijsen, S., Wirtz, B. W., & Welch, E. W. (2022). Algorithmic transparency and trust in government: Legitimacy challenges in automated decision-making. *Public Policy and Management*, *5*(3), 232–246. DOI: 10.1093/ppmg/pwac021

GSA. (2025). The Home of the U.S. Government's Open Data. Retrieved June 22, 2025 from https://data.gov/

Gualdi, F. and Cordella, A. (2022). Techno-legal entanglements as new actors in the policy-making process.. DOI: 10.24251/HICSS.2022.298

Guazzo, G., & Çekani, V. (2023). How nudge can support smart governance in smart cities ecosystems: an a4a framework. Itm Web of Conferences, 51, 02002. DOI: 10.1051/itmconf/20235102002

Guezouli, L., Guezouli, L., & Bentahrour, A. (2024). (PDF) IoT and AI for Real-time Water Monitoring and Leak Detection. *Journal of Renewable Energies*, *27*(2), 243–281. DOI: 10.54966/jreen.v27i2.1210

Hackity. (2025). Hackity App. Eusebio Reyero. Retrieved July 1, 2025 from https://hackityapp.com/

Haghbin, S., Lundmark, S., Alakula, M., & Carlson, O. (2012). Grid-connected integrated battery chargers in vehicle applications: Review and new solution. *IEEE Transactions on Industrial Electronics*, *60*(2), 459–473. DOI: 10.1109/TIE.2012.2187414

Hartanti, F., Abawajy, J., Chowdhury, M., & Shalannanda, W. (2021). Citizens' trust measurement in smart government services. *IEEE Access : Practical Innovations, Open Solutions*, *9*, 150663–150676. DOI: 10.1109/ACCESS.2021.3124206

Häseler, S., & Wulf, A. J. (2024). Promoting real-time electricity tariffs for more demand response from German households: A review of four policy options. *Energy, Sustainability and Society*, *14*, 59. DOI: 10.1186/s13705-024-00490-z

Hayat, P. (2016). Smart cities: A global perspective. *India Quarterly*, *72*(2), 177–191. DOI: 10.1177/0974928416637930

Helbing, D., Frey, B. S., Gigerenzer, G., Hafen, E., Hagner, M., Hofstetter, Y., & Zwitter, A. (2021). Will democracy survive big data and artificial intelligence? *Scientific American*, *317*(2), 25–33.

He, Y., Liu, C., Liu, C.-C., & Wang, Y. (2023). Smart Monitoring and Fault Diagnosis in Smart Grids: A Review. *Energy Reports*, *9*, 584–596. DOI: 10.1016/j.egyr.2022.11.071

He, Y., Yang, F., & Hua, Q. (2022). A survey on Zero Trust architecture: Challenges and future research directions. *Wireless Communications and Mobile Computing*, *6476274*(1), 6476274. Advance online publication. DOI: 10.1155/2022/6476274

Hierro, L. (2013, July 4). Congreso 2.0. EL Pais. Retrieved July 4, 2025 from https://elpais.com/politica/2013/07/04/actualidad/1372930254_072779.html

Hochstetter-Diez, J., Negrier-Seguel, M., Diéguez-Rebolledo, M., Vásquez-Morales, F., & Sancho-Chavarría, L. (2023). Governance Democratic and Big Data: A Systematic Mapping Review. *Sustainability*, *15*(16), 12630.

Hoheisel, A., Betterman, B., Dunham, I., O'Leary, H., & Mahmoud, M. (2022).. . *Green Computing from a Holistic Perspective.*, *1299–1302*, 1299–1302. Advance online publication. DOI: 10.1109/CSCI58124.2022.00233

Hope, O., Jiang, S., & Vyas, D. (2021). Government transparency and firm-level operational efficiency. *Journal of Business Finance & Accounting*, *49*(5-6), 752–777. DOI: 10.1111/jbfa.12563

Hutahaean, M., Eunike, I., & Silalahi, A. (2023). Do social media, good governance, and public trust increase citizens' e-government participation? dual approach of pls-sem and fsqca. *Human Behavior and Emerging Technologies*, *2023*, 1–19. DOI: 10.1155/2023/9988602

Ibarra Vazquez, A., Lara Ramos, B. G., & Soto Karass, J. G. (2025). Transparencia en México mediante inteligencia artificial: La ruta digital emergente hacia una nueva rendición de cuentas. *Encrucijada Revista Electrónica del Centro de Estudios en Administración Pública*, (50), 98–122. DOI: 10.22201/fcpys.20071949e.2025.50.90895

Ibrahimy, M. M., Norta, A., & Normak, P. (2024). Blockchain-based governance models supporting corruption-transparency: A systematic literature review. Blockchain: Research and Applications, 5(2), 100186. https://doi.org/https://doi.org/10.1016/j.bcra.2023.100186

IDPAC. (2025). El Sistema de Votación Electrónica Ciudadana. Retrieved July2, 2025 from https://votec.participacionbogota.gov.co/votec-ciudadano

IECM. (2025). Plataforma Digital de Participación Ciudadana del Instituto Electoral de la Ciudad de México. Retrieved June 1, 2025 from https://plataformaciudadana.iecm.mx/#/inicio

IEEE Public Safety Technology. (2025). AI and ethical considerations in public safety technologies. IEEE. https://publicsafety.ieee.org/

Igbokwe-Ibeto, C., & Osakede, K. (2017). Public policy and citizens participation in ngor okpala local government area of imo state, nigeria 2011 - 2015. *Management Studies and Economic Systems*, *3*(3), 149–158. DOI: 10.12816/0040228

İkizer, İ. (2022). Do Smart City Solutions Contribute to the Achievement of the Sustainable Development Goals?: Case of Istanbul. In Pego, A. C. (Ed.), *Smart Cities, Citizen Welfare, and the Implementation of Sustainable Development Goals* (pp. 22–44). IGI Global Scientific Publishing., DOI: 10.4018/978-1-7998-7785-1.ch002

Ilhami, R., Marlovia, E., & Achmad, W. (2022). Smart government policy implementation for smart city concept realization. *International Journal of Health Sciences*, *6*(S5), 8379–8389. DOI: 10.53730/ijhs.v6nS5.11753

INAFED. (2024, April 12). Datos abiertos. Retrieved May 30, 2025 from https://www.gob.mx/inafed/documentos/datos-abiertos-347532#:~:text=Los%20Datos%20Abiertos%20son%20los,redistribuidos%20por%20cualquier%20persona%20interesada

INAI. (2025). Plataforma Nacional de Transpaencia. Retrieved June 29, 2025 from https://www.plataformadetransparencia.org.mx

INE. (2024). Voto de mexicanos residentes en el extranjero. Retrieved June 2, 2025 from https://votoextranjero.mx/web/vmre/modalidades-de-voto

INEGI. (2023). Censo Nacional de Transparencia, Acceso a la Información Pública y Protección de Datos Personales. Retrieved July 4, 2025 from https://www.inegi.org.mx/programas/cntaippdpf/2023/

INEGI. (2025). Datos abiertos. Retrieved June 25, 2025 from https://www.inegi.org.mx/datosabiertos/

Instituto Nacional de Estándares y Tecnología (NIST). (2012). *Computer Security Incident Handling Guide* (SP 800-61 Revision 2). U.S. Department of Commerce. https://nvlpubs.nist.gov/nistpubs/SpecialPublications/NIST.SP.800-61r2.pdf

Institutodeinnovaciondigital.ar. (2025). Informe sobre la protección de los neuroderechos. Instituto de Innovación Digital. https://www.institutodeinnovaciondigital.ar/neuroderechos

Inter-American Development Bank (IDB). (2023). Smart Infrastructure for Latin America: Policy Priorities and Lessons Learned. https://www.iadb.org

Inter-American Development Bank. (2023). *The economics of electricity losses in Latin America and the Caribbean*. IDB Publications.

International Energy Agency (IEA). (2023). Grid integration of variable renewable energies: a key priority for system stability. https://www.iea.org

International Energy Agency (IEA). (2023). Latin America Energy Outlook 2023. https://www.iea.org/reports/latin-america-energy-outlook-2023

International Energy Agency (IEA). (2023). Monitoring the reliability of the energy system. https://www.iea.org/reports/tracking-power-system-reliability

International Renewable Energy Agency (IRENA). (2023). Smart grid policy frameworks for the energy transition. https://www.irena.org

Irwin, V., Wang, K., Cui, J., & Thompson, A. (2024, July). Report on Indicators of School Crime and Safety: 2023 (NCES 2024-145/NCJ 309126). National Center for Education Statistics, U.S. Department of Education, and Bureau of Justice Statistics, Office of Justice Programs. Retrieved 7 August 2025, from https://nces.ed.gov/pubs2024/2024145.pdf

Ishengoma, F., & Shao, D. (2025). A framework for aligning e-government initiatives with the sustainable development goals. Journal of Innovative Digital Transformation. DOI: 10.1108/jidt-09-2024-0025

ITU. (2021). ITU smart sustainable cities brochure. International Telecommunication Union. Retrieved from https://www.itu.int/en/ITU-T/ssc/united/Documents/Reports-on-SSC/ITU_smart_sustainable_cities_brochure.pdf?csf=1&e=yIueWP

Janssen, M., Charalabidis, Y., & Zuiderwijk, A. (2017). Benefits, adoption barriers and myths of open data and open government. *Information Systems Management, 29*(4), 258–268. DOI: 10.1080/10580530.2012.716740

Janssen, M., & van der Voort, H. (2020). Agile and adaptive governance in crisis response: Lessons from the COVID-19 pandemic. *International Journal of Information Management, 55*, 102180. DOI: 10.1016/j.ijinfomgt.2020.102180 PMID: 32836637

Jasso López, L. C. (2023). Vigilar al vigilante: Transparencia y rendición de cuentas sobre las tecnologías de vigilancia pública en México. *Revista Estudios en Derecho a la Información*, (15), 31–53. DOI: 10.22201/iij.25940082e.2023.15.17470

Jin, M., & Aletras, N. (2020). Complaint Identification in Social Media with Transformer Networks. arXiv:2010.10910. https://arxiv.org/abs/2010.10910 DOI: 10.18653/v1/2020.coling-main.157

Johnson, P., Acedo, A., & Robinson, P. (2020). Canadian smart cities: Are we wiring new citizen-local government interactions? *The Canadian Geographer. Geographe Canadien, 64*(3), 402–415. DOI: 10.1111/cag.12623

JRC (Joint Research Centre). (2022). *Smart Grid Interoperability Laboratory—Annual Report 2022*. Publications Office of the European Union., DOI: 10.2760/066580

Kabbara, N., Zografopoulos, I., & Antoniou, A. (2022). Towards software-defined protection, automation, and control in power systems: A survey. *Energies, 15*(24), 9362. DOI: 10.3390/en15249362

Kabeyi, M. J. B. (2023). Smart grid technologies and application in the sustainable power sector. *Energy and Environment Research, 10*(2), 123–139. DOI: 10.1080/14786451.2023.2222298

Kaiser, Z. R. M. A. (2024). Smart governance for smart cities and nations. *Journal of Economy and Technology, 2*, 216–234. DOI: 10.1016/j.ject.2024.07.003

Khalid, M. (2024). Smart grids and renewable energy systems: Perspectives. *Energy Reports*. Advance online publication. DOI: 10.1016/j.egyr.2024.05.105

Khan, F. & Ahmed, Z. (2024). Smart grid integration with Industry 5.0: Applications, challenges. Sustainable energy systems. .DOI: 10.1016/j.sesj.2024.02.031

Khattak, H. A., Farman, H., Jan, B., & Din, I. U. (2019). Toward integrating vehicular clouds with IoT for smart city services. *IEEE Network, 33*(2), 65–71. DOI: 10.1109/MNET.2019.1800236

Kirmani, S., Khurshid, F., & Karim, S. (2022). A survey on IoT-enabled smart grids: Technologies, architectures, applications, and challenges. *Sustainability (Basel), 15*(1), 717. DOI: 10.3390/su15010717

Kitchin, R. (2019). *The data revolution: Big data, open data, data infrastructures & their consequences*. Sage Publications Ltd., DOI: 10.4135/9781473909472

Kitchin, R. (2021). *Data lives: How data are made and shape our world*. Bristol University Press.

Kitchin, R. (2021). *Data Lives: How Data Are Made and Shape Our World*. Bristol University Press., DOI: 10.1080/02513625.2024.2510128

Klinger, E., Wiesmaier, A., & Heinemann, A. (2023). *A Review of existing GDPR Solutions for Citizens and SMEs*. https://doi.org/https://doi.org/10.48550/arXiv.2302.03581

Kraft, J., & Luh, P. Y.-S. (2024). Improving energy access in rural areas: Smart microgrid in Tanzania. *Energy for Sustainable Development*. Advance online publication. DOI: 10.1016/j.esd.2024.100452

Krawczyk, K., & Sweet-Cushman, J. (2016). Understanding political participation in west africa: The relationship between good governance and local citizen engagement. *International Review of Administrative Sciences, 83*(1, suppl), 136–155. DOI: 10.1177/0020852315619024

Krizanovic, V., Pejković, A., Pracny, P. (2024). Smart Street Lighting for Enhancing Energy Efficiency in Urban Environments. 1–6. DOI: 10.23919/SoftCOM62040.2024.10721821

Kropf, M., Pope, J., Shepherd, M., & Mohr, Z. (2020). Making every vote count: The important role of managerial capacity in achieving better election administration outcomes. *Public Administration Review, 80*(5), 733–742. DOI: 10.1111/puar.13216

Lamrini, M., Ben Mahria, B., Chkouri, M. Y., & Touhafi, A. (2024). Towards Reliability in Smart Water Sensing Technology: Evaluating Classical Machine Learning Models for Outlier Detection. *Sensors (Basel), 24*(13), 4084. DOI: 10.3390/s24134084 PMID: 39000863

Larsen, A. G., & Følstad, A. (2024). The impact of chatbots on public service provision: A qualitative interview study with citizens and public service providers. *Government Information Quarterly, 41*(2), 101927. https://doi.org/https://doi.org/10.1016/j.giq.2024.101927

LATINNO. (2017a). MexicoLeaks. Berlin: WZB. Retrieved July 5,2025 from https://latinno.wzb.eu/en/case/13145/

LATINNO. (2017b). Yoveoveo. Berlin: WZB. Retrieved July 5,2025 from https://latinno.net/es/case/8091/

Latour, B. (1987). *Science in action: How to follow scientists and engineers through society*. Harvard University Press.

Law, J. (1992). Notes on the theory of the actor-network: Ordering, strategy and heterogeneity. *Systems Practice*, *5*(4), 379–393. DOI: 10.1007/BF01059830

Leal Filho, W., Dibbern, T., Pimenta Dinis, M. A., Coggo Cristofoletti, E., Mbah, M. F., Mishra, A., & Aina, Y. A. (2024). The added value of partnerships in implementing the UN sustainable development goals. *Journal of Cleaner Production*, *438*, 140794. DOI: 10.1016/j.jclepro.2024.140794

Lee, T. L. C. (2023). Redesigning streets for micromobility: improving mobility and access to transportation for less able users. DOI: 10.32920/24085086.v1

Lee, S., & Kim, B. (2023). Machine Learning Model for Leak Detection Using Water Pipeline Vibration Sensor. *Sensors (Basel)*, *23*(21), 8935. DOI: 10.3390/s23218935 PMID: 37960635

Lee, W. H., & Chiu, C. Y. (2020). Design and implementation of a smart traffic signal control system for smart city applications. *Sensors (Basel)*, *20*(2), 508. DOI: 10.3390/s20020508 PMID: 31963229

Lei, Z., Xie, Y., & Ji, X. (2025). Design and implementation of smart iot water Meter based on LoRa. EITCE '24: En Proceedings of the 2024 8th International Conference on Electronic Information Technology and Computer Engineering (pp. 1447-1451). Association for Computing Machinery. DOI: 10.1145/3711129.3711371

Leiva Vilaplana, J. A., Kabbara, N., & Coste, T. (2024). Virtualized Protection, Automation, and Control in Electrical Substations: An Open-Source Dynamic Cost-Benefit Assessment Model. *IEEE Access : Practical Innovations, Open Solutions*, *12*, 1–1. DOI: 10.1109/ACCESS.2024.3435972

León Lazo, R. I., & Macancela Sumba, J. G. (2024). Construcción de un medidor de agua inteligente mediante Arduino para reducir las pérdidas en la distribución de agua. https://dspace.ucacue.edu.ec/handle/ucacue/16769

LeoTronics Robotics. (2022). Patrol robot M01: Features and capabilities. LeoTronics Robotics. https://www.leotronics.eu/

Letki, N., & Steen, T. (2021). Social-psychological context moderates incentives to co-produce: Evidence from a large-scale survey experiment on park upkeep in an urban setting. *Public Administration Review*, *81*(5), 935–950. DOI: 10.1111/puar.13340 PMID: 34690373

LGPDPPSO. https://www.diputados.gob.mx/LeyesBiblio/pdf/LGPDPPSO.pdf (2025). https://www.diputados.gob.mx/LeyesBiblio/pdf/LGPDPPSO.pdf

Libert-Amico, A., Trench, T., Rodríguez, A., & Martínez-Morales, M. (2018). Experiencias de gobernanza multinivel en méxico: Innovación para la reducción de emisiones de carbono de los ecosistemas terrestres. *Madera y Bosques*, *24*. Advance online publication. DOI: 10.21829/myb.2018.2401909

Lim, K. Y. H., Zheng, P., Zheng, P., & Chen, C.-H. (2020). A state-of-the-art survey of Digital Twin: Techniques, engineering product lifecycle management and business innovation perspectives. *Journal of Intelligent Manufacturing*, *31*(6), 1313–1337. DOI: 10.1007/s10845-019-01512-w

Liopa-Tsakalidi, A., Thomopoulos, V., Barouchas, P., Boursianis, A. D., & Goudos, S. K. (2024). A LoRaWAN-based IoT platform for smart irrigation in olive groves. *Smart Agricultural Technology*, *9*, 100673. DOI: 10.1016/j.atech.2024.100673

Liu, C.-C., McArthur, S. J., & Lee, S.-J. (2023). *Smart Grid Handbook* (Vol. 1–3). Wiley.

Liu, S., & Yuan, Q. (2015). The evolution of information and communication technology in public administration. *Public Administration and Development*, *35*(2), 140–151. DOI: 10.1002/pad.1717

Li, Y., & Cao, J.. (2023). Operational risk awareness planning for rural multi-energy microgrids. *Frontiers in Energy Research*, *11*, 112164. DOI: 10.3389/fenrg.2023.112164

Llamas-Valenzuela, A. C., de la Rosa, J. I., Moreno-Chávez, G., Gonzales-Ramírez, E., Villa, J., & Celaya-Padilla, J. M. (2025). Predicting urban expansion in Zacatecas-Guadalupe cities: A support vector machine approach enhanced by SHAP values. *International Journal of Combinatorial Optimization Problems and Informatics*, *16*(1), 75–89. DOI: 10.61467/2007.1558.2025.v16i1.500

Löfgren, K., & Webster, C. W. R. (2020). The value of Big Data in government: The case of 'smart cities'. *Big Data & Society*, *7*(1), 1–14. DOI: 10.1177/2053951720912775

López-Aguado, M., Gutiérrez-Provecho, L., Quintanal-Díaz, J., & García-Llamas, J. L. (2022). *Social exclusion and the digital divide.* Journal of e-Learning and Knowledge Society, 18(3), 74–82. https://doi.org/DOI: 10.20368/1971-8829/1135660

Losada-Puente, L., Blanco, J. A., Dumitru, A., Sebos, I., Tsakanikas, A., Liosi, I., & Rodríguez, E. (2023). Cross-case analysis of the energy communities in Spain, Italy, and Greece: Progress, barriers, and the road ahead. *Sustainability*, *15*(18), 14016. DOI: 10.3390/su151814016

Losa, I., & Cossent, R. (2024). Scalability and replicability analysis in smart grid demonstration projects: Lessons learned and future needs. *Energies*, *17*(21), 5312. DOI: 10.3390/en17215312

Lostal Martínez, F. R. (2024). *The Impact of Artificial Intelligence on Mexico's Logistics Sector: Challenges and Opportunities* (pp. 95–114). https://doi.org/DOI: 10.1007/978-3-031-71993-6_7

Lum, K., & Isaac, W. (2016). To predict and serve? *Significance*, *13*(5), 14–19. DOI: 10.1111/j.1740-9713.2016.00960.x

Luong, H. T., ... (2023). Innovating the Smart Grid: A SmartSacramento Utility Case Study from SMUD. EBA-Net Reports https://www.smud.org/en/Corporate/About-Us/News-and-Media

Mabillard, V., & Pasquier, M. (2015). Transparency and trust in government: A two-way relationship. *Yearbook of Swiss Administrative Sciences*, *6*(1), 23. DOI: 10.5334/ssas.78

Maciél, C., Roque, L., & García, A. (2010). Interaction and communication resources in collaborative e-democratic environments: The democratic citizenship community. *Information Polity*, *15*(1,2), 73–88. DOI: 10.3233/IP-2010-0197

Macintosh, A., & Whyte, A. (2008). Towards an evaluation framework for eParticipation. *Transforming Government: People. Transforming Government*, *2*(1), 16–30. DOI: 10.1108/17506160810862928

Maestre-Góngora, G., & Nieto, W. (2015). Factores clave en la gestión de tecnología de información para sistemas de gobierno inteligente. *Journal of Technology Management & Innovation*, *10*(4), 109–117. DOI: 10.4067/S0718-27242015000400012

Mahmood, Z. Mahmood, & Wheeler. (2018). Smart Cities. Springer.

Mair, P. (2013). *Ruling the void: The hollowing of Western democracy*. Verso Books.

Makanadar, A., & Shahane, S. (2023). Urban Mobility: Leveraging AI, Machine Learning, and Data Analytics for Smart Transportation Planning- A case study on New York City. 1–6. DOI: 10.1109/ICCCNT56998.2023.10307632

Make.org. (2025). Make.org. Retrieved June 4, 2025 from https://make.org/US

Maldonado-Meléndez, M. A. (2023). La regulación (necesaria) de la actuación administrativa automatizada: el uso de la robótica mediante chatbots y asistentes virtuales en la administración pública peruana. Revista Iberoamericana de Gobierno, 23(Junio· 2023).

Mansour, R. F., Mafarja, M., Bruzzone, A., & Al-Azab, M. (2023). Digital twins and IoT-assisted smart electric power systems: A review. *IET Generation, Transmission & Distribution, 17*(23), 5581–5597. DOI: 10.1049/gtd2.12940

MAPLE. (2025). Massachusetts Platform for Legislative Engagement (MAPLE). Retrieved June 4, 2025 from https://www.mapletestimony.org/

March, H., & Ribera-Fumaz, R. (2016). Smart contradictions: The politics of making Barcelona a Self-sufficient city. *European Urban and Regional Studies, 23*(4), 816–830. DOI: 10.1177/0969776414554488

Márquez, M., Velasco, M., Ochoa, R., & Delfin, F. (2024). Inteligencia artificial en el sector público en México: Actos de fiscalización. *Newman Business Review, 10*, 124–147. DOI: 10.22451/3002.nbr2024.vol10.2.10103

Matasick, C., Alfonsi, C., & Bellantoni, A. (2020). Governance responses to disinformation: How open government principles can inform policy options. OECD Working Papers on Public Governance(39), 46. https://doi.org/https://doi.org/10.1787/d6237c85-en

Mateo, J. J. (2025, January 1). La transparencia se atasca en el Madrid de Ayuso: reclamaciones sin resolver desde 2022 y 335 casos en un limbo. elpais.com. Retrieved July 4, 2025 from https://elpais.com/espana/madrid/2025-01-02/la-transparencia-se-atasca-en-el-madrid-de-ayuso-reclamaciones-sin-resolver-desde-2022-y-335-casos-en-un-limbo.html?utm_source=chatgpt.com

Mbuy, H., O'Neil, M., & Theodosiou, M. (2022). Algorithmic impact assessment for an ethical use of AI in SMEs. In *Proceedings of the 35th British HCI and Doctoral Consortium 2022* (pp. 1–8). https://doi.org/DOI: 10.14236/ewic/HCI2022.34

McCool, S., Freimund, W., & Breen, C. (2019). Beneficios del pensamiento complejo.. https://doi.org/DOI: 10.22459/GGAP.2019.10

Mchirgui, M., Frikha, M., Dhaou, I., & Jemaa, M. B. (2024). Digital twin for smart grid: A comprehensive review. *Applied Sciences (Basel, Switzerland), 14*(23), 10933. DOI: 10.3390/app142310933

Mehrabi, N., Morstatter, F., Saxena, N., Lerman, K., & Galstyan, A. (2021). A survey on bias and fairness in machine learning. *ACM Computing Surveys, 54*(6), 1–35. DOI: 10.1145/3457607

Mehta, K. S., Raj, K. N., & Brahmbhatt, K. N. (2024). Machine learning solutions for adaptive traffic signal control: A review of image-based approaches. *World Journal of Advanced Engineering Technology and Sciences, 13*(1), 476–481. DOI: 10.30574/wjaets.2024.13.1.0437

Meijer, A. (2021). *The algorithmic state: Towards a new digital democracy*. Oxford University Press.

Meijer, A., & Bolívar, M. (2015). Governing the smart city: A review of the literature on smart urban governance. *International Review of Administrative Sciences, 82*(2), 392–408. DOI: 10.1177/0020852314564308

Meza-Jiménez, A., Vázquez, M., Verschoor, G., Lugo, E., & García-Barrios, L. (2021). Hacia una gobernanza adaptativa centrada en los grupos domésticos rurales que habitan las áreas naturales protegidas. el caso de la sepultura, chiapas, méxico. Sociedad Y Ambiente, (24), 1-30. https://doi.org/DOI: 10.31840/sya.vi24.2340

Minguijon, J., & Serrano-Martinez, C. (2022). La inteligencia artificial en los servicios sociales: Estado de la cuestión y posibles desarrollos futuros. *Cuadernos de Trabajo Social, 35*(2), 319–329. DOI: 10.5209/cuts.78747

Ministerio de Modernización. (2024). Derecho de Acceso a la Información Pública. Boletín Nacional. Retrieved Sep 5, 2025 from https://www.argentina.gob.ar/normativa/nacional/decreto-780-2024-403572

Ministerio para la Transformación Digital. (2025). Portal de la Transparencia de la Administración del Estado. Retrieved June 28, 2025 from https://transparencia.gob.es/

Ministry of Economic Affairs and Employment of Finland. (2021). Finland's artificial intelligence program. https://tem.fi/en/artificial-intelligence

Min, Q., Lu, Y., Liu, Z., Su, C., & Wang, B. (2021). Machine learning-based digital twin framework for smart water management. *Water Research, 197*, 117060. DOI: 10.1016/j.watres.2021.117060

Mishra, R., & Varshney, D. (2024). Consumer Protection Frameworks by Enhancing Market Fairness, Accountability and Transparency (FAT) for Ethical Consumer Decision-Making: Integrating Circular Economy Principles and Digital Transformation in Global Consumer Markets. *Asian Journal of Education and Social Studies, 50*(7), 640–652. DOI: 10.9734/ajess/2024/v50i71494

Mittelstadt, B., Floridi, L., & Taddeo, M. (2023). A systematic review of artificial intelligence impact assessments. *Artificial Intelligence Review, 42*(5), 1021–1056. DOI: 10.1007/s10462-023-10420-8

Mohd Yussof, N. A., & Ho, H. W. (2022). Review of Water Leak Detection Methods in Smart Building Applications. *Buildings (Basel, Switzerland), 12*(10), 1535. DOI: 10.3390/buildings12101535

Mohler, G., Short, M. B., Malinowski, S., Johnson, M. E., Tita, G. E., Bertozzi, A. L., & Brantingham, P. J. (2015). Randomized Controlled Field Trials of Predictive Policing. *Journal of the American Statistical Association, 110*(512), 1399–1411. DOI: 10.1080/01621459.2015.1077710

Molobela, T. and Uwizeyimana, D. (2023). E-governance as a new public administration paradigm: a rhetoric or reality?. International Journal of Research in Business and Social Science (2147-4478), 12(8), 348-356. DOI: 10.20525/ijrbs.v12i8.2931

Monzon, A. (2015). *Smart cities concept and challenges: Bases for the assessment of smart city projects.* IEEE., DOI: 10.1007/978-3-319-27753-0_2

Mora, L., Deakin, M., Aina, Y. A., & Appio, F. P. (2019). Smart City Development: ICT Innovation for Urban Sustainability. In Leal Filho, W., Azul, A., Brandli, L., Özuyar, P., & Wall, T. (Eds.), *Sustainable Cities and Communities. Encyclopedia of the UN Sustainable Development Goals.* Springer., DOI: 10.1007/978-3-319-71061-7_27-2

Morales, M. (2021). Firmas digitales en México: conceptos, oportunidades y desafíos. En Jornadas de Divulgación – TopTamaulipas 2021 (pp. 9–18). https://ccc.inaoep.mx/~mmorales/divulg/JD05.pdf

Morley, J., Floridi, L., Kinsey, L., & Elhalal, A. (2020). From What to How: An Initial Review of Publicly Available AI Ethics Tools, Methods and Research to Translate Principles into Practices. *Science and Engineering Ethics, 26*(3), 2141–2168. DOI: 10.1007/s11948-019-00165-5 PMID: 31828533

Moya-Martínez, J. (2024). Metaverso: Amenazas internacionales y cooperación en la digitalización. Barataria. *Revista Castellano-Manchega de Ciencias Sociales,* (35), 1–20. DOI: 10.20932/barataria.v0i35.687

Muttaqee, M., Stelmach, G., Zanocco, C., Flora, J., Rajagopal, R., & Boudet, H. S. (2024). Time-of-use pricing and likelihood of shifting energy activities, strategies, and timing. *Energy Policy, 187*, 114019. DOI: 10.1016/j.enpol.2024.114019

MYSOCIETY. (2024). FixMyStreet. In (Version 3.0.2) https://play.google.com/store/apps/details?id=org.mysociety.FixMyStreet

Nam, T., & Pardo, T. A. (2011). Conceptualizing smart city with dimensions of technology, people, and institutions. In *Proceedings of the 12th Annual International Digital Government Research Conference* (pp. 282–291). ACM. DOI: 10.1145/2037556.2037602

Natalya, V. B., & Ella, M. L. (2020). Conceptualization of Smart Government: A scientometric approach. *Upravlenets, 11*(3), 33–45. DOI: 10.29141/2218-5003-2020-11-3-3

National Urban Security Technology Laboratory & DAGER Technology, LLC. (2024, January). Augmented reality (AR) training systems for first responders: Market survey report (SAVER-T-MSR-45) [PDF]. Science and Technology Directorate, U.S. Department of Homeland Security. Retrieved from https://www.dhs.gov/sites/default/files/2024-02/24_02_16_st_artrainingsystemsmsr_0.pdf

Navaratna, A. R., & Deepak Saxena. (2025). From policy to practice in digital governance: A three-level analysis of citizen-centric applications. *JeDEM - EJournal of EDemocracy and Open Government, 17*(1), 33–64. https://doi.org/DOI: 10.29379/jedem.v17i1.906

Nayak, S. K. (2019). *Electric vehicle charging topologies, control schemes for smart city application. In 2019 IEEE transportation electrification conference (ITEC-India)*. IEEE.

Negri-Ribalta, C., Lombard-Platet, M., & Salinesi, C. (2024). Understanding the GDPR from a requirements engineering perspective—A systematic mapping study on regulatory data protection requirements. *Requirements Engineering, 29*(4), 523–549. DOI: 10.1007/s00766-024-00423-4

New, J., Castro, D., & Beckwith, M. (2017). *How national governments can help smart cities succeed.* Center for Data Innovation.

Ngatikoh, S., Kumorotomo, W., & Retnandari, N. (2020). Transparency in government: a review on the failures of corruption prevention in indonesia.. https://doi.org/DOI: 10.2991/aebmr.k.200301.010

Nieuwenhuijsen, M., de Nazelle, A., Cirach Pradas, M., Daher, C., Dzhambov, A. M., Echave, C., Gössling, S., Iungman, T., Khreis, H., Kirby, N., Khomenko, S., Leth, U., Lorenz, F., Matkovic, V., Müller, J., Palència, L., Pereira Barboza, E., Pérez, K., Tatah, L., & Mueller, N. (2024). The Superblock model: A review of an innovative urban model for sustainability, liveability, health and well-being. *Environmental Research, 251*(Part 1), 118550. DOI: 10.1016/j.envres.2024.118550 PMID: 38432569

NIST. (2023). Post-quantum cryptography standardization. National Institute of Standards and Technology. https://csrc.nist.gov/projects/post-quantum-cryptography

Normas, I. S. O. (2007). Esquema Nacional de Seguridad. *Normas ISO*. https://www.normas-iso.com/esquema-nacional-de-seguridad/

North America, E. D. F. (2022). *Evaluation framework for smart grid deployment plans*. EDF.

Novelli, C., Taddeo, M., & Floridi, L. (2024). Accountability in artificial intelligence: What it is and how it works. *AI & Society*, *39*(4), 1871–1882. DOI: 10.1007/s00146-023-01635-y

Nurbojatmiko, N., Karimiyah, M. S. K., Asnadi, N. M., & Anisyah, R. (2025). ISO 27001 As Information Security Solution In Society 5.0 Era: Systematic Literature Review. *Sinkron*, *9*(1), 484–492. DOI: 10.33395/sinkron.v9i1.14448

Nuutinen, M., Kaasinen, E., Hyvärinen, J., Mölsä, A., & Siltanen, S. (2022). Making a Building Smart with a Co-Created and Continuously Evolving Enjoyable Service Entity—Insights from a Collaborative Study. *Smart Cities*, *5*(1), 1–21. DOI: 10.3390/smartcities5010001

NYC Office of Data Analytics. (2022). NYC Open Data Portal. https://opendata.cityofnewyork.us

Ocaña, Y., Valenzuela-Fernández, L., Vera, M., & Lozano, R. (2021). Inteligencia artificial (IA) aplicada a la gestión pública. *Revista Venezolana de Gerencia*, *26*(94), 25–40. DOI: 10.52080/rvgv26n94.14

OECD. (2020), Smart Cities and Inclusive Growth: Building on the outcomes of the 1st OECD Roundtable fon Smart Cities and Inclusive Growth, OECD Regional Development Papers, No. 91, OECD Publishing, Paris, DOI: 10.1787/267a6231-en

OECD. (2020). *Digital government index: 2019 results*. OECD Publishing., DOI: 10.1787/4de9f5bb-

OECD. (2020). Smart Cities and Inclusive Growth: Building on the outcomes of the OECD Roundtable. https://www.oecd.org/cfe/cities/smart-cities.htm

OECD. (2020a). *The OECD Digital Government Policy Framework: Six dimensions of a Digital Government*. OECD Publishing. DOI: 10.1787/f64fed2a-

OECD. (2020b). Policy Framework on Sound Public Governance: Baseline Features of Governments that Work Well. OECD Publishing. https://www.oecd.org/en/publications/policy-framework-on-sound-public-governance_c03e01b3-en.html

OECD. (2022). Harnessing the power of AI and emerging technologies: Background paper for the CDEP Ministerial meeting. In *OECD Digital Economy Papers, No. 340*. OECD Publishing., DOI: 10.1787/f94df8ec-

OECD. (2023). *OECD digital government policy framework: Towards a digitally enabled state.* OECD Publishing.

OECD. (2025). *Closing Broadband Connectivity Divides for All: From Evidence to Practice*. OECD Publishing., DOI: 10.1787/d5ea99b2-

OECD. (2025). *Recommendation of the Council on Digital Government Strategies.* OECD.

OECD. (2025). *Regulatory sandbox toolkit: A comprehensive guide for regulators to establish and manage regulatory sandboxes effectively.* OECD Publishing., DOI: 10.1787/de36fa62-

O'Flaherty, K. (2018). Taiwan's revolutionary hackers are forking the government. Wired, (July 2, 2025).

Ogbodo, E. U., Abu-Mahfouz, A. M., & Kurien, A. M. (2022). A Survey on 5G and LPWAN-IoT for Improved Smart Cities and Remote Area Applications: From the Aspect of Architecture and Security. *Sensors (Basel)*, *22*(16), 6313. DOI: 10.3390/s22166313 PMID: 36016078

OGP. (2025). *Foundations for Open Government* OGP National Handbook.

Ogunkan, D. V., & Ogunkan, S. K. (2025). Exploring big data applications in sustainable urban infrastructure: A review. *Urban Governance*, *5*(1), 54–68. DOI: 10.1016/j.ugj.2025.02.003

OHCHR. (2025). OHCHR and good governance. Retrieved May 20, 2025 from https://www.ohchr.org/en/good-governance

OLACEFS & EFS. (2024, July). Chatbot DCI: Chatbot de denuncia ciudadana idónea. Retrieved July 1, 2025 from https://olacefs.com/giz/iniciativa/chatbot-de-denuncia-ciudadana-idonea/

Oliha, J. S., Biu, P. W., & Chimezie, O. (2024). Securing the smart city: A review of cybersecurity challenges and strategies. Open Access Research Journal of Multidisciplinary Studies, 7(1), 094–101. DOI: 10.53022/oarjms.2024.7.1.0013

Onufreiciuc, R. (2022). Principle of Transparency as reflected in OGP National Action Plans in Romania. Logos Universality Mentality Education Novelty. *Law*, *10*, 60–71. DOI: 10.18662/lumenlaw/10.1/71

Organisation for Economic Co-operation and Development. (2020). *Digital government in Latin America: Transforming public services and institutions*. OECD Publishing., DOI: 10.1787/6e1b64a3-

Organisation for Economic Co-operation and Development. (2021). The impact of AI on the labour market. OECD. https://www.oecd.org/employment/impact-of-ai-on-jobs.htm

ORNL (Oak Ridge National Laboratory). (2013). Chattanooga Electric Power Board Smart Grid Analysis. Technical report. .DOI: 10.2172/1376469

Ostrom, E. (1990). *Governing the commons: The evolution of institutions for collective action*. Cambridge University Press. DOI: 10.1017/CBO9780511807763

Ostrom, E. (2010). Beyond markets and states: Polycentric governance of complex economic systems. *The American Economic Review*, *100*(3), 641–672. DOI: 10.1257/aer.100.3.641

Otamendi, U., Maiza, M., Olaizola, I. G., Sierra, B., Flores, M., & Quartulli, M. (2024). Integrated Water Resource Management in the Segura Hydrographic Basin: An Artificial Intelligence Approach. *Journal of Environmental Management*, *370*, 122526. DOI: 10.1016/j.jenvman.2024.122526 PMID: 39357444

Othengrafen, F., Sievers, L., & Reinecke, E. (2023). Using augmented reality in urban planning processes: Sustainable urban transitions through innovative participation. *Gaia (Heidelberg)*, *32*(1), 54–63. DOI: 10.14512/gaia.32.S1.9

Pan, T. H., Aung, M. N., & Nam, E. W., & al., e. (2024). Digital inclusion among community older adults in the Republic of Korea: Measuring digital skills and health consequences. *European Journal of Investigation in Health, Psychology and Education*, *14*(8), 2314–2336. DOI: 10.3390/ejihpe14080154

Pantanowitz, L., Hanna, M., Pantanowitz, J., Lennerz, J., Henricks, W. H., Shen, P., Quinn, B., Bennet, S., & Rashidi, H. H. (2024). Regulatory Aspects of Artificial Intelligence and Machine Learning. *Modern Pathology*, *37*(12), 100609. DOI: 10.1016/j.modpat.2024.100609 PMID: 39260776

Parliament, E. (2016, April 27). Reglamento General de Protección de Datos (RGPD – UE 2016/679). Retrieved April 4, 2025 from https://eur-lex.europa.eu/eli/reg/2016/679/oj

Parliament, E. (2022, October 19). Reglamento de Servicios Digitales. European Parliament. Retrieved April 12, 2025 from https://eur-lex.europa.eu/eli/reg/2022/2065/oj

Peixoto, T. (2007). Peixoto, Tiago, Stocktaking of Social Accountability Initiatives in OECD Countries. *SSRN.*

Peña, J., Giraldo, S., Arango, C., & Bucheli, V. (2022). Un chatbot para asistir a las necesidades de información en tiempos de COVID-19. *Revista Ingeniería y Competitividad*, *24*(1), 1–15. DOI: 10.25100/iyc.v24i1.11004

Peña-López, I. (2023). *Crowdlaw: Casos de participación legislativa digital.* Editorial UOC.

Pereira, G., Eibl, G., Stylianou, C., Martínez, G., Neophytou, H., & Parycek, P. (2018). The role of smart technologies to support citizen engagement and decision making. *International Journal of Electronic Government Research, 14*(4), 1–17. DOI: 10.4018/IJEGR.2018100101

Pereira, G., Parycek, P., Falco, E., & Kleinhans, R. (2018). Smart governance in the context of smart cities: A literature review. *Information Polity*, *23*(2), 143–162. DOI: 10.3233/IP-170067

Pérez-Lara, M. D., Trejo-Macotela, F. R., & Ruiz-Vanoye, J. A. (2023). Digital twins for participatory governance in smart cities. *Journal of Urban Technology*, *30*(3), 115–133.

Peter, O., Pradhan, A., & Mbohwa, C. (2024). Smart Mechatronics: Innovating Sustainable Solutions for the Future. In Proceedings 5th African international conference industrial engineering & operations management (pp. 1037-1047).

Petrović, N., Milić, P., & Prlinčević, B. (2022). Using open government data for economic development. *The European Journal of Applied Economics*, *19*(2), 129–141. DOI: 10.5937/EJAE19-39004

Phonsitthangkun, S., & Arreeras, T. (2024). Mobility as a Service (MaaS): A Bibliometric Analysis of Research Trends, Technology Acceptance, and Urban Logistics Integration. 1–6. DOI: 10.1109/DASA63652.2024.10836433

Piemonte, R. (2025). Open Data della Regione Piemonte. Retrieved June 15, 2025 from https://www.dati.piemonte.it/#/home

Pillai, R., Islam, M., Sreejith, S., & Al-Malkawi, H. A. (2025). Comparative analysis of environmental, social and governance (ESG) ratings: Do sectors and regions differ? *The Journal of Management and Governance*, *29*(1), 69–109. DOI: 10.1007/s10997-023-09692-7

Preotiuc-Pietro, D., Gaman, M., & Aletras, N. (2019). Automatically Identifying Complaints in Social Media. arXiv:1906.03890. https://arxiv.org/abs/2308.11138 DOI: 10.18653/v1/P19-1495

Públicas, A. D. P. (2019). *Herramientas para la transparencia y la rendición de cuentas. Claves para un Gobierno abierto. LABgobar*. Subsecretaría de Innovación Pública y Gobierno Abierto, Secretaría de Modernización.

Purwanti, Y., Purwanto, B., & Jamaludin, M. (2022). Citizen participation in electronic public administration: The considerations of functionality and the technology acceptance model. *International Journal of Public Policy and Administration Research*, *9*(4), 90–101. DOI: 10.18488/74.v9i4.3206

Radtke, J., & Renn, O. (2024). Participation in energy transitions: A comparison of policy styles. *Energy Research & Social Science*, *114*, 103743. DOI: 10.1016/j.erss.2024.103743

Rajamäe-Soosaar, K., & Nikiforova, A. (2024). Exploring Estonia's Open Government Data Development as a Journey towards Excellence. https://doi.org/https://doi.org/10.48550/

Rajith, A., Soki, S., & Hiroshi, M. (2018). Real-time optimized HVAC control system on top of an IoT framework. In 2018 Third international conference on fog and mobile edge computing (FMEC) (pp. 181-186). IEEE. DOI: 10.1109/FMEC.2018.8364062

Rajitha, A. K. A., Nagpal, A., Kalra, R., Maan, P., Kumar, A., & Abdul-Zahra, D. S. (2024). Machine Learning and AI-Driven Water Quality Monitoring and Treatment. 3rd International Conference on Applied Research and Engineering (ICARAE2023). E3S Web of Conferences. Volume 505, 2024. DOI: 10.1051/e3sconf/202450503012

Ramírez-Alujas, Á. V., & Dassen, N. (2014). Vientos de cambio: el avance de las políticas de Gobierno Abierto en América Latina y el Caribe. Banco Interamericano de Desarrollo. Retriev July 20, 2025 from https://short-link.me/196zA

Ramírez-Hernández, U. A., Trejo-Macotela, F. R., & Robles-Camarillo, D. (2025). Intelligent system for management and optimization of residential water consumption: Master's thesis summary. International Journal of Combinatorial Optimization Problems and Informatics, 16(1), 226–236. DOI: 10.61467/2007.1558.2025.v16i1.906

Ramírez, J., Neri-Suárez, M., & Torres, M. (2024). Automatización de la auditoría fiscal en las PYMES mediante un algoritmo secuencial para extracción de comprobantes fiscales: Un enfoque en la economía digital. *International Journal of Combinatorial Optimization Problems and Informatics*, *15*(5), 146–154. DOI: 10.61467/2007.1558.2024.v15i5.565

Redacción. (2025, 8 June). Así es el nuevo robot urbano diseñado para la Policía de Dubai. El Correo del Golfo. Retrieved 7 August 2025, from https://www.elcorreo.ae/articulo/emiratos-arabes/asi-es-nuevo-robot-urbano-disenado-policia-dubai/

Reddy, S., Harivardhagini, & Sreelakshmi. (2024). IoT and Cloud Based Sustainable Smart Irrigation System. International Conference on Renewable Energy, Green Computing and Sustainable Development (ICREGCSD 2023). Volume 472. DOI: 10.1051/e3sconf/202447201026

Renuka, O. RadhaKrishnan, N., Priya, B. S., Jhansy, A., & Ezekiel, S. (2025). Data Privacy and Protection. In *Emerging Threats and Countermeasures in Cybersecurity* (pp. 433–465). Wiley. https://doi.org/DOI: 10.1002/9781394230600.ch19

Reza, S. (2021). Investigating electronic government maturity models. Sociología y tecnociencia, 11(Extra_1), 160-176. https://doi.org/https://doi.org/10.24197/st.Extra_1.2021.160-176

RICI. (2024, August). Participación Ciudadana Digital. https://redciudad.org/posts/post-4/

Ríos, A. M., Guillamón, M. D., & Benito, B. (2024). The influence of local government transparency on the implementation of the sustainable development goals in municipalities. Journal of Public Budgeting, Accounting &amp. *Financial Management*. Advance online publication. DOI: 10.1108/jpbafm-12-2023-0229

Riquelme, R. (2025, March 3). Gobiernos en México usan al menos 119 aplicaciones de Inteligencia Artificial. Retrieved July 3, 2025 from https://www.eleconomista.com.mx/tecnologia/gobiernos-mexico-119-aplicaciones-inteligencia-artificial-20250311-750004.html

Rivera, R. M., Amorim, M., & Reis, J. (2020). Robotic Services in Smart Cities: *An Exploratory Literature Review. Iberian Conference on Information Systems and Technologies*. DOI: 10.23919/CISTI49556.2020.9141099

Robertson, S. P., Bertot, J. C., & Nahon, K. (2013). Introduction to Open Government and Participation Minitrack. 2013 46th Hawaii International Conference on System Sciences

Rodríguez, A. (2024). Medidor inteligente de agua | Telcel Empresas. https://www.telcel.com/empresas/tendencias/notas/funcion-de-medidor-inteligente-de-agua

Rojas Flores, G. (2020). Plataformas digitales: mecanismos de acceso a la información en lo subnacional (Veracruz 2000-2018). Revista de Estudios de Políticas Públicas, 6(2), 99-115. ISSN edición web: 0719-6296 DOI: 10.5354/0719-6296.2020.58242

Rose, S., Borchert, O., Mitchell, S., & Connelly, S. (2020). Zero trust architecture (NIST Special Publication 800-207). National Institute of Standards and Technology. DOI: 10.6028/NIST.SP.800-207

Royo, S., Bellò, B., Torres, L., & Downe, J. (2024). The success of e-participation: Learning lessons from Decide Madrid and We asked, You said, We did in Scotland. *Policy and Internet*, (16), 65–82. https://doi.org/https://doi.org/10.1002/poi3.363

Royo, S., Pina, V., & Garcia-Rayado, J. (2020). Decide Madrid: A Critical Analysis of an Award-Winning e-Participation Initiative. *Sustainability*, *12*(4), 1674. DOI: 10.3390/su12041674

Ruggieri, R., Ruggeri, M., & Vinci, G. (2020). Efficient energy and electric transport in a Smart City: Evaluation of sustainability and competitiveness. *International Conference on Environment and Electrical Engineering*. DOI: 10.1109/EEEIC/ICPSEurope49358.2020.9160676

Ruijer, E., Détienne, F., Baker, M., Groff, J., & Meijer, A. (2019). The politics of open government data: Understanding organizational responses to pressure for more transparency. *American Review of Public Administration*, *50*(3), 260–274. DOI: 10.1177/0275074019888065

Ruiz-Vanoye, J. A., & Díaz-Parra, O. (2022). Editorial comments about safe cities. *International Journal of Combinatorial Optimization Problems and Informatics*, *13*(3), 1. Advance online publication. DOI: 10.61467/2007.1558.2022.v13i3.314

Ruiz-Vanoye, J. A., Díaz-Parra, O., Marroquín-Gutiérrez, F., Rodríguez-Lara, B. M., Fuentes-Penna, A., Barrera-Cámara, R. A., Ramos-Fernández, J. C., Xicoténcatl-Pérez, J. M., & Aguilar-Ortiz, J. (2023). Smart Government and Future Trends. In Ruiz-Vanoye, J. (Ed.), *Management, Technology, and Economic Growth in Smart and Sustainable Cities* (pp. 37–59). IGI Global Scientific Publishing., DOI: 10.4018/979-8-3693-0373-3.ch003

Ruiz-Vanoye, J. A., Díaz-Parra, O., Ramos-Fernández, J. C., Trejo-Macotela, F. R., & Xicoténcatl-Pérez, J. M. (2023). Editorial: A brief panorama of water smart cities. *International Journal of Combinatorial Optimization Problems and Informatics*, *14*(1), 1. DOI: 10.61467/2007.1558.2023.v14i1.332

Ruiz-Vanoye, J. A., Fuentes-Penna, A., Barrera-Cámara, R. A., Díaz-Parra, O., Trejo-Macotela, F. R., Gómez-Pérez, L. J., Aguilar-Ortiz, J., Ruiz-Jaimes, M. Á., Domínguez Mayorga, C. R., & Toledo-Navarro, Y. (2025). Digital Security and Stability as a Foundation for Emotional Well-Being in an AI-Driven Society. *International Journal of Combinatorial Optimization Problems and Informatics*, *16*(1), 14–37. DOI: 10.61467/2007.1558.2025.v16i1.932

Rwanda, T. I. (2025). Transparency International Rwanda web site. Retrieved May 30, 2025 from https://www.tirwanda.org/#

Ryalat, M., Franco, E., Elmoaqet, H., Almtireen, N., & Al-Refai, G. (2024). The integration of advanced mechatronic systems into Industry 4.0 for smart manufacturing. *Sustainability (Basel)*, *16*(19), 8504. DOI: 10.3390/su16198504

SABG. (2025). Gobierno diogital o electrónico. Retrieved June 1, 2025 from https://www.gob.mx/buengobierno/documentos/gobierno-digital-o-electronico

Sadoway, D., & Shekhar, S. (2014). (Re) prioritizing citizens in 'smart cities' governance: Examples of smart citizenship form India. *Journal of Community Informatics*, *10*(3). Advance online publication. DOI: 10.15353/joci.v10i3.3447

SafetyCulture Content Team. (2024). Top emergency management tools in 2024. SafetyCulture. https://safetyculture.com/topics/emergency-management/

Salvador, M. (2021). Inteligencia artificial y gobernanza de datos en las administraciones públicas: Reflexiones y evidencias para su desarrollo. *Gestión y Análisis de Políticas Públicas*, (26), 20–32. DOI: 10.24965/gapp.i26.10855

Sánchez-Ixta, C., Vázquez-Abarca, J. R., López-Sosa, L. B., & Golpour, I. (2024). Analysis of the Restoration of Distribution Substations: A Case Study of the Central–Western Division of Mexico. *Energies*, *17*(16), 4154. DOI: 10.3390/en17164154

Sánchez, R., González, F., & Ortiz, T. (2021). *Uso responsable de la IA para las políticas públicas: Manual de ciencia de datos*. Banco Interamericano de Desarrollo., DOI: 10.18235/0002876

Sandoval-Almazán, R. (2015). Gobierno abierto y transparencia: Construyendo un marco conceptual. *Convergencia*, *22*(68), 203–227. https://www.researchgate.net/publication/321893741_Gobierno_abierto_y_transparencia_construyendo_un_marco_conceptual. DOI: 10.29101/crcs.v0i68.2958

Sandoval-Almazán, R. (2019). Gobierno abierto y transparencia en México: Estudio longitudinal 2015-2018. *Innovar (Universidad Nacional de Colombia)*, *29*(74), 115–131. DOI: 10.15446/innovar.v29n74.82097

Sandoya, L., & Mawyin, M. (2025). La inteligencia artificial y su impacto en la gestión pública. *LATAM Revista Latinoamericana de Ciencias Sociales y Humanidades*, *6*(1), 710–718. DOI: 10.56712/latam.v6i1.3373

Santos Pinacho, M., Rentería-Gaeta, R., & García García, L. M. (2022). La Política Nacional de Datos Abiertos como instrumento para la consolidación de un Gobierno Abierto en México. *Encrucijada Revista Electrónica Del Centro De Estudios En Administración Pública*, (40), 34–57. DOI: 10.22201/fcpys.20071949e.2022.40.81278

Schneider, N., De Filippi, P., & Frey, S. (2020). Modular politics: Toward a governance layer for online communities. arXiv. https://arxiv.org/abs/2005.13701

SCIDSG. (2025). Distributed Denial of Secrets. Retrieved July 7, 2025 from https://ddosecrets.com

Secretaría General Iberoamericana. (2023). Carta Iberoamericana de Principios y Derechos en los Entornos Digitales. https://www.segib.org/wp-content/uploads/Carta_iberoamericana_derechos_digitales_ESP_web.pdf

Segovia, N., & Guzmán, A. (2025). Evaluación de un chatbot basado en aprendizaje supervisado: Impacto en la satisfacción y propuestas de mejora. Revista Electrónica de Tecnología Educativa, (92), e3849. DOI: 10.21556/edutec.2025.92.3849

Sernani, P., Cossiri, A., Di Cosimo, G., & Frontoni, E. (2025). Analyzing Digital Political Campaigning Through Machine Learning: An Exploratory Study for the Italian Campaign for European Union Parliament Election in 2024. *Computers, 14*(4), 126. DOI: 10.3390/computers14040126

Serra, J., Pubill, D., Antonopoulos, A., & Verikoukis, C. (2014). Smart HVAC control in IoT: Energy consumption minimization with user comfort constraints. *TheScientificWorldJournal, 2014*(1), 1–11. DOI: 10.1155/2014/161874 PMID: 25054163

Setiya, R., Pandey, S., Singh, A. K., & Sharma, D. K. (2021). Citizen e-governance using blockchain. In Krishnan, S., Balas, V. E., Julie, E. G., Robinson, Y. H., & Kumar, R. (Eds.), *Blockchain for Smart Cities* (pp. 119–152). Elsevier. https://doi.org/https://doi.org/10.1016/B978-0-12-824446-3.00010-7

Setyarto, D. B., Alimuddin, A., Mulyaningsih, M., & Judijanto, L. (2025). The role of e-government in increasing transparency and accountability of public administration in the digital era. *Edelweiss Applied Science and Technology, 9*(2), 1771–1783. DOI: 10.55214/25768484.v9i2.4908

SFP. (2023). Política Nacional de Datos Abiertos. https://canalonce.mx/REST/data/transparencia/datosabiertos/politica-nacional-de-datos-abiertos-dof-09102023-dof-10112023.pdf

SGMM Team. The. (2011, September 1). Smart Grid Maturity Model, Version 1.2: Model Definition (Technical Report CMU/SEI-2011-TR-025). Institute of Software Engineering. DOI: 10.1184/R1/6583835.v1

Shafik, M. B., Elbarbary, Z. M. S., Bu, S., Azmy, A. M., & Hussien, M. G. (2023). Distribution network's reliability assessment considering distributed automation system with penetration of DG units and SOP devices. *Energy Reports, 9*, 6199–6210. DOI: 10.1016/j.egyr.2023.05.224

Shaharudin, A. A. A. (2020). Open Government Data: Principles, Benefits and Evaluations. Khazanah Research Institute, 12(20).

Shah, J., Kothari, J., & Doshi, N. (2019). A survey of smart city infrastructure via case study on New York. *Procedia Computer Science, 160*, 702–705. DOI: 10.1016/j.procs.2019.11.024

Shaikh, I. N., & Ahammed, M. M. (2020). Quantity and quality characteristics of greywater: A review. *Journal of Environmental Management, 261*, 110266. DOI: 10.1016/j.jenvman.2020.110266 PMID: 32148323

Sharifi, A., Allam, Z., Bibri, S. E., & Khavarian-Garmsir, A. R. (2024). Smart cities and sustainable development goals (SDGs): A systematic literature review of co-benefits and trade-offs. Cities, Volume 146, 2024, 104659, ISSN 0264-2751, DOI: 10.1016/j.cities.2023.104659

Sharma, S., Sharma, S. K., Sahu, A. K., & Sharma, A. (2024). Internet of Things (IoT) and Smart Cities. *Deleted Journal, 2*(08), 2526–2531. DOI: 10.47392/IRJAEM.2024.0365

Sheller, M. (2020). Chapter 1 Mobility justice. In Handbook of Research Methods and Applications for Mobilities. Cheltenham, UK: Edward Elgar Publishing. Retrieved Jul 25, 2025, from DOI: 10.4337/9781788115469.00007

Sherif, S., & Labib, G. (2025). Digital Transformation and the SDGs: A Case Study on Egypt's E-government and SDG-16. *Governance and Politics, 3*, 8–20. DOI: 10.24833/2782-7062-2024-3-4-8-20

Shladover, S. E. (2020). Connected and automated vehicle systems: Introduction and overview. *Journal of Intelligent Transport Systems, 22*(3), 190–200. DOI: 10.1080/15472450.2017.1336053

ShotSpotter Wikipedia. (2024). ShotSpotter. In Wikipedia. https://en.wikipedia.org/wiki/ShotSpotter

Siano, P., De Marco, C., Rola, P., Loia, V., & Vasirani, M. (2022). Advanced smart metering infrastructures for distribution networks: A review. *Electric Power Systems Research, 211*, 108000. DOI: 10.1016/j.epsr.2022.108000

Sievers, T., Mata-Vázquez, M., & Schuller, A. (2023). A systematic review of data-driven energy management in distribution grids. *Energies, 16*(4), 1688. DOI: 10.3390/en16041688

Silos, J., Ramírez-Hernández, U. A., Reyes-Hernández, Y., Ortiz-Suarez, L. A., Gómez-Pérez, L. J., Cruz-Rojano, D., Trejo-Macotela, F. R., & Robles-Camarillo, D. (2023). Analysis of the feasibility of smart contracts in Mexico's legal and social framework: A study on the future of trade agreements. *International Journal of Combinatorial Optimization Problems and Informatics, 14*(3), 71–90. DOI: 10.61467/2007.1558.2023.v14i3.404

Silva, J. M., Ribeiro, D., Ramos, L. F., & Fonte, V. (2024). *A worldwide overview on the information security posture of online public services*. En Bui, T. X. & Sprague, R. H. (Eds.), *Proceedings of the 57th Hawaii International Conference on System Sciences* (pp. 1881–1890). Disponible en SSRN: https://ssrn.com/abstract=4577703

Silva, C., Faria, P., & Vale, Z. (2023). Demand response implementation: Overview of Europe and United States status. *Energies, 16*(10), 4043. DOI: 10.3390/en16104043

Singapore Government. (2025). Singapore's open data portal. Retrieved Jun 23, 2025 from https://data.gov.sg

Singh, Y., & Walingo, T. (2024). Smart Water Quality Monitoring with IoT Wireless Sensor Networks. *Sensors (Basel), 24*(9), 9. Advance online publication. DOI: 10.3390/s24092871 PMID: 38732981

Skjølsvold, T. M., Ryghaug, M., & Heidenreich, S. (2023). Citizen participation in smart grid pilots: A review of frameworks and impacts. *Energy Research & Social Science, 98*, 103123. DOI: 10.1016/j.erss.2023.103123

Sloat, S. (2025, mayo 1). Farmers are using IoT to take the guesswork out of growing. Business Insider. https://www.businessinsider.com/iot-technology-precision-agriculture-transforming-farming-2025-5

Smart energy. (2024, February). IEC 61850 – The standard for digitizing and automating power grids. Smart energy.

Smart energy. (2025, June). IEC 61850 Ed. 2.1: A new milestone in smart grid interoperability. Smart energy.

Smith, J. (2020). The Future of Smart Cities: Integrating Mechanical Systems with IoT. *American Journal Of Mechanical Engineering And Technology, 1*(6), 8–15.

Smith, M., & Miller, S. (2021). The ethical application of biometric facial recognition technology. *AI & Society*, •••, 1–9. DOI: 10.1007/s00146-021-01199-9 PMID: 33867693

Solmaz, S., Innerwinkler, P., Wójcik, M., Tong, K., Politi, E., Dimitrakopoulos, G., Purucker, P., Höß, A., Schuller, B. W., & John, R. (2024). Robust Robotic Search and Rescue in Harsh Environments: An Example and Open Challenges. DOI: 10.1109/ROSE62198.2024.10591144

Song, E. & Lee, K. B. (2024). Interoperability testing based on hardware-in-the-loop simulation of smart sensors. IEEE ICPS 2024 Proceedings.

Song, J.-U., Oh, Y.-S., Ahn, J.-G., & Lee, S.-I. (2023). A topology-based local identifier mapping scheme for power system resources in a CIM framework for interoperability. *Applied Sciences (Basel, Switzerland)*, *13*(18), 10341. DOI: 10.3390/app131810341

Srivastava, S., Brar, S. K., Rao, S., & Kumar, P. (2024). Assessing operational issues in a modular sewage treatment plant and providing remedies via comprehensive modeling and simulation through GPS-X. *Journal of Water Process Engineering*, *57*, 104678. DOI: 10.1016/j.jwpe.2023.104678

Steibel, F. (2018). Brazil Midterm Progress Report 2016–2018. https://www.opengovpartnership.org/wp-content/uploads/2018/10/Brazil_Mid-Term_Report_2016-2018_EN.pdf

Stringhini, A. (2020). Open government, emerging technologies and public information. Revue internationale des Gouvernements Ouverts, 9, 121-132.

Sundharakumar, K. B., Bhalaji, N., & Mirunalini, P. (2024). Spatio Temporal Modelling of Repeat Crimes and Hotspots Prediction Using Recurrent Deep Neural Networks. DOI: 10.1109/ICITIIT61487.2024.10580830

Sunkel, G., & Ullmann, H. (2019). Older adults in the digital age in Latin America: Bridging the digital age divide. *CEPAL Review*, *127*(127), 215–236. DOI: 10.18356/e9ed7f26-en

Swiss Post. (2024). E-voting: Online voting and elections. Retrieved July 3, 2025 from https://digital-solutions.post.ch/en/e-government/digitization-solutions/e-voting

Sysoyeva, L., & Martínez-Usarralde, M.-J. (2025). From security to digital governance in OECD: Evolution and some current considerations since the digital transformation. *Salud, Ciencia y Tecnología*, *4*(1401). Advance online publication. DOI: 10.56294/sctconf20251401

Tangi, S., Majumdar, A., & Das, D. (2024). Smart distribution network voltage estimation using PMU measurements. *PLoS One*, *19*(2), e0293616. DOI: 10.1371/journal.pone.0293616

Tao, F., Zhang, H., Liu, A., & Nee, A. Y. C. (2019). *Digital twin driven smart manufacturing*. Academic Press.

Taqi, H. M., Naeem, M., & Javaid, N. (2022). Implementation of IoT in smart grids. *Future Energy Proceedings*, *1*(2), 66–78. DOI: 10.1016/j.fep.2022.04.006

Tera, T., Kelvin, K., & Tobiloba, B. (2024). Privacy Preserving Machine Learning Algorithms Using Local Information Privacy. https://doi.org/DOI: 10.31234/osf.io/x5mc4

ThamaraiSelvan M, & Ambikapathy, A. (2025). Literature Review And *Identification Of Research Gaps In Cybersecurity Risk Management. IAPQR Transactions, 89–95.* https://www.researchgate.net/publication/392831911_LITERATURE_REVIEW_AND_IDENTIFICATION_OF_RESEARCH_GAPS_IN_CYBERSECURITY_RISK_MANAGEMENT

The GovLab. (n.d.). The GovLab. https://thegovlab.org/

Tikkinen-Piri, C., Rohunen, A., & Markkula, J. (2018). EU General Data Protection Regulation: Changes and implications for personal data collecting companies. *Computer Law & Security Review*, *34*(1), 134–153. DOI: 10.1016/j.clsr.2017.05.015

Tiwari, S., Jain, A., Ahmed, N. M. O. S., Charu, , Alkwai, L. M., Dafhalla, A. K. Y., & Hamad, S. A. S. (2021). Machine learning-based model for prediction of power consumption in smart grid-smart way towards smart city. *Expert Systems: International Journal of Knowledge Engineering and Neural Networks*, *39*(5), e12832. DOI: 10.1111/exsy.12832

TOJIL. (2024). Teo Chatbot. Retrieved July 1, 2025 from https://tojil.org/teo/

Touil, S., Richa, A., Fizir, M., & Gómez, S. (2022). A review on smart irrigation management strategies and their effect on water savings and crop yield. https://onlinelibrary.wiley.com/doi/10.1002/ird.2735

Travez-Tipan, A., & Villafuerte-Garzon, C. (2023). Industria 5.0, revisión del pasado y futuro de la producción y la industria. *Ciencia Latina Revista Científica Multidisciplinar*, *7*(1), 1059–1070. DOI: 10.37811/cl_rcm.v7i1.4457

Trimble, M. and Plummer, R. (2019). Evaluación participativa para la gobernanza adaptativa de sistemas socio-ecológicos. Tekoporá Revista Latinoamericana De Humanidades Ambientales Y Estudios Territoriales, 1(1). https://doi.org/DOI: 10.36225/TEK.1.1.5

Trimble, M. and Plummer, R. (2019). Evaluación participativa para la gobernanza adaptativa de sistemas socio-ecológicos: participatory evaluation for adaptative governance of social-ecologic systems. Tekoporá Revista Latinoamericana De Humanidades Ambientales Y Estudios Territoriales, 1(1). https://doi.org/DOI: 10.36225/tekopora.v1i1.8

Tseng, Y. (2022). Algorithmic Empowerment: A Comparative Ethnography of Two Open-Source Algorithmic Platforms – Decide Madrid and vTaiwan. *Big Data & Society*, *9*(2). Advance online publication. DOI: 10.1177/20539517221123505

U.S. Department of Energy (DOE). (2022). Cybersecurity Capability Maturity Model (C2M2). https://www.energy.gov/ceser/c2m2 (2022).

U.S. Department of Transportation. (2024, April 17). Connected Vehicle Pilot Deployment Program (2024 update). ITS Knowledge Resource Service. Last updated May 2025. Retrieved 26 July 2025, from https://www.itskrs.its.dot.gov/briefings/executive-briefing/connected-vehicle-pilot-deployment-program-2024-update

UN & ESCAP. (2009). What is good governance? Retrieved May 11, 2025 from https://hdl.handle.net/20.500.12870/3794

UN. (1948). Universal Declaration of Human Rights, Article 19. Retrieved July 4, 2025 from https://www.un.org/en/about-us/universal-declaration-of-human-rights

UN. (2024). A Digital Government Model Framework for Sustainable Development. In Affairs, U. N. D. E. S. (Ed.), *United Nations E-Government Survey 2024 Accelerating Digital Transformation for Sustainable Development - With the addendum on Artificial Intelligence* (pp. 1–33). United Nations Department of Economic and Social Affairs. DOI: 10.18356/9789211067286

UNDRR. (2022). Global Assessment Report on Disaster Risk Reduction 2022. United Nations Office for Disaster Risk Reduction. https://www.undrr.org/gar2022

UNESCO. (2020). Recommendation on the Ethics of Artificial Intelligence. https://unesdoc.unesco.org/ark:/48223/pf0000379920

UN-Habitat. (2021). People-Centered Smart Cities. https://unhabitat.org/people-centered-smart-cities

UN-Habitat. (2021). Smart Cities for All: Bridging the Urban Digital Divide. https://unhabitat.org

UN-Habitat. (2022). *World Cities Report 2022: Envisaging the future of cities.* United Nations Human Settlements Programme.

United Nations Environment Programme. (2022, 3 May). Build Back Better: Using green and digital technologies to reduce food waste at consumer level. UN Environment Programme. Retrieved 26 July 2025, from https://www.unep.org/explore-topics/green-economy/build-back-better

United Nations. (2019). *World Urbanization Prospects: The 2018 Revision.* Department of Economic and Social Affairs, Population Division.

United Nations. (2019). World Urbanization Prospects: The 2018 Revision. https://population.un.org/wup

United Nations. (2021). Sustainable Development Goals: Goal 11. https://sdgs.un.org/goals/goal11

United Nations. (2021). *The Sustainable Development Goals Report 2021.* United Nations.

United States government. (2025). The official source of government spending data. Retrieved June 27, 2025 from https://www.usaspending.gov/

US Dept of Labor. (2000). *Occupational outlook handbook.* JIST Publishing.

Use of Blockchain Technologies in Smart Cities. (2023). International Journal For. *Kexue Jishu Yu Gongcheng, 11*(5), 4942–4947. DOI: 10.22214/ijraset.2023.52111

Vani, S., Joshi, P., Shinde, R., Kadam, S., & Matkamwad, M. (2024). *Smart Water Management Grid.* International Journal of Innovative Science and Research Technology., DOI: 10.38124/ijisrt/IJISRT24MAY931

Vasuki, M., Victoire, T. A., & Seventhi, S. (2024). *Forecasting Criminal Activity Using Machine Learning Approaches.* International Journal of Innovative Science and Research Technology., DOI: 10.38124/ijisrt/IJISRT24MAY645

Veoci. (n.d.). Veoci emergency management platform overview. Veoci Inc. https://veoci.com/

Viani, F., Polo, A., Robol, F., Giarola, E., & Ferro, A. (2016). Experimental validation of a wireless distributed system for smart public lighting management. In 2016 IEEE International Smart Cities Conference (ISC2) (pp. 1-6). IEEE. DOI: DOI: 10.1109/ISC2.2016.7580852

Villanueva, E., Andrea, M. C., & Edith, F. G. Sandra, & Martínez Bermeo, José Roberto. (2016). La participación digital en la construcción de la e-democracia y ciudadanía digital. RIDE. Revista Iberoamericana para la Investigación y el Desarrollo Educativo, 7(13), 126-146. ISSN 2007-7467. Retriev July 20, 2025 from https://www.scielo.org.mx/scielo.php?script=sci_arttext&pid=S2007-74672016000200126&lng=es&tlng=es

Ville de Paris. (2025). Paris Open Data. Retrieved June 2, 2025 from https://opendata.paris.fr/pages/home/

Voitenko, O., Shults, S., Bilyk, I., & Kaplenko, H. (2022). Government transparency as ukrainian territorial communities' economic development factor. *Financial and Credit Activity Problems of Theory and Practice*, *5*(46), 387–397. DOI: 10.55643/fcaptp.5.46.2022.3879

Volk, R., Stengel, J., & Schultmann, F. (2014). Building Information Modeling (BIM) for existing buildings — Literature review and future needs. *Automation in Construction*, *38*, 109–127. DOI: 10.1016/j.autcon.2013.10.023

von Bertalanffy, L. (1968). *General system theory: Foundations, development, applications*. George Braziller.

Von Jouanne, A., Agamloh, E. B., & Yokochi, A. (2023). Power hardware-in-the-loop (PHIL): A review to advance smart inverter-based grid-edge solutions. *Energies*, *16*(2), 916. DOI: 10.3390/en16020916

VVK. (2025). Internet voting in Estonia: i-Voting. Retrieved July 1, 2025 from

Wahl, H. (2025, 2 April). A flexible robot can help emergency responders search through rubble. MIT News. Massachusetts Institute of Technology. Retrieved from https://news.mit.edu/2025/sprout-flexible-robot-help-emergency-responders-search-rubble-0402

Wanden-Berghe Lozano, J. L., & Fernández Daza, E. (2020). Blockchain: instrumento de transparencia y control del sector público.

Wang, Z., Yang, Q., & Qiu, S. (2024). The construction effect of ultra-high-voltage power grid based on multilevel index analysis method. *Sustainability*, *16*(18), 8083. DOI: 10.3390/su16188083

Waza, A. M. (2024). Examining the Role of Artificial Intelligence in Improving Decision Making Processes in Governance. DOI: 10.59890/ijatss.v2i7.2319

Webster, C., & Leleux, C. (2018). Smart governance: Opportunities for technologically-mediated citizen co-production. *Information Polity*, *23*(1), 95–110. DOI: 10.3233/IP-170065

What is ShotSpotter? Controversial gunshot-detection technology facing increasing scrutiny. (2024, 20 May). Boston.com. Retrieved 7 August 2025, from https://www.boston.com/news/local-news/2024/05/20/what-is-shotspotter-controversial-gunshot-detection-technology-facing-increasing-scrutiny/

White, G. B., & Sjelin, N. (2022). The NIST Cybersecurity Framework. In *Research Anthology on Business Aspects of Cybersecurity* (pp. 39–55). IGI Global., DOI: 10.4018/978-1-6684-3698-1.ch003

White, Z. M. (2023). Re-envisioning digital equity and connection literacy for older adults. *North Carolina Medical Journal*, *84*(2). Advance online publication. DOI: 10.18043/001c.73013 PMID: 39302329

Wickert, J., & Lewis, K. (2013). An introduction to mechanical engineering. Cengage learning.

Wiener, N. (1948). *Cybernetics: Or control and communication in the animal and the machine*. MIT Press.

WikiLeaks. (2015, November 3). What is WikiLeaks. Retrieved July 5, 2025 from https://wikileaks.org/What-is-WikiLeaks.html

Wilson-Menzfeld, G. (2025). Digital inclusion and governance frameworks for community resilience. *Behaviour & Information Technology*, *44*(1), 1–18. DOI: 10.1080/0144929X.2024.2368087

Wirtz, B. W., Weyerer, J. C., & Sturm, B. J. (2023). Algorithmic transparency in the public sector: Toward responsible artificial intelligence. *Government Information Quarterly*, *40*(2), 101824. DOI: 10.1016/j.giq.2022.101824

Woinaroschy, A. (2016). Smart cities will need chemistry. Acta Marisiensis. *Seria Technologica*, *13*(1), 5.

World Bank. (2022). Energy Data Landscape – Latin America and the Caribbean. https://databank.worldbank.org/source/sustainable-energy-for-all)

World Bank. (2022). Energy Infrastructure Cost Benchmarking Toolkit. https://www.worldbank.org)

World Economic Forum, & Deloitte. (2021, 13 July). Governing Smart Cities: Policy benchmarks for ethical and responsible smart city development. In collaboration with Deloitte. Retrieved 26 July 2025, from https://www.weforum.org/publications/governing-smart-cities-policy-benchmarks-for-ethical-and-responsible-smart-city-development/

World Economic Forum. (2020). Exploring Blockchain Technology for Government Transparency: Blockchain-Based Public Procurement to Reduce Corruption. https://www3.weforum.org/docs/WEF_Blockchain_Government_Transparency_Report.pdf

World Economic Forum. (2023). The global public impact of GovTech: A $9.8 trillion opportunity (Global Technology Governance Report). World Economic Forum. https://www.weforum.org/publications/the-global-public-impact-of-govtech/

Wray, S. (2022, July 25). LinkNYC programme gets a reboot with 5G kiosks. ITU. Retrieved from https://www.itu.int/hub/2022/07/linknyc-5g-kiosks-cities-today/

Wu, J., Li, Y., & Xu, H. (2023). Design and implementation of the Zero Trust model in power IoT networks. *International Transactions on Electrical Energy Systems, 6545323*, 1–13. Advance online publication. DOI: 10.1155/2023/6545323

Wu, Y.-C., Chang, C.-S., & Li, W.-H. (2024). Development of a Low-Cost Automated Demand Response Controller for Home Energy Management. *Applied Sciences (Basel, Switzerland), 14*(23), 11434. DOI: 10.3390/app142311434

WWF Peru. (2024, June 11). Justina del Mar. Retrieved July 1, 2025 from https://www.wwf.org.pe/?389250/

Xia, S. (2017). E-governance and political modernization: An empirical study based on asia from 2003 to 2014. *Administrative Sciences, 7*(3), 25. DOI: 10.3390/admsci7030025

Xia, W., Chen, X., & Song, C. (2022). A framework of blockchain technology in intelligent water management. *Frontiers in Environmental Science, 10*, 909606. Advance online publication. DOI: 10.3389/fenvs.2022.909606

Xu, L., Lam, Y. Y., Ng, D. T. K., Peng, P., Suen, W. L., Lee, C. S., & Chu, S. K. W. (2024). Digital literacy education for older adults: A scoping review. *Proceedings of the Association for Information Science and Technology, 61*(1), 691–696. DOI: 10.1002/pra2.1081

Yang, K., & Pandey, S. (2011). Further dissecting the black box of citizen participation: When does citizen involvement lead to good outcomes? *Public Administration Review, 71*(6), 880–892. DOI: 10.1111/j.1540-6210.2011.02417.x

Yeung, K. (2018). Algorithmic regulation: A critical interrogation. *Regulation & Governance, 12*(4), 505–523. DOI: 10.1111/rego.12158

Yoldaş, Y., Önen, A., Muyeen, S. M., Vasilakos, A. V., & Alan, İ. (2023). Improving Smart Grid Flexibility with Virtual Power Plants: Recent Developments and Future Directions. *Renewable & Sustainable Energy Reviews, 180*, 113298. DOI: 10.1016/j.rser.2022.113298

Yu, M. Y. (2024). Key Challenges and Potential Solutions in Smart City Governance. *Scientific and Social Research Articles., 6*(8), 2024. DOI: 10.26689/ssr.v6i8.7818

Zendejas, R. (2024). Ciberpolítica: Estrategias de gobernanza para el empoderamiento de la ciudadanía digital. Ediciones Universidad de Xalapa. https://www.researchgate.net/publication/390137588_CIBERPOLITICA_Y_GOBERNANZA_Estrategias_de_gobernanza_para_el_empoderamiento_de_la_Ciudadania_Digital

Zendejas, R. (2024). *Ciberpolítica: Estrategias de gobernanza para el empoderamiento de la ciudadanía digital*. Ediciones Universidad de Xalapa.

Zeng, X., Chen, L., Wang, D., Zhang, Z., He, S., Liu, S., & Wang, L. (2024). An effective method of equivalent load-based time-of-use electricity pricing strategy. *Mathematics, 12*(9), 1408. DOI: 10.3390/math12091408

Zevallos Apaza, A. A., Onque Gárate, S. S., Canaza Cuadros, A. E. J., & Choqueneira Ccasa, P. M. (2022). Predictive model of water potability through a decision tree in Artificial Intelligence. *Revista Innovación y Software, 3*(2), 121–131. DOI: 10.48168/innosoft.s9.a72

Zhang, W., Lim, G., Perrault, S., & Wang, C. (2022). A Review of Research on Civic Technology: Definitions, Theories, History and Insights. arXiv.Org.

Zhang, X., He, L., Gioia, F. D., Choi, D., Elia, A., & Heinemann, P. (2022). LoRaWAN based internet of things (IoT) system for precision irrigation in plasticulture fresh-market tomato. *Smart Agricultural Technology, 2*, 100053. DOI: 10.1016/j.atech.2022.100053

Zhao, L., Wang, X., Li, Z., & Li, Z. (2022). Self-healing control strategy in intelligent distribution networks based on data-driven decision-making. *Applied Energy, 313*, 118807. DOI: 10.1016/j.apenergy.2022.118807

Zheng, Y., Capra, L., Wolfson, O., & Yang, H. (2020). Urban computing: Concepts, methodologies, and applications. *ACM Transactions on Intelligent Systems and Technology, 11*(4), 1–33. DOI: 10.1145/3383261

Zuboff, S. (2019). The Age of Surveillance Capitalism: The Fight for a Human Future at the New Frontier of Power. Harvard Business School Faculty & Research. Retrieved 26 July 2025, from the Harvard Business School website.

About the Contributors

Ruiz-Vanoye is a Professor and Researcher at Universidad Politécnica de Pachuca (UPP), a National Researcher under the CONAHCYT program, and an Adjunct Researcher at the National Laboratory of Autonomous Vehicles and Exoskeletons (LANAVEX). Additionally, he holds the title of Lecturer-level Researcher for the Agency for the Quality of the University System of Catalonia (Generalitat de Catalunya). His research interests include Smart Cities, Smart Water, Smart Education, Smart Government, Smart Healthcare, Smart Farming, Smart Energy, Smart Sports, Smart Food, Smart Tourism, Algorithmic Finance, Algorithmic Portfolio Management, Applications and Theory of Algorithms, Bio-inspired Algorithms, Combinatorial Optimization Problems, Compilers, Computational Intelligence, Computational Complexity Theory, Computational Financial Intelligence, Complexity of Algorithms, Complexity of Instances, Computational Statistics, Computer Networks, Computer Science Security, Cybercrimes, Data Mining, Education, Evolutionary Computation, Heuristic Optimization Techniques in Bioinformatics, Hybrid Evolutionary Algorithms, Hybrid Optimization Algorithms, Machine Learning, Meta-heuristics, Operations Research, Operations Management, Parallel & Distributed Computing, Production Planning and Logistics Optimization, Project Scheduling Problems, Software Engineering, and Transgenic Algorithms.

Diaz-Parra is a Professor and Researcher at Universidad Politécnica de Pachuca (UPP), a National Researcher under the CONAHCYT program, and an Adjunct Researcher at the National Laboratory of Autonomous Vehicles and Exoskeletons (LANAVEX). His research interests include Smart Cities, Smart Water, Smart Education, Smart Government, Smart Healthcare, Smart Farming, Smart Energy, Smart Sports, Smart Food, Smart Tourism, Algorithmic Finance, Algorithmic Portfolio Management, Applications and Theory of Algorithms, Bio-inspired Algorithms, Combinatorial Optimization Problems, Compilers, Computational

Intelligence, Computational Complexity Theory, Computational Financial Intelligence, Complexity of Algorithms, Complexity of Instances, Computational Statistics, Computer Networks, Computer Science Security, Cybercrimes, Data Mining, Education, Evolutionary Computation, Heuristic Optimization Techniques in Bioinformatics, Hybrid Evolutionary Algorithms, Hybrid Optimization Algorithms, Machine Learning, Meta-heuristics, Operations Research, Operations Management, Parallel & Distributed Computing, Production Planning and Logistics Optimization, Project Scheduling Problems, Software Engineering, and Transgenic Algorithms.

Eric Simancas Acevedo is Full Research Professor at the Polytechnic University of Pachuca (UPP), where he teaches in the Master's Degree in Information and Communication Technologies, as well as in Telematics and Software Engineering.

***

Jaime Aguilar-Ortiz holds a Ph.D. in Mathematics and is a recognized researcher with an extensive academic and scientific trajectory, currently a member of Mexico's National System of Researchers. His scholarly output includes over 40 peer-reviewed research and dissemination articles, complemented by the authorship and co-authorship of more than 40 educational and scientific books across mathematics, financial education, programming, artificial intelligence, and applied technologies. He has also contributed to the creation of digital and educational resources, including academic portals, videogames, and over 100 educational films, always combining rigorous mathematical foundations with innovative applications of artificial intelligence. His current research focuses on deep tabular learning, fuzzy logic, reinforcement learning, natural language processing, and neural networks, seeking to apply cutting-edge AI methodologies to address social problems and foster technological development, while strengthening postgraduate education and research in Mexico and beyond.

Ricardo Barrera-Cámara, Ph.D. in Computer Systems from the Universidad del Sur. Master in Informatics from the Universidad Autónoma of Carmen. Research professor at the Autonomous University of Carmen in Mexico. National System of Researchers level 1. Leader of the academic group of scientific and technological computing. Leader of the Academy of Administration and information processing. His research areas are Scientific Computing, Data Science, Optimization, Quality and Information Technology

Ana L. Cortes, Master in Systems Engineering and PhD in Computer Systems, currently completing a Doctorate in Public Administration and Policy. She is a lecturer and trainer at various higher education institutions and has promoted the creation of spaces for discussion, analysis, and proposal development on topics related to education, entrepreneurship, and social economy. She has collaborated with the National Technological Institute of Mexico on various professional and academic projects. She also participated in the development and design of the curriculum for the Diploma in Social and Solidarity Economy and the Master's in Social Economy. Currently, she serves as the regional coordinator of NODESS (Territorial Nodes of Social and Solidarity Economy) for the central region at INAES. She has published book chapters, essays, and articles in national and international academic journals, where she explores in depth the principles and practices of the social economy.

Manuel Erazo Valadez holds a Master of Science in Computer Science from the National Center for Research and Technological Development (CENIDET). He is a full-stack developer with experience in building Android applications and web systems that integrate Internet of Things (IoT) technologies such as FIWARE. He has contributed to projects involving indoor geolocation, academic subject validation, and sensor-based data visualization in real time. Currently, he is involved in a research project focused on analyzing and predicting compatibility between heavy and light antibody chains using deep learning techniques and numerical amino acid representations. This work aims to optimize the design of intelligent agents for bioinformatics analysis. He is known for his analytical mindset, ability to solve complex problems, and continuous pursuit of technical and professional growth.

Alcjandro Fuentes-Penna, distinguished Mexican academic and researcher specializing in strategic planning, artificial intelligence, and educational technology. He earned his Ph.D. in Strategic Planning and Technology Management from the Universidad Popular Autónoma del Estado de Puebla (UPAEP) in 2012. Prior to that, he completed a Master's degree in Computer Science at the Instituto Tecnológico y de Estudios Superiores de Monterrey (ITESM), where he published two articles in international conferences and secured first place in the Technology category of the Third Banamex Award for Internet Evolution. Dr. Fuentes Penna has held various academic positions, including serving as a Full-Time Research Professor at the Escuela Superior de Tlahuelilpan of the Universidad Autónoma del Estado de Hidalgo (UAEH). His research interests encompass educational management, educational technology, complexity in social sciences, and bio-inspired intelligent scientific computing. He has contributed to multiple publications, including articles indexed in JCR and Scopus, as well as books in his areas of expertise. Throughout his career, Dr. Fuentes Penna has received numerous national and international recognitions for academic and research excellence. He has been awarded the PRODEP Profile (formerly PROMEP) three times, is a member of the State System of Researchers in Morelos, and was recently included in the National System of Researchers at the Candidate level. Additionally, he has collaborated with various universities and research institutes, including the Universidad Nacional Autónoma de México (UNAM) and the Mexican Institute of Transportation. Dr. Fuentes Penna has extensive experience in teaching at both undergraduate and graduate levels, in both face-to-face and online modalities. He has supervised theses, coordinated educational programs, and organized significant academic events such as the International Space Week and the National Science and Technology Week.

David H. Fuque-Ehuan, Professor of Information Technology at Universidad Autónoma del Carmen. Develops technology solutions for enterprise and institutional process optimization, with research focus on Machine Learning, Database Systems, Computer Vision, and Internet of Things (IoT). Background includes graduate studies in Education.

Justo Fabián Montiel Hernández holds a degree in Materials Science Engineering from the Autonomous University of Hidalgo State. During this period, he completed a research internship at the Center for Research in Optics A.C. in León, Guanajuato, Mexico. He subsequently pursued a direct PhD in Materials Science at the same institution. During this period, he completed a doctoral internship with the Applied Electrochemistry and Electrocatalysis Group at the University Institute of Electrochemistry at the University of Alicante, in Alicante, Spain. Upon completing his credits, he received the 2015 Academic Merit Award for the highest grade point average in his doctoral class (9.67). His work has been published by national and international publishers, and he has written numerous research articles, book chapters, and conference proceedings. He has also supervised master's theses.

Miguel Ángel Ruiz Jaimes is a Professor and Researcher at the Universidad Politécnica del Estado de Morelos (UPEMOR), Mexico. He holds a Ph.D. in Computer Systems Engineering and is a member of the National System of Researchers (SNI Level I). His work focuses on information technologies, computer networks, cybersecurity, artificial intelligence, and digital governance. He has authored and co-authored scientific articles and book chapters published by IGI Global, MDPI, IEEE, and other international publishers. He also serves as a peer reviewer for journals such as IJCoPI and BEEI. His research interests include AI ethics, cybersecurity in critical infrastructures, algorithmic transparency, and digital transformation in the public sector.

Evelin Gutiérrez Moreno studied Chemical engineering at the Technological Institute of Pachuca. She collaborated for some years in the chemical industry. She studied a Master's Degree and a Ph.D. in Chemistry at the Autonomous University of the State of Hidalgo. Her interest area is the analysis of corrosion in acidic media.

Jesús Patricio Oliver, He obtained the title of engineer in Electronics and Telecommunications from the Autonomous University of the State of Hidalgo and the M.Sc. in Automatic Control at the same university. In 2012, he received the PhD in Sciences in Automatic Control at CINVESTAV, Mexico City. His research interests are intelligent systems, adaptive control, nonlinear control, robust control, system identification and observation. He is currently a Professor at the Autonomous University of the State of Hidalgo, Pachuca, Mexico.

Daniel Robles-Camarillo, He has conducted research in the field of electronic interfaces and intelligent systems, leading multidisciplinary projects that include: * Smart technologies applied to energy efficiency. * Autonomous navigation for ground vehicles. * Assistive technologies for personal safety. * Automatic classifiers for identifying entomological vectors causing Dengue and Chagas disease. * Biomedical systems for processing and applying biosignals. He is a two-time winner of the "Premio Hidalgo de Ciencia, Tecnología e Innovación" (Hidalgo Prize for Science, Technology, and Innovation) both in the area of Technological Development, in 2019 and 2014. The award was granted by the Government of the State of Hidalgo and CITNOVA. He won the "Premio CANIFARMA" in Technological Development in 2015, an award given by the National Chamber of the Pharmaceutical Industry and CONACYT. He also received the "Premio al Registro de Patentes" (Patent Registration Award) in 2010, granted by the Institute of Science and Technology of DF

Jazmín Rodríguez Flores, PhD Candidate in Applied Engineering. Master of Science in Computer Science, specializing in systems analysis and design, has more than 17 years as a full time researcher at UPP, teaches undergraduate and graduate courses.

Yadira Toledo Navarro is a professor and researcher at the Universidad Politécnica del Estado de Morelos (UPEMOR), with academic and professional experience in educational technologies, business administration, and innovation in higher education. She holds a Ph.D. in administration and has coordinated several interdisciplinary projects. Dr. Toledo has also served in leadership roles within academic bodies and committees, contributing to the development of institutional programs.

Trejo-Macotela is a Professor and Researcher at Polytechnic University of Pachuca (UPP), a National Researcher under the CONAHCYT program, and an Adjunct Researcher at the National Laboratory of Autonomous Vehicles and Exoskeletons (LANAVEX). Dr. Trejo-Macotela received the PhD. Degree in Electronics from the National Institute of Astrophysics, Optics and Electronics (INAOE), Puebla, Mexico. His main research interests are Integrated Circuit Design, Analog and Digital Design, Embedded Systems, RF Electronics, Telecommunications Systems, Precision Agriculture, Internet of Things, among others.

Index

A

B

C

D

E

G

I

L

M

O

P

R

S

T

U

V

W

www.ingramcontent.com/pod-product-compliance
Lightning Source LLC
LaVergne TN
LVHW081535300926
849161LV00006B/1432